JEWISH REFUGEES FROM GERMANY AND AUSTRIA IN BRITAIN, 1933–1970

D1471395

Jewish Refugees from Germany and Austria in Britain, 1933–1970

Their Image in *AJR Information*

ANTHONY GRENVILLE

VALLENTINE MITCHELL
LONDON • PORTLAND, OR

First published in 2010 by Vallentine Mitchell

Middlesex House,	920 NE 58th Avenue, Suite 300
29/45 High Street, Edgware,	Portland, Oregon,
Middlesex HA8 7UU, UK	97213-3786, USA

www.vmbooks.com

Copyright © 2010 Anthony Grenville
reprinted 2014

British Library Cataloguing in Publication Data

Grenville, Anthony.
   Jewish refugees from Germany and Austria in Britain,
   1933-1970 : their image in AJR information.
   1. Jewish refugees—Great Britain—History—20th
   century. 2. Jews, German—Great Britain—Social
   conditions—20th century. 3. Jews, Austrian—Great
   Britain—Social conditions—20th century. 4. World War,
   1939-1945—Jews—Germany. 5. World War, 1939-1945—
   Jews—Austria. 6. Great Britain—Civilization—Jewish
   influences. 7. Jews, German—Great Britain—History—
   20th century—Sources. 8. Jews, Austrian—Great Britain—
   History—20th century—Sources. 9. Association of Jewish
   Refugees in Great Britain. 10. Association of Jewish
   Refugees Information.
   I. Title
   941'.004924-dc22

ISBN 978 0 85303 842 9 (cloth)
ISBN 978 0 85303 852 8 (paper)

All rights reserved. No part of this publication may be reproduced, stored in or introduced into a retrieval system, or transmitted, in any form or by any means, electronic, mechanical, photocopying, recording or otherwise without the prior written permission of the publisher of this book.

Printed by CMP (UK) Ltd, Poole, Dorset

In memory of my parents, Arthur and Trude Grenville,

and to my wife, Eva Urbach-Grenville

Contents

List of Illustrations

Preface

Between January 1933, when Hitler came to power, and the outbreak of war in September 1939 over 60,000 Jews from territories under Nazi control – Germany, Austria and, in smaller numbers, Czechoslovakia – fled to Britain, of whom approaching 50,000 settled there permanently. They formed (and still form) the most obvious living reminder of the Holocaust to be found on British soil, where they represented a continuation, in exile, of the great traditions of the Jewries of the German-speaking countries. Although the great majority came before 1939 and were not camp survivors, they were victims of Nazi persecution who had to build new lives in Britain.

The refugees from Central Europe proved to be an extraordinarily valuable bonus to British society. Their contribution to British culture has been enormous, out of all proportion to their numbers (about 0.1 per cent of the population). One only needs to cite names such as Sigmund and Anna Freud, Paul Hamlyn and George Weidenfeld, Lucian Freud and Frank Auerbach, Richard Tauber and Max Rostal, Elias Canetti and Arthur Koestler, Ernst Gombrich and Nikolaus Pevsner, Karl Popper and Norbert Elias, Ernest Chain, Hans Krebs and Max Perutz, or Emeric Pressburger, Anton Walbrook and Lilli Palmer.

These great names did not exist in a vacuum; they formed the tip of the iceberg of a culturally and intellectually vibrant community whose collective history has hitherto remained unwritten. This book aims to tell that history from the point of view of the mass of the 'ordinary' refugees from Hitler in Britain, using material from *AJR Information*, the journal of the refugees' own organization, amongst other sources, to build up a picture of the communal identity that they developed and the social culture that they established in the first quarter-century after the war. Whereas there are many studies of prominent individual refugees, there is as yet no history of the bulk of the refugees, the largely anonymous foot soldiers, as it were, of the emigration from Central Europe. This book is intended to fill that gap, outlining in its opening two chapters the experience of the refugees during their initial reception in Britain and during the war, and then focusing in its main part on their post-war settlement and the way in which they adapted to and integrated into British society.

I have tried to write a social history of the refugee community as a whole, which no existing study has so far done. My book is based on a systematic working through of the best and richest source of material on the refugees, the *Association of Jewish Refugees Information*, the monthly journal of the Association of Jewish Refugees, which has been appearing since January 1946. The AJR was founded in 1941 to represent the interests of the Jews from the German-speaking lands in Britain, becoming over the decades the largest and longest-lived of the refugee organizations.

The journal, originally eight pages long, gradually expanded to sixteen, consisting of three columns per page. Its format remained fairly constant over the first quarter-century of its existence. The front page carried a feature resembling an editorial in its left-hand column, and the other two columns were devoted to a substantial article on another subject. The contents of the inside pages reflected the changing concerns of the refugees. Initially, when the refugees' daily lives were still affected by government decisions, the first inside page contained information about debates in parliament and other official pronouncements that were relevant to the refugees. Though interaction with British society always occupied much space in the journal, by the early 1950s, when the refugees' official status in Britain was secure, the second page was largely turned over to news from Germany and Austria, including restitution matters. There was a column containing news about Anglo-Jewry as well as reports from Israel.

The main focus outside the refugee community in Britain remained the refugees' native countries, particularly their culture: there was a regular column intended to keep readers in touch with the actors, writers and other figures in the arts known to them from pre-emigration days, as well as numerous reviews of books and exhibitions that sought to maintain the contact with pre-Hitler German-speaking high culture. The journal also published letters to the editor, reports on the work of the AJR, and many advertisements, both personal and commercial. *AJR Information* carefully recorded the achievements of its members, which it featured in articles published on occasions such as their sixtieth birthdays and in their obituaries.

Throughout the period 1946–70 the editor of the journal was Werner Rosenstock, initially alongside Herbert Freeden (Friedenthal), who left for Israel in 1950. Rosenstock also served as General Secretary of the AJR. In this capacity, and also as editor of the journal, Rosenstock was responsible to the AJR's Executive, the elected committee of management that formed the Association's governing body. Until his retirement in 1982, Rosenstock was the key figure in the day-to-day administration of the AJR, while also finding time to edit the journal, much of which he wrote himself. His pride in the past achievements of German Jewry and his continuing attachment to its native culture marked the journal fundamentally, as did a painful awareness of the community's losses during the Nazi years.

AJR Information is a quite unrivalled source of material, as it has throughout its existence been written almost entirely by refugees for refugees and is devoted to issues that concern the refugee community, to its interests, activities and general patterns of life. Because *AJR Information* is unique in its coverage of refugee life from the specific viewpoint of the refugees themselves, I have given it a privileged position among the sources that I have used.

Indeed, given the paucity of statistics and similar material, official or otherwise, relating to the period of the post-war settlement of the refugees, it is hard to see how a history of the refugees in Britain after 1945 can be written without using the journal. Official British documents provide information about the admission of the refugees in the 1930s, about their internment and wartime service. But after their post-war naturalization, the refugees drop out of government records (with the exception of certain matters relating to restitution payments) and are treated not much differently from other groups of British citizens. Unfortunately for historians (though fortunately for civil liberties), the British government did not place the newly naturalized refugees under surveillance, so their communal life after the 1940s is not well documented in the files at the National Archives.

In attempting to cover the history of the refugees from Central Europe in Britain as a whole, this book differs fundamentally from previous studies. Some of these are well known and authoritative studies of particular aspects of the refugees' history: accounts of British immigration policy, of relations between the refugees and Anglo-Jewry, of wartime internment, of refugees serving in the British forces, of the Kindertransport children, as well as the many books on distinguished individual refugees and on specific areas in which refugees have contributed to British society.

By definition, none of these offers an overall history of the settlement of this group of refugees in Britain in the post-war years. Studies of Anglo-Jewry and studies of immigrant communities and minorities in Britain cover the Jewish refugees from Central Europe, of necessity, only relatively briefly. Other studies have drawn on interviews conducted with surviving refugees several decades after the events of their early settlement. But none of these claims to be a history of the refugees, nor do they attempt to supply an in-depth historical narrative covering the experience of the refugees over the early decades of settlement.

There are two aspects of refugee life that this book does not investigate in detail. The first is restitution, a complex area requiring specialist understanding of German and Austrian restitution and social welfare law. The second is religion. This study concentrates on that majority of the refugees who were represented by organizations like the AJR and can be termed assimilated, even if, as in many cases, they remained observant. Many of these refugees were secularized, retaining from their homelands a common social culture and lifestyle that was highly distinctive, but no longer primarily religiously based. The smaller groupings of Orthodox Jewish refugees that grew up in areas like Stamford Hill in London or parts of Manchester will not be considered here. Nor will there be any detailed discussion of refugee religious life; for that, readers are referred to specialist studies of institutions like Belsize Square Synagogue, the principal refugee synagogue.

Because synagogues and other specifically Jewish institutions (like Jewish schools) were no longer at the heart of the refugee community, their records tell us far less about that community than they do about Anglo-Jewry. Anglo-Jewish records generally are of limited use, since the refugees from Central Europe mostly maintained their distance from British Jewry, certainly as far as their communal identity is concerned. I have preferred instead to draw on sources like *AJR Information* and other documents by refugees from the period, where possible. For it is here that the authentic voice of the refugee community can be heard, and it is on the basis of these sources that one can best approach a historical recreation of refugee life.

Acknowledgements

It is a pleasure to acknowledge the assistance that I have received from numerous organizations and individuals in the completion of this book. Pride of place among the organizations goes to the Association of Jewish Refugees, which welcomed me into its fold long before I joined its staff. The AJR's Charitable Trustees generously supported my research financially from 2000 to 2005, then smoothed the way to my book's appearance by helping to cover the costs of publication. I was also the grateful recipient of a scholarship from the Harold Hyam Wingate Foundation in 2005. Members of staff at the British Library, the Wiener Library and the National Archives assisted me in my research, as did Ken Emond at the British Academy and Judith Curthoys at Christ Church, Oxford. Special thanks go to Vallentine Mitchell for publishing the book, and in particular to Heather Marchant.

I owe a debt of gratitude to many friends and colleagues. I have greatly enjoyed and benefited from the friendship and expertise of my long-standing colleagues at the Research Centre for German and Austrian Exile Studies, Charmian Brinson, Richard Dove, Marian Malet, Hamish Ritchie and Jennifer Taylor. Collaborating with Bea Lewkowicz on the exhibition 'Continental Britons' and the AJR's 'Refugee Voices' project has enhanced and enriched my understanding of the field. I would also like to thank all the colleagues at the Institute of Germanic and Romance Studies (and the former Institute of Germanic Studies), University of London.

My research has gained immeasurably from the many Jewish refugees who have shared their experiences with me, as friends and as interviewees. The late Richard Grunberger, my predecessor as editor of *AJR Journal*, was a model and an inspiration to me, as well as a very dear friend. Above all, I must thank my wife Eva for her support and advice and for her unfailing confidence in my ability to produce this book over the years that it took me to write.

Anthony Grenville
July 2009

The Jews from Germany and Austria in Britain, 1933–1939

The position of the Jewish community in Germany came under immediate threat when Hitler was appointed chancellor of Germany in January 1933 and the Nazis gained control of the machinery of state. Jews at once began to seek to escape the hostile regime by emigrating; Britain was to become host to one of the largest settled communities of German-speaking Jews who fled abroad before the war. The conditions under which the Jewish refugees came to Britain and the procedures by which they were admitted were very important to the nature and development of that community; immigration to Britain proved to be a kind of selection process that determined the community's composition, dictating who was admitted and who was not.

The most important factor determining the admission and reception of the Jewish refugees from Hitler's Reich who sought entry to Britain was the attitude of the British government and people. The British government was in the uncomfortable position of having to wait on the initiatives of an unpredictable and potentially hostile power, which dealt. with the Jewish issue as it saw fit, regardless of any difficulties this might cause Britain. To understand the development of British immigration policy after 1933 properly, one must take account of Nazi policy towards the Jews, for Nazi policy effectively dictated the pace of emigration, the varying levels of persecution which it imposed determining the number of Jews wishing to emigrate and the urgency of their desire to do so.[1]

At first, Nazi intentions towards the Jews were unknown. It was clear that Germany's Jews would suffer, for hatred of the Jews was fundamental to Nazi ideology and to Hitler's entire thinking. Yet it was quite unclear in 1933 what forms of persecution that hatred would take. While the Führer plainly believed that Jews had no place within the German national community (*Volksgemeinschaft*) and that they should be removed from German society, there is no evidence at this stage that he intended to exterminate the entire Jewish population of Germany, let alone of Europe. Nazi policy was certainly to persecute the Jews and make life increasingly difficult for them, but it evolved piecemeal, in response to external events and internal party pressures, not according to a master plan for genocide. What Karl Schleunes has called 'the twisted road to Auschwitz' (see note 1) was anything but a highroad to mass murder.

As Nazi policy towards the Jews developed, it determined the varying levels of persecution they suffered, and these in turn dictated their attitude to emigration, which the Nazis sought to encourage, if inconsistently. A significant and surprising feature of Jewish emigration from Germany was the relatively modest number emigrating in the first five years of Nazi rule, up to 1938. It is perhaps helpful to think of Nazi policy towards the Jews before the outbreak of war in two phases: 1933–38, the phase of relatively restrained persecution, and the period after the annexation of Austria (March 1938) and the 'Crystal Night' pogrom in Germany (November 1938), the period of open terror. In turn, emigration to Britain proceeded in two phases: in the first, 1933–38, numbers were small, but in the second, from March 1938 to the outbreak of war in September 1939, Jews fled to Britain at the rate of some thousands per month.

In response to the Nazi takeover of power and the initial excesses of Nazi rule, 37,000 Jews (of some 570,000) left Germany in 1933. But as the situation stabilized, numbers fell, and for the next five years the annual rate of emigration never exceeded 25,000.[2] The officially inspired boycott of Jewish businesses and professions of 1 April 1933, the series of laws and decrees passed in the same month that purged the civil service, the legal and medical professions and the education system of Jews, and even the Nuremberg Laws of September 1935, institutionalizing racial discrimination, failed to overcome the reluctance of many German Jews to emigrate. It took a campaign of real and sustained brutality to drive the assimilated Jews of Germany out of their native land en masse, and that campaign commenced in 1938.

On 12 March 1938 German forces marched into Austria. The *Anschluss*, the incorporation of Austria into the Reich, met with the enthusiastic approval of large numbers of Austrians and provoked an orgy of anti-Semitic excesses, especially in Vienna, where mob fury was let loose on the defenceless Jews. The looting and violence was on a scale not seen in Germany, and it shocked observers like the American journalist William Shirer and his British colleague G.E.R. Gedye.[3] The anti-Jewish excesses in Vienna represented a step change in the level of persecution. Now frantic Jews queued for hours at the consulates of all countries that might conceivably grant them entry visas. When the young Viennese Jew Georg Klaar (George Clare) arrived in Berlin with his family after the *Anschluss*, he found the relaxed conditions in Germany a blessed relief after Vienna.[4] That was not to last. On 7 November 1938 a young Polish Jew, Herschel Grynszpan, shot and fatally wounded a German diplomat in Paris. In revenge, the Nazis unleashed a state-inspired pogrom on the Jewish community. During the night of 9/10 November, hundreds of Jewish shops were plundered and nearly 300 synagogues burned; because of the broken glass, Goebbels cynically named the pogrom the *Reichskristallnacht* ('Crystal Night').

For the first time there was large-scale violence carried out against Jewish communities nationwide. The resulting orgy of violence affected hundreds of Jewish communities and spelt the end of any hope that Jews might lead an ordered existence inside Germany. Hundreds of Jews were murdered and some 30,000 Jewish men arrested, many sent to concentration camps for a time. A series of regulations were issued in the wake of the November pogrom, designed to intensify the elimination of Jews from the German economy, thus depriving them of their livelihood, to curtail their activities and to limit their interaction with Germans, and generally to subject them to harassment, humiliation and misery.

Jews now sought desperately to escape from the Reich. But they faced serious obstacles, not least because most foreign countries were closing their doors to Jewish refugees. In addition, the Nazi authorities subjected those wishing to emigrate to a bureaucratic paper-chase; to satisfy the requirements for emigration, a refugee had to have a sheaf of documents, including an exit permit, a certificate of good conduct (*Führungszeugnis*), a document certifying that all tax payments had been made (*steuerliche Unbedenklichkeitsbescheinigung*), as well as a passport (stamped with the obligatory 'J' for *Jude*) and the documents necessary for admission abroad. Jews were subject to various taxes on leaving Germany, the tax on 'flight from the Reich' (*Reichsfluchtsteuer*) and that on Jewish wealth (*Judenvermögensabgabe*), and were only permitted to take personal effects and ten Reichsmarks with them. The difficulties confronting would-be emigrants were exacerbated when the number of Jews under Hitler's control increased with the German occupation of the Sudetenland in autumn 1938, followed by the invasion of the rump of Czechoslovakia in March 1939.

Much as the Nazis wished to rid themselves of 'non-Aryans', the brutality and sheer malice with which they conducted the process of emigration impeded the departure of many Jews. And time was now of the essence. Within ten months of the 'Crystal Night', Hitler invaded Poland and provoked the Second World War. Under wartime conditions, emigration became vastly more difficult. Then, after the invasion of the Soviet Union in 1941, the Nazis turned to other means to realize their 'Final Solution'. Nevertheless, by September 1939 a considerable portion of Germany's 570,000 Jews had emigrated; of the Austrian Jews, who had only the eighteen months between the *Anschluss* and the outbreak of war in which to leave, some two-thirds, almost 130,000, succeeded in emigrating. The number that found refuge in Britain, often with considerable difficulty, was surprisingly large.

The entry of Jewish refugees into Britain from 1933 depended on the government; governments could refuse them entry on principle, as the USSR did, or apply rigid quota limits on the American model. Britain adopted neither of these expedients. With the Aliens Act of 1905, designed to limit Jewish immigration from Eastern Europe, Britain had abandoned its policy of allowing free entry to immigrants. This act, together with other legislation and the detailed regulations set out in the Aliens Order of 1920, provided the legislative framework within which the government approached the problems created by the sudden demand for entry from German Jews after 1933.

British government policy towards the Jewish refugees from the Third Reich has been the subject of several substantial academic studies, often notably critical of its shortcomings. The pioneering works were A.J. Sherman's *Island Refuge: Britain and the Refugees from the Third Reich 1933–1939* (1973) and Bernard Wasserstein's *Britain and the Jews of Europe 1939–1945* (1988). Sherman's study, which covers the pre-war years when the great majority of the immigrants from the German-speaking countries were admitted, reached the relatively mild judgement that, on balance, Britain's record in admitting over 60,000 refugees was compassionate, even generous, at least by comparison with other nations. Wasserstein, on the other hand, concentrated on the wartime years, when very few Jews were admitted to Britain, and on British policy on Jewish immigration to Palestine, which was anything but generous. The more recent, authoritative study by Louise London, *Whitehall and the Jews, 1933–1948* (2000), is a model of exhaustive research on official documents, but so consistently critical of government policy that it does not do justice to the relative generosity of that policy in the immediate pre-war period.

For the first five years of Nazi rule, British government policy was, broadly, to restrict the admission of refugees to a modest number, while trying to maintain an appearance of humanity in its approach to the refugee problem: a manageable compromise between humanity and expediency. On 5 April 1933 the Cabinet discussed the increasing number of Jewish refugees from Germany seeking entry to Britain and appointed a committee to examine the proposals presented to the Home Office by representatives of Anglo-Jewry, who demanded free entry for the refugees and offered to cover all the costs of maintaining them.[5] On 7 April the committee recommended to the Cabinet that the existing arrangements for the admission of German-Jewish refugees be maintained, rejecting both the alternative of tightening the restrictions on entry and that of relaxing them, as demanded by the Jewish representatives; the only change was that refugees had to register with the police on reaching their destinations in Britain. This compromise was largely maintained until 1938; it allowed the government to claim both that it was safeguarding British interests and that, by considering each case on its merits, it was proceeding in accordance with humanitarian traditions.

This was a time of very high unemployment when, the government feared, groups like Oswald Mosley's British Union of Fascists might exploit an influx of Jewish refugees to create instability by appealing to the undercurrents of anti-Semitism prevalent in much of British society. Ministers were not insensitive to the plight of the refugees, especially when Nazi brutality outraged public opinion and provoked waves of sympathy for the refugees. But ultimately British interests came first. The Cabinet favoured the admission of refugees who could bring some benefit to Britain, for example if they had distinguished themselves in an artistic, scientific or technological field or might create new industrial enterprises. Those who had sufficient financial resources to provide for themselves were at an advantage throughout. Otherwise, and especially if they lacked any obvious means of supporting themselves, refugees risked being turned back at their port of entry by immigration officers. It was these officials who were, up to 1938, at the front line in deciding who could and could not enter Britain.

Consequently, it is not surprising that the relatively few refugees who settled in Britain between 1933 and 1938 included a number of persons with capital, industrialists who would set up firms and provide employment, established figures in the arts like the writer Stefan Zweig, and a significant element of scientific and academic talent brought over under the auspices of the Society for the Protection of Science and Learning.[6] Less eminent refugees were allowed in as students and domestic servants, or to fill specific job vacancies, or on condition that they did not take employment. The early refugees also included a significant number of political opponents of the regime, often non-Jewish. Accurate figures are not available, but best estimates suggest that by 1938 there were less than 10,000 refugees from Germany in Britain.

The Jewish community in Britain assisted the refugees substantially. In 1933 it set up the Jewish Refugees Committee (later German Jewish Aid Committee) under Otto M. Schiff, a banker of Anglo-German origin, which was funded by the Central British Fund for German Jewry.[7] To this body must go much of the credit for administering the admission of many thousands of Jewish refugees. Leading figures in the Jewish community, like Simon Marks, Viscount Samuel and Lord Bearsted, raised money for the cause. The Board of Deputies of British Jews provided an organizational base for the project of rescue at Woburn House. By early 1939 the organizations involved had multiplied so greatly that new premises had to be found for them, and they moved to Bloomsbury House, which provided accommodation, employment and subsistence for many a desperate refugee. Most importantly, the Jewish community undertook in April 1933 to bear all the expenses of maintaining and accommodating the Jewish refugees, thus ensuring that they would not become a burden on the state.[8] This guarantee to the Treasury greatly eased the position, though the number of those admitted ultimately involved expenditure beyond the capacity of the community, and in September 1939 the government took it over.

Richard Bolchover's study of Anglo-Jewish responses to the arrival of the refugees and to the Holocaust, *British Jewry and the Holocaust* (1993), was the first scholarly work in this area, and was particularly valuable in its analysis of the anxieties underlying the reception accorded by British Jews to the new immigrants. Pamela Shatzkes viewed Anglo-Jewry's efforts more favourably in her study, *Holocaust and Rescue: Impotent or Indifferent? Anglo-Jewry 1938–1945* (2002). One of the merits of Shatzkes' book is that it differentiates clearly between the pre-war period, when the Anglo-Jewish organizations achieved a measure of success in securing entry for refugees from Nazism, and the wartime period, when its demands met with government intransigence.

Government policy underwent a marked change in 1938, in response to the waves of refugees caused by the *Anschluss* and the 'Crystal Night'. In March 1938 the Jews of Austria were the first to flee in large numbers, overwhelming the resources of the British consul general in Vienna, who reported that his building was 'literally besieged every day by hundreds of Jews',[9] conditions which were to be repeated in Germany after November 1938. At the insistence of the Home Office, the government reacted in April 1938 by instituting a visa system, which required refugees to obtain a visa from the British authorities before they left the Reich. It is often argued that this was intended to restrict further the number of refugees entering Britain. If so, it was a conspicuous failure. Whereas at most 10,000 refugees had been admitted in the five years since 1933, some 60,000 were admitted in the eighteen months between March 1938 and the outbreak of war. To move from admitting some 2,000 refugees a year to admitting over 3,000 a month is, even by Home Office standards, a curious way of effecting a reduction in numbers.

If the government had wished to limit the numbers admitted to the pre-1938 level, or even to reduce them further, it could easily have done so. Instead, Britain was virtually alone in increasing sharply the number of refugees it admitted, and it did so just when the Nazis intensified their persecution of the Jews and caused a massive upsurge in the number of Jews desperate to emigrate. One can argue that as Nazi policy towards the Jews moved into its second, more brutal phase, British immigration policy also took on a new dimension, largely in response.

Britain now admitted various groups of Jewish refugees in some numbers. Nearly 10,000 children were admitted without visas and other formalities on rail and sea transports that became known as *Kindertransports*. An unknown number, probably greater, were women admitted as domestic servants. Some 5,000 men, housed at Kitchener Camp in Richborough, Kent, were admitted as 'transmigrants', on the understanding, mostly never fulfilled, that they would re-emigrate; most of them had been released from Nazi concentration camps because they had been granted transit visas that allowed them into Britain.[10] A considerable number of Jews were able to obtain visas by finding guarantors willing to offer a financial guarantee to cover their expenses, while others came to take up specific offers of employment in industry, commerce and the academic, artistic, scientific and other fields. Trainees were given visas, as were nurses and some persons over 60.

This does not mean that entry to Britain was easy; far from it. The process of securing a visa while still in the Reich was arduous, time-consuming and nerve-wracking. The attitude of the British government to the Jewish refugees was far from welcoming; it remained grudging and ungenerous, at least in the sense that too few were admitted and those only with some reluctance. The prevailing tinge of anti-Semitism, official obstructionism and hostility to foreign refugees never vanished, and it was reinforced by those sections of public opinion that opposed the admission of Jews from Europe.

Nevertheless, possession of a visa did guarantee entry, whereas before April 1938 a refugee arriving at a British port had run the risk of being refused entry by the immigration officer. Take the case of the Austrian actress Hanne Norbert (Nussbaum), later to marry the distinguished refugee actor Martin Miller. She was performing in Innsbruck at the time of the *Anschluss*, took a train to the Channel ports and travelled on by boat to Britain, where she was promptly deported back to France. Later, however, her parents came to Britain with a visa that included her, and she then entered Britain without a hitch.[11]

Historians have been slower to acknowledge Britain's crucial role in admitting Jews emigrating from the Reich in the period 1938/39 than were the refugees themselves.[12] As early as 1946, a letter to the editor of

the journal of the Association of Jewish Refugees, *AJR Information*, recalled
the situation from personal experience:

> Tens of thousands of applications had been submitted to the American
> and British consulates and to a dozen other consulates in all parts of
> Germany and tens of thousands of desperate men and women were
> beleaguering them day by day. In this situation the countries overseas
> raised the walls of their frontiers higher and higher and made them
> more and more insurmountable for the deplorable people. Only
> Great Britain was a glorious exception, particularly in favour of
> Jewish children, but only after November 1938, which was very late
> for many people.[13]

A more considered historical appraisal by the journal's editor, Werner
Rosenstock, appeared on the twentieth anniversary of the 'Crystal Night'
pogrom, emphasizing the greatly increased rate of immigration in the last
nine months before the war and adding that many Jews who perished
would have been saved if more countries had followed Britain in relaxing
their immigration policies. Rosenstock wrote with authority on this subject, for from November 1938 till August 1939 he had worked for the
Reichsvertretung der Juden in Deutschland, the organization of the
German Jews under the Nazis, in a department responsible for emigration
to Britain. He also had figures to back up his argument:

> The frontiers of most countries were barred. The United States and
> Palestine were restricted in their immigration policies by the quota
> and certificate systems. The only country which really reached [out]
> a helping hand and which thus lived up to the emergency, was Great
> Britain. Of the 100,000–150,000 Jews who left Germany between
> the pogroms and the outbreak of war, about 40,000 found refuge in
> this island, and in addition a further 40,000 from Austria and
> Czechoslovakia. One must have experienced what it meant in those
> days of anxiety if a letter from a guarantor or from a British immi-
> gration authority arrived in a Jewish household.[14]

Of the 250,000 or so Jews who escaped from Germany before September
1939, at least two-fifths emigrated after November 1938, and of those not
far short of 40 per cent came to Britain.

One might have expected that the proportion of German Jews who survived would have been considerably greater than that of the Jews from
Austria, given that the latter had only the eighteen months between the
Anschluss and the outbreak of war in which to emigrate. But the figures,
approximate though they are, show that the proportion of Austrian Jews

who survived was at least as great; of the Jews of Vienna, where some 90 per cent of Austrian Jewry lived, about two-thirds, 120,000 of 180,000, emigrated. This can be explained by the timing of historical events; the Austrian Jews were driven to emigrate over a period of eighteen months, from March 1938 to September 1939, whereas the German Jews only came under comparable pressure after the 'Crystal Night' pogrom in November 1938. That difference of eight months represented nearly half of the precious window of opportunity for emigration, before the outbreak of war blocked the emigration route to Britain, the largest recipient country in those critical months.

The number of Austrian Jews who found refuge in Britain before the war has been calculated at 27,293 (the figure given by Jewish organizations to the Nazi authorities in November 1941), or, more reliably, as 30,850 (the figure arrived at by a post-war study).[15] More pre-war Jewish refugees from Vienna came to Britain as their first country of refuge than to any other, though since some moved on, the final number in America exceeded that in Britain. Nevertheless, it is a fact that something approaching one in six of Vienna's 180,000 Jews found refuge in Britain, and that of those who survived the Nazi years (some 120,000), almost one in four survived by fleeing to Britain. As a result, anyone familiar with the refugee community in the post-war decades would have observed a compact block of Viennese Jews, clustering especially in north-west London, with their own unmistakable culture.

The procedures of emigration also played a key role in determining the composition of the Jewish refugee community that settled in Britain, as they favoured some groups of potential refugees while disadvantaging others. Obvious beneficiaries of the visa system were scientists, scholars and artists with international reputations, like Sigmund Freud or Richard Tauber, or industrialists willing to set up new enterprises, though these were few in number. More numerous were those able to find British citizens who would provide them with the financial guarantee that secured a visa or those who found employment with British firms on account of their specialized skills. It was predominantly the affluent, middle-class, cosmopolitan sections of the Jewish community who were able to take advantage of such contacts, while poorer Jews tended to lack the life-saving benefits of wealth, contacts abroad, bankable qualifications and familiarity with the mechanics of foreign travel. Younger Jews, energetic and flexible, and those without children were also at an advantage, whereas the elderly were often reluctant to emigrate.

Those who found jobs in domestic service for their daughters or who sent their children to Britain as students were also largely middle-class people, sometimes with contacts in Britain, as were those able to find positions in households for themselves because they knew enough of Britain to advertise their services in British newspapers. Even those who sent their children on Kindertransports were predominantly those who had some familiarity with travel to a foreign country, unlike the poor Jews in the city slums, for whom the journey to Britain would have been a leap into the unknown. In the bureaucratic obstacle race of emigration, the advantages lay with those who possessed money, skills, education, awareness of the outside world and the readiness and adaptability to exploit any opportunity to gain admission to Britain. Those still living in the traditional lifestyle of Eastern Europe would have been unfamiliar even with the procedure for applying for a passport.

The Jews who fled to Britain in 1938/39 were not representative of German and Austrian Jewry as a whole. This is of great importance for the development of the refugee community in Britain, for that community would have been very different if it had reflected more exactly the social and occupational structure of Jewry in its native lands. That the emigration from Vienna, to take an obvious example, was unrepresentative of Viennese Jewry as a whole and drew disproportionately on middle-class groups is easily demonstrated. The largest concentration of Jews in any district of Vienna was to be found in the Leopoldstadt or 'Mazzesinsel', the Second District, where the Jewish population tended to be poorer, working class, Orthodox and closer to the traditions and customs of the East. But among the refugees in Britain there was a marked preponderance of those from the more prosperous inner districts of Vienna, such as the first, eighth and ninth, where the Jews were more assimilated, secularized, middle class in lifestyle, prosperity and occupation, well educated and wedded to the German-speaking culture of the city to which they had contributed so notably.[16]

It is a common perception that one only had to scratch a Viennese Jew to discover a Freud, a Popper, a Gombrich or at the very least a budding member of the Amadeus Quartet. This is, however, an illusion, resulting not least from the fact that the less assimilated, lower-class Jews from the poorer districts of Vienna, though more numerous, were far less successful than assimilated, middle-class, 'culture-bearing' Jews in overcoming the obstacles to emigration in the short period between the *Anschluss* and the outbreak of war. In the lapidary phrase of Georg Stefan Troller, describing the Leopoldstadt and the fate of its Orthodox residents, 'Waren wir Assimilanten nach Westen emigriert, so die frommen Chassidim geschlossen nach Auschwitz' ('While we assimilated Jews emigrated to the West, the observant Hassidic Jews went en masse to Auschwitz').[17]

Middle-class, professional Jews entered Britain in considerable numbers despite the instructions circulated by the Foreign Office's Passport Control Department to officials responsible for issuing visas. According to these, applicants unsuitable for admission were small shopkeepers, retail traders, artisans and persons likely to seek employment, minor musicians and commercial artists of all kinds, and the rank and file of professional men, lawyers, doctors and dentists. Yet one of the features of the refugee community in Britain was precisely the number of small businessmen, traders and entrepreneurs it contained, as a walk in the post-war years up the Finchley Road in north-west London, the area around which refugee shops, cafés and businesses clustered most densely, would have demonstrated.

Lawyers and medical and dental practitioners faced additional opposition from British professional bodies bent on defending their members' interests; however, they arrived in some numbers, reflecting, as did the businessmen, the patterns of employment and vocational choice common among middle-class German and Austrian Jews. Considerable numbers of medical practitioners from these countries eventually practised in Britain, though by no means all of them were able to.[18] Fewer lawyers were able to practise, on account of the two countries' differing legal systems, but their skills still enabled many of them to build careers in commerce, industry and management, and in dealing with the legal side of post-war restitution claims. The wealth of musical and artistic talent that this wave of immigration famously brought to Britain also made light of Foreign Office instructions.

During the early period of settlement in Britain before the war, the refugees faced formidable difficulties in their initial efforts to establish themselves. Much of British society was at best ignorant about and indifferent to their plight, at worst unsympathetic and hostile. The sense of distance between Britain and the continent of Europe was far greater than it is now, and the prevailing attitude towards foreigners was instinctively suspicious and hostile. Jews in particular were the butt of prejudice, viewed with distaste by a population that knew little about them and cared less. Though the level of prejudice did not compare with that from which the refugees had escaped, and was significantly lower than in much of Europe, the reception accorded to the refugees in Britain initially was in general far from welcoming.

Public attitudes to the refugees in Britain were divided. The number of extreme right-wingers, ideologically committed anti-Semites or outright supporters of Nazism was very small. Mosley's British Union of Fascists was vocal, but electorally insignificant; the government remained nervous, however, about the potential of such groups for stirring up trouble over the refugee issue. More widespread was an ugly layer of anti-Semitism that pervaded right-wing sections of the social and political establishment and the right-wing press. Those sections of the middle classes affected by what is termed 'golf club anti-Semitism' disliked and distrusted Jews, indulging in the discourse of casual racism and in acts of petty but wounding discrimination. They mostly drew the line at outright violence and the institutionalization of racial discrimination, however: men like G.K. Chesterton and Hilaire Belloc, the mouthpieces of such attitudes, could not stomach Nazi measures. But there is no doubt that much of the traditional right was opposed to the settlement of 'alien Jews' in Britain, and the Chamberlain government paid heed to its views. The government's policy of seeking to avoid war by appeasing Hitler also militated against the favourable treatment of known enemies of Germany.

Hard-line right-wingers in parliament critical of government immigration policy declared that Britain could support only very few refugees and argued that large-scale immigration would lead to an increase in anti-Semitism and to public disorder. At a time of mass unemployment, the trade unions also opposed immigration that threatened 'British jobs', as did professional bodies intent on defending the interests of their members against an influx of well-qualified refugee practitioners. Often, such arguments cloaked a deeper hostility to the integration of foreigners, especially Jews, into British society, whose cohesion was seen to depend on adherence to a core of homogeneously 'British' values from which 'aliens' were excluded.

The refugees also had their supporters, though these were a minority and, with the possible exception of periods like the aftermath of the 'Crystal Night' pogrom,[19] had to fight an uphill battle against public attitudes of indifference or hostility. Those who spoke up for the refugees in the House of Commons included Eleanor Rathbone, Colonel Josiah Wedgwood and Commander Oliver Locker-Lampson, and Lord Marley in the Lords. Bishop George Bell of Chichester was among the churchmen who championed their cause, as did a steadfast band of liberal and progressive notables who could be relied on for their support. The Society of Friends (Quakers) was particularly active in bringing refugees to Britain and supporting them. The refugees experienced much kindness and generosity from men and women across the country who acted in a spirit of humanity and charity, responding with sympathy and compassion to the plight of penniless, disorientated Jews escaping from the Reich.

Such people stood guarantor for refugees trapped in Germany, took in refugee children, provided accommodation or employment for adults, or simply offered the support of friendship to newcomers struggling to come to terms with an unfamiliar environment. Not surprisingly, refugee memories of such generosity remain vivid and warm. The distinguished historian Peter Pulzer, who came to Britain from Vienna as a boy in 1939, stated categorically that the private and voluntary efforts made in Britain were second to none.[20] He described the Hertfordshire vicar and his wife who took him in as 'the absolute salt of the earth, of the sort one is familiar with from the British middle class', the wife in particular being 'an absolutely tireless carer for other people's welfare'. But the experience of another distinguished refugee historian, Professor John Grenville, who came as a boy from Berlin and is now a colleague of Peter Pulzer at the Leo Baeck Institute in London, was very different: as a young refugee, he had to battle hard for his education against an environment that displayed disdain for his abilities, suspicion of his ambitions and indifference to his personal development.

The element of chance and luck often played a crucial role in refugees' lives, as demonstrated by the strikingly different beginnings from which these two academics built successful careers. The imponderable factors of character and temperament also conditioned refugees' reactions to the experience of exile. The life stories of two cousins from Vienna, Adolf Placzek and Ernst Philipp, illustrate this very clearly; though both men were from very similar backgrounds, had broadly similar experiences up to and including the early stages of emigration and retained a lifelong close relationship, their lives took very different directions. Adolf Placzek, whose temperament inclined him to be positive and life-affirming, fled to Britain after the *Anschluss*, then went on to America, where he enjoyed a distinguished career as Professor of Architecture at Columbia University; he was married to the writer Jan Struther, creator of the figure of Mrs Miniver, until her death in 1953. Ernst Philipp also fled to Britain, saw active service in the forces, but made no attempt to revive his academic career after the war, though he had a doctorate in mathematics; he took a job at a small private boys' school in Seascale, Cumbria, in which remote location he remained for the rest of his life, isolated and often depressed. The cousins' lives were shaped by their contrasting personalities.[21]

The difficulties with which the refugees had to cope varied widely, according to factors such as their age on arrival. The children who came on Kindertransports were the most obviously innocent victims of Nazi persecution. The strange and often frightening world to which they escaped was, unavoidably, very different from that in which they had been growing up, and many of them never entirely overcame the shock and disorientation of the rupture. As children, they were heavily dependent on the adults immediately around them, in foster families, schools or hostels. The children either went straight to foster-parents or were housed in temporary accommodation, like Dovercourt holiday camp near Harwich, the main port of arrival, where places were then found for them with families, schools or hostels or in employment. A large number of hostels sprang up in towns and cities across the country, with a noticeable cluster in the Willesden area of north-west London. The Refugee Children's Movement tried to monitor the children's well-being, but the scale of the task was beyond its resources.

Some children suffered emotional neglect, even abuse, from unsuitable foster-parents; others encountered warmth and love. For example, Martha Blend, née Immerdauer, who came from Vienna aged 9, recorded at length the kindness with which she was enveloped by the Jewish foster family of modest means who took her in and the neighbourliness that characterized the whole area of the East End where they lived.[22] In her detailed study of six cousins from Leipzig who came on Kindertransports, Gertrude Dubrovsky recounts how Vera Nussenbaum, née Ribetski, found a loving surrogate family in the home of Bertha and Arthur Staff of Norwich. But Dubrovsky also unearthed a serious case of sexual abuse.[23] The pain endured by the many children who were placed in ill-suited or uncaring homes, thus accentuating their awareness of the loss of their parents, comes across vividly in the volumes that record their memories, as does the difficulty they had in adapting to the largely indifferent and uncomprehending society around them.[24]

The experience of the (mostly older) children placed in schools and residential institutions was in some respects different. Though they lacked the family surroundings, hostels like the Bradford Jewish Refugee Hostel in Parkfield Road, Manningham, created a happy environment in which a supportive communal spirit developed. The arrival of a group of refugee boys in Bradford attracted sympathetic publicity in the local press, which may have contributed to the warmth of their reception. Their recorded memories are full of gratitude for the friendliness they encountered: 'People were extremely kind to us. I have never met anything but kindness in Bradford. People of all levels went out of their way to help us.'[25] Living among other refugees, they escaped the isolation that affected children living alone in a British environment, and the morale-boosting effect of life in such a collective doubtless helped retrospectively to shape their recollections of it.

Otto Tausig, later an actor in Austria, who arrived aged 16 in 1939, experienced a not untypical admixture of callousness and helpfulness, hardship and support.[26] The man whose job offer allowed the boy into

Britain turned out to be a paedophile, though Tausig fortunately escaped his attentions; as well as abusing the children, the man was a swindler who took the guarantee money posted by the guarantors (£50), sent the boys to a third-rate school in Whitby at minimal expense and pocketed the rest. Tausig and two other refugee pupils went miserably hungry, but were saved by the generosity of Quakers who opened their house to them. When the school was closed down, Tausig tried to survive as a string player in a local orchestra, then worked on a chicken farm. From this ill-rewarded toil he was rescued by a benefactress, who invited him to live in her house in Oxford, where he managed to secure a scholarship to study economics at London University – only to be interned in 1940.

The Kindertransportees' own perceptions of their experiences in Britain are strikingly favourable. It is hard not to be moved by the pages of grateful tributes to benefactors in the brochure published to accompany the sixtieth anniversary celebration in 1999: 'Alice Boddy (now in USA) remembers with gratitude her wonderful foster family, the Lewis family, and is still in contact with her English brothers who welcomed little sister Alice into their midst.' 'Professor Fanni Bogdanow remembers with thanks the kindness of her loving and adoptive family, Mr and Mrs H.A. Clement and children in Houghton Green. To this day, the Clement family are still Fanni's own family.'[27] But although many of the children have gone on to lead happy, productive and successful lives, it is probably fair to say that the trauma of separation from their families, growing up in a strange environment and in some cases adopting a new, 'British' identity inevitably left its mark. 'After all', states a recent survey, 'the tale of the Kindertransport is not only one of triumph, but also one of trauma and diversity'.[28]

The large group of women who came as domestic servants often experienced bad treatment, resulting from their station in the households in which they worked; some, however, encountered kindness and would dispute the charge of exploitation levelled against their British employers.[29] Many of the women came from comfortable middle-class homes and found the indignities of life as a domestic intolerable, though they were probably treated no worse than other servants, including servants in middle-class households in Vienna or Berlin. All too often underpaid, underfed and overworked, they were exposed to callous and inhuman treatment by employers who ignored the emotional trauma of their forced emigration and their anxious separation from endangered families at home. The memories of those who came as young girls from sheltered backgrounds frequently dwell on specific experiences: living in unheated rooms, or sharing rooms with no private space; struggling to survive on wages below £1 a week; having only one free afternoon a week; suffering constant hunger; having to empty chamber pots and perform other degrading tasks; above all, the sense that their employers saw them as second-class human beings, oblivious to their feelings and sensitivities at a time when they were desperate for human warmth and support.

These features of thankless drudgery, of acute loneliness and homesickness and of being barred from participation in normal family life and activities have remained central to such analyses of domestic service as there are. This is true both of recent studies and accounts written closer to the time, such as the reflections of Lily Wagner, who in 1938 set up a boarding house for refugees in Hampstead, where she was able to observe the difficulties encountered by the wide range of refugees who lodged with her, not least domestic servants between jobs.[30]

Many of these women were wholly unprepared for domestic service. Hortense Gordon, née Heidenfeld, who came from Breslau in 1939 aged 19, was the daughter of a well-to-do doctor's family who had found her a job with an affluent British family in Surrey; they kitted her out with an evening dress and parting instructions to learn bridge, the key to social life in England.[31] But during the two and a half years she spent as cook-general in Farnham, she toiled from dawn to near midnight to supply a series of copious and frequent meals, and was treated strictly in accordance with her status in the kitchen.

Edith Argy, née Tintner, who came from Vienna in 1938 also aged 19, could not cope at all:

> I had never so much as held a broom, and I was supposed to keep a fairly large house clean, and heaven knows what else I was meant to do. I wasn't used to eating in the kitchen – poor though we were we had had all our meals, except perhaps for a hasty breakfast, in the living room – nor was I used to eating alone. I found the food hard to swallow – quite tasteless; and I had never had malt vinegar before. I was cold in bed. I missed my duvet. The thin blankets seemed to provide no warmth at all. I was desperately homesick. I wanted to die.

She even applied for a German passport with the intention of returning to Vienna.

Edith Argy had a string of short-lived jobs, which she recalls with undiminished bitterness:

> But in many households, particularly the British non-Jewish middle-class ones, servants were considered to be some sub-species of the human race. One could speak freely in front of them because a) they were not equipped intellectually to follow the conversation, and b)

they did not exist as equal human beings. For most of the time they were invisible and untouchable, barely spoken to, unless to receive orders, or if they happened to incur the displeasure of the master or the mistress.[32]

Some of the worst experiences that domestics endured were at the hands of those who had lived in the colonies, where they had learnt to treat servants as an inferior breed of human being and where right-wing, hierarchical views fostered anti-Semitic and racist attitudes.[33] Most refugees, like Edith Argy, left domestic service as soon as they could after the outbreak of war.

The refugees tended to congregate in certain areas, principally north-west London, in the postal districts of NW3 (Belsize Park, Swiss Cottage and Hampstead), NW6 (West Hampstead) and NW11 (Golders Green), with a perceptible presence in the adjacent areas of NW2 (Willesden Green), NW8 (St John's Wood) and W9 (Maida Vale). Those with more Orthodox beliefs settled as a distinct group in Stamford Hill and Stoke Newington. Cities like Manchester and Glasgow had sizeable refugee communities, and they were a presence in the university towns of Oxford and Cambridge. The areas of settlement pointed strongly to the middle-class self-image and aspirations of many refugees; in north-west London, they tended to avoid adjacent working-class areas like Kilburn or Cricklewood, Kentish Town or Camden Town. But at the start they mostly had to lower their expectations sharply. Many of them, being young, accepted this as a temporary loss of status, confident that they would in time be able to work their way up to positions more in line with the aspirations they had inherited from their home backgrounds. Those who came as young couples in particular displayed resilience and resourcefulness, probably because they had partners with whom they could share their troubles and on whom they could rely for support in times of crisis.

The age profile of those who left the Reich was heavily skewed towards the younger age groups; the more elderly, less acceptable as immigrants, were inclined to stay behind, fearful of emigration and believing that the Nazis had no incentive seriously to mistreat harmless old folk. The younger refugees lived in bedsitting rooms, furnished rooms, boarding houses and cheap rented flats, relying on such casual employment as they could find; the women often worked as cleaners or charwomen, while the men tried to gain some professional foothold on which to build a secure existence. Sometimes they were reliant on handouts from the Jewish Refugees Committee in Bloomsbury House. The Lyons Corner Houses in the West End were favoured establishments, both as meeting places and as relatively generous employers. Jewish-owned but not kosher, they harboured so many budding lawyers and other professionals from Germany that refugees joked that the Amtsgericht Berlin Mitte (Central Berlin District Court) had transferred to Lyons Corner House, Piccadilly Circus.

The majority of the adult refugees who made their way to Britain alone or with families faced a daily battle for subsistence. Though there were many for whom this hand-to-mouth existence was far from a joke, most of the younger refugees coped with the unaccustomed poverty and hardship of the early years with surprising resilience. Refugees would later describe their first rooms or flats, with gas rings as cooking facilities, packing crates as storage, mantelpieces as bookshelves, with gas meters, wholly inadequate gas and coal fires, draughty widows and primitive plumbing, in a tone of humorous, even affectionate recollection: as if that initial stage of émigré life were a rite of passage through which they had had to pass on the road to a better, settled life in Britain. There was a widespread sense that such disadvantages were a small price to pay for escaping the fear, discrimination, humiliation and persecution that had been their lot under the Nazis.

The section on accommodation in the study *Changing Countries*[34] contains several vivid descriptions of living conditions in the early days, like that by Adelheid Schweitzer, née Schoenewald, who recalled that she and her husband shared a house in St John's Wood that was let to several other tenants and was 'also inhabited by various flourishing families of mice who came out of the gas fire connection and ran around the room'. Hanna Singer, née Cohn, came on a Kindertransport, followed by her mother; they found a top-floor room in a house, with a shared bathroom on the floor below and a sink that doubled as a washbasin: 'It was just one room, a tiny window looking on to a wall, and we called it the Black Hole of Calcutta, but it was wonderful.' Relief at having escaped the Nazis and a sense of liberation and re-empowerment caused a shabby rented room to seem like the foundation for a new and happier life.

Poverty was the lot of most refugees. Even after the outbreak of war, when she found work as a typist with a printer's business in Exeter, Edith Argy earned one pound and five shillings (25/-) a week, 23/6d after deductions, of which £1 went on board and lodging – she shared a rented room with an aunt – leaving her 3/6d (17½p) for all other expenses. Early in the war, all the furniture Otto Tausig and his new wife possessed was a table, in reality an old door with four sections of a beam from a bombed-out house nailed on to it as legs, a bed, which was an old wire frame resting on bricks, and a bedside table, a beer crate decorated with coloured crown corks. When they were bombed out, they were delighted to receive a few items of real furniture from the authorities.[35]

There were, however, many refugees who suffered grievously from their new situation. These were often older people, who were affected less by the physical deprivations of exile than by a psychological inability to adapt to unfamiliar conditions and a strange lifestyle – there were cases of elderly refugees who were so adrift in Britain that they chose to return to Germany – and especially by the loss of status that shattered their confidence, on which their very identity rested.[36] The expression 'the difficult early years' became something of a set formula in later accounts of the initial experiences of middle-aged refugees forced to leave established positions in Germany. They suffered keenly from a loss of professional dignity: scientists forced to take employment as laboratory technicians; men who had held senior and responsible positions working as bookkeepers and office drudges; scholars and intellectuals like the writer Ernst Sommer working as waiters or menials in the struggle to keep their families. Many refugees saw their professional ambitions destroyed forever; there were even suicides.

Even if they were permitted to work, most refugees could not easily sell their labour on the employment market, coming as so many of the older refugees did from the professional and commercial worlds. The Jewish refugees, young and old, rarely competed in the market for manual or unskilled labour, except as a temporary expedient or to help the war effort. Some of the older refugees, like the doyen of Berlin's theatre critics, Alfred Kerr, never succeeded in gaining settled employment. One of the saddest aspects of his daughter Judith's semi-autobiographical account of the family's early years in Britain is her description of her father's decline into enforced idleness, his inability to find work robbing him of his status within the family and reducing him to dependence on his wife's hard-earned wages.[37] More flexible and adaptable than their husbands, women like Julia Kerr shouldered the burden of providing for their families, often in dead-end jobs and demeaning conditions, while their husbands struggled to find suitable employment. The trials of emigration brought out previously unexpected strengths in the women who took jobs as secretaries, seamstresses, cooks or cleaners.[38]

The refugees had to bridge the substantial gulf between the social culture of their countries of origin and their country of refuge. Britain in the late 1930s was a vastly different society and country from today, more insular, dismissive of European culture and customs and, as befitted an imperial power, almost unquestioningly confident of the superiority of its institutions, traditions and way of life over those of mere Continentals. Refugee memoirs and autobiographies repeatedly record the new arrivals' struggle to adapt to the unfamiliar clothes, climate and customs. The inadequacy of the heating and the inedibility of the food were standard themes: refugees were bewildered by Bovril and Marmite or depressed by the tasteless white bread, while Andrew Sachs, the future actor, was confronted with Shredded Wheat on arrival from Berlin aged 8, and assumed that the English ate straw with milk for breakfast.[39] The young Marianne Elsley, née Josephy, arrived from Rostock on a Kindertransport and stayed with a widow, Elizabeth Carter, and her daughter Irene in north-west London. She was lovingly looked after, but recorded that she was 'totally unprepared for the rigours of the English indoor climate':

> The Carters' house was comfortable enough by pre-war London stan-
> dards. There was an open fire in the sitting-room, an Ideal Boiler
> which gave out a blissful heat in the kitchen, and a gas-fire, rarely in
> use, in a small dining room. The bedrooms were completely unheat-
> ed, and how I shivered during those first months. I should have
> brought a hot water bottle, unheard of in Germany except in the case
> of illness. Irene kindly shared hers with me; that is, I borrowed it to
> get my bed warm and then put it out for her to use. It was not an
> entirely satisfactory arrangement.[40]

Such unaccustomed arrangements were, however, outweighed by the kind-
ness she experienced from the Carters and from the lady who acted as guarantor for her, Miss Courtauld.

The sheer size and anonymity of London, the drab slums and the apparently endless monotony of the suburbs added to the refugees' sense of estrangement. In smaller towns and cities, on the other hand, where refugees were fewer, they could easily feel even more cut off from all that was familiar and reassuring; English manners, with their aloofness and reserve, induced a keen sense of isolation. Many refugees probably suffered more from the invisible barriers created by coolness and politely impenetrable distance than from outright hostility and insult, which seem on the whole to have been rare. Lily Wagner observed how this affected her:

> I had not been long in England and still had a good deal of natural,
> exuberant feeling and warm readiness for friendship. In the mean-
> time the English climate and mentality, which demand a certain
> reserve and cool balance, have changed and to some extent subdued
> me too. The longer one lives in a country, the more readily and nat-
> urally does one grow like its inhabitants. We feel that our English
> hosts do not appreciate extravagance or passion and prefer a distant

> friendliness, which is none the less sincere. And so we try to control
> our overwhelming feelings and keep in check our too warm hearts,
> however hard this enforced reserve may seem.[41]

She also noted how the older refugees struggled to cope with emigration:

> It is pathetic to watch these people who want to settle in England,
> and to see how they, sometimes very old, try hard to adapt themselves
> to their surroundings, to learn the foreign language, to be as little
> conspicuous as possible . . . If you think of it, you realise the tragedy
> of these people, who so well deserve a rest, both physically and men-
> tally, and now in their old age have to learn strange languages, new
> habits and foreign customs.[42]

Language was one of the greatest barriers. Even refugees who had learnt
English at school were at first baffled by the everyday jargon and the Cockney
or local dialects they encountered. Others were barely able to communicate at
all. The refugees themselves proclaimed their foreignness as soon as they
opened their mouths, and their accents often accompanied them through
their lives. For many, it remained a matter of regret, surprise or anger that they
were instantly recognizable as 'foreigners' even after many years of residence
in Britain. Interviewed after half a century of life in south-west London, Klary
Friedl, a refugee from Prague born in Košice, pronounced herself so tired of
being asked where she came from that she regularly replied – in a strong
Slovakian accent – 'I come from Kew Gardens'.[43]

Younger refugees tended to approach the problem of language in a
lighter, more resilient manner. Their struggles with English soon gave rise
to one of the most characteristic features of refugee life, the large body of
jokes that turned on the newcomers' unwitting mangling of the English
language. Some of these jokes became very well worn: for example, the
misuse of the word 'become' to mean 'receive' or 'get' (the meaning of the
German word *bekommen*), as in the oft-recounted tale of the indignant
refugee lady who swept out of an overpriced butcher's declaring 'I can
become a sausage much cheaper round the corner'. The refugees' battle to
decipher the complex cultural patterns encoded in the English language,
and then to imitate them, formed a central part of depictions of the interaction between refugees and British, from George Mikes's *How To Be an Alien*
(1946) and Victor Ross's *Basic British* (1956) to Carl F. Flesch's *'Where Do You
Come from?'* (2001). This stock of jokes passed into refugee lore, veiling the
hardships of the early years behind a bilingual humour that assumed a
certain mastery of both languages and cultures. The element of humour

indicated a relatively relaxed attitude to the problems of integration; it helped to defuse the feeling of otherness.

Perhaps surprisingly, many refugees came to remember the early days in Britain as a happy time. Through the alchemy of memory, acts of kindness now figure prominently in interviews with former refugees: railway porters, taxi drivers or policemen who helped them on arrival; strangers who extended hospitality to them; colleagues at work who took them under their wing. This is not to minimize the frequent incidents of insensitivity, indifference, hostility, prejudice and sheer unfeeling callousness. But in the main, admiration, even affection, for certain aspects of pre-war British life pervade the life stories of refugees: the orderliness of the queues, with their aura of fair play for all; the public insistence on courtesy, especially the habit of saying 'sorry' in the street even when not at fault; the approachability of the 'bobbies', so different from their authoritarian German counterparts; the tolerance of dissenting views and the right of free speech.

Expressions of gratitude to Britain have become something of a standard feature in refugee memoirs, concluding a narrative that is structured to start with an inauspicious arrival in an unfamiliar and unwelcoming country and leads on through a successful struggle against adversity to a happier and fulfilled life. Irene White, née Michelson, who arrived in 1938 via Palestine to train as a nurse, chose to introduce the story of her life in this way:

> I chose *I Came as a Stranger* as the title of my story because in some ways it reflects my life. One day I went unannounced to visit an old lady, when I was working as a welfare officer. She would not let me into her flat, as she did not know me. I therefore made an appointment by letter with her for the next week, and enclosed a recommendation from her congregation. As I was leaving her, after an hour's visit, she said to me, 'You came as a stranger, and you left as a friend.' These were exactly my feelings when I came to England, with only a slight variation. I came as a stranger, and I stayed as a friend. May it remain a country of freedom and fair play for ever.[44]

The deliberate structuring of experience here and the prominent concluding reference to 'British' values clearly reflect this preconceived collective narrative.

Edith Argy, whose early experiences in Britain were far from happy and who left the country for several years after the war, marrying a French-speaking Jew from Egypt in Australia, nevertheless gave her adopted home town a place above all others: 'Vienna will forever be the city of my dreams

– and nightmares – and the beauty of Paris takes my breath away on every visit, but my heart and loyalty very firmly belong to London.' The balance that she drew from her experiences in Britain, happy and unhappy, was unmistakably positive:

> There is much disparaging talk these days about asylum seekers and illegal immigrants. I shall never forget that I was once an asylum seeker, and my father and brother were illegal immigrants. It is fashionable now to talk approvingly of the wave of Continental Jewish refugees in the thirties, and quite a few of them have been made knights and even peers of the realm, but it was not always so. Britain, like every other country, was nervous of being 'swamped' by Jewish foreigners at the time. But Britain gave me life, and I, personally, have never encountered anything but civility, tolerance and friendship in my dealings with the British. Thank you, Britain![45]

The causes of this pronounced shift in so many refugees' perception of Britain, from reluctant host to cherished homeland, lay to a considerable extent in the wartime period. There were also factors that dated back to the pre-war period, not least the strong sense of solidarity and shared identity that grew up among the refugees from Central Europe at an early stage. Clear evidence of the close-knit cohesion of refugee society is the high incidence of marriages among refugees. Of the twenty-eight Jewish refugees interviewed for the study *Changing Countries*, a not untypical group, the great majority married other refugees; a handful married British partners, while only one married a British Jew.

The refugees' collective identity developed at a distance from that of existing Anglo-Jewry; indeed, one of the principal factors constituting the 'Continental' identity of the Jews from Germany and Austria was arguably their continuing separateness from Anglo-Jewry. As already stated, the organ-izational response of Anglo-Jewry to the arrival of Jewish refugees from the Reich[46] was in many respects admirable; the Central British Fund and the Jewish Refugees Committee did especially valuable work. But Anglo-Jewish attitudes towards the refugees were ambiguous. British Jews, the largest section of whom were descendants of the immigrants from Tsarist Russia who had come to Britain at the turn of the previous century, continued to share the misgivings of Eastern Jewry about the assimilated Jews of Central Europe, with their middle-class aspirations and pretensions to high culture.

British Jews were concerned that the arrival of a fresh wave of immigrants would provoke an anti-Semitic backlash and undermine the more secure existence that they had built up over the decades by gradually winning acceptance from gentile society. Richard Bolchover has shown how this anxiety about domestic anti-Semitism exercised a determining influence on Anglo-Jewish attitudes towards the refugees. The fear that an influx of conspicuously alien Jews would arouse the sleeping demons of anti-Semitism led much of Anglo-Jewry to favour restricting the number of refugees permitted to enter the country and to treat those admitted with considerable reserve, even with concealed hostility.[47] This pervasive anxiety found clear expression in the pamphlet *Helpful Information and Guidance for Every Refugee*, published in January 1939 by the German Jewish Aid Committee (the renamed Jewish Refugees Committee) and the Board of Deputies of British Jews. This earnestly exhorted the refugees not to give offence to the British, not to make themselves conspicuous in public by their speech, behaviour or appearance – 'Talk halting English rather than fluent German – and *do not talk in a loud voice*' – and on no account to criticize the British way of life: 'be loyal to England, your host'.

Werner Rosenstock, who served as General Secretary of the AJR from 1941 to 1982 (with a break in the 1940s), was made aware of the divide between the two communities when he met an Anglo-Jewish family from the East End during the war:

> When they realised that I was a refugee, they told me the story of their own experience. In the wake of the November pogroms they offered to take in a refugee child. They expected a downtrodden impoverished child. Instead their guest was not only well clad but also brought with her several cases with beautiful new dresses and other articles. Her first request was for a hot bath after the journey, unable to imagine that there were houses without private bathrooms. Later, the family sat down for the Friday evening meal. It turned out that the girl had never heard the Sabbath blessings. The family was outraged: There we are told of the poor Jews in Germany, who are persecuted because they are Jews, and now we learn to our dismay that they still lived in comfort and had no Jewish bonds though their Jewishness was the reason of their plight. This episode made me aware of the difference between the majority of English Jews, who were immigrants or the children of immigrants and in those days of a modest living standard, and the middle class, assimilated German Jews. This difference resulted in a great amount of misunderstandings between the two groups.[48]

It would appear that greater even than the difference between the two groups in class and wealth were the differences in the degrees of their assimilation, in their attitudes to traditional customs and values and in their understanding of what it meant to be a Jew. One can discern a dual mechanism of rejection and attraction at work in the refugees' attitudes here: the sense of their distance from Anglo-Jewry played its part as one of the factors that fuelled the eagerness with which many of them approached middle-class British society, resolving that in Britain they could hope to continue the process of integration begun in countries now under Nazi rule. That perception of Britain was to emerge greatly reinforced from the war.

Before the war, the refugees were concentrated to a considerable extent in London, but few were securely established. Adult refugees moved between rented rooms, flats and boarding houses, domestic servants moved from position to unsatisfactory position, and Kindertransport children, especially those not placed with families, lacked permanent homes. The precarious economic situation of most refugees, few of whom enjoyed steady employment or a guaranteed income, effectively denied them the possibility of stable settlement. On arrival, a number of refugees were distributed around the country in locations not of their choosing; Kindertransport children and domestic servants were again obvious examples. Glasgow and Manchester, with sizeable existing Jewish communities, were early areas of settlement outside London. A considerable proportion of the refugees whose first places of residence were outside London later gravitated to the capital, but conversely there was also a gradual spreading of refugees outwards from the south-east across the country; according to its annual report for 2006, the AJR boasts no fewer than thirty-five fully-fledged local groups nationwide.[49] But before the refugees could settle securely anywhere in Britain, the coming of war brought fresh disruption to their lives.

NOTES

1. S. Friedländer, *Nazi Germany and the Jews. Volume I: The Years of Persecution, 1933–1939* (New York: HarperCollins, 1998), and especially the pioneering study by K. Schleunes, *The Twisted Road to Auschwitz: Nazi Policy toward German Jews 1933–1939* (Urbana and Chicago, IL: University of Illinois Press, 1990 [1970]).
2. Schleunes, *Twisted Road to Auschwitz*, p.199.
3. W. Shirer, *The Rise and Fall of the Third Reich: A History of Nazi Germany* (New York: Fawcett Publications, 1962 [1959]), p.477, and G. Gedye, *Fallen Bastions: The Central European Tragedy* (London: Gollancz, 1939), pp.300ff.
4. G. Clare, *Last Waltz in Vienna: The Destruction of a Family 1842–1942* (London: Macmillan, 1981), pp.208f.
5. A. Sherman, *Island Refuge: Britain and Refugees from the Third Reich 1933–1939* (London: Frank Cass, 1994 [1973]), pp.29ff.
6. On the SPSL, see R. Cooper, *Refugee Scholars* (Leeds: Moorland Books, 1992), and J. Seabrook, *The Refuge and the Fortress: Britain and the Flight from Tyranny* (London: Palgrave Macmillan, 2008).
7. The files of World Jewish Relief, the renamed Central British Fund, are held at the AJR offices in Stanmore, London.

8. When representatives of the Jewish community undertook in April 1933 that it would bear all the expenses of the refugees' accommodation and maintenance, they estimated the likely numbers of refugees at 3–4,000. See Sherman, *Island Refuge*, p.30.

9. NA (National Archives, Kew), FO371/21635.

10. On the transmigrants, see the short account by Anthony Grenville, 'Saved by a Transit Visa', *AJR Journal* (May 2009), pp.1f.

11. Interview with Hanne Norbert-Miller in the Oral History collection of the Research Centre for German and Austrian Exile Studies at the Institute of Germanic and Romance Studies, University of London.

12. Friedländer, for example, concentrates on the refusal of the British to admit more Jews from the Reich to Palestine and to the British Empire generally, while omitting any mention of the sharp increase in admissions to Britain in 1938/39 (*Years of Persecution*, p.299).

13. *AJR Information* (October 1946), p.5.

14. *AJR Information* (November 1958), pp.1 and 4.

15. W. Muchitsch, *Österreicher im Exil – Großbritannien 1938–1945: Eine Dokumentation* (Vienna: Österreichischer Bundesverlag, 1992), p.8.

16. Similarly, Jews who came to Britain from prosperous districts of Berlin like Charlottenburg, Wilmersdorf or the Hansaviertel far outnumbered those from the Scheunenviertel, a poor district where recent arrivals from Poland tended to congregate.

17. Quoted in G. Troller, 'Eine Art Venedig ohne Lagune', in U. Seeber (ed.), *Ein Niemandsland, aber welch ein Rundblick!: Exilautoren über Nachkriegswien* (Vienna: Picus, 1998), pp.87–90 (p.87).

18. Refugee medical practitioners have been thoroughly researched by P. Weindling. See 'Gebrochene Lebenswege. Erfahrungen medizinischer Flüchtlinge in Großbritannien und anderen Ländern', *Medizin und Judentum*, 7 (2004), pp.9–18, and 'Medical Refugees as Practitioners and Patients: Public, Private and Practice Records', *Yearbook of the Research Centre for German and Austrian Exile Studies*, 9 (2007), pp.141–56.

19. It was in the wake of the pogrom of November 1938 that public outrage, allied to a sense of guilt at Britain's betrayal of Czechoslovakia to Hitler at Munich a few weeks previously, allowed the creation of the Movement for the Care of Children from Germany, later Refugee Children's Movement, which with government assistance organized the Kindertransports.

20. Interviews with Professors Pulzer and Grenville in the archive of filmed interviews 'Refugee Voices: The AJR Audio-Visual Testimony Collection'.

21. *Cousins in Exile: An Anthology. Poems by Adolf Placzek and Ernst Philipp*, with an introduction by M. Ives (Lancaster: Lancaster University, Department of European Languages and Cultures, Occasional Papers in German Studies [2005]).

22. M. Blend, *A Child Alone* (London: Vallentine Mitchell, 1995).

23. G. Dubrovsky, *Six from Leipzig* (London: Vallentine Mitchell, 2004), pp.58f. and 130f. Bertha Staff was Jewish, married to a non-Jew.

24. K. Gershon, *We Came as Children* (London: Gollancz, 1966), B. Leverton and S. Lowensohn, *I Came Alone: Stories of the Kindertransport* (Brighton, Sussex: Book Guild, 1990), and M. Harris and D. Oppenheimer, *Into the Arms of Strangers: Stories of the Kindertransport* (London: Bloomsbury, 2000). The best overall study of the Kindertransports in English to date is B. Turner . . . *And the Policeman Smiled: 10,000 Children Escape from Nazi Europe* (London: Bloomsbury, 1990). See also R. Göpfert, *Der jüdische Kindertransport von Deutschland nach England 1938/39: Geschichte und Erinnerung* (Frankfurt-on-Main/New York: Campus, 1999).

25. Sandor Grünhut from Vienna, in 'Bradford Jewish Refugee Hostel 1939–1989: A Souvenir Brochure Commemorating the 50th Anniversary Reunion, March 1989' (typescript with no publication details or pagination).

26. O. Tausig, *Kasperl, Kummerl, Jud: Eine Lebensgeschichte* (Vienna: Mandelbaum Verlag, 2005), pp.33ff.

27. *Sixtieth Anniversary of the Kindertransport 1939–1999* (London: Reunion of Kindertransport, 15–17 June 1999), pp.34ff.

28. C. Sharples, 'Kindertransport: Terror, Trauma and Triumph', *History Today* (March 2004), pp.23–9 (p.29).

29. A. Grenville, 'Underpaid, Underfed and Overworked: Refugees in Domestic Service', *AJR Journal* (December 2008), pp.1f. This article prompted numerous letters in defence of the way domestic servants were treated.

30. M. Malet and A. Grenville (eds), *Changing Countries: The Experience and Achievement of German-speaking Exiles from Hitler in Britain from 1933 to Today* (London: Libris, 2002), pp.91ff.; L. Wagner, 'Emigrants' Daily Life' (c. 1940), typescript copy of the English translation of the German original, p.30, kindly

provided to me by the late Irene Bloomfield, Dr Wagner's daughter; also T. Kushner, 'An Alien Occupation – Jewish Refugees and Domestic Service in Britain', in W. Mosse (ed.), *Second Chance: Two Centuries of German-speaking Jews in the United Kingdom* (Tübingen: Mohr, 1991), pp.553–78.

31. Interview with Hortense Gordon in the 'Refugee Voices' collection.
32. E. Argy, *The Childhood and Teens of a Jewish Girl in Inter-war Austria and Subsequent Adventures* (Charleston, SC: BookSurge, 2005), pp.145 and 147.
33. See the experience of Hilde Ainger, née Salomon, in Malet and Grenville, *Changing Countries*, p.91, or that of Bina Wallach in a family that had seen service with the police in the Middle East (interview in the possession of the author).
34. Malet and Grenville (eds), *Changing Countries*, pp.99ff.
35. Argy, *Childhood and Teens*, p.151; Tausig, *Kasperl, Kummerl, Jud*, p.70.
36. See, for example, Sir Ken Adam's description of his father, in his interview in the 'Refugee Voices' collection.
37. J. Kerr, *The Other Way Round* (London: Collins, 1995), the second part of the trilogy *Out of the Hitler Time*, following *When Hitler Stole Pink Rabbit*.
38. E. Tucker, *Becoming English* (London: Starhaven, 2009) describes movingly the difficulties confronting a refugee girl and her mother.
39. Interview with Andrew Sachs carried out for the exhibition 'Continental Britons: Jewish Refugees from Nazi Europe', held at the Jewish Museum, London, May–October 2002 (in the possession of Dr Bea Lewkowicz). Famous as the Spanish waiter Manuel in *Fawlty Towers*, he has since played such quintessentially British roles as Doctor Watson in a BBC Radio 4 version of the Sherlock Holmes stories in 2004 and P.G. Wodehouse's Jeeves in 2006.
40. M. Elsley, *A Chance in Six Million* (privately published, 1989), p.44.
41. Wagner, *Emigrants' Daily Life*, p.18.
42. Ibid., p.27.
43. Interview with Klary Friedl held at the Research Centre for German and Austrian Exile Studies.
44. I. White, 'Introduction', *I Came as a Stranger* (London: Hazelwood, 1991).
45. Argy, *Childhood and Teens*, pp.139f.
46. R. Stent, 'Jewish Refugee Organisations', in Mosse, *Second Chance*, pp.579–98.
47. Richard Bolchover, *British Jewry and the Holocaust* (Cambridge: Cambridge University Press, 1993), especially pp.42ff.
48. Typescript copy of the unpublished autobiography of Werner Rosenstock, Part II, pp.7f., kindly supplied by his son Michael Rosenstock. Part II of the autobiography was written in 1986 and covered the years 1941–86; Part I, covering the years up to 1941, was written around the end of the war.
49. *AJR Journal* (May 2006), p.4.

2

The Jewish Refugees and the War, 1939–1945

The outbreak of war in September 1939 was a major turning point for the refugees, though they, like the rest of the civilian population, did not come face to face with the full reality of war until the end of the 'Phoney War' in May/June 1940, when the Nazis overran the Low Countries and France and prepared to invade Britain. This brought those on the home front into the front line, and swept many thousands of refugees into internment camps. Initially, however, the impact of the war on the Jewish refugees was less severe, but those of German and Austrian (though not Czech and Polish) nationality were now 'enemy aliens', nationals of a power with which Britain was at war.

The British government wished to avoid interning enemy aliens en masse, as it had in the First World War. It therefore set up tribunals before which all German and Austrian nationals had to appear and which allocated them to one of three categories. Only a tiny minority, mostly those with Nazi sympathies, was allocated to Category A and interned. The vast majority of refugees were classed as victims of Nazi oppression and allocated to Category C, which left them at liberty. Those whose cases the tribunals judged unclear were allocated to the intermediate Category B and were subject to certain restrictions.[1]

New regulations were introduced that affected all enemy aliens: their freedom of movement was subject to stricter control and they were forbidden to possess certain items, such as cameras, maps or radios. With the end of emigration from Germany to Britain, refugees realized with foreboding that a lifeline for relatives who had not escaped had been cut. Some refugees welcomed the coming of war as heralding the end of the Nazi regime, but for more it was a development of ill omen. The initial impact of the war on the refugees' material circumstances was very damaging. Many hundreds of domestic servants lost their jobs, and most refugees who had started their own business ventures had to abandon them or reduce them greatly in scope. But the demand for labour created by the war soon reversed that trend; many refugees found work in factories, firms and offices, while others joined the British armed forces, though at this stage refugees could serve only in the non-combatant Pioneer Corps.

The period of mass internment has already been more thoroughly researched than any other aspect of the refugees' experience,[2] and it will be covered here only briefly. In the early summer of 1940, the collapse of France brought the German army to the Channel, within sight of the British coast, and the German air force within bombing range of Britain's cities. Under pressure from the right-wing press, increasingly hostile to the refugees, the government gave way to those who argued that the refugees posed a threat to national security, as potential fifth columnists who might sabotage British defences as their counterparts supposedly had in the Low Countries and France.

In May 1940 the newly installed coalition government under Winston Churchill first decreed the internment of male enemy aliens between 16 and 60 living in 'Protected Areas' on the threatened sectors of the coast, then issued the notorious order to 'collar the lot'. Male refugees in Category B were interned, as were Category B women; the detention of male refugees in Category C, ordered in June, was under way when the policy of internment was halted the following month. This measure, to some extent a panic response to the extreme situation of national emergency prevailing in May/June 1940, ultimately caused the internment of some 27,000 enemy aliens, including some 4,000 women, most of whom were Jews who plainly posed no security risk whatsoever.

The mass internment of enemy aliens in 1940 was, it is now generally agreed, indefensible. It was a measure that was as cruel and inhumane as it was stupid and pointless. The best that can be said for it is that it was an unthinking response taken in panic, with little heed to the consequences for its victims, at a time of national obsession, largely irrational, with internal security risks, largely imaginary. At worst it can be seen as the control of policy, albeit temporarily, by illiberal, xenophobic, anti-Semitic elements in right-wing political, military and security circles bent on targeting the Jewish refugees from Germany and Austria.[3] To intern as potential Nazi sympathizers the Jewish refugees, who had been the most prominent targets of Nazi persecution and had the greatest reason to oppose the Nazi regime, was almost perversely insensitive. Among its worst aspects was the trauma that a fresh bout of detention inflicted on those of the internees who had already experienced imprisonment in Nazi concentration camps.

The incompetence and inefficiency that characterized the entire episode were apparent from the outset, as was a distinctly illiberal hostility to the Jews from Germany. The decisions of the tribunals that classified refugees into categories were sometimes alarmingly arbitrary. The process of arresting detainees was conducted with a combination of heartless bureaucracy and disorganized muddle. Refugees were often detained in the early morning, so some suffered the dawn knock on the door that would carry them off to an uncertain fate, while others adopted the simple expedient of leaving home early to avoid arrest. The police notoriously raided Hampstead Public Library on 13 July 1940 to detain its refugee readers, but failed to round up those who congregated for an early breakfast at Lyons Corner House at Marble Arch.

After their arrest, most refugees were first held at temporary camps, like the racecourses of Kempton Park and Lingfield for those in the London area. In Edinburgh, the composer Hans Gál was incarcerated in the grim surroundings of the Donaldson Hospital, where he was shocked to find himself surrounded by barbed wire and armed sentries; in his internment diary he gave vent to a sense of outraged fury and disbelief at this betrayal of trust by the British, whom he had come to consider as welcoming and humane hosts.[4] Conditions were bad at Prees Heath in Shropshire, where internees lived under canvas, and indescribable at Warth Mill, a disused cotton mill at Bury, Lancashire, where dirt, squalor and lack of food and facilities reigned. The chaos of these makeshift arrangements was matched by the disorganization of the entire exercise; the internees soon realized that the military authorities had no real idea why they had been interned, what was to be done with them, and how long they were to be held. Some were detained in prison, in particular women who were held at Holloway Prison in London; a contemporary account by Ruth Borchard, written in 1942 and recently reprinted, gives a vivid account of what they went through there.[5]

Worst of all was the psychological blow of being unjustly imprisoned. The deprivation of liberty, the confinement and humiliation were made more wounding by the apparent willingness of the authorities to identify Jewish refugees with the agents of Nazism. Hans Gál, for one, found the experience traumatic, probably the worst experience of his life. Paul Jacobsthal, a refugee classical archaeologist who had obtained a position at Christ Church, Oxford, conveyed the shock of his arrest in the opening sentence of his internment memoir: 'On Friday July 5th 1940 in the morning when I was peacefully writing on Celtic Geometric Ornament a knock came at my door in Christ Church and a plain clothes Police Officer entered producing a warrant of arrest.'[6] Jacobsthal, an optimist by nature, was better equipped to cope with the crisis of internment.

The authorities soon started moving the internees from the temporary camps to the Isle of Man, where, as in the First World War, they were to be held; the people of Liverpool greeted them with insults and missiles as they were marched through the streets to be shipped across. Many spent some time at a makeshift camp at Huyton on Merseyside, a newly built council estate hastily and inadequately converted into a camp. The internees were housed in camps in Douglas and other resorts on the Isle of Man, mostly in groups of boarding houses requisitioned for the purpose. Camp names like Central Promenade, Hutchinson, Onchan, Sefton, Mooragh and Rushen (the women's camp comprising Port Erin and Port St Mary) became common refugee usage.

Conditions in the camps on the Isle of Man were considerably better than in the temporary camps, not least because some semblance of order and stability could be established there. The internees lived in small groups in individual boarding houses, where the food and accommodation was spartan but adequate; many refugees slept two to a double bed. The summer months on the Isle of Man were pleasant, and free from air raids. Walks in the country were permitted, under armed guard, as was swimming in the sea. There were adequate sanitary arrangements and some medical care. The camps were run through a system of self-administration by the internees, though under the close control of the British military command. This allowed the internees to develop a remarkable array of cultural activities, including concerts, lecture courses and other educational activities organized by 'camp universities', and even a musical revue, *What a Life!*, staged in Central Promenade Camp to music by Hans Gál. The galaxy of academic, musical and artistic talent available in the internment camps made for a wide and attractive selection of lectures for those eager to put their enforced idleness to good use.[7]

But the emotional and psychological impact of detention remained powerful and hurtful. The internees were confined on an island remote from the mainland cities, far from their families whose safety was at serious risk from German bombing and who had been deprived of their main breadwinner. Cut off from reliable sources of news by the censorship, the internees fell prey to all sorts of rumours and fears, not least that Britain would surrender and hand them over to the Nazis, 'like rats in a trap', as had happened in France. A particular problem in the women's camps was the presence of Nazi sympathizers, who, because of the far smaller number of female refugees interned, represented a perceptible proportion of the inmates of the women's camps; initially, they made life unpleasant for the Jewish inmates.[8] The difficulty of communicating with the outside world, especially the long delays to which letters and telegrams to families were subject, was a source of great frustration. The military administration had erected its own impenetrable barriers of procedure and bureaucracy between the refugees and the outside world, making it very difficult, for example, for refugees to set about securing their release. Such arbitrary inefficiency was one of the aspects of camp life that relentlessly ground down the internees' morale.

The government took the process a stage further when it started to deport internees overseas. Four ships carrying some 4,400 men sailed to Canada, while some 2,400 were sent to Australia on the ill-famed *Dunera*, a troopship on which conditions were extremely poor; on this vessel the internees were robbed and seriously mistreated by the military escort, and eventually court-martial proceedings were taken against the officer in charge and two of his subordinates. On 2 July 1940 the liner *Arandora Star*, bound for Canada, was sunk off the Irish coast with the loss of several hundred lives, mostly German and Italian deportees. Though the government first claimed that all Germans on board had been Category A internees, it soon became known that many of the dead were Jewish refugees in Category C.

The resulting furore crystallized opposition to internment and led to a determined campaign against it in parliament, culminating in a celebrated debate on 22 August 1940, as German bombs fell on the capital. By then, public opinion had swung sharply against internment and the government had reversed its policy, issuing a White Paper in late July listing a variety of categories of internees eligible for priority release; these were widened over the following months. The release of the interned refugees proceeded reasonably speedily, especially for those who had expertise that would benefit the war effort, who were elderly or in ill health, or who had influential voices speaking on their behalf. The first fifty were released from the Isle of Man on 5 August 1940. Paul Jacobsthal and Hans Gál were released in September 1940, though more refugees were detained until late 1940 or early 1941. By August 1941 only about 1,300 refugees were still interned in Britain, while many of those deported overseas had returned, often to join the armed forces.

Internment aroused widely differing reactions, and the judgements passed on it have also varied greatly. Many of the younger refugees, single men, recalled the months spent on the Isle of Man almost as a kind of enforced holiday to which they reconciled themselves once they had accustomed themselves to it; its restrictions were irksome, but they felt able to take them in their stride. Older refugees, concerned about their families, found the anxieties and humiliation of imprisonment harder to bear; some experienced serious mental crises.

Some refugees went so far as to defend internment as an understandable measure not incommensurate with the national emergency facing Britain in 1940. More common was the view that internment was a wholly misconceived, unjust and stupid measure taken in panic and implemented inefficiently, but that events had soon caused the government to reconsider and reverse its policy, and that relatively little serious damage had been done. Even when the nation was fighting for survival, British liberalism had reasserted itself. But some refugees retained a lasting sense of grievance. Walter Eberstadt, who later served with distinction in Normandy, was a student at Oxford when he was interned. Though he was impressed by the way in which the government had been brought to abandon an unjust policy, internment permanently coloured his view of Britain and contributed to his post-war decision to emigrate to America: 'Still, since internment I have felt different about the English. No doubt it was my fault that I had foolishly fancied that a few years at public school and a year at Oxford had made me part of them.'[9]

The predominant attitude towards internment among the refugees inclined strongly towards understanding and forgiving and has for that reason been strongly contested by academic studies. Reminiscences like that by F.I. Wiener,[10] which described his internment with some humour and affection, concluding in the serene light of hindsight that it had done little serious harm, found no favour with later academic critics of British policy. Discussing the articles published in *AJR Information* on the twenty-first anniversary of internment in 1960, the editors of a volume of essays on the subject, Tony Kushner and David Cesarani, claimed that the refugees had 'sanitized [internment] into a jolly jape';[11] the implication was that the refugees had refused to face up to the truth about internment, fearing to confront the reality of their treatment by the British government.

The underlying issue was not the rights and wrongs of internment, but two contending views of Britain as a homeland to immigrant groups. Kushner and Cesarani did not believe that internment was a temporary aberration from the mainstream of British liberalism. For them, it stood in an established tradition of repressive hostility to small and defenceless minorities at times of war and crisis, exemplified by the Aliens Act of 1905 aimed at Jews from Eastern Europe, the internment of enemy aliens in the First and Second World Wars and the detention of Arab suspects during the first Gulf War. Behind the complacent fiction of Britain as a generous haven for the persecuted, they perceived a series of illiberal and discriminatory measures taken against 'alien' immigrants and minorities. Refugee commentators, by contrast, mostly saw internment as a passing and exceptional episode that was rapidly overturned once public opinion had reverted to its traditional values; an underlying sense of fair play and tolerance had, they believed, reasserted itself, overcoming the illiberal prejudices that had led to the initial injustice. Their view of Britain was conditioned by confidence in its democratic institutions and trust in the basic decency and humanity of its people.

Given the gulf between these two views, it came as no surprise that the refugee historian Ralph Blumenau adopted a tone of mild bafflement when reviewing Cesarani and Kushner's volume:

> And yet it seems to this reviewer that there is something awry when the book makes illiberalism and injustice so much more central than the idea, conveyed by so many Jewish ex-internees, that in the end they were more impressed by the liberalism and fairness which ended their ordeal. This reviewer is inclined to align himself with the quotation in the book from Lord Beloff: 'The reaction of the refugees themselves proved considerably more understanding than that of the historians who were not even born at that time, or were infants then.'[12]

The Second World War was a key formative experience that in considerable measure determined the attitudes of the refugees from Central Europe to Britain and conditioned the subsequent development of their community here. It was during the war, at least after internment was over, that an abiding affection for their country of refuge took root among the Jews from Germany and Austria in Britain, partly as a result of the refugees' admiration for the behaviour of the British people during the war. But the war also brought the refugees a sense of pride and renewed self-worth at being able to participate with the British in a common cause: the war effort to defeat National Socialism, the regime that had degraded the Jews to the status of pariahs and robbed them of their dignity and self-respect. The war, a time of unusual solidarity across British society, reinvested the refugees with a feeling of belonging lost under the Nazis and with the confidence that, broadly speaking, they faced the hardships and suffering of war on the same terms as the rest of society and could share once again in a common national purpose.

The first, crucial factor to make a favourable impact on the refugees was psychological: the unmistakable determination of the British people from 1940 to resist Hitler by all means and at all costs. This stubborn refusal to contemplate defeat or surrender made a profound impression on the refugees. Few groups were more painfully aware than the German-speaking Jews of the unbroken series of Hitler's victories, which seemed to endow him with a semblance of invincibility. Few groups were more influenced by the spirit of 1940, which punctured that aura for the first time: refugee memories of the war repeatedly invoke Churchill's speeches, the ritual of gathering round the radio to listen to the news, and the air battles of summer 1940.

The unity of purpose and the confidence in ultimate victory that formed a bond extending from stateless refugees to Battle of Britain pilots are conveyed in Judith Kerr's *The Other Way Round*, as the refugee residents of a Bloomsbury hotel listen to the evening news. Anna, Judith Kerr's semi-autobiographical narrator, senses an unfamiliar note in the stately tones of the announcer, Bruce Belfrage, as he reads the news bulletin after a decisive day in the Battle of Britain:

> The voice did not sound quite as usual and Anna thought, what's the matter with him? It had a breathlessness, a barely discernible wish to hurry, which had never been there before. She was listening so hard to the intonation of each word that she hardly took in the sense. Air battles over most of England ... Heavy concentrations of bombers ... An official communiqué from the Air Ministry ... And then it came. The voice developed something like a tiny crack which completely robbed it of its detachment, stopped for a fraction of a second and then said slowly and clearly, 'One hundred and eighty-two enemy aircraft shot down'. There was a gasp from the people in the lounge, followed by murmured questions and answers as those who did not understand much English asked what the news-reader had said, and the others checked with each other that they had heard aright. And then the elderly Pole was leaping up from his chair and shaking Mr Chetwin by the hand. 'It is success!' he cried. 'You English show Hitler he not can win all the time! Your aeroplanes show him!'[13]

The Battle of Britain and the Blitz that followed showed that Hitler had failed to break the morale of the British people or force Britain to surrender; this was most evident to those at the eye of the storm, the civilian population in the British cities.

From the summer of 1940 the refugees found themselves in the front line of a population facing the Blitz, the first large-scale campaign of aerial bombardment aimed at civilian towns and cities over an extended period; London was bombed nightly almost without interruption from September 1940 till May 1941. The stolid endurance and companionable good humour of the British and the unflustered coolness of quite ordinary people under fire immensely impressed many refugees. Klary Friedl from Czechoslovakia, in hospital with serious wounds sustained during an air raid on Belsize Park, remembered how her spirits were raised by an old man who urged her to 'keep smiling, young woman'; an hour later he had died of his own injuries.[14]

In interviews and memoirs, refugees who experienced the Blitz in London and other British cities repeatedly expressed their admiration for the behaviour of the British civilian population. The war, it seemed to the newcomers, brought out the best in the British, their coolness under fire, their understated humour and their indomitable will to win through – all key elements of the much mythologized 'spirit of the Blitz'. The strong sense of solidarity, the kindness and readiness to help those who were in distress or fell victim to the bombing made a particularly strong impression on the Jewish refugees, whose recent experiences as defenceless victims of state terror and public ostracism in their native lands made them especially sensitive to such qualities. British humour also served to cut the arrogant posturing of the Nazis down to size, which was particularly gratifying to their erstwhile victims.

Lucie Kaye, née Schachne, an intellectual prone to observing others with a cool and not uncritical eye, pronounced herself 'enormously amazed' by the way the British conducted themselves during the Blitz. She listened whenever possible to speeches by Churchill, who became the living personification of the spirit of defiant resistance to Hitler.[15] As German speakers familiar with the Führer's public image and speech-making, the refugees perhaps sensed early on the superiority of the British Prime Minister in the rhetorical duel that developed between the two men, when for the first time Hitler was exposed by Churchill's inspirational oratory for the shallow, ranting bully that he was; the public persona of Germany's 'man of destiny' was for the first time overshadowed by another leader, whose claim to speak for his people rested on genuine consent, not on a grandiose propaganda apparatus backed by coercion.

The actor Otto Tausig, hardly one of nature's shrinking violets, found his excitable temperament cooled by the phlegmatic stoicism with which Londoners faced the bombing:

> We owed it to the unbelievable composure of the English, who put up with the daily horrors with no sign of fear, that we grew accustomed to it all. Their calmness was catching. When a V2 hit our house while we were at the factory and there was nothing left of our house but a tattered volume of English poetry and a solitary lady's stocking hanging over a wire, we looked at each other, bought ourselves a kilo of cherries and went to the cinema.[16]

Refugees were aware, with some pride, that they shared the dangers and suffering of the Blitz with the British, and tended to tailor their reactions accordingly.

At the end of the war, Werner Rosenstock described his return to London some four years earlier after six weeks of internment; writing close to the events recounted, he gave a dispassionate, largely factual account of his experiences, but his admiration for the British shone through:

I myself was greatly impressed by the state of nerves and the discipline of the population. On the morning after a grave attack you could see the workmen cleaning [up] the mess with cigarettes in their mouths as if it was quite an ordinary job. This was not lack of emotion on their side but the typical self-discipline achieved during the long history of the nation.[17]

Recalling the Blitz decades later, Edith Argy painted a not dissimilar picture. Though she arrived in London just in time for the bombing – she lived in Maida Vale, near Paddington station, a Luftwaffe target – her memories of the Blitz were coloured by her perception of the exceptional nature of the qualities displayed by the British:

On the whole, I remember the blitz with some, dare I say it? – nostalgia. All that has been said and written about the British during that period is, in my experience, true. Like other people, I was often very scared during those noisy raids and praying that I might survive the night; yet, on my way to work in the morning, when I witnessed people's stoicism and courage and sense of humour, amidst all the devastation, I felt proud, almost privileged, to live in London – among the English – at that moment in time. Also, I was very aware of the fact that here I shared the fate of millions as an equal, and not, as I would have done in Austria, as an *Untermensch* [subhuman].

However, there was evidently a limit to the acceptance of outsiders, even in the basement that acted as a shelter during air raids: 'Sometimes, the boyfriend of the daughter of one of the lodgers joined us; he was a tall, handsome, well-educated Indian. Two spinster ladies recoiled in horror. White Jewish refugees, although "foreign", were just about tolerated, but they drew the line at "coloureds".'[18]

Marga Brodie, who came on a Kindertransport, experienced the Blitz as a young domestic in Manchester. Her memories were tinged with nostalgia for a bygone time when people felt able to trust one another in the face of common danger; anyone who has conducted interviews with former refugees will have heard elderly ladies regretfully recalling that they felt less at risk in the total darkness of the blackout, bombing or no bombing, than they do now on the streets at night:

It's true, it was a different mentality, a totally different outlook. If I was in town, if I wanted to walk to Broom Lane, if there was a blitz on, or something, or in a blackout, I used to walk it, I used to walk up Cheetham Hill Road. The town was full of foreign soldiers, of every colour, of every creed, or everything. You didn't look over your shoulder, you didn't have to be scared, nobody attacked you. I mean, today I don't go from here up to Channah's [her daughter-in-law] if it's dark, it was a different world in that respect. So when I arrived it was scary, when you heard the bombers going over, but you were never scared to look over your shoulder, we had a different mentality altogether. It is like the people in London who sat in the Underground singing, you know, the planes were dropping bombs and they were singing. I am not sure if they would be like that today. I don't think so, I think that everything that has been going on in the world and so on, we have a different mentality. A bomb would drop down and it didn't hit, and we would say, 'You see, Adolf, you see what you have done?' And really, I think today is different, you wouldn't be like that, we had a very refined attitude. It is a very good attitude to have, yes.[19]

For all the danger and loss of life, refugees have come to see the war predominantly as a time of common purpose, high morale and even a certain devil-may-care happiness, beside which the post-war decades represented a decline into a meaner-spirited world of decreasing social cohesion.

The principal figures symbolic of wartime Britain came to loom large in refugee perceptions of the war. Churchill's speeches inspired them with confidence in ultimate victory, while the Spitfire was the most potent symbol of successful resistance to the Nazis. Peter Pulzer, the distinguished refugee historian, recalled watching 'Spits shooting down Messerschmidts' over south-west London as a boy.[20] In October 1940 the warden of the Bradford Jewish Refugee Hostel wrote to the Lord Mayor of the city, enclosing the sum of one pound and five shillings that the boys had collected from their pocket money as a donation to the Lord Mayor's Spitfire Fund.[21] As a 10-year-old in Kingston, Pulzer took a 'rather Churchillian view' of the impossibility of defeat; he later conjectured that Churchill had boosted the morale of the refugees even more than that of the general British public, as he ruled out both defeat and a compromise peace with the Nazi dictator.

For a group of immigrants, the refugees developed a surprising degree of regard for the British royal family, the ultimate symbol of the British state. On the occasion of the Queen's Golden Jubilee in 2002, Ruth Sellers, a former Kindertransportee, had herself photographed proudly holding a Union Jack in the garden of her home in Stock, near Chelmsford in Essex; on the rear of the photo she wrote 'Continental Briton!', an inscription that expressed the strong sense of adherence to Britain that has come to infuse the dual identity of the 'Continental' Jewish refugees.[22] Though some refugees never felt any affection for the monarchy or any allegiance to the British state beyond the formalities of nationality and residence, for many the wartime experience led them to identify strongly with the symbols of that state.

The link between loyalty to the monarchy and the war was movingly demonstrated in a later account. Gretel Salinger had been invited to a garden party held at Buckingham Palace in 1945 for those who had done notable war work. She set her heart on speaking to the Queen (the late Queen Mother), who duly spoke to her:

> 'Where have you come from?' I ought to have said: 'From Paddington', but what did I say? I said: 'I come from Germany.' She looked at me and said 'And you are invited here to this party?' Very strict with me. I said: 'Yes, Your Majesty. I have worked very hard during the war and I have collected millions [sic] of pounds for the war effort.' 'Oh', she said, 'you mean you are a refugee from Germany'. 'Of course, Your Majesty.' 'That's different, my dear child. I'm glad you have escaped and made your way here.' Where I took my courage from I still cannot say, but I said: 'Yes, Your Majesty, but may I tell you what happened to my family?' She said: 'Yes.' 'All my family have been killed in Auschwitz.' She made a gesture, like shielding herself. She said: 'If only I hadn't asked you.' I said: 'On the contrary, Your Majesty, this is my kaddish, the prayer we Jews have for the dead, that I could tell their fate to my Queen.' She took both my hands and she pressed them and said 'My darling child, I hope nothing else bad will happen to you and that you will enjoy your life and God bless you.' I stood there crying, crying.[23]

Recognition by the Queen seemed to mark a stage for Gretel Salinger in the process of grieving for her losses in the Holocaust.

Professions of regard for Britain and the symbols of its wartime past became part of the stock of refugee images. In her poem 'At Dover Harbour', the title of which evoked the white cliffs emblematic of national defiance of the Nazis, the refugee poet Lotte Kramer conveyed the perception of Britain as the land which held tyranny at bay: 'Behind this rough sleeve of water / There lies the heart's island, set in / A harvest of stone, its work done. Ahead, the broad hand of Europe / Opens her lined landscape, the skin / Hard and calloused with bitter blood'. The description of Britain as 'the heart's island' could hardly be bettered as a declaration of patriotic affection.[24]

A recent article in the AJR Journal, entitled 'My Country', reflected on a refugee's sense of national allegiance, returning again to the war. The author, Peter Prager, considered his evolving attitude to the three countries that had claims to his loyalty, Germany, Israel and Britain.[25] His sense of Jewish identity, and such German identity as he has, now exist within the context of his life in Britain. It is Britain to which he feels his deepest allegiance, and this he related explicitly to his wartime experience of emotional solidarity with the British:

> I am of course a cosmopolitan, but England always had a special attraction for me. My father spent several years as an apprentice in Bond Street and always spoke highly of English tolerance. When I came to England I not only fled persecution but came to a country for which I had the greatest regard. I have lived most of my life in England, my wife and children are English, and the English way of life is my way of life. In 1940 I was at an Old Vic production of Shakespeare's *Richard II*. When John of Gaunt recited the famous lines 'this blessed plot, this earth, this realm, this England', the audience burst into applause. I joined in. I have no doubt that my country is England.

Many refugees were eager to serve in the British armed forces during the war (or to make some contribution in civilian war work or civil defence), though initially they met with a cool reception. At first, refugees were only allowed to serve in the non-combatant Auxiliary Military Pioneer Corps, but after 1942 they could be enlisted directly into combatant and technical units and special forces. As the war progressed they were admitted to almost all branches of the forces. The history of the refugees in the forces has been well enough documented not to require detailed recapitulation here. Norman Bentwich's account, *I Understand the Risks: The Story of the Refugees from Nazi Oppression Who Fought in the British Forces in the World War*, appeared as early as 1950. A full-length study by Peter Leighton-Langer, *X steht für unbekannt: Deutsche und Österreicher in den britischen Streitkräften im zweiten Weltkrieg*, was published in 1999, appearing in English in 2006 as *The King's Own Loyal Enemy Aliens: German and Austrian Refugees in Britain's Armed Forces: 1939–45*; it was followed by Helen Fry's *The King's Most Loyal Enemy Aliens: Germans Who Fought for Britain in the Second World War* (2007).

The two volumes compiled by Wolfgang Muchitsch, *Österreicher im Exil – Großbritannien 1938–1945: Eine Dokumentation* and *Mit Spaten, Waffen und Worten: Die Einbindung österreichischer Flüchtlinge in die britischen Kriegsanstrengungen 1939–1945* (both 1992), have documented the contribution of the Austrian refugees very fully. Helen Fry's study *Jews in North Devon during the Second World War* (2005) contains much useful information on the training centres set up for the Pioneer Corps in West Country towns like Ilfracombe, where many members of its Alien Companies underwent their training. Books about those branches of the forces where refugees were prominent are numerous, for example Ian Dear's *Ten Commando* (1987), a study of the German-speaking commando units manned almost entirely by refugees.[26] The many memoirs written by refugee service personnel also provide much information about their wartime service.

During the war, the refugees' language skills and familiarity with conditions in Germany and Austria proved valuable to the British authorities in such areas as the BBC's German-language broadcasting and the propaganda war that was fought out over the airwaves, including the 'black' propaganda produced under the aegis of the Political Warfare Executive.[27] Government bodies also drew on the wealth of information contained in the archives of the Wiener Library, which its founder, Alfred Wiener, had brought over to Britain in 1939 and which remains the world's oldest documentary resource for the study of National Socialism and the Holocaust.[28] After the war, the British forces in Germany badly needed German speakers. Areas where former refugees were especially useful were intelligence and the investigation of war crimes. A considerable number of refugees, including women, came to Germany to work for the Allied occupation forces as translators, interpreters, telephone operators or office staff.

It is estimated that some 10,000 refugees from Germany and Austria, about 7,000 Germans and 3,000 Austrians, men and women, volunteered for the British forces, a proportion of the total number of refugees from those countries that compared favourably with that for the British population as a whole. It is understandable that the Jewish refugees were particularly keen to join the fight against Hitler; they had greater reason to hate the Nazis than any other group in Britain. Joining the forces also gave a major psychological boost to refugees condemned otherwise to an aimless existence. Lily Wagner was amazed at the transformation in her newly enlisted son-in-law:

> He seemed a different man. All that weakness, that lack of courage, the weariness and feeling of uselessness has gone. He is no longer the foreigner, the outsider, who is only suffered and does not belong. Now he is a man who has a duty to do, a task to fulfil, he is again part of the community, and has a place in the world.[29]

More unexpected was the close identification of the refugee volunteers with the British units with which they fought, with the British war effort and with the British cause in the Second World War as such. Pride in taking part in the war against Nazism took on a specifically British dimension, with a marked sense of loyalty to Britain as the adopted homeland and of admiration for the British people. It developed into pride at being part of the British war effort and part of British society at war – despite the obstructive attitude of the British authorities, who refused, for example, to follow the American example and grant British citizenship to refugees from Germany and Austria who were risking their lives in the British forces. Those refugees who fell fighting in the forces were proudly remembered by their community.

Pride in wartime service has remained an important feature of the refugee experience, as the numerous articles on the subject in *AJR Information* in the post-war years showed.[30] Few groups of immigrants would have expressed their allegiance to Britain and to British values as unconditionally as did Fred Pelican in the foreword to his account of his wartime experiences:

> I also wish to express my personal pride at having served the Crown and worn the uniform of the finest army in the world. I pay tribute to the heroic British people who at the most critical time of my life granted me refuge, and never showed malice or hostility towards us. They welcomed and embraced us on account of our exemplary conduct, because we respected the rule of law, and thus adjusted to freedom and democracy.[31]

This conveyed the refugees' sense of identification with Britain accurately; less so the reality of their reception in Britain.

Refugees gradually found their way into a wide variety of units, showing that the British forces had largely overcome their suspicion of 'enemy aliens'; the main exception was the Royal Navy, which largely maintained its refusal to take non-British-born recruits. Refugees served with the grandest of British guards' regiments, with the Commandos, the airborne forces – Louis Hagen, a glider pilot at the Battle of Arnhem, wrote a successful book, *Arnhem Lift*, based on his experiences – and even as fighter pilots: Klaus Adam (Sir Kenneth Adam) flew Typhoons over north-western Europe after the Normandy invasion. Proof of this turnaround in British attitudes was the admission of refugees into highly sensitive areas. Alice Anson, née Gross, who had come from Vienna aged 14 in 1938, volunteered for the WAAF (Women's Auxiliary Air Force) in March 1943, was trained as a photographer at Farnborough and worked in photographic reconnaissance at RAF Bomber Command in High Wycombe, where she was involved in developing the first aerial photographs of the launching pads for V1s and other top-security targets.[32]

One of the most important functions of wartime service was greatly to accelerate the integration of refugees into British society, by promoting their adherence to British attitudes, values and customs. In researching his engrossing book about Marianne Strauss, Mark Roseman encountered an arresting example of this in her three cousins, Alexander, Alfred and Otto Weinberg.[33] Alexander and Otto volunteered for the British forces, where they changed their names to Eric and Gerald Alexander. Refugees on active service had to change their names in case they were captured by the Germans; but the change of name not infrequently went hand in hand with a pronounced shift in identity. Gerald fought in Germany with the Glasgow Highlanders and Eric served in the Middle East. Alfred, however, was interned and deported on the *Dunera* to Australia, then settled in Israel, where he changed his first name to Uri.

The contrast between Eric Alexander and Uri Weinberg, as portrayed by Roseman, was striking. Eric Alexander, though still conscious of his German origins, had married an Englishwoman and converted to Anglicanism; he lived in the picturesque English market town of Stamford, in a bright, attractive flat decorated with floral designs, the sofa and curtains in chintz, and of 'generally a slightly old-fashioned, genteel English feel'. Uri Weinberg, on the other hand, far from relinquishing his Jewish identity, lived in Me'a Sharim, Jerusalem's ultra-Orthodox quarter, spoke Yiddish-accented German and lived in a flat that 'could have been in a Polish ghetto town', with peeling wallpaper and little furniture apart from cupboards full of books in Hebrew.

While it would be an oversimplification to attribute the differing identities assumed by the brothers in exile solely to their wartime experiences, there can be little doubt that service in the British forces powerfully reinforced the assimilationist tendency of refugees like Eric Alexander, who came to feel that they shared in the systems of values and attitudes of those with whom they fought. The stories of two more refugees from Germany who first emigrated to Palestine further illustrate the point. Marianne Geernaert, née David, was the daughter of Orthodox Jews from Hamburg who left for Palestine in 1939. But in 1943, aged 20, she joined the WAAF where a thoroughgoing process of anglicization commenced. The majority of her unit were Jews from Germany, who proceeded to establish close relations with their English counterparts, despite initial reservations on both sides:

> After some months we were told that we were to be joined by a number of WAAFs from England; we were excited, but also a bit apprehensive. We need not have worried, because they were a particularly nice group of girls and we soon became really good pals. We had a good laugh much later, after we had got to know each other well,

when they told us that they had expected us all to be black! What does that say about English education at the time?[34]

That Marianne David integrated comprehensively into the social milieu of the British forces is evident here in the very style of her narrative; her sense of ease in those circles also emerges in the humour with which she brushed off a potentially racist remark that might have offended someone less confident of acceptance by her British peers. While still in the Middle East, she married Flight Sergeant John Geernaert, son of a bespoke tailor from Colchester, returning with him in 1945 to Britain, where she fell into the lifestyle of a small English town indistinguishable from that of count-less young post-war couples. Marianne Geernaert did not drop her German-Jewish identity lightly: she was aware that her marriage to a Gentile would break her father's heart. Her adoption of an English identity was a conscious decision, though the fact that she later chose to write an account of the first thirty years of her life showed the value she placed on her origins.

Arnold Paucker, born in Berlin in 1921, also emigrated to Palestine, where he joined the British forces, serving with the Royal Engineers in Italy. He only came to live in Britain in 1950, when he also got married. He described himself in a part-autobiographical essay as well and happily assimilated, despite his ineradicable refugee accent:

> I do not see myself as an exile. When I return to Germany I feel that I am visiting a foreign country where it so happens that I speak the language rather well – and without an accent. Yet here in London after more than fifty years I am asked in, say, my bank, in the most friendly manner by a new cashier, how long have I been in this coun-try. And do I like it here? I do!

Paucker directly attributed the smooth integration into British society of refugee service personnel to the shared experience of wartime service:

> On their return to civilian life, their accents more or less intact, the émigrés, men and women alike, found that their service in the Forces had speeded the process of integration and acceptance. To be able to say: 'I was in the Navy', 'I was in the ATS', 'I was with the Eighth Army', 'I was in the Royal Engineers', took away the stigma of the accent.[35]

Director of the London branch of the Leo Baeck Institute for over forty years and author of a major study of German Jewry's fight for its rights, Paucker has devoted his life's work to the history and heritage of his native community. Nevertheless, he plainly feels that Britain is his homeland and that his easy assumption of a British identity, within the limits set by his age at arrival, was made possible by his service with the forces – and, as in Marianne Geernaert's case, by a happy marriage to a British partner. It is worth noting that if he had been among the refugees who joined the Jewish Brigade in Palestine, his socialization would have progressed very differently.

Many of the refugees who did not join up contributed to the war effort in a civilian capacity. From 1940 many took part in fire-watching and Air Raid Precautions duties on an equal footing with the British, and were proud to do so, proving their loyalty under fire. The turnaround in British attitudes was illustrated by the cases of refugees who had been maliciously denounced to the authorities during the internment period for allegedly signalling to the Luftwaffe during the blackout, but who were later accepted for civil defence duties; a development from suspicion to acceptance that naturally gratified them. Irene White, newly married, lived in Temple Fortune, north of Golders Green, where everyone in the street took turns fire-watching:

> At night it was the time of the Molotov cocktail bombs. The German planes came over and dropped a stick of fire bombs which lit up all the streets. They followed these with large bombers to drop the really destructive bombs, which wrecked houses, caused a lot of damage and cost lives. It was one of our jobs to take the metal dustbin lids and cover the fire bombs before they exploded and illuminated everything. The house next door to us caught fire. We formed a bucket chain and, with the help of our neighbours using hosepipes, stirrup pumps and very primitive equipment, the fire was put out.[36]

Fire-watching was commonplace among refugees; some of those inter-viewed for the study *Changing Countries* recounted as a matter of course that they or their partners had volunteered to do fire-watching at night, while working during the day.[37] A number of women refugees became nurses, including Marianne Elsley and Irene White, who in May 1940 found her-self nursing casualties from Dunkirk at a military hospital near Basingstoke. Josephine Bruegel from Czechoslovakia was one of a number of refugees who had had their medical training interrupted by the Nazis and who turned to nursing in Britain, later practising as a doctor.[38]

The refugees viewed wartime austerity surprisingly positively, as the cat-alyst for a display of national solidarity in which people accepted shortages and discomfort, in the knowledge that they were shared broadly equally and in the interest of the successful prosecution of the war. In this spirit, many refugees willingly took jobs in factories manufacturing munitions or other

products for the war effort. Women were required in large numbers by tailoring and garment firms for the production of uniforms and other items;
so great was the demand from employers that Zeitspiegel, the weekly newspaper of the refugee Austrian Centre, was by 1942 carrying lists of advertisements in German for women for tailoring and leatherwork, for seamstresses, cutters, machinists, milliners and, so common had the rag trade
jargon become in refugee circles, Finisherinnen.

Refugee women also worked for armaments and munitions firms. Bina
Wallach worked for four years with Clews Petersen in West Hampstead, an
engineering firm producing piston rings and cylinder liners for the tank
landing craft that played a key part in the Normandy invasion. In 1943 the
directors awarded her the substantial bonus of £25 'for your untiring services in the past year', to which the firm's secretary added his personal
thanks 'for your excellent work, co-operation, and loyalty to me'.[39] Many
male refugees did war work in munitions factories; most were middle-
class, sometimes no longer young, and ill prepared for exacting manual
labour on engineering machinery. But their satisfaction at being able to
contribute, however ineptly, to the war effort was greatly increased by the
friendly reception they often enjoyed from their British fellow workers.

Fifteen years after the war, Ernest Schaefer, a former lawyer who had
arrived in Britain no longer young, described his experiences in war
work.[40] Released from internment, he was first sent to the Park Royal
Government Training Centre in Acton, to be trained for work in a munitions factory. Schaefer was greatly impressed by the atmosphere and attitudes prevailing in the factory to the east of London to which he next
went:

> Altogether the relationship between the workers and the foremen
> and the shop manager was very different from the spirit I had seen
> in German factories. No worker would have tolerated being shouted
> at, even if he had made a mistake. No superior would have dreamed
> of bullying. The workers called their superiors by their Christian
> names and vice versa. It is a matter of course that I, too, was soon
> 'Ernie', 'cock', 'chum' or 'mate'.

He was astonished by the degree of acceptance he encountered from his
fellow workers:

> I shall never forget the splendid attitude of my colleagues in the
> machine shop. They knew, of course, that I was a refugee from
> Germany and had a different background. They at once saw that I was
> far from gifted for the work I did on various machines. Right from

the start they helped and advised me as much as possible whenever I got into trouble. On the other hand, in the beginning they completely abstained from personal queries. After some weeks this changed. During breaks they eagerly talked with me about Germany, Hitlerism, the war and so on.

Only after an air raid that killed a number of schoolchildren did one worker turn on Schaefer, but with unexpected consequences: 'It was significant that all the other mechanics sided with me, squashed him, and made it clear to him that I, of all people, was not responsible for such outrages. My adversary soon became one of my many friends in the shop.'

Gina Gerson from Vienna, also bent on contributing to the war effort, took a factory job in Colindale, north-west London, where the workers were 'incredibly nice' to her. For a very young woman, she had an extraordinary number of wartime jobs, ending up as a trained comptometrist. Edith Argy also had a bewildering succession of jobs, including that of dishwasher at one of the wartime British Restaurants, and eventually found a contented niche as a secretary in an engineering firm in Maidenhead; she was befriended by another secretary who took her to social events where she was initiated into English customs and manners from the inside.[41] It is impossible to say how representative these friendly receptions were of the overall refugee experience of wartime work; there were certainly instances of indifference and hostility. But a significant factor was the eagerness of refugees like Ernest Schaefer to highlight the positive aspects of their reception by the British, to internalize the image of the refugees' acceptance into the society of wartime Britain and to anchor that narrative in the collective memory of the refugees by committing it publicly to print.

The organizations set up by refugees came into their own in the later stages of the war. The Austrian Centre, founded in 1939 to represent those from Austria, became the largest and arguably the most successful of all these wartime organizations, with several thousand members and an extensive range of social and cultural services. Its German counterpart was the Freie Deutsche Kulturbund (Free German League of Culture), which attracted a number of high-profile figures from the arts – Oskar Kokoschka was its president.[42] These organizations were both largely controlled by Communists, and both had active youth wings, Young Austria and Free German Youth, which they sought to build up in preparation for the post-war reconstruction of their homelands. Once their leading activists left for Germany and Austria after 1945, both organizations became defunct in Britain. The Association of Jewish Refugees, founded in 1941, was the principal organization representing those who stayed in Britain and became by far the most important of all, still numbering several thousand members at the turn of the millennium. Once internment was over, many refugees became actively involved in these organizations, established to represent and promote their interests.

The effect of the war in advancing the integration of the refugees from already well-integrated backgrounds in Germany and Austria becomes even clearer when one compares them with refugees with strongly Jewish backgrounds. Whereas the identity of the former as assimilated German or Austrian Jews was shattered by the Third Reich, preparing the way for their willing integration into British society, the identity of the latter, which had not been so strongly German or Austrian, remained broadly the same in Britain. The story of Eli and Eva (Chava) Fachler, a devout Orthodox couple from Frankfurt, exemplified the different path taken in Britain by those whose identity remained centred on traditional Jewishness. The Fachlers' account of life in wartime Britain differed sharply from that of the other refugees previously cited. There was little hint of the identification with the British and their war effort that was such a marked feature in other accounts, little admiration for the British and little sense of sharing in the values and experiences of British society at war. Instead, the Fachlers' lives remained dominated, as they had been before emigration, by Jewish concerns.

Though strongly opposed to Nazism, Eli Fachler showed no urgency in joining the British war effort. Only when he was threatened with compulsory enlistment into the Polish forces in 1942 – his family had retained Polish nationality – did he choose to be called up into the British Army instead. Joining the British forces was for Eli Fachler primarily a means of escaping the notorious anti-Semitism of the Polish Army. Eager to stay in the Jewish world of the school where he was teaching, he delayed his call-up by over a year by appealing for exemption, beginning his basic training only in March 1944. His account of these events revealed his somewhat lukewarm attitude to the British Army:

> When the Polish Army informed me that it demanded my presence in its ranks, I point blank refused. There was no way I would take up arms for a nation that was so blatantly anti-Semitic. I took my subsequent call-up to the British Army philosophically. While I was certainly not keen on engaging in hand-to-hand combat with the enemy, I was not overly apprehensive, certainly not to the point of debilitating worry or anxiety.[43]

Eli Fachler was no shirker. He performed his military duties conscientiously, but lacked any sense of identification with the British forces. His repeated requests for a transfer to the Jewish Brigade showed where his true loyalties lay. He was proud of family members who fought for the state of Israel and of Jewish Brigade members in Italy who smuggled Jews to Palestine and supplied the Jewish underground there with weapons (for use against the British). The crucial issue here was one of identity: Eli Fachler had been raised as a devout Jew in Frankfurt, and this remained at the core of his identity in Britain, stable and unshaken, making any assumption of a new, British identity unnecessary. Consequently, he was untouched by the enthusiasm with which the assimilated refugees embraced the British cause during the war; unlike him, they had lost their former, assimilated identity, and they seized the opportunity to forge a new one while facing the experience of war side by side with the British. Significantly, refugee service personnel even formed their own association, separate from specifically Jewish associations like AJEX, the association of Jewish ex-servicemen and women; this was the Ex-Service (1943) Association, also known as the Ex-Service (NB) Association (NB standing for non-British), which ran a club in Circus Road, St John's Wood, and proudly embodied its members' service for many years after the war.

Even those assimilated refugees who found it hard to adapt to British society did not remain as emotionally distant from the British war effort as did Eli Fachler. Heinz Cassirer, son of the celebrated philosopher Ernst Cassirer, returned from internment to north Oxford, where he and his family lived in something of a refugee bubble, half-insulated from the British world outside. The Cassirers were consequently astonished to be approached at the end of the war by the local Victory Party committee, who, realizing that victory meant more to the Cassirers than to anyone else on their street, asked him to be president of the committee. Beatrix Walsh recorded their reaction to the celebrations:

> The delighted Cassirers told us about it afterwards, in the deliciously patronising tones taken by all Continentals when talking of the British: how touching it had been to listen to those simple chaps singing about Lambeth Walks and Rolling Barrels and then to wonder what the German people would have been singing at their street parties, had they won, instead of us.[44]

The Cassirers were plainly outsiders to whom British ways were a cause for puzzlement and some amusement, but their willingness to bridge the divide and their affection for the British come across clearly here, as does the characteristic undertone of appreciation for the British at war. Lacking an established Jewish identity like the Fachlers', the Cassirers were preparing to evolve a new identity in interaction with British society around them.

Arguably, it was the war against Nazi Germany that laid the foundations for the relatively smooth post-war settlement of the refugees in Britain and their broadly successful integration into British society. After the difficult pre-war years and the open hostility of the internment period, the later wartime years created a lasting bond between many of the refugees and their adopted homeland, where they were to build new lives for themselves and their families after the war.

NOTES

1. Some 600 people were allocated to Category A, 6,800 to Category B and 64,200 to Category C, of whom 55,460 were classed as refugees from Nazi oppression.
2. F. Lafitte, The Internment of Aliens (London: Penguin, 1940), P. and L. Gillman, 'Collar the Lot!': How Britain Interned and Expelled its Wartime Refugees (London: Quartet Books, 1980), R. Stent, A Bespattered Page: The Internment of 'His Majesty's Most Loyal Enemy Aliens' (London: Deutsch, 1980), D. Cesarani and T. Kushner (eds), The Internment of Aliens in Twentieth-century Britain (London: Frank Cass, 1993), and R. Dove (ed.), 'Totally Un-English'? Britain's Internment of 'Enemy Aliens' in Two World Wars: Yearbook of the Research Centre for German and Austrian Exile Studies, 7 (2005).
3. It was, however, not only the right-wing press that advocated internment; the Jewish Chronicle explicitly approved the measure in May 1940, presumably reflecting Anglo-Jewish anxieties.
4. H. Gál, Musik hinter Stacheldraht: Tagebücher aus dem Sommer 1940 (Berne: Lang, 2003).
5. R. Borchard, We Are Strangers Here: An 'Enemy Alien' in Prison in 1940 (London and Portland, OR: Vallentine Mitchell, 2008).
6. P. Jacobsthal, typescript account of his internment (p.4) written some three months after his release on 30 September 1940, in his file in the archives of Christ Church, Oxford. The archivist, Judith Curthoys, kindly drew this document to my attention.
7. Artists, too, suffered in internment, as the case of Fred Uhlman makes clear; see C. Brinson, A. Müller-Härlin and J. Winckler, 'HM Loyal Internee': Fred Uhlman in Captivity (London and Portland, OR: Vallentine Mitchell, 2008).
8. C. Brinson, '"In the Exile of Internment" or "Von Versuchen, aus einer Not eine Tugend zu machen": German-Speaking Women Interned by the British during the Second World War', in W. Niven and J. Jordan (eds), Politics and Culture in Twentieth-Century Germany (Rochester NY/Woodbridge, Suffolk: Camden House, 2003), pp.63–87.
9. W. Eberstadt, Whence We Came, Where We Went: From the Rhine to the Main to the Elbe, from the Thames to the Hudson (New York: W.A.E. Books, 202), p.163.
10. F.I. Wiener, 'Hutchinson Square Revisited', AJR Information (September 1957), p.11.
11. T. Kushner and D. Cesarani, 'Alien Internment in Britain during the Twentieth Century: An Introduction', in The Internment of Aliens, p.7.
12. AJR Information (October 1993), p.4.
13. J. Kerr, Out of the Hitler Time: One Family's Story (London: Collins, 1995), pp.364f. This is the omnibus edition containing When Hitler Stole Pink Rabbit, The Other Way Round and A Small Person Far Away.
14. Interview with Klary Friedl held at the Research Centre for German and Austrian Exile Studies.
15. Interview with Lucie Kaye in the possession of the author.
16. O. Tausig, Kasperl, Kummerl, Jud: Eine Lebensgeschichte (Vienna: Mandelbaum Verlag, 2005), pp.67f. and p.72 (my translation).
17. Rosenstock, unpublished autobiography, Part I, p.88.
18. E. Argy, The Childhood and Teens of a Jewish Girl in Inter-war Austria and Subsequent Adventures (Charleston, SC: BookSurge, 2005), p.154 and p.153.
19. Interview with Marga Brodie in the 'Refugee Voices' collection.
20. Interview with Peter Pulzer in the 'Refugee Voices' collection.

21. Letter from the warden, Herbert Eger, to the Lord Mayor, 7 October 1940, *Bradford Jewish Refugee Hostel, 1939–1989*, n.p.
22. Interview with Ruth Sellers in the 'Refugee Voices' collection.
23. *AJR Information* (November 1990), p.4.
24. L. Kramer, 'At Dover Harbour', in *The Shoemaker's Wife and Other Poems* (Sutton, Surrey: Hippopotamus Press, 1987), p.13.
25. *AJR Journal* (June 2005), p.3.
26. The German-speaking unit was 3 Troop of 10th (Inter-Allied) Commando, known as X-Troop.
27. C. Brinson and R. Dove (eds), *'Stimme der Wahrheit': German-language Broadcasting by the BBC: Yearbook of the Research Centre for German and Austrian Exile Studies*, 5 (2003).
28. B. Barkow, *Alfred Wiener and the Making of the Holocaust Library* (London: Vallentine Mitchell, 1997).
29. Wagner, 'Emigrants' Daily Life' (typescript, c. 1940), p.19.
30. See for example the report about Sergeant John Taylor (Johann Schneider) cited in Chapter 5.
31. F. Pelican, 'Foreword' to *From Dachau to Dunkirk* (London: Vallentine Mitchell, 1993).
32. Alice Anson is my cousin, the daughter of my aunt Edith Shelton, née Grünfeld, and her first husband, Otto Gross.
33. M. Roseman, *The Past in Hiding* (London: Penguin, 2001), pp.40ff.
34. M. Geernaert, 'Marianne: The First 30 Years...' (unpublished typescript, 2004, kindly supplied to me by Mrs Geernaert), p.15.
35. A. Paucker, 'Speaking English with an Accent', in *Deutsche Juden im Kampf um Recht und Freiheit: Studien zu Abwehr, Selbstbehauptung und Widerstand der deutschen Juden seit dem Ende des 19. Jahrhunderts* (Teetz: Hentrich und Hentrich, 2003), pp.339–53 (p.340 and p.348). This is the published version of a conference paper delivered in 1993.
36. I. White, *I Came as a Stranger* (London: Hazelwood, 1991), pp.34f.
37. M. Malet and A. Grenville (eds), *Changing Countries: The Experience and Achievement of German-speaking Exiles from Hitler in Britain from 1933 to Today* (London: Libris, 2002), pp.156f.
38. M. Elsley, *A Chance in Six Million* (privately published, 1989), pp.77ff.; White, *I Came as a Stranger*, pp.22ff.; and the brief biography of Josephine Bruegel in Malet and Grenville (eds), *Changing Countries*, p.xiv.
39. Letter from Clews Petersen Piston Ring & Engineering Co. Ltd to Albine Wallach, 8 October 1943, kindly supplied to me by Bina Wallach.
40. *AJR Information* (February 1960), p.9.
41. Interview with Gina Gerson in the 'Refugee Voices' collection; Argy, *Childhood and Teens*, pp.150–63.
42. On the Austrian Centre, see M. Bearman, C. Brinson, R. Dove, A. Grenville and J. Taylor, *Out of Austria: The Austrian Centre in London in World War II* (London and New York: I.B. Tauris, 2008). On the FDKB, see the forthcoming study by C. Brinson and R. Dove, *Politics by Other Means: The Free German League of Culture in London, 1939–1946* (London and Portland, OR: Vallentine Mitchell).
43. Y. Fachler, *The Vow: Rebuilding the Fachler Tribe after the Holocaust* (Victoria, BC: Trafford Publishing, 2003), p.161. See also the interviews with Eli and Eva Fachler in the 'Refugee Voices' collection.
44. B. Walsh, 'From Outer Darkness: Oxford and Her Refugees', *Oxford Magazine* (eighth week, Michaelmas Term, 1992), pp.5–11 (pp.10f.).

3

British Citizens: The Refugees and the British State after 1945

The end of the war in 1945 arguably represented even more of a turning point for the Jewish refugees from Nazism in Britain than it did for the British population at large, most of which reverted after the hardships and emergencies of war to a peacetime existence not so very different in most respects from that of pre-war days. For the refugees, however, victory over Hitler opened the door to a completely new life in Britain, where they would no longer be constrained by their wartime status as 'enemy aliens' and where they could rebuild the settled existence that they had enjoyed in pre-Nazi days in their home countries, though in a very different form and under utterly changed social, material and psychological conditions. For this to happen, the refugees had first to be formally accepted into British society as British citizens; the process of naturalization, by which the great majority of them applied for and were granted British citizenship in the years 1946–50, was therefore a crucial landmark in the history of the refugees, probably the most significant after their life-saving admission to Britain before the war.

But before the British government decided to offer the refugees the possibility of naturalization, it had to make an even more fundamental decision: were the refugees to be allowed to stay and settle in Britain at all? It may come as a surprise to many that the question of returning the refugees to their home countries was ever raised. The idea that a British government fresh from victory over Nazism could have contemplated returning Jewish refugees against their will to Germany and Austria, the breeding grounds of the Holocaust, would strike most people today as grossly inhumane. From today's perspective, it would also appear little short of deranged for a government to consider deporting a group that turned out to include Anna, Clement and Lucian Freud, George Weidenfeld and Paul Hamlyn, the refugee members of the Amadeus Quartet, Arthur Koestler and Anton Walbrook, Ernst Gombrich and Nikolaus Pevsner, to say nothing of such public favourites as Gerard Hoffnung and the cartoonist Vicky (Victor Weisz), and Nobel Prize-winning scientists like Ernst Chain, Hans Krebs and Max Perutz.

Yet it is beyond question that such a policy was under serious discussion within the government in the later years of the war.[1] The principal proponent of the repatriation of the refugees to their home countries was Herbert Morrison, home secretary in the wartime coalition government, who throughout the war remained mulishly obstructive where the refugees were concerned, repeatedly rejecting proposals to remove or alleviate the restrictions and handicaps placed on them as 'enemy aliens'. He opposed the granting of British citizenship even to German and Austrian refugees fighting in the British forces, on the grounds that naturalization had been suspended for the duration of the war. He also refused to offer any guarantee of post-war security to refugees wishing to settle in Britain. Obviously, if the refugees were not allowed to stay in Britain in the first place and were returned to their countries of origin, the question of their naturalization would become academic.

The refugees themselves would not have known that Morrison's views were not shared by officials responsible for refugee matters at the Home Office. In particular, E.N. Cooper, head of the Home Office's Aliens Department, became a firm friend of the refugees and spoke out in internal Home Office discussions against the repatriation of the refugees; after his retirement, Cooper married a refugee from Germany. Morrison's statements in parliament on the subject naturally caused some anxiety among the refugees, but most remained optimistic, believing, correctly as it proved, that the prospect of a British government forcibly deporting refugees – men, women and children resident for years in Britain – back to Germany and Austria at the end of a victorious war against fascism was too fantastical to carry conviction. This is the light in which anxieties about repatriation were depicted in a post-war publication by the refugees' own organization, the Association of Jewish Refugees. To mark its tenth anniversary in 1951, the AJR published a small volume, *Britain's New Citizens: The Story of the Refugees from Germany and Austria*, where the subject of repatriation, now safely in the past, was discussed:

> Having no organisation, meeting place, or news sheet of their own at the beginning, the German refugees allowed the most unlikely rumours to get around. Most of them were convinced that they had found temporary shelter only and doubted whether they would ever be naturalised. One man who had quite early on been able to settle down with a home, permits and everything, destroyed his own morale by toying for nine years with the idea of re-emigration, as somebody had told him for certain that divorced people were never naturalised in this country. As late as May 1945 a man of seventy who

had brought over a fortune was found packing – though he didn't know where he would go – as he had heard that in the next two weeks all refugees were to be expelled. This feeling of insecurity did not stop until the first naturalisations actually took place. And all the time these people were only too anxious to be loyal. 'Civis Britannicus sum' was their ideal.[2]

Two points highlighted here had shaped the attitude of most refugees to these issues throughout the later years of the war: their belief that talk of their imminent repatriation was based on idle rumour rather than political reality (though they recognized that their naturalization was by no means a certainty); and the unusual intensity of their loyalty to Britain, reflected in their eagerness to be integrated into British society, if possible as British citizens. This marked them out from most other groups of immigrants to Britain, whose sense of their collective identity, as in the case of the Irish or the Jews from Eastern Europe, continued to assert a degree of separateness from British society. It also indicated how easy it would be, relatively speaking, for the refugees from Central Europe – and still more their children – to integrate into British society: white, predominantly middle class, well educated, and socially and professionally upwardly mobile, they were in a quite different situation from later immigrants from New Commonwealth and Third World countries, who found it far more difficult to integrate into the host population, if only because the colour of their skin excluded them from the broad measure of acceptance extended in time to the refugees from Central Europe.

A principal cause of this newfound loyalty to Britain was the radical nature of the breach between the refugees and their countries of origin. Few groups of immigrants to Britain had experienced anything approaching the ruthless and systematic state-directed persecution to which the Nazi regime had subjected the Jews of Germany and Austria: it had declared them biologically unfit to be members of German society, had excluded them rigorously from that society and had ultimately implemented policies designed to eliminate every last trace of their existence, physical, social and cultural. The AJR, representing the refugees, took their exceptional situation as the starting point of its wartime campaign to secure their right to settle in Britain once the war was over. When in August 1944 it spoke in a circular to its members of 'the special problems and hopes of the Jewish refugees from Germany and Austria which of necessity differ in many respects from the problems and hopes of other refugees',[3] it was pointing to the fact that the Jews from Germany and Austria were unique among the many groups of exiles congregated in Britain for the duration of hostilities, in that they mostly did not wish to return to their home countries once these were liberated from Nazi rule. Whereas the Free French, Dutch or Norwegians could return to countries purged of the taint of German occupation, the Jews from Germany and Austria would have had to return to live among people who had perpetrated or colluded in the liquidation of their entire communities.

It was thus not only a hostile and hated regime that stood between the Jewish refugees from Germany and Austria and a return to their homelands, but a deep-felt repugnance at the prospect of consorting on an everyday basis with the accomplices to the murder of their families. This difference between the refugees from the German-speaking lands and the other wartime exiles was of the greatest sensitivity for them. Many reacted with indignant fury at the merest hint that they might happily return 'home'. The writer Hilde Spiel, later a *grande dame* of Austrian letters, recalled in her memoirs her horrified disbelief when at the end of the war Kingsley Martin, editor of the *New Statesman*, casually assumed that she and her husband would now be returning to 'their own country'; this total failure to understand the changed feelings of Jewish refugees towards their former homelands left her with an almost traumatic sense of outrage and betrayal.[4]

The AJR accorded the highest priority to lobbying for the refugees' right to remain in Britain if they so chose (or to emigrate to Palestine or elsewhere); this naturally meant that it rejected any suggestion that they should be compulsorily repatriated to their home countries. The first reference in an AJR circular to the question of settlement in Britain occurred in May 1942, when the organization informed its members that it was in contact with similar organizations overseas about 'questions of refugee life now and after the war', notably their demand that Jews should be allowed to remain in the 'refugee countries' where they were now resident. The urgency here was probably caused by the promulgation of the Nazi *Ausbürgerungsgesetz* of 25 November 1941, which had definitively stripped the refugees of their German citizenship.[5] The issue of settlement grew increasingly important in the later stages of the war when plans for peacetime began to be laid.

By mid-1944, with the end of the war in sight, the refugees were campaigning systematically against repatriation; in Britain, the AJR coordinated its efforts with those of its fellow refugees in the USA, calculating no doubt that their influence on the American administration might help to sway the British government in a direction favourable to refugee demands. Speaking before the House Foreign Affairs Committee, the representative of the American Federation of Jews from Central Europe, the AJR's sister organization in the USA, declared:

On various occasions, the return of the Jews to Central Europe after the war has been advocated as a proper way for at least a partial solution of the Jewish problem. Those in favour of such a return forget that many ... will refuse to live in countries which to them hold out no prospects of liberty, dignity and happiness. They lose sight of the fact that German education for more than ten years has been most thorough. For those subjected to that sort of education it will be easier to cross continents and oceans than to overcome the distance to people whom they have learned to despise and to murder. The same difficulty exists for Jews with regard to their persecutors. Again, the same small amount of energy left in a Nazi victim ... will not be sufficient to have him resume his life in Germany and to have him fight against the background of ghastly memories, unredeemed souls, and of a slowly if at all receding flood of bias and hatred. Therefore, the majority of those who will survive the dreadful camps as well as those who have found temporary refuge in various parts of the world will want to stay away from the land of their persecutors.

This statement was quoted at length in the AJR's own publication.[6]

By now the issues of repatriation and naturalization were clearly seen as interlinked. The refugees' refusal to be repatriated went hand in hand with their rejection of any proposal to reimpose German citizenship on them; and their aim of remaining in their countries of refuge naturally entailed the right to acquire citizenship there, since otherwise they would remain stateless. A further AJR circular quoted at length from a letter to the *New York Times* from the president of the American Federation of Jews from Central Europe, with whose arguments it strongly concurred:

There will be no doubt that among the problems which Jewish Refugees from Central Europe all over the world will be confronted with after the war, the problem of their nationality will be of great importance. This question concerns all who, after having been deprived of their citizenship by Nazi law, are now stateless. Should they, against their will, automatically become German citizens again? I believe that nobody who considers nationality more than a mere matter of form would advocate that anyone should be forced to resume citizenship of a nation with which he no longer is connected through any formal or emotional ties whatsoever. No one should be compelled to return to his former country after having experienced such dreadful persecution as was and still is imposed on the Jews by the Nazis. It would mean almost a mental cruelty to force citizenship upon people who do not and cannot feel any kind of allegiance towards their former country and a new 'deportation' to compel them to return there.[7]

At the end of the war, the AJR agreed with the other two main representative organizations, the American Federation of Jews from Central Europe and the Irgun Olej Merkas Europa in Palestine, to set up a council to protect the rights and interests of the Jewish refugees from Central Europe. The Council of Jews from Germany promptly submitted to the San Francisco Conference of the United Nations a statement laying down the aims of the refugees as regards their future. The statement's guiding principle was that Jews from Germany, regardless of where they lived, should not be treated as Germans, but as allies of the United Nations; high among the demands deriving from this principle were the right to remain in the country of refuge and the recognition that those deprived of their citizenship by the Nazis should not automatically revert to the status of German nationals.[8]

As the war neared its end, the AJR grew more confident of securing the right of its members to settle in Britain, as is demonstrated by the advice it gave in August 1944 about filling in a questionnaire sent out by the Jewish Refugees Committee, the principal organization responsible for the Jews from Germany who had emigrated to Britain and for maintaining them in this country. Some members were concerned by a question about the future intentions of so-called transmigrants, refugees who had been admitted to Britain in 1938/39 on a temporary basis, in the expectation that they would re-emigrate. If the British government had been bent on repatriation, then these people, whose status as immigrants was openly and officially temporary, would have been the first to go. But most of the transmigrants were by now integrated into British society, and many were serving in the British forces or contributing in other ways to the war effort; they had become indistinguishable from refugees who had been admitted on a more permanent basis, and the AJR doubted that they would be treated differently. Accordingly, it confidently advised those wishing to stay to state openly that they wished to make Britain their permanent home, as almost all did.[9]

The unimaginable horrors revealed by the liberation of the Nazi concentration camps in 1945 provided an almost irresistible argument against repatriation, helped by the fact that Herbert Morrison had left the coalition government with his Labour colleagues. The AJR issued a powerfully worded press statement:

> To the Jews from Germany their former country is the graveyard of their families. There are no bonds left between them and Germany. In their overwhelming majority they have no desire to return to the

country where these atrocities were committed and be compelled to live amongst people who perpetrated the murder of the Jews or connived in these crimes. They prefer to live anywhere else in the world rather than in Germany.[10]

When hostilities in Europe ceased, the refugees were to achieve their aim. Before the end of the war, repatriation of Jews to Germany and Austria had not been a practical possibility, but the cessation of hostilities in Europe confronted the British government with a new situation, which it resolved rapidly. Only a week after the war's end, on 15 May 1945, Winston Churchill faced a question in the House of Commons from Austin Hopkinson MP, who asked whether, in view of the destruction of National Socialism, arrangements could be made for the immediate repatriation of all Jewish refugees who had been victims of persecution in their country of origin. Speaking with all the authority of the man who had led Britain to victory, Churchill responded with a blunt 'No, Sir'. He went on to say that apart from considerations of humanity, the practical difficulties of carrying out such a suggestion were very great.

When Hopkinson pressed the prime minister further, the Jewish Labour MP Sydney Silverman came to Churchill's support: 'Would the right honourable gentleman bear in mind that it would be difficult to conceive of a more cruel procedure than to take people who have lost everything they have – their homes, their relatives, their children, all the things that made life decent and possible – and compel them against their will, to go back to the scene of those crimes?' The prime minister replied simply: 'I agree with that.'[11] This was a landmark moment in the history of the refugee community in Britain: with repatriation ruled out by government at the highest level, the greatest obstacle to the permanent settlement of the Jewish refugees from Central Europe in Britain had been removed. Churchill's statement in parliament opened the way for the community of 'Continental' Jewish refugees, as we now know it, to develop.

It may be that, not for the first time, Churchill had gone further than his ministers and officials would have liked; the Foreign Office minister George Hall gave a far more non-committal answer to a parliamentary question about repatriation from Commander Oliver Locker-Lampson on 16 May 1945.[12] But the decision not to repatriate the refugees had in practice been taken, and it was buttressed by a tide of opinion in the refugees' favour, as is shown by exchanges during a debate on 'alien questions' in the House of Lords on 22 May. The Jewish peer Lord Reading made an emotional plea for allowing the refugees to stay. If the refugees had not been in Britain, he said, they would have been in concentration camps; their only fault was to have belonged to a people considered as racially inferior and singled out for liquidation. He stressed both that the ties that had bound the refugees to Germany had been cut and that their contributions to the economic life of Britain had created new bonds of mutual obligation between them and their adopted country. He ended by declaring that the refugees might have been Germans of the Germany of years ago, but that they were not Germans of the Germany of today or tomorrow: they could not go back.[13]

The Earl of Munster, speaking on behalf of the government, made no attempt to mount any counter-argument, effectively conceding the case by saying that most of the government's speech had already been made by Lord Reading. Under the conditions obtaining in 1945, repatriation had become impossible, both practically and politically. The Labour government that replaced Churchill's administration in July 1945 never tried to revive it. The way was open for the refugees to settle in Britain. This is not to say that there was no popular backing for the repatriation of 'alien' refugees. The 'anti-alien' petition launched in the Borough of Hampstead in north-west London in October 1945 (discussed in Chapter 5) was an example – one of very few – of organized action against the refugees. Repatriation of refugees was the express aim of the petition; as Graham Macklin has demonstrated, the petition was fuelled by a prevailing current of anti-alien sentiment, with clear anti-Semitic overtones, and it seized on the shortage of accommodation in the borough that was allegedly exacerbated by the concentration of refugees there.[14] As the failure of the petition indicated, however, anti-alien and anti-Jewish sentiments remained restricted both in their extent and their intensity. Had there been a deep and widespread groundswell of such sentiment, the government could hardly have dismissed the proponents of repatriation in parliament as readily as it did.

It is sometimes claimed that if Herbert Morrison had remained at the Home Office, the refugees would not have been permitted to stay in Britain. Apart from the fact that the home secretary alone could never have pushed so controversial a measure through Cabinet, this argument ignores the reality of the situation obtaining at the time. Germany and Austria lay in ruins, their economies shattered and their populations short of the very essentials of life. There were already several million displaced persons in Germany, as well as some ten million people of German origin who had fled there from territories now to the east of the new German borders. That the British government would choose to add another 60,000 deportees to this scene of monumental disruption and misery seems at the very least improbable. One can readily imagine the reaction of the military commanders who administered the

British zone of occupation, men like Field Marshal Montgomery and General Sir Brian Robertson, to the proposal that they provide subsistence and accommodation for 60,000 unwilling Jewish refugees who wanted nothing better than to stay in Britain. The British authorities had every incentive to discourage refugees wishing to travel to Germany and Austria, let alone seeking to settle there permanently; initially, travel permits were unobtainable, except for key personnel, and the procedure involved in obtaining one remained obstructive until as late as 1948.

In the post-war years the first barrier to be surmounted on the road to integration in Britain was the bureaucratic but essential process of naturalization, which gave the stateless refugees British nationality and formal equality of status with British-born citizens. Not surprisingly, naturalization is one of the dominant topics in the early years of *AJR Information*: a front-page article in May 1949 unambiguously declared that securing 'the right of permanent residence in Great Britain for all those who wished to stay here after the war' was 'the first central task for whose accomplishment the AJR had been founded', an instructive indication of the association's integrationist agenda. Freedom to acquire British citizenship removed the lingering threat of the reimposition of German or Austrian nationality and of compulsory repatriation to those countries, and gave the refugees who settled in Britain the secure anchorage they desired. It was important both officially, as a recognition by the British state of their new status, and psychologically, as the underpinning of the new lives that they could now build in Britain.

The departure of Herbert Morrison from the Home Office, the end of the war and the appointment of James Chuter Ede as home secretary in the new Labour government marked the opening of a new chapter, the process of mass naturalization that began, albeit slowly, in 1946 and was largely complete by 1950. The importance of this to the refugees can hardly be overstated. The very first issue of *AJR Information*, which appeared in January 1946, quoted at length from the home secretary's announcement in parliament on 15 November 1945 of the setting up of procedures to resume naturalization after its wartime suspension, beginning with certain priority categories of refugees.[15] These included those who had served in the forces; those who had contributed in a civilian capacity to the war effort, such as scientists and technicians; and those who were contributing to the country's economy, in commerce and industry, in providing employment and in assisting trade, especially the all-important export trade. Those who had lodged their claims before the wartime suspension of naturalization in November 1940, and whose applications would normally have long since been processed, were also to be granted priority consideration.

In the same issue, the very first published letter from a reader proceeded from the assumption that naturalization for all refugees irrespective of categories was imminent, as proved to be the case. 'What the Press Says', a column devoted to press coverage of issues relevant to the readership, quoted an article from the *New Statesman* commenting favourably on the procedures adopted, on the judicious balance that the home secretary had struck between the claims of the various priority categories while shielding his department from unmanageable thousands of claims, and on his tone and manner, 'which should entirely allay the widespread fears that the Government might suddenly expel those who had come to this country on "transit" visas'. It continued: 'It is clear that no one, who obeys the laws of the land, need fear sudden expulsion, and that the Government's naturalization policy will be based on the sound principle that we shall accept as citizens men and women who can adapt themselves to our way of life', a broad but vague integrationist promise of welcome that many refugees were only too happy to take up.

The Home Office opted for the customary process of checking each application for naturalization individually, which, slow and time-consuming as it was, resulted in considerable initial anxiety and frustration. In March 1946 a front-page report in *AJR Information* on progress to date made dismal reading: a mere 220 certificates of naturalization had been granted; of those applications made before the war and now reactivated, a paltry 300 were under examination; and the other priority categories could only be promised that plans for dealing 'expeditiously' with their applications were 'in an advanced state'. Commenting in April 1946 on the priority categories for naturalization, a front-page article in the journal recognized that those many refugees not included in these categories would naturally feel disappointed; by referring to the efforts that had been called for to have naturalization resumed at all, it hinted at the existence of residual opposition to it in influential quarters. Its expression of hope that non-priority cases would attain naturalization 'in due course' scarcely concealed its concern to the contrary. Detailed evidence of the slow progress of the naturalization process, and hence of what could be interpreted as official obstructionism similar to that practised over immigration before the war, was noted several times. For example, the journal contrasted the home secretary's statement of 30 May 1946 that so far that year 250 certificates of naturalization had been granted to pre-war refugee applicants with the 22,000 applications still awaiting decision, figures that spoke for themselves.[16]

But a key factor on the positive side of the balance was the government's preservation of the requirement of five years' residence in Britain or Crown service as the central condition for naturalization. This was a condition that the refugees who had arrived before September 1939 could hardly fail to satisfy, thanks to the war, which had stopped most civilians from leaving the country. As is well known, the abandonment of the almost automatic granting of citizenship to those resident here for five years marked a crucial step in the tightening of government policy on immigrant settlement from New Commonwealth countries in later decades. It is profoundly significant that no such removal of the effective right to citizenship from the Jewish refugees from Hitler long resident in Britain was invoked in 1946; on the contrary, the home secretary affirmed the residence qualification as the principal requirement for naturalization in his written reply to a parliamentary question on 31 July 1947.[17]

The home secretary's subsequent announcement of 28 February 1946 made plain that the priority categories for naturalization claims would be fairly broadly defined; they now included those who were making a substantial contribution to the interests of the country, as directors of companies, members of the professions (for example doctors, nurses, teachers), persons in business on their own account and other self-employed persons, as well as 'salaried officials or employees of industrial or commercial concerns'.[18] The cautiously qualified optimism expressed on the front page of *AJR Information* of May 1946, on the occasion of the fifth Annual General Meeting of the Association since its foundation, was to prove justified: 'The outstanding event for refugees in Great Britain during the year under review was the resumption of naturalization. Even if many will have to wait a considerable time until they will become British subjects, the barriers which have hitherto blocked the way to legal absorption are removed.'

The year 1947 did indeed see a dramatic speeding up of naturalization. AJR members could read that more cases were dealt with in the first three months of that year than in the whole of 1946.[19] The total for the year was five times more than in 1946.[20] By September 1947, the journal could report that 1,600 cases – a case would often be an entire family, with the wife and children covered by the husband's application – were being dealt with per month, and that overall 13,415 certificates had been granted, over one-third of those applying, leaving 23,070 outstanding; of the 3,630 people newly naturalized in 1946, the bulk had come from Germany (1,521) and Austria (512), with a further 162 coming from Czechoslovakia; confidence in the procedures would have been boosted by the tiny number of applications rejected, only 160, or just over 1 per cent of those processed.[21] This convincingly refutes the argument that the government was keen to reject applications from refugees, or even to deport them; granting citizenship is not, after all, the way in which governments treat people whom they only recently wished to deport. As the only alien minority resident since pre-war days, applicants of German and Austrian origin naturally made up by far the largest group of candidates for naturalization as individuals and continued to do so until 1949, by which time their naturalization was largely complete.

The official machinery now worked through the backlog of applications steadily: in April 1947, over 9,200 of some 37,600 applications had been processed, or roughly one-quarter,[22] while by November 1947 the number outstanding had fallen to some 19,200, after 15,200 applications had been granted in the period January–October 1947.[23] In 1947 well over 6,000 applicants of German origin had been naturalized, over 3,200 from Austria and over 1,700 from Czechoslovakia, well over 10,000 Jewish refugees in all.[24] Mass naturalization had become routine by mid-1948, no longer worth more than the briefest report: 'On April 26, Mr. Ede stated that since January 1, 1946, up to April 17, 1948, inclusive, 28,189 certificates of naturalization have been granted.'[25] Some two-thirds of those granted British citizenship during this period were former refugees from the German-speaking lands, a proportion that fell as the number of applications from that group still outstanding dwindled. As early as August 1947, AJR Information published the first of what was to become over the years a considerable number of letters proposing that the Association change its name, as the term 'refugee' was no longer applicable to its members; in this case the reason was precisely the security afforded the former refugees by their naturalization:

> At the time of the foundation of the A.J.R. the position of its Members was unsettled. The 'Refugees' had lost the protection of the State of their origin without acquiring a new status, and they were rather doubtful whether their stay in this country would be a permanent one. Today our Members feel secure in the knowledge that if they so desire they have reached the end of their journey. Naturalisation and liberal granting of work permits make 'Association of Jewish Refugees' a misnomer.[26]

The final statistics published by the journal in 1950 tell their own story: overall, a few hundred certificates of naturalization were granted in 1945 (May–December), 3,630 in 1946, 17,742 in 1947, 15,108 in 1948, 9,593 in 1949, and 3,582 in January–May 1950.[27] The figures for former Germans and Austrians alone show a very similar pattern, demonstrating that they were not treated any differently from other groups of applicants: 2,033 certificates were issued to refugees from these countries in 1946, 9,548 in 1947, 7,171 in 1948, and 2,942 in 1949, a total of 21,694 over four years.[28] The number of former Germans and Austrians naturalized declined over this period as a proportion of the overall number of those granted British citizenship, as they were replaced in the later years by other groups of applicants, mainly from Eastern Europe. The figures for the refugees from Central Europe peaked in the years 1947–48, then fell back, as did those for applicants overall. The fact that the proportion of certificates issued to former Germans and Austrians fell from over half of the total in 1946–47 to well under a third in 1949 indicates that applications from former Germans and Austrians, the bulk of the early applicants, were processed promptly at a correspondingly early stage, leaving applicants from elsewhere as the majority in the later years.

The government had been somewhat slow to embark on naturalization after the war, and progress had at first been sluggish. But the dramatic increase in the number of cases dealt with from 1947/48 onward meant that the process was effectively complete by 1950; it seems fair to say that it was mostly carried through as smoothly and rapidly as can reasonably be expected of a state bureaucracy dealing with many thousands of individual cases. Very few refugees complain in interviews or memoirs about any undue delays or difficulties in the granting of citizenship; when asked, almost all recall only that they went through the requisite procedures of application, emerging as British citizens at the end. Klary Friedl, who had come in 1939 from Czechoslovakia shortly after her husband Ernst, recalled that they did not even bother to apply for naturalization until 1954; asked whether they had encountered any problems, she replied emphatically: 'Not at all, not at all.'[29]

On the other hand, memories of how it felt to become a British passport-holder for the first time often remain very vivid. For many refugees, getting their first British passport was a major event in their lives. Adelheid Schweitzer, who had emigrated from Germany in 1933, was naturalized in 1948 with her family and her husband's: 'It was a wonderful relief. I have been loath to give up my – I've still got it, the old British passport – it was a wonderful thing to have a British passport'. Her sense of pride when she returned from abroad made walking through the gate marked 'British Citizens' for the first time seem 'wonderful. It was a great, great, great moment. Unforgettable.' Doris Balacs, who arrived in 1939 on a domestic service visa after her family had been brutally deported to Poland in October 1938, fell in love with Britain immediately: 'I thought it was wonderful . . . I loved it, I really loved it.' This was reflected in her decision to stay in Britain, again associated with the later acquisition of a passport, and not to make use of her visa for the USA, a decision she never regretted: 'And I don't mind. I don't mind. No, no, no. I remember getting my passport,

1. Bernard and Flora Grünfeld and their maid, Vienna, 1930s. Photo in the possession of the author.

2. Trude and Paul Strassberg (seated left and centre) and their three cousins, Vienna, c. 1929. Photo in the possession of the author.

3. The Birken family, Berlin, 1938. Courtesy of the Jewish Museum.

4. Gertrude Landshoff on her first day at school, holding her *Schultüte*, the cone-shaped box of sweets customary on that occasion, c. 1902. Courtesy of the Jewish Museum.

5. Lore Sulzbacher's parents on honeymoon in Venice, 1910. Courtesy of the Jewish Museum.

6. Gerson Simon with other leading Berlin businessmen, 1920s. Courtesy of the Jewish Museum.

7. Sigmund Freud had to pay the Reichsfluchtsteuer before being permitted to leave Vienna in 1938. Courtesy of the Freud Museum.

8. Advertisements for positions in domestic service from Jews desperate to come to Britain, *Jewish Chronicle*, 1938. Courtesy of the Jewish Museum.

9. Kindertransport children housed at Dovercourt, a holiday camp near Harwich. Courtesy of the Jewish Museum.

10. Refugee Boys' Hostel, Minster Road, London NW2. Courtesy of the Jewish Museum.

11. Refugees classed as 'enemy aliens' being marched to internment camp, summer 1940. Courtesy of the Jewish Museum.

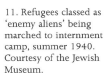

1. Spend your spare time immediately in learning the English language and its correct pronunciation.	**Betrachten Sie sie bitte als Ehrenpflichten:**
2. Refrain from speaking German in the streets and in public conveyances and in public places such as restaurants. Talk halting English rather than fluent German—and *do not talk in a loud voice.* Do not read German newspapers in public.	1. Verwenden Sie Ihre freie Zeit unverzüglich zur Erlernung der englischen Sprache und ihrer richtigen Aussprache.
3. Do not criticise any Government regulations, nor the way things are done over here. Do not speak of "how much better this or that is done in Germany". It may be true in some matters, but it weighs as nothing against the sympathy and freedom and liberty of England which are now given to you. Never forget that point.	2. Sprechen Sie nicht deutsch in den Strassen, in Verkehrsmitteln oder sonst in der Öffentlichkeit, wie z.B. in Restaurants. Sprechen Sie lieber stockend englisch als fliessend deutsch—und sprechen Sie nicht laut. Lesen Sie keine deutschen Zeitungen in der Öffentlichkeit.
4. Do not join any Political organisation, or take part in any political activities.	3. Kritisieren Sie weder Bestimmungen der Regierung noch irgendwelche englischen Gebräuche. Sprechen Sie nicht davon, "um wieviel besser dies oder das in Deutschland getan wird". Es mag manchmal wahr sein, aber es bedeutet nichts gegenüber der Sympathie und Freiheit Englands, die Ihnen jetzt gewährt werden. Vergessen Sie diesen Punkt niemals.
5. Do not make yourself conspicuous by speaking loudly, nor by your manner or dress. The Englishman greatly dislikes ostentation, loudness of dress or manner, or unconventionality of dress or manner. The Englishman attaches very great importance to modesty, under-statement in speech rather than over-statement, and quietness of dress and manner. He values good manners far more than he values the	4. Treten Sie weder einer politischen Organisation bei, noch nehmen Sie sonst Anteil an politischen Bewegungen.
	5. Benehmen Sie sich nicht auffallend durch lautes Sprechen, durch Ihre Manieren oder Kleidung. Dem Engländer missfallen Schaustellungen, auffallende oder nicht-konventionelle Kleidung und Manieren.
Page 12	Seite 13

12. The booklet *Helpful Information and Guidance for Every Refugee* was issued to all refugees by the Jewish Board of Deputies and the German Jewish Aid Committee. In the possession of the author.

being British, that was terrific for me.' Asked why, she replied: 'Because I liked it, you see, I loved the people. And having been successful [as a restaurant owner] ... No, no, no. I loved England, I loved England. I don't think I would have been that happy in America.' These are cases where pleasure in acquiring British citizenship was rooted in a deep-seated affection for the country and pride in integrating successfully.

Ilse Wolff, later well known as a publisher, also took British citizenship as a matter of course soon after the war, as her first husband, Ernst Lowenthal, had been naturalized immediately after the war so that he could return to Germany, in British uniform, to work with the Jewish Relief Unit. But the memory of receiving her first passport and of becoming formally British remained with her. Asked whether she was British, she replied: 'Oh yes. One of the very highlights was my first British passport. Yes, I am British, but I am not English.' The granting of citizenship allowed the generation of the parents to become British, and it also opened up the way for the generation of their children to grow up as English, which meant a great deal to the parents. Hanna Singer, who had come on a Kindertransport from Germany in 1939, expressed this clearly: 'I think one of the times that I remember with great relish was when our children were very young and I thought "Oooh, they're English" and that was sort of good.'

One particular group that did encounter problems in securing British citizenship consisted of those with left-wing political views who had not applied for naturalization before the authorities became almost obsessively concerned about the communist threat. The case of Klaus Fuchs, a non-Jewish refugee scientist discovered to have been passing atomic secrets to the USSR, made the security services acutely fearful of allowing communist spies to infiltrate into Britain as refugees seeking naturalization. Accordingly, left-wingers who delayed their applications until the 1950s routinely endured suspicion and obstructionism wholly different from the experience of the bulk of refugee applicants. Ernst Flesch, a committed socialist from Austria, had his application turned down; after the Special Branch officer sent to interview him in the late 1950s accused him of delaying his application so as to avoid doing his National Service – an offensive assumption that showed a mentality quite unlike that encountered by refugees in the 1940s – he never applied again.[30]

Alfred Dörfel, a one-time Communist from Germany, also never took British nationality, because of a lasting sense of outrage at his treatment by the British authorities as an 'enemy alien' and by the Home Office after the war, and at the even worse treatment to which he was subjected when he was interned and deported to Canada on board the SS Ettrick.[31] The case of

Dörfel, a non-Jew, is included here as an informative contrast with the many Jewish refugees who underwent similar experiences as wartime internees and deportees to Canada and Australia, but who put those experiences behind them and became loyal and contented British subjects. One reason for the difference was that Dörfel, whose family had endured harsh discrimination in Germany before 1918, transferred his hatred of the ruling classes to the British state, and the upper classes who controlled it, which he saw, in class-conscious terms, as hostile to the refugees.

But it is equally true that Dörfel, unlike most Jewish refugees, was able after many years to make his peace with Germany and to reassume German nationality, persuaded by the argument that Germany had changed politically beyond all recognition. This was not a path that was open to Jewish refugees who felt that the destruction of German Jewry in the Holocaust had opened up an irreconcilable gulf between them and their homeland; whereas Dörfel, a political refugee, could conclude that post-war Germany's progress towards social democracy had reintegrated it into Western traditions of parliamentary self-government acceptable to left-wing socialists, the Jewish refugees could find no such common ground, for after the Nazi years there was no Jewish tradition left in Germany, no shared heritage to which they could re-establish ties of loyalty and citizenship. Dörfel's case also illustrates the contrast that not a few refugees perceived between the attitude of the authorities and the British state towards them and that of the majority of the British people with whom they came into contact. Dörfel remained convinced of 'a profound official hostility that for him far outweighs the friendly reception he has received from other sectors of British society',[32] an important reminder that the ungenerous, unwelcoming and even downright hostile attitude sometimes displayed by the British government and its apparatus towards the refugees in the early years left a lasting residue of disaffection in the minds of many.

In contrast to Ernst Flesch and Alfred Dörfel, Herbert Lowit, a Jew and convinced left-winger who had to flee from the Sudetenland after the Munich Agreement of 1938, was ultimately successful in his application for naturalization. Lowit knew only too well that his case for naturalization was gravely compromised by political factors that would have counted heavily against him in the 1950s.[33] While serving in the Czech forces during the war, he had little doubt that the British authorities had become aware of his socialist views, since he had made no secret of his belief that his future lay in a socialist Czechoslovakia closely allied to the USSR, the only major power not to have betrayed it at Munich. After the war he had settled in Czechoslovakia. He had then been allowed to leave Czechoslovakia legally in autumn 1947 for a visit to Britain, with a permit

from the Ministry of Labour to work abroad; the fact that his Czech passport was renewed in 1948 *after* the Communist takeover of government in
Czechoslovakia must have been damning proof in the eyes of the British
security service that he was *persona grata* with the Communist authorities. In
a word, if ever a refugee looked like a spy planted by the Communists, it
was Herbert Lowit – though in fact his connections with the West made
him thoroughly suspect to the Communist regime in Prague, which was
shortly to embark on the notorious 'anti-Zionist' purges that targeted Jews
throughout the party and state apparatus.

Herbert Lowit was fortunate. His father had settled very happily in
Yorkshire, where his connection with the Labour party made the local MP
more than willing to put his son's case to the Home Office. Lowit was
given permission to stay in Britain in 1948, on condition that he agreed to
work in the textile industry, where factories were experiencing a severe
shortage of labour. When he applied for naturalization in the 1950s, he
found unexpected allies whose personal goodwill towards him materially
assisted his application. He first struck up something of a friendship with
the Special Branch officer sent to interview him, who told Lowit that he
intended to report that he knew him to be personally reliable, though he
added that the thickness of Lowit's file might well weigh more heavily
against him with those responsible for deciding on his case. But a colleague
of Lowit's at work – he had now moved to London – came forward with
an offer to vouch for him; he was a former military man with, Lowit
strongly suspected, connections to British intelligence, and his intervention
may well have been decisive, for after three years of waiting Lowit was
offered British citizenship in 1955, on condition that he renounced his
Czech nationality. In the years after his return to Britain he had been reluctant to give up Czech nationality, but when, many years later after the Velvet
Revolution and the fall of communism, he was offered a Czech passport
again, he refused it, on the grounds that he now prized his British passport
too highly. Herbert Lowit had come to love Britain; his vivid evocation of
his feelings of homecoming every time he returned to Britain from abroad
formed a memorable passage in the interview that I conducted with him.

There was no shortage of evidence to show that the process of naturalization was being carried out in what the refugees would have seen as a
reasonably generous and fair-minded spirit. When, for example, the home
secretary was asked in 1947 about the naturalization of refugee children
who had originally been admitted as transmigrants (that is, on the understanding that they would not settle in Britain), he replied,

When these children were brought here in the early days of 1939, the intention was that many of them would emigrate to other countries, but the position was entirely altered by the war. Many of the older boys and girls at the age when they would have been emigrating joined His Majesty's Forces and the younger ones have grown up in our schools and often have become, in effect, adopted children of their British hosts.[34]

Home Secretary Chuter Ede made no attempt to use the special position of former transmigrants to refuse them naturalization, which would have been harsh indeed; he preferred instead to follow the path of fairness and natural justice – not always the British government's course in immigration policy.

Rumours of delays and other disadvantageous developments often turned out to be false, as in the case of stories that consideration of applications had been delayed on account of the wedding of Princess Elizabeth (the present queen). *AJR Information* reported that the home secretary had had to declare these rumours untrue in parliament; the truth was that the number of cases dealt with in the months in question had been much larger than in preceding months. In the same issue, an erudite article by C.C. Aronsfeld contrasted the failure of the bill of 1753 to naturalize resident Jews, the 'Jew Bill' that came to grief amidst an eruption of anti-Semitic xenophobia, with the smooth implementation of the present procedures:

> Naturalisation is now proceeding at an even pace. Not a ripple is caused by the steady procession of capital 'N's which, often two or three abreast, grace the columns of the press, daily and weekly, locally and in *The Times*: 'Notice is hereby given ...'. He would indeed be an unmitigated madman who were to suggest that the naturalisation thus carefully enacted was calling for anything but sympathy and approval, and the thought that Englishmen would rise in revolt over the issue must seem the ludicrous extravagance of a hopelessly unbalanced mind. Yet the very proposal of naturalisation once did gravely upset the people of England.[35]

Even allowing for an element of rhetorical exaggeration, Aronsfeld's point about the general acceptance of naturalization by the British public and its largely uncontested progress would have chimed with the experiences of much of his readership.

Under the title 'Equal Citizenship', the journal of June 1948 quoted on its front page a resolute defence by the home secretary of the principle of equal treatment of all British subjects, whether naturalized or British-born. Speaking in the Commons debate on the Representation of the People Bill, Chuter Ede spoke out forcefully:

> In my view a person is either a British subject or he is not ... If he is
> a British subject, that, in my view, suffices, and I, as one who is
> responsible for having to admit into British nationality persons who
> are other than British subjects by birth, would deprecate an action
> which differentiated, after naturalisation, between one British subject
> and another.[36]

When the bill was discussed in committee, the home secretary emphatically
rejected a proposal that parliamentary candidates should be compelled
to state their nationality by birth, which he saw as opening the door to
discrimination on grounds of nationality or race: 'What is important is not
where a man was born, but that he is a naturalized citizen ... The only
purpose of making him declare where he is born is the hope of creating
prejudice against him.'

The refugees themselves were not slow to recognize how favourably the
process of their naturalization had developed from 1947 onwards. In
January 1948 a front-page article in *AJR Information* stated with evident satisfaction that it might well be only 'one or two years until the whole problem of naturalization has been settled'. This turned out to be a correct
prognostication: by January 1950 the journal's regular feature on legal
matters, 'Law and Life', could state with some finality that 'every refugee
who applied for it and had not made himself personally objectionable to
the authorities has become a British subject'.[37]

A new tone of relaxed confidence made itself felt in *AJR Information*'s
reports. By March 1949 the column 'From My Diary', written by the editors under the pseudonym 'Narrator', could afford to treat the subject with
humour, a sure sign of anxieties defused. Surveying the register of aliens
naturalized in 1947, the authors came across celebrities like the pianist
Franz Osborn and the actor Adolf Wohlbrück, 'known as Anton Walbrook'
(famous for his roles in *The Life and Death of Colonel Blimp*, *The Red Shoes* and *La
Ronde*) and a battery of aristocratic 'vons', Bethmann-Hollweg, Neurath,
Etzdorf, Westarp, and even, lurking 'von'-less among the commoners, a
grandson of Kaiser Wilhelm II, Friedrich Georg Wilhelm Christoph
Hohenzollern, 'known as George Mansfield'. Commenting on the changes
of name that often accompanied the acquisition of British citizenship, the
article, tongue-in-cheek, chided those who took the process of anglicization to extremes: 'Without wishing to hurt anybody's sentiments, one feels
tempted to ask, whether people do not overdo the expression of their gratitude to their new country if they adopt names like Eden or Kipling, and
whether names starting with "Mac" should not rather be left to Members
of the Scottish Clans.'[38] 'Narrator' concluded with an altogether serious

assessment of the importance of the register of aliens for future historians: 'It vividly illustrates the legal absorption of thousands of individuals who, in times of their greatest peril, found refuge in this island.'

Those eager to detect evidence of hostility to the refugees from the native population often seize on this type of discourse as proof of an excessive desire to express loyalty and gratitude to Britain, arising out of the perceived need to propitiate potential or actual anti-Semitism among the host population. Examples cited by such scholars include the refugees' surprisingly benign attitudes to wartime internment (discussed in the previous chapter) and the establishment by the refugees in the 1960s of the 'Thank-You Britain' Fund (discussed in Chapter 10), on the grounds that this was a servile gesture aimed at airbrushing British xenophobia out of history. *AJR Information*, however, seldom reads in that ingratiating way. A defensive tone did sometimes appear, as in a front-page article on natu-ralization in December 1946, which was evidently concerned to damp down criticism of the authorities and to display an attitude of loyal appre-ciation of the efforts of the Home Office at this early stage. The article was at pains to point out the scale and complexity of the task confronting the department and attributed the slowness of the naturalization process to 'the limitation of man-power with which the Home Office, no less than any other public or private body, has to contend', while assuring readers that 'no doubt, every effort is being made to tackle the many thousands of applications'.

While recognizing its readers' 'ardent' desire to acquire the status of 'cit-izens of a country in which they and their children want to live', the arti-cle went on to urge them not to give voice to their dissatisfaction, nor to spread 'rumours' critical of the government, and to contain their impa-tience, in the interest of 'see[ing] things in their right perspective' and avoid-ing friction with their hosts. Such protestations of well-ordered loyalty can be seen as evidence of an excessive concern not to 'rock the boat', itself the product of an uneasy awareness of the hostile reaction that an over-vocal insistence on their rights by the refugees might have provoked among the host population. This issue of discourse has taken us to the central question of relations between the refugees and the native British, as defined by the interplay between friendly acceptance and hostile rejection, between harmonious integration and anti-Semitic prejudice, between trust and fear.

The discourse of fear, driven by a consciousness of the threat of anti-Semitism, was certainly not the rule in *AJR Information*. Thus another major article entitled 'A Mirror of Our Time' described the machinery set up to deal with naturalization and the progress made in an even and matter-of-fact tone wholly lacking the between-the-lines anxiety discernible in the previous article, then abandoned all defensiveness in favour of a confidently optimistic prediction: 'Here, at last, we can see the end of a problem which for a long time was a serious preoccupation of ours. A liberal principle has been evolved and the technical apparatus to carry it out is gradually gathering speed. No doubt, in the coming year, the number of naturalization certificates granted will greatly exceed last year's figure.'[39] As indeed it did.

The Jewish refugees from Central Europe, most of whom had already progressed far along the road to secularization and assimilation before they were forced to emigrate, were notably keen to integrate themselves more fully into British society, resuming in their adopted homeland the process of assimilation that had been interrupted by Nazism in their countries of origin. The eagerness with which they seized the chance to become British citizens was proof of this. Within a few short years, those refugees who had not become British subjects almost took on the role of relics from a bygone age, a species so rare that it deserved to be exhibited in museums, as in the humorous reminiscence that 'Narrator' shared with his readers in 1950: 'Do you still remember the joke about the two refugees who were exhibited at Madame Tussaud's, because they had not applied for naturalization under one of the priority categories?'[40]

The other main factor in this equation was the degree of willingness of the British to accept newly naturalized refugees into British society and to allow them to integrate. *AJR Information* certainly contained material pointing to the prevalence of native anti-Semitism and other forms of hostility to the newcomers, but it also contained much material casting their reception in the more positive light of acceptance, mutual respect and tolerance. On the specific subject of naturalization, the balance of the journal's coverage indisputably lay on the positive side, with little mention of opposition to the process of the granting of citizenship.

A particularly striking example of this occurred in 1946, when naturalization was entering its phase of decisive acceleration and, as a topical issue, came under discussion in that venerable forum of intellectual and moral guidance to middle Britain, the BBC Home Service's *Brains Trust*. The published extracts from the debate on the question 'Is Naturalisation Good for this Country?' occupied nearly a page of the journal's October 1946 issue, and the responses of the panellists were remarkable for their unanimity. The political scientist Sir Ernest Barker, the editor of the *New Statesman* Kingsley Martin, the conductor Malcom Sargent and the scientist Julian Huxley, leaders of British thought and opinion for millions of listeners, were at one in their approval of the proposition that naturalization brought the greatest benefits to the country and in their abhorrence of any discrimination on grounds of race or national origin that undermined the principle of the equality of all British citizens.

But it was the novelist and broadcaster E. Arnot Robertson whose heated response to the premises underlying the question took even the question master John Gloag by surprise:

> This is the sort of subject that brings the hair up on the back of my neck and I think on a lot of other people. Does the writer of the question really feel that he has distinguished – I presume that he is English … that he has really distinguished himself by being in the right bedroom of the right parents – therefore he deserves automatically the honour of being what he considers the member of a good race – why should people who have come over to our country because they preferred it and have perhaps given the whole of their lives to work in this country, be regarded as any more undesirable than people who just happen to be born here. Surely, one of the first things is to admit your indebtedness to other great races … I don't feel that a refugee should in any way distinguish himself for his being allowed to become an English citizen if he has lived over here for some considerable time.[41]

It was of course one thing for privileged intellectuals to express such admirable sentiments in the rarefied surroundings of a BBC radio studio, another thing entirely for a Jewish refugee to experience in everyday life the petty prejudices and animosities that beset post-war British society. Nevertheless, the published extracts, which would have been quite unimaginable on a comparable radio programme in the refugees' countries of origin even before Hitler, would have brought cheer to their hearts, and it says much about the journal's perception of the values and attitudes of British society that it chose to present the extracts as it did. Tony Kushner uses the fact that the subject of anti-Semitism was banned from the 'Brains Trust' during the war as part of his evidence for the conclusion that 'The government's inability to confront the issue of domestic antisemitism directly revealed the limitations of a liberal democracy.'[42] If that was so, then the emphatic approval of the naturalization of Jews from Central Europe on the programme in 1946 was evidence that those limitations no longer applied and that liberal values had regained their dominance, allowing the process of naturalization to go ahead smoothly.

That said, naturalization was no magic formula that removed all obstacles to the refugees' integration into British society. Even as naturalization was well under way, the AJR was becoming aware that the refugees' special position would necessitate the continued existence of the organization that catered for their needs:

At a moment when a number of refugees have been naturalised and others may expect their naturalisation within the near future, the question may arise, as to whether an organisation, which had been created for the purpose of protecting the interests of the refugees, still has its *raison d'être* ... Naturalisation does not solve all our difficulties with one stroke of the pen. It is far from being a panacea. Taken by itself it does not alter the economic situation nor does it settle the professional worries of those that had to acquire a new profession or trade. The financial problems of those that were compelled to build up a new life without reserves remain.[43]

Thirteen months later, the journal returned to this theme, broadening it out into a snapshot view of the situation of the refugees within British society:

If naturalisation, the outcome of manifold endeavours in which the AJR took a prominent part, had been the only and final object of the AJR, there would hardly have been a reason left for keeping the organisation going. Experience showed, however, that acquisition of citizenship, important as it may be, is only a milestone on the road the newcomer has to go, whereas the ultimate integration is a very slow process. If an advertiser in a local paper offers a furnished room 'for British people only', hardly any naturalised immigrant with common sense would apply for it. In the field of administration and legislation the distinction between British born and British naturalised persons is not unknown either ... Fortunately, the number of incidents which affect the Community as a whole is, at present, comparatively small. This is due, however, not only to a certain adaptation of our people to their environment, but also to the fact that this country now enjoys a period of full employment. Whenever, for one reason or another, political tension should grow, we, being foreigners and Jews at the same time, would be amongst the most suitable scapegoats.[44]

This vision of an explosion of anti-Semitism fuelled by an economic crisis, deriving from the experience of Germany during the economic depression of the early 1930s, never became reality; but the quotation revealed how precarious the refugees still felt their acceptance in British society to be in the late 1940s. Only gradually did this sense of a provisional existence give way to the greater confidence of permanent settlement.

Scholars critical of British policy on immigration and refugees would dispute this broadly positive view of the treatment of the refugees after

1945. They tend to give greater weight to evidence of official distaste for and discrimination against the Jewish refugees from Central Europe, seeking to show that in the early post-war years the Home Office was reluctant to admit the refugees to permanent residence and more than ready to take measures that intensified their sense of insecurity. Louise London examines in detail the Home Office's attempts to impose on refugees returning from visits abroad a time limit on the length of stay permitted them in Britain. (This would have been possible until refugees acquired British passports on their naturalization.) Refugees returning from abroad would be landed subject either to the word 'visit' being endorsed on their travel document or to a time limit not exceeding one year, even if they were industrialists or entrepreneurs whose trips abroad brought economic advantage to Britain.[45]

But there is little evidence to show that the Home Office actually attempted in practice to curtail the right of the great majority of refugees returning from abroad to stay in Britain unconditionally. One refugee who went abroad on business was my father, Arthur Grünfeld, who travelled to Vienna in December 1946, in part to look into the state of the family business, Adolf Lichtblau & Co. As he was not yet naturalized and had no British passport, he travelled on a Certificate of Identity issued by the Home Office, known as a travel document or travel paper. *AJR Information* had given its readers advice on how to apply for these certificates, with no hint that any problem might arise on re-entry into Britain, provided that a re-entry permit had been obtained.[46]

Arthur Grünfeld's certificate was issued by the Home Office in October 1946, and it shows that he left for Vienna two months later, returning in January 1947. As he had also been issued with the requisite return visa by the Passport Office in November 1946, had registered with the Metropolitan Police on his return and had refunded his unused foreign currency, he encountered no problems whatsoever re-entering the country; his travel document bears no sign of the imposition of any limitation of the stay allowed him in Britain (or the word 'visit'). Given that the AJR, which watched with an eagle eye for regulations disadvantageous to its members, also said nothing in its advice about travel documents to warn its members of the imposition of a time condition if they travelled abroad, one can say with some confidence that the imposition of a time condition was far from universal. In many years of research in the field, I have yet to encounter a refugee who recalls being subject to one.

In fact, ministerial intentions towards the refugees seem to have been more benign than those of some officials, as statements by the home secretary made clear, for example his statement in parliament in early 1946 on this question of the temporary absence of aliens. Asked by John Lewis MP why, in cases where aliens were granted permission to leave the country for a temporary period, their passports were stamped on their return as being valid only for six months, Chuter Ede replied that aliens unconditionally resident in this country were allowed to land unconditionally on return from abroad; aliens whose stay was on a temporary basis would normally be given leave to land on a temporary basis, though it was open to them to apply for an extension if the period granted were insufficient. This did not satisfy Mr Lewis, who asked again why it was the practice that aliens allowed to leave temporarily had their passports stamped for a specific period, irrespective of the condition referred to by the home secretary. Chuter Ede replied bluntly: 'That is not my information, nor is it my instruction.' On readmission, he reiterated, aliens normally returned on the same conditions as those under which they were here before they left.[47] This statement, by which Home Office officials were bound, would have lifted any threat of insecurity in this regard from the refugees.

Most refugees look back on the process of their formal acceptance as citizens by the British state as one where an initial sense of some anxiety and insecurity gave way to growing confidence. In January 2003 I received a letter from a former refugee, in which he briefly stated how he saw himself in terms of his national identity. The letter was particularly moving because the writer was in the last stages of terminal illness and appeared in his letter to be drawing a balance of the development in his sense of national allegiance. He rejected the description 'Continental British', which is now often used of the former refugees from Central Europe,[48] using instead a striking form of words to capture his experience of passing from formal admission to Britain to a deeper attachment and emotional integration: 'I would not agree to consider myself "Continental" British, but British by immigration and now admiration.'[49] A sentiment that is widespread, perhaps surprisingly so, among the Jewish refugees from Germany and Austria, who initially felt that they had been admitted into Britain very much as foreign immigrants who had to clear the hurdle of official procedures like naturalization, but had then mostly settled contentedly into British society, while remaining conscious of the social and cultural characteristics that distinguished them from the British.

The refugees from Germany and Austria experienced, on balance, the more generous side of the British state and British society, partly perhaps because they had undergone the perils and hardships of war alongside the British, shouldering their share of the common burden and establishing themselves as willing partners to the native British. For the pre-war refugees from Germany and Austria were also to experience a process of integration into British society very different from that of the next waves of immigrants, those from the Caribbean and the Indian sub-continent. This was not only because the German and Austrian Jews, being white, were less obvious targets for racial discrimination and could more easily blend into their new social environment, but also because so many of them, and even more so their children, opted to embrace full-scale integration into British middle-class life, occupationally and, with certain important areas where they preserved their difference, in their everyday life and their public identity.

NOTES

1. L. London, *Whitehall and the Jews, 1933–1948: British Immigration Policy, Jewish Refugees and the Holocaust* (Cambridge: Cambridge University Press, 2000), pp.252ff.
2. G. Tergit, 'How They Resettled', in *Britain's New Citizens: The Story of the Refugees from Germany and Austria. Tenth Anniversary Publication of the Association of Jewish Refugees in Great Britain* (London: Association of Jewish Refugees, 1951), pp.61–9 (p.67). Gabriele Tergit (Elise Hirschmann), a journalist and writer, had achieved her literary breakthrough in Germany with the novel *Käsebier erobert den Kurfürstendamm* (1931), but had had to flee in 1933 with her husband, the architect H.J. Reifenberg. In London she became the doyenne of refugee writers in Britain and acted for many years as secretary of the PEN Centre of German-speaking Authors in Exile.
3. 'Be Ready for the Future', circular of the AJR to its members (August 1944), p.8. These wartime circulars are held in safe keeping at the AJR offices in Stanmore, London.
4. H. Spiel, *Die hellen und die finsteren Zeiten: Erinnerungen 1911–1946* (Munich: List, 1989), p.206.
5. 'Co-operation with Organisations Overseas', AJR circular (May 1942), p.9. An item on the 'German Denaturalisation Law' appeared on p.8.
6. AJR circular (August 1944), p.5.
7. AJR circular (November 1944), pp.5f.
8. 'A World Council of Refugees', AJR circular (June 1945), pp.5f.
9. AJR circular (August 1944), p.6.
10. 'Jewish Refugees and Atrocities', AJR circular (June 1945), p.4.
11. References to proceedings in parliament are taken from *Parliamentary Debates*, Commons, 5th Series. See for these exchanges 410 H.C. Deb. 5s, cols 2266–7.
12. 410 H.C. Deb. 5s, col. 2441.
13. AJR circular (June 1945), p.5.
14. G. Macklin, '"A Quite Natural and Moderate Defensive Feeling"? The 1945 Hampstead "Anti-Alien" Petition', *Patterns of Prejudice*, 37, 3 (September 2003), pp.277–300.
15. 415 H.C. Deb. 5s, cols 2305–7. The material cited in this and the following paragraph appears in *AJR Information* (January 1946), p.6, 'Naturalisation', p.7, 'Solidarity', and p.3, 'What the Press Says'.
16. 423 H.C. Deb. 5s, col. 1330, and *AJR Information* (July 1946), p.5.
17. 441 H.C. Deb. 5s, cols 175–6.
18. 419 H.C. Deb. 5s, cols 2085–7.
19. *AJR Information* (June 1947), p.3.
20. The statistics for naturalization in the following pages are taken from the annual returns for certificates of naturalization granted by the Home Office, held at the National Archives, Kew. The post-war series begins with HO 409/8 'Aliens (Naturalization)' for 1945; the annual returns were published by His Majesty's Stationery Office, London, dated the year following that for which the return was made. *AJR Information* also drew on this source for much of the statistical material on naturalization that it quoted. The figures for 1946 and 1947 quoted here are taken respectively from *Index to Certificates of Naturalization 1946* and HO 409/10 'Aliens (Naturalization)' for 1947. The number of cases processed per month had already increased sharply during 1946, from 78 in January to 793

in December (*AJR Information* [March 1947], p.3).

21. *AJR Information* (September 1947), p.2. The number of certificates of naturalization revoked was also insignificant, numbering just three by June 1947 (*AJR Information* [August 1947], p.3). The figures for refugees from Central Europe naturalized were taken from the *Index to Certificates of Naturalization* 1946.
22. *AJR Information* (June 1947), p.3.
23. *AJR Information* (January 1948), p.2.
24. HO 409/10 'Aliens (Naturalization)' for 1947 (London: HMSO, 1948).
25. *AJR Information* (June 1948), p.2.
26. Letter to the editor from Dr H. Capell, *AJR Information* (August 1947), p.5.
27. *AJR Information* (July 1950), p.2, quoting figures for the years 1945–49 that tally with those in the annual returns for those years.
28. Figures taken from the breakdown of those naturalized according to their country of origin, from the Home Office's annual returns.
29. Interviews with Klary Friedl, Adelheid Schweitzer, Ilse Wolff and Hanna Singer in the collection of the Research Centre for German and Austrian Exile Studies and interview with Doris Balacs in the 'Continental Britons' collection.
30. Interview with Ernst Flesch in the collection of the Research Centre for German and Austrian Exile Studies.
31. Interview with Alfred Dörfel in the same collection.
32. M. Malet and A. Grenville (eds), *Changing Countries: The Experience and Achievement of German-speaking Exiles from Hitler in Britain from 1933 to Today* (London: Libris, 2002), p.200.
33. Interview with Herbert Lowit in the possession of the author.
34. Written reply, 10 February 1947, 433 H.C. Deb. 5s, col. 213.
35. *AJR Information* (December 1947), p.3, 'Naturalisation', and p.5, 'Naturalisation – A Historical Reminiscence'.
36. 450 H.C. Deb. 5s, col. 289.
37. *AJR Information* (January 1950), p.4.
38. *AJR Information* (March 1949), p.6.
39. *AJR Information* (January 1947), p.3.
40. *AJR Information* (March 1950), p.6.
41. *AJR Information* (October 1946), p.3.
42. T. Kushner, *The Persistence of Prejudice: Antisemitism in British Society during the Second World War* (Manchester: Manchester University Press, 1989), pp.139 and 141.
43. *AJR Information* (November 1947), p.5.
44. *AJR Information* (February 1949), p.1.
45. London, *Whitehall and the Jews*, pp.261ff.
46. *AJR Information* (April 1946), p.4.
47. 418 H.C. Deb. 5s, cols 1088–9.
48. The first scholar to use the term was M. Berghahn in *Continental Britons: German-Jewish Refugees from Nazi Germany* (Oxford: Berg, 1988); it was used, with permission, for the exhibition 'Continental Britons: Jewish Refugees from Nazi Europe' (2002).
49. Letter to the author of 22 January 2003. I have kept the writer anonymous.

4

The Decision to Settle:
Taking the British Option

The British government's decision to allow the Jewish refugees from Central Europe to stay in Britain and to take British citizenship meant that the state had largely played its part in providing the external conditions essential to the settlement of the refugees. The legal and official framework for settlement was now in place, and the refugees as a group were to experience no further intervention from the government and its bureaucratic machinery, which was in future to treat them no differently from other British citizens (except for government involvement in their restitution claims against foreign states). This has the disadvantage from the historian's point of view that the refugees largely ceased to feature as a separate group in government documents or statistics. Historians are consequently dependent on material such as the memoirs or testimonies of individual refugees or the records of institutions and other bodies in which refugees were involved, which are either private, individual stories or records that shed light only on limited segments of refugee life. In view of this shortage of contemporary documentation, which has till now made it virtually impossible to write a historical narrative covering the development of the refugee community, a published record as rich in material on the refugees over the entire post-war period as *AJR Information* is a rare and valuable resource.

The other obvious condition for settlement was the willingness of the refugees themselves to remain in Britain, once the option of settling elsewhere had become available to them again after the end of the war. That in turn depended on the refugees' attitude to the country that had harboured them during the war and on their perception of it as a potential homeland where they could expect a reasonable degree of security and acceptance from the majority population, and where they could with some confidence expect to establish a rooted existence, to fulfil at least some of their material aspirations and to build a new life for themselves and their families. Looking further ahead, it would also have to offer them an environment within which they could preserve their communal sense of Central European Jewish identity.

At the outset one must recognize that there were several options open to the refugees after 1945 other than that of remaining in Britain and forming there a distinct group defined by the culture of its Central European origins. It might have been expected that a community of uprooted Jews would prefer to settle in Palestine, especially once it became the new Jewish state of Israel, rather than to stay in solidly gentile Britain; indeed, two of the founding members of the executive of the AJR, Adolf Michaelis and Salomon Adler-Rudel, emigrated there soon after the war, as did Herbert Freeden (Friedenthal),[1] one of the original editors of *AJR Information*. Another possibility open to the refugees was to return to their countries of origin, as most of the other European émigrés exiled in Britain for the duration of the war hastened to do. Even given the terrible rift that the period of Nazi rule had created between the refugees and their homelands in Germany and Austria (and the effective elimination of all things German from post-war Czechoslovakia), there were those, like the journalist and AJR executive member Ernst Lowenthal, who went back; Lowenthal, who had briefly acted as co-editor of *AJR Information*, returned in 1946 to work with the Jewish Relief Unit in Germany. A trickle of other Jews also returned, mainly communists and social democrats who saw their political future in their native lands, and those who went back when their businesses or professional practices were restored to them.[2]

Another attractive alternative to the drab, constrained life of post-war Britain was emigration to third countries, most commonly to the USA, where economic and professional opportunities beckoned; another leading figure in the AJR, Kurt Alexander, a founder member of its executive and general secretary from 1943, left for America in 1949. America was certainly the object of considerable interest to the refugees. However, although *AJR Information* published prominent front-page articles on conditions in America, such as those by Rabbi Joachim Prinz in August 1946 and by Kurt Alexander in December 1948, the attraction of the USA remained largely limited to those who wished to rejoin family members there and those who managed to obtain affidavits permitting entry. The reluctance of many refugees to undertake a second emigration so soon after resettling in Britain was compounded by the difficulties of entry posed by the American immigration system, while some would have been deterred by the materialism and competitiveness of American society, captured in Kurt Alexander's image of the 'wild race for the dollar which dominates everything in the States'.[3]

The refugees' perception of America, as reflected in *AJR Information*, was primarily that of a foreign country with a substantial refugee community, not a prospective homeland.[4] A strong sense of gratitude to and identification with Britain, the wartime country of refuge, also came into play: significantly, few of the hundreds of refugees admitted to Britain in 1939 as 'transmigrants' who had applied for American visas chose to reactivate those visa applications after the war and re-emigrate. The clear inference is that the great bulk of the refugees now felt themselves comfortably settled in Britain. That was certainly the case with two refugees, Robert Norton (Neubauer) and Gina Gerson (née Bauer), who had come to Britain as children before the war, Robert Norton from Teplitz-Schönau in the formerly German-speaking part of Czechoslovakia, Gina Gerson from Vienna. Robert Norton's parents decided in 1945 not to use the affidavit that the family had secured for the USA, as they had been in Britain for several years and were happily settled in Leicestershire, where they felt secure and well accepted by the local community. Gina Gerson and her older half-sister had been sent an affidavit in 1945 by an uncle, a distinguished eye specialist in the USA, but they too decided not to make use of it. Gina Gerson half-jokingly put this down to their refusal to leave behind their cat, on whom they doted; one can read this as an indication of the ties that bound two young women, virtually alone in the world, to the small haven of security that they had created in London and of their reluctance, having lost their parents in the Holocaust, to cut themselves adrift from familiar surroundings again.[5]

Finally, there was the option of absorption into Anglo-Jewry, which might have had a strong appeal to a relatively small group of Jewish refugees confronting a new and strange post-war world where their ties with their past lives, their communities at home and all too often their families had been brutally severed. In 1941 the founding objectives of the Association of Jewish Refugees had included the integration of the refugees into the communal life of Anglo-Jewry: 'It is our aim to enable Jewish refugees to take part in the activities of the Anglo-Jewish Community so that they may share the life and fate of British Jewry in all respects.'[6] It was the sole aim to remain unattained, an important pointer to the development of a distinct and discrete refugee community in post-war Britain. That relations between Anglo-Jewry and the majority, though by no means all, of the refugees from Central Europe remained distant, never approaching the embrace of total amalgamation, is a central strand in the refugees' history.

The German-speaking Jews in Britain thus found themselves after 1945 at a crossroads, where several avenues of opportunity lay open to them. Material such as that available in *AJR Information* throws light on the process by which the great bulk of the refugees opted to remain in Britain – though a number did not – and the reasons why they chose to do so. The result of this opting for Britain was the development in this country of a clearly defined, independent community of erstwhile refugees from the German-speaking lands, held together primarily by the culture and language of their homelands and by their common fate as Jewish victims of Nazi persecution who had survived the wartime years on British soil. A useful starting point for an understanding of the refugees' decision to stay in Britain is to consider in detail the various alternative options open to the refugees and the reasons why they were rejected in favour of settling here. Starting with the rejected option of returning to the countries of birth, these avenues not taken reveal a great deal about the developing self-image and identity of the refugee community as it began to take root in Britain; that identity, more fully developed, will be examined in greater detail in Chapter 8.

The first, essential precondition for the psychological integration of the Jewish refugees from Hitler into British society, for their emotional attachment to their adopted homeland and their establishment of a new communal identity, was that they discarded their former identity from their country of origin, at least in the formal sense of refusing to return there or to reassume German or Austrian citizenship, as members of those national communities. Even before 1945, the Nazis, who had persecuted the refugees, driven them from their homes and finally liquidated the communities to which they belonged, had succeeded in making pariahs of them in their own countries and in alienating them psychologically from the society in which they had lived; all of this, it should be added, with the evident approval of the bulk of their non-Jewish fellow citizens. This separation from their former nationality and fellow nationals was cemented for most refugees by post-war developments in Germany and Austria: the failure of de-Nazification, the continuing anti-Semitism, the often shamelessly lenient treatment of Nazis by the courts, the reluctance to make restitution to the victims, and above all the refusal to confront the guilt and crimes of the Nazi years and to assume moral responsibility for what had been done in the name of the German people – all this was reflected in great and frequently depressing detail in *AJR Information*'s many reports from Germany and Austria.

The failure of so many Germans and Austrians to make a fresh start morally after 1945, by undertaking the change of attitude that would have allowed their Jewish former fellow citizens to reintegrate into the society of their native lands, effectively destroyed the possibility of the refugees' readopting their former German or Austrian identity in the post-war years. This left the refugees with little option but to become British citizens, for all their distinctive Central European social culture. While such features as their accent and dietary preferences clearly marked the refugees out as being of Central European origin, the great majority of them no longer felt themselves to be German or Austrian after 1945, nor did they wish to be designated as such, given all that had happened since 1933.[7] This is a crucial element in the development of the refugees' collective sense of identity, and historians who understate it are missing a point of fundamental importance.

That so very few refugees chose to return is irrefutable evidence of the permanent break with the former homelands. As late as 1953, it was reported that a mere 603 Austrian Jews had gone back, of the many thousands who had come to Britain.[8] On 8 May 1946 the Chancellor of the Duchy of Lancaster, John Hynd, stated in the House of Commons that the Control Office had received a paltry 197 written applications for repatriation to Germany and Austria, adding rather vaguely that 'many thousands' had applied 'in various ways' to return there;[9] many of these would have been political exiles and non-Jewish, while others presumably progressed no further than registering their applications. The *Zionist Review*, quoted in *AJR Information* of May 1946 (p.3), found that the Communist-controlled Free German Movement, which was encouraging refugees to return 'home', had received only 600 applications from an estimated 26,000 German refugees in Britain, to which were added between 500 and 600 applications made directly to the Foreign Office; the Austrian equivalent, the Austrian Centre, had registered 1,600 applications for return from some 13,000 Austrians in Britain (a figure that considerably understated the Austrian Jewish immigration, as the earlier figure understated that from Germany).

The article quoted was unequivocal in its conclusion that both Austrian and German Jews rejected overwhelmingly 'the idea of going back to a country which has murdered their families and where the poison of Anti-Semitism is as virulent as ever'. Unlike 'the political fugitives who had sought temporary shelter from Hitler's storm', the Jewish refugees were not eager to return, and their reluctance could only have been strengthened by regular warning voices exhorting them not to do so. An early letter to the editor of *AJR Information*, published in April 1947, asked bluntly:

> [W]ho can expect that a self-conscious Jew would or should return to a country which has inflicted upon him and his community sufferings unparalleled in history ... He is bound to meet people in Germany who either have taken part in the atrocities or have profiteered by them and with whom he naturally would not have any contact. But he will also meet people who had not the courage and strength ... to

make a stand against the disgraceful actions and who now ought to blush with shame and penitence. Every Jew who wants to be respected must avoid such encounters for psychological or ideological reasons. All the more so as the poison of Nazism has not been eliminated and may become effective at any time.[10]

Many refugees would have taken to heart the warning expressed by a former welfare worker for the Jewish Relief Unit from Britain about conditions in Vienna: 'Jews are coming back – and bitterly regretting it.' His condemnation of those who returned was unambiguous: 'To me it is simply impossible to understand the mentality of young persons who willingly come back to a city where their families underwent every humiliation and insult a bare few years ago, and which sent amidst the plaudits of the Viennese many thousands of their own parents, relatives and friends to a nameless end in the death camps.' This grim account extended over the first two pages of the November 1948 issue of *AJR Information*. Though the refugees could not throw off the social culture, lifestyle and customs that they had brought with them from the German-speaking lands, it was plain by the late 1940s that they would carry on that very specifically Central European Jewish culture, now vanished from its lands of origin, in a new British environment.

In March 1949, C.C. Aronsfeld, one of the respected intellectuals writing for *AJR Information*, expertly analysed the strange phenomenon whereby Jews had returned time and again over the centuries to the places where persecution had been visited upon them. Counselling insistently against repeating this historical pattern after 1945, Aronsfeld nevertheless understood the reasons behind it: 'It is almost impossible to understand, and only to be explained by the Jews' deep-felt attachment to their homesteads, that in spite of the sad experiences and terrible catastrophes, they yet again returned to the old places.'[11] Unable to return to the physical environment of their native towns and cities after the Holocaust, the Jewish refugees from Central Europe were yet deeply attached to the culture, customs and spiritual values in which they had grown up, and it was above all through the German-language culture which they had brought with them that they created and retained a sense of their own distinct identity in their adopted country.

A poem entitled 'Der Flüchtling' ('The Refugee'), published in *AJR Information* under the pseudonym 'Inquit' (Moritz Goldstein),[12] captures this combination of rejection and attachment, the painful pairing of an abhorrence of the Nazi past of Germany and Austria with a continued longing for what was valued in the lost *Heimat*. The poem's first stanza expresses a strong revulsion against the besmirched homeland:

Kehr nicht zurück in das verfluchte Land,
Den Unterschlupf der abgefeimten Horde.
Um seine Trümmer wittert noch gebannt
Der Blutgeruch der Schlachten und der Morde.
(Do not return to the accursed land, the hideout of that devious
horde. Around its ruins there hangs yet the blood-stench of battles
and killings.)

But the final stanza evokes by contrast the lonely refugee's despairing longing for that part of the once beloved homeland which lived on in memory
alone, for the values and community of a past now destroyed forever:

Bleib, wo du bist, vereinsamt und verkannt.
Wach auf aus deinen Träumen sehnsuchttrunken.
Kehr nicht zurück in das geliebte Land.
Was Heimat war, ist ach so tief versunken.
(Stay where you are, lonely and unrecognised. Wake from your
dreams drunk with yearning. Do not return to the beloved land. What
once was homeland has sunk, alas, so low.)

The refugees were able to salvage enough of their cultural, social and intellectual heritage to build from it a new identity and existence that would
draw both on the lost homeland and on the new country of refuge.

After 1945 the countries of origin were alien territory, separated by a
psychological chasm that could not be bridged by the post-war resumption
of transport and communications. This was a frequent topic in *AJR
Information*. Returning to Berlin after a gap of eight years, as Adolf Schoyer,
chairman of the AJR, told readers of the journal in a front-page article in
November 1946, had been like 'travelling into an unknown and uncannily
foreign land'; and a German Jew who returned to Germany with the
British forces of occupation was unable to feel any connection between
pre- and post-war Germany.[13] Reflecting in the same issue on his disap-
pointment on seeing the German film *Maskerade* again after an interval of
seven years, 'Narrator' (the pseudonym used by the editors) conveyed a
similar sense of the gulf between his German-Jewish past and the present:
'Sometimes it is as if the films, books, streets, towns and people
we remember existed only in our memory'.[14] The adage that the past is
another country was doubly true in the case of the Jewish refugees.

The German-speaking Jewish refugees had not only suffered the material
loss of their homes and familiar surroundings in the war; by destroying the
entire communities in which they had lived, the Holocaust had also
robbed them of the possibility of re-establishing emotional and spiritual

contact with the past. The refugees' pre-war lives had been irreparably severed from the post-war present, and the realization of this was often traumatic, as in the case of Werner Rosenstock, General Secretary of the AJR for
some forty years and editor of its journal, who received 'the shock of my
life' on returning to his native district of Berlin, the badly bombed Hansa-
Viertel in 1950:

> Before 1933 there was hardly a house in which one did not know at
> least one family. Jews in the Hansa-Viertel formed a closely knit com-
> munity. First, when Hitler came, the Jews had to go, partly to strange
> countries, partly to the extermination camps. Now their dwellings
> have also ceased to exist. A centre of Jewish life has been erased
> entirely. What is left is the memory of the happy days which many of
> us once spent in Berlin's Hampstead[15]

The positive note on which this piece closed, perhaps implying that the
refugees had found an alternative to the Tiergarten in Hampstead Heath,
was not maintained in its sequel, where Rosenstock described his visit to
the Jewish cemetery at Weissensee:

> The cemetery is again as peaceful and dignified as it was before the
> war ... There is only one difference: you do not meet a single person
> when wandering around. What struck me most were the tombstones
> whose inscriptions were unfinished. Half of the space had been left
> blank for the husband or wife until his or her turn would have come.
> Now we know that this space will remain blank for ever.[16]

Small wonder that refugees like Rosenstock preferred to live out their lives
in north-west London rather than amidst the ghosts of their vanished
native communities.

In June 1950 *AJR Information* published a major front-page article, tellingly
entitled 'Beginning or End?', that discussed the future, if any, of the Jewish
community in post-war Germany, which by then consisted mainly of displaced persons from other countries, concentration camp survivors and
Jews who had survived as partners in mixed marriages. The number of
German Jews remaining was described as 'infinitesimally small'; those
returning to Germany from all allied countries were estimated at 'no more
than three to four hundred'. The survey reached the sombre conclusion
that German Jewry, once one of the jewels in the crown of Judaism, had
disappeared:

> Community life cannot be compared with that in the former Jewish
> communities . . . There are no central institutions, no teachers and

theological seminaries and it is not to be expected that such institutions will be established. All this cannot be taken as a continuation of the history of German Jewry, which has come to an end once and for all.

But German-speaking Jewry, though extinguished in Germany and Austria, was not dead. Indeed, one of the recurrent key themes in *AJR Information* was the survival of precious parts of the German-Jewish heritage in the alien, but not entirely unwelcoming environment of Britain. A front-page article in September 1947 by a leader of Berlin's Jews, Hans-Erich Fabian, made this point powerfully; it is the more convincing as it was written by an outsider with no interest in lauding the settled conditions enjoyed by the Jewish refugees in Britain. Viewed from post-Hitler Berlin, Britain offered conditions enviably favourable to the recreation of a form of German-Jewish life, albeit adapted to its new setting, as well as sadly truncated by the Nazi terror:

> No doubt in Great Britain, too, the Jews originating from Germany lived through difficult times, being subjected to the 'Blitz' and internment, yet they never ceased to enjoy a certain measure of security. The world around them was by no means hostile; on the contrary, in many cases distinctly friendly even. Despite all the hardships that were occasioned by the war, they were able to proceed with their plans for settlement and had, at the same time, an opportunity for reconstructing Jewish life, as they had known it in Germany. In short, they were able to adjust themselves to their new surroundings.

Fabian foresaw a transplantation of German-Jewish culture to Britain, a combination of the heritage of the past with the demands of the present, which meant both that the refugees must 'remain conscious of their origin' and also that they must 'take root' in their new homeland, becoming 'integrated into the world around them' as 'British citizens in the full meaning of the term'. But this was not a straightforward statement of the old assimilationist agenda, transmuted into a demand for a far-reaching integration into British society. For Fabian exhorted the refugees to preserve those parts of their communal identity which had historically given German Jewry its lustre, to carry their Central European culture on into the future in Britain: 'Such a policy does obviously not mean that the refugees should deny their origin or write off their past. On the contrary, German Jewry can be proud of its history. It can, indeed, it should build on its meritorious achievements. Yet we must not be content with retrospection.'

Thus a leader of Germany's principal surviving Jewish community entrusted the continuation of the traditions and values particular to the German-speaking Jews of Central Europe in considerable measure to those of them who had settled in Britain, where they would preserve their own heritage, at least for the lifetime of the German-speaking generations. A further front-page article in *AJR Information* of July 1947 had the title 'Trustees of an Heritage', quoting a phrase from Rabbi Leo Baeck's speech opening the first plenary session of the Council for the Protection of the Rights and Interests of Jews from Germany, the international organization representing the dispersed remnants of German Jewry. Fittingly, this body was based in London, then the key bridgehead between the continent of Europe and the Jews overseas, and, again fittingly, its president was Rabbi Dr Baeck, the spiritual leader of the German Jews. In a sombre address, he declared the history of the Jews in Germany to be at an end, but went on to proclaim the London-based Council 'the trustee of [their] spiritual heritage'; the refugees in Britain would play a leading part in ensuring that their creative legacy passed on into the future.

That legacy, emancipated and secular in its subordination of adherence to traditional Jewish religious practices and beliefs to the goal of integration into the German-speaking *Bildungsbürgertum*, the educated middle class, set its refugee heirs in Britain apart from many other Jewries, including Anglo-Jewry. This emerged clearly in *AJR Information*'s attitude to Palestine, and later Israel, which, though overwhelmingly positive and supportive, was plainly not Zionist, in that it notably refrained from encouraging its readers to emigrate there; nor was it informed by a strong sense of shared traditional values binding the Jewish refugees to their co-religionists in Israel, since the values of the refugees drew so heavily on the German-speaking culture and lifestyle that their community had embraced in the era of emancipation and assimilation.

The great majority of the refugees in Britain evidently preferred to continue to live as Diaspora Jews in Britain. The number who re-emigrated to Israel was relatively small, very much smaller than the number who went to the USA; and some took the reverse route and left the nascent Jewish state for Britain. Some of these, like the writer and journalist Robert Weltsch, were out of sympathy with the nationalistic turn of Jewish policy in Palestine, especially towards the Arab population. Others, like the psychotherapist Irene Bloomfield, who was to pioneer the development of encounter groups for the second generation, the British-born children of refugees, spent the war years in Palestine, but then came to London and stayed to exploit professional and career openings. Others again, like the writer Gabriele Tergit and her architect husband H.J. Reifenberg, came to Britain after they and their child all fell ill in pre-war Palestine. Even an ardent Zionist like Edith

Fairfield, who had freely chosen to emigrate to Palestine from Vienna before the *Anschluss*, found the climate so damaging to her health that she came to live in Britain; she stayed here until her death in 2004, though her continued adherence to her convictions meant that her life developed along more obviously Jewish lines than was the case with the more secularized, non-Zionist refugees, whose allegiance came to lie with Britain.[17]

Material conditions certainly played a part in dissuading those in Britain from emigrating to Israel in the post-war years: the pervasive threat to the security of the Jewish state and the lives of its inhabitants, the low standard of living, the primitive conditions and the shortages of goods and services taken for granted even in post-war Britain, the poor economic prospects for professional people, and the fact that so much of the new state had, almost literally, to be built from scratch were powerful disincentives to emigration to Israel. Yet that presented no obstacle to the many thousands of Jews who flocked to Israel with pioneering enthusiasm from a multitude of lands; indeed, the challenge of creating a new communal life against all the odds was for many an added spur to their dedication to Israel. The conclusion must be that such enthusiasm was largely absent among the Jewish refugees in Britain, who had mostly not come from Zionist backgrounds in their countries of origin and whose loyalty to Britain, established during the war years, outweighed their sense of solidarity with the state of Israel. The barriers that kept the overwhelming majority of the Jewish refugees from Central Europe from leaving Britain for Israel were not primarily material; they were cultural and historical.

It goes without saying that a refugee publication like *AJR Information* was very supportive of the Jewish cause in Palestine, as were its readers. The journal was often severely critical of British policy towards the Jews in Palestine, especially of the inhumanity of the restrictions on immigration into Palestine that left Jews to rot in thousands in DP camps in Europe.[18] But at the same time it condemned unreservedly the use of terrorist violence in the struggle for independence against the British mandatory authority. This reflected a deeper ambiguity towards the concept of a Jewish homeland: before 1948 the journal did not endorse the principle of the establishment of a Jewish state, stopping short at the humanitarian demand that homeless Jews be admitted to Palestine in the framework of a peaceful compromise accord.

As late as February 1947, an editorial article on the front page, tellingly entitled 'Plough *versus* Gun', argued passionately against the use of terror and violence and in favour of cooperation with the British authorities in Palestine; by ruling out the use of violence, it could be argued, the journal was effectively abandoning the means to an independent Jewish state:

> We still hope that the views of ... those who believe in negotiation
> as the medium of political struggle will in the end prevail. A policy
> based on violence is alien to Judaism, opposed to our ethical con-
> ception of a Jewish National Home and objectionable even from the
> point of view of practical expediency. We know what terror means.
> Terror has driven us from land to land, has made us flotsam and jet-
> sam, has murdered our families and killed our dearest. We condemn
> terror in whatever form it may appear and whoever may exercise it.
> For us there is no compromise with violence. It is no mere coinci-
> dence that our corresponding organisation in Palestine [the Irgun
> Olej Merkas Europa] has always been in the forefront of the struggle
> against terrorism and in the attempts to come to a workable arrange-
> ment with the Mandatory Power.

Terror in Palestine received here the ultimate condemnation of being mentioned side by side with Nazi terror, even though terror was the means by
which much of the Jewish community in Palestine was seeking to throw
off British rule; by contrast, the preservation of working relations with the
British remained a central requirement, as it did for the refugees when it
came to ordering their communal life in Britain.

Clearly, the establishment of a Jewish state claiming to represent all Jews
would pose a serious problem for those Jews whose loyalties lay elsewhere
and who had opted to settle in host countries like Britain and to integrate
into British society. The uneasy balance among the Jewish refugees between
loyalty to Britain and support for the Jewish cause in Palestine was reflected
in two contrasting items on the front page of the January 1947 issue of *AJR
Information*. The first, resoundingly entitled 'Testimony of Faith', quoted
from Chaim Weizmann's proud account to the Zionist Congress in Basle of
the progress made towards the establishment of a free Jewish state; the second recorded that the Pioneer Corps had been granted the privilege of the
title 'Royal' in recognition of its war service, a distinction that would have
gratified the many refugees who had served in its 'Alien Companies'.
Together, these items neatly encapsulated what Herbert Freeden termed
'the intricate problem of "double loyalty"',[19] the divide between pride in
the nascent Jewish state on the one hand and the refugees' pleasure in official recognition and acceptance by Britain on the other. Loyalty to Britain
proved the stronger, even with the foundation of the Jewish state in 1948,
at least for the majority whose natural enthusiasm for Israel did not extend
to resettling there.

Lutz Weltmann, a journalist and theatre critic in Germany who emigrated and became a teacher and lecturer in Britain, where he contributed

literary reviews of elegant erudition to *AJR Information*, recognized this pull of conflicting loyalties: 'The Zionists have achieved their chief aim with Israel's statehood. But for the greater number of Jews in the Diaspora the problem of a dual loyalty still exists.'[20] Weltmann was surely typical of the majority of his fellow refugees when he went on to defend stoutly the 'healthy middle course', midway between Zionism and total integration, taken by the German-speaking Jews concerned to preserve their own culture and identity in Britain, as they had in Central Europe. Rather than embarking on a fresh emigration to Israel, the refugees from Germany and Austria preferred to continue along their chosen path of adaptation to the society around them, which was now that of their new homeland, Britain. The importance of the Jewish state to the refugees could of course hardly be overstated. This was especially the case in the late 1940s, with the seismic impact on Jews worldwide of the creation of the state of Israel. As a front-page article in *AJR Information* of October 1948 made clear, however, the impact of the foundation of Israel on the refugees from Hitler in Britain was twofold and potentially divisive. On the one hand, some welcomed the establishment of Israel unreservedly as 'the fulfilment of dreams they have cherished throughout their lives'. But for others, who 'react to the new situation with qualified rejoicing', Israel also represented a threat to the security of their identity as Jews settled in the Diaspora, since it called into question the claim to full Jewishness of those communities that remained outside the Jewish state; they must 'hope that the conception of a Jewish State may not impair the position of the majority of Jews outside Israel, who feel themselves politically integrated into their countries of residence'. These included the heirs to the German-Jewish tradition, many of whom, though by no means all, had by now too little in common with the core values of the Jewish state to be easily transplanted there.

Consequently, statements in the journal emphasising the role of Israel as the sole true homeland of all Jews were counterbalanced by reassuring statements stressing the continuing validity of community life in Britain. On the one hand, *AJR Information* reported Chaim Weizmann's impassioned appeal for a massive 'ingathering of the exiles', in his first address to the Knesset as president of Israel, on the front page of its March 1949 issue, and the following month's front page celebrated the feast of Passover as 'the passing over of innumerable homeless Jews from the insecurity of their existence into the security and freedom of Israeli citizenship'. On the other hand, however, a steady stream of items reflected the sense among the refugees that they were no longer among the 'homeless' and that they now enjoyed 'security and freedom' as British citizens. Thus in March 1949 the column 'Anglo-Judaica', which kept readers informed about events in

Anglo-Jewry, quoted at some length from a speech by Maurice Edelman MP about divided loyalties: 'Emotionally, Jews could feel sympathy and, indeed, affection for the State of Israel. Politically, the Jew had a single allegiance and that was to the country of which he was a citizen.' In February 1950 the same column reported the stout defence of Diaspora Jewry mounted by the Chief Rabbi, couched in traditionally religious terms: 'Jews outside the land of Israel will continue to exist; they will be regarded as Jews and will feel far from being cut off from the Land of Israel; they will still form the people designed by God Himself to fulfil a purpose for Mankind.'[21]

As long as immigration to Palestine was limited by the restrictions on entry imposed by the British authorities and by the general uncertainty of conditions there, the Jewish refugees were under little immediate pressure to opt for settlement in the Jewish homeland. But by 1948, when an independent Jewish state had become a reality, they were faced with a clear choice between their attachment to Britain, their country of settlement, and the appeal of Israel to all Jews in the name of their common heritage and as the land of their historic destiny. In a major front-page article in *AJR Information* of January 1948, Robert Weltsch, distinguished editor of the *Jüdische Rundschau* in pre-emigration Germany and a Zionist of long standing who had come to Britain from Palestine after the war, struggled to find a form of words that celebrated the 'birth of the Jewish State' while at the same time justifying the continued existence of Jewish communities elsewhere. His key sentence was awkwardly hedged about with reservations that convey this dilemma: '[The UN resolution on Israel] means the official recognition of the legitimate right of – not the Jewish people as a whole, but – a certain Jewish community on ancient Jewish soil to free national life in its own state.' This was hardly calculated to rouse his readers to set sail for Tel Aviv; rather, it accorded with the fact that most refugees preferred to resolve the clash of loyalties by opting for Britain.

When Weltsch returned to the subject in 1950, in a lecture entitled 'Zweierlei Judentum (Two Kinds of Jewry) – Israel und Diaspora', he saw the division between Diaspora and Israeli Jews as an established fact. The challenge posed by the establishment of the Jewish state had, he said, led a number of Jews in Britain to emphasize the independence of their community and to regard Israel as a separate entity, which they supported in a spirit of philanthropy, but which could not match 'the sole political allegiance to the country of residence'.[22] Significantly for the refugees, he added that the problem of dual loyalty 'was eased by the very undogmatic conception held in English speaking countries of the relationship between the State and the individual', one of many tributes from refugees weaned on Germanic authoritarianism to easy-going British pragmatism as a factor that smoothed the path to integration into British society. It was that path that the refugees mostly chose to take.

The Jews from Central Europe were both less emotionally committed to Israel than was established Anglo-Jewry and less reliant for their collective identity on a sense of being a traditionally Jewish community preserving traditional customs and practices. It is, for example, hard to imagine a leading figure among the refugees declaring as unambiguously as did Professor Selig Brodetsky, president of the Board of Deputies of British Jews, that 'Jewish education in this country should be associated with Jewish life in Palestine and that the Jewish child should be made to feel that he is a part of the unity of the Jewish people'.[23] It is also unlikely that the Board of the Association of Jewish Refugees would, as the Board of Deputies did, have burst spontaneously into a rendition of the Hatikvah, the Jewish anthem, to welcome the proclamation of the Jewish state. The development of the collective identity of the refugees from Hitler kept them at arm's length from Israel, and the relative weakness of their allegiance to traditional Jewish religious and social practices was also to distance them from Anglo-Jewry.

In the initial post-war period, expectations of close and friendly relations between Anglo-Jewry and the refugees were high, as is shown by the welcome extended to *AJR Information* on its appearance in 1946 by such organs of Anglo-Jewry as the *Jewish Chronicle* and the *Zionist Review*. Front-page articles in *AJR Information* of November 1949 and September 1950 recalling the generous financial support extended by British Jews before the war to the often destitute refugees were evidence of the latter's gratitude, though already here the heavy emphasis on charitable support in material terms pointed up the relative failure of human and organizational contacts to develop on a wide scale. The refugees' refusal to integrate into Anglo-Jewry is a key indicator of their developing communal identity. The very fact that the two groups of Jews were in many respects so close throws into sharp relief the factors that kept them apart; at the same time these elements formed part of the core values and attitudes that defined the self-image and communal identity of the refugees from Germany and Austria.

This is not to overlook the evident fact that many refugees from Central Europe did become involved with Anglo-Jewry, through synagogues and other institutions, in their careers, their pastimes, their friendships and social relations, and not least by marrying Anglo-Jewish partners. But the majority remained separate from British Jewry, retaining a distinct Continental identity that pervades *AJR Information*, with its highly cultured and largely secularized brand of journalism, designed to appeal to an intellectually sophisticated and largely assimilated readership not bound by specifically Jewish concerns and interests. The refugees from Central Europe did not on the whole build their communal organizations around religious institutions, as Anglo-Jewry had done around its synagogues, nor was their social and cultural life determined to the same extent by customs and values deriving from traditional Jewish religious practice.

Attitudes towards the prospect of integrating the more recent refugees into Anglo-Jewry varied very widely, as is evident from the statements of congratulation from eminent well-wishers that were published on the first two pages of *AJR Information* in January 1947, on the occasion of the first anniversary of its appearance. On the one hand, a leading figure in Anglo-Jewry like Professor Selig Brodetsky warmly welcomed AJR members into the common fold of the Jewish community: 'I hope that as long as a special Bulletin for Refugees is needed, it will continue its unifying work successfully, but I hope even more that the membership of the Association in Britain may soon become an integral part of the Anglo-Jewish Community.' This reflected the assumption, still common in the immediate post-war years, that the refugees from Central Europe would amalgamate smoothly and rapidly into Anglo-Jewry. In the event, though, this fusion of the two communities never materialized.

On the other hand, people close to the refugee community like the Anglo-German banker Otto Schiff, chairman of the Jewish Refugees Committee that had been responsible for organizing the emigration of Jews from Nazi Germany to Britain, clearly anticipated that the refugees would integrate into British society, rather than into Anglo-Jewry. Schiff looked back on 1946 as 'a momentous year for the refugees from Nazi oppression who found sanctuary in this country, because it has seen the recommencement of naturalization', the process that marked a key step in the integration of the refugees into British society.

Those who welcomed that process of integration also foresaw that the refugees could and would preserve their distinct Central European cultural heritage in Britain. An example of this was the message received from E.N. Cooper, formerly head of the Home Office's Aliens Department and now chairman of the London Regional Refugee Council (and a valued friend of the AJR, as an affectionate obituary in its journal later showed):

> Now that the refugees are being rapidly absorbed into our British national life, I find myself asking what contribution they can make in the years to come to the life and work of the country of their adoption. It is my great hope that they may become a living link between this country and the best of the culture that derives from Germany and Austria.

An accurate analysis, coming from a man who had played a leading part in implementing Home Office policy towards the refugees and had come to appreciate their qualities, and who eventually married a refugee wife.

Relations between the refugees, who came from the Westernized cities of the German-speaking world, and the British Jews, who were largely descended from immigrants from Eastern Europe, were affected by the historical friction between the assimilated, secularized, middle-class Jewish communities in Germany and Austria, prosperous and cultured, and the Eastern Jews, mostly poor, Orthodox in their religion and traditional in the practices that governed their social culture. There are clear traces of this in *AJR Information*, which occasionally reflected an awareness of the disapproval felt by Eastern Jews, and their British-born descendants, for the German Jews. In the eyes of the Eastern Jews, their German-speaking cousins had abandoned their ancestral religion and its associated practices, opted headlong for integration into German-speaking society and culture, and assumed a sense of patronizing cultural superiority towards their allegedly more backward cousins, whom they styled *Ostjuden*. Diplomatically, the journal chose to confine overt references to this delicate area largely to certain of its reports from faraway Palestine/Israel, where it was common knowledge that Jews from Eastern Europe often viewed the 'Prussian Jekkes'[24] with ill-concealed disfavour.

In the post-war years fear of anti-Semitism continued to be a factor contributing to the mixed nature of the reception extended by Anglo-Jewry to the refugees from Hitler. A striking example of this discourse of fear, right down to the image of Jews being forced to slink along by the side of the street, is given by a German-speaking Jewish refugee from Prague, quoting the accusation levelled at her and her husband by a British Jew that the new arrivals from Central Europe threatened the tenuous security painstakingly achieved over the years by Anglo-Jewry:

> I remember in Anson Road [Willesden] there was a house next to us which belonged to some English Jewish people ... They had some friends in one evening and we were also invited, Andrew and I, and we had a rather unpleasant conversation because they told us they didn't want us. They, the Jews, didn't want us to come in here ... So he said, he explained to me. My family came from Poland or Russia, I don't know, at the beginning of the century. He described it rather sort of picturesquely, he had to go in the street quite by the wall ... slink along by the wall, and then as he grew up and made his way, he was by now proudly walking in the middle of the road. Now we came and pushed them back to the wall. That was their explanation

> ... Because we didn't speak English, we were not English ... our
> habits ... That's how we pushed them back to the wall and they held
> this against us.[25]

With their foreign accents and appearance and their demands on resources
like housing, health care and employment, the refugees seemed to British
Jews all too likely to fuel the anti-Semitic feelings latent in British society.
But fears that the refugees from Nazism would arouse the prejudices of the
native British soon evaporated – not surprisingly, given the refugees' evident fondness for Britain and its ways, their rapid adaptation to British
society, and the speed with which their very considerable contribution to
that society transformed their image in the eyes of the British public. This
significantly undercut the threat of their provoking anti-Semitism and
earned instead the respect of at least the more educated and open-minded
sections of that public.[26]

A central issue in the post-war years was the route to integration into
British society chosen by the refugees from Central Europe, which differed
very greatly from the experience of the earlier immigrants from Eastern
Europe, whose descendants composed the bulk of British Jewry. As the
German-speaking refugees were predominantly drawn, in socio-economic
terms, from the commercial and professional middle classes, it was perhaps natural that they sought to integrate into British society at a broadly
comparable level. This represented a sharp contrast with the immigrants
from Tsarist Russia, who initially tended to settle in poor working-class
districts like London's East End and thus started out at the lower end of the
social scale. Nowhere was this class difference more clearly visible, as the
editors of *AJR Information* had noticed as early as 1948, than in the tendency
of the refugees from Germany and Austria to congregate in predominantly
middle-class areas of north-west London:

> In Germany, the Jew was assimilated and belonged to the middle
> class; even when losing his fortune, he did not become a proletarian
> but a petty bourgeois. In the London East End ... he belonged to a
> Yiddish speaking proletarian stratum, though at a later stage either he
> or his children managed to improve their position. Many misunder-
> standings between the refugees from Germany ... and other sections
> of the Anglo-Jewish community may be explained by this different
> background. The dispossessed refugee did not start at the lowest rung
> of the ladder in Whitechapel, but, penniless as he was, took his fur-
> nished room in Hampstead or other North-Western parts of the
> town.[27]

Even allowing for an element of generalization, this analysis does point to a key feature in the development of the self-image and identity of the refugee community, which can in many ways be seen as following naturally on from the type of assimilated, urban, middle-class, professional communities that the Jews in pre-Hitler Germany and Austria had evolved. Continuing the strong tradition of upward social mobility and social adaptation in their countries of origin, the majority of the Central European Jews aimed almost instinctively to integrate into the broadly equivalent strata of British society, the educated, cultured, professional middle classes. This socio-cultural orientation proved stronger than any religious or traditionally Jewish allegiance that might instead have bound them into Anglo-Jewry.

AJR Information's column 'Events in Anglo-Jewry', which in December 1948 became 'Anglo-Judaica' and under that name was for many years its source of information about Anglo-Jewry, was full of evidence of the enduring distance between the refugees from Hitler and the British Jews. Though intended to inform the journal's readers about Anglo-Jewry, the column's coverage was in the event scarcely calculated to bring the two communities together. Almost from the start, the selection of items about Anglo-Jewry in the column, drawing mainly on the Jewish press, was surprisingly weighted towards the negative aspects of the community: positive items about support for Israel or resistance to Mosley's fascists were often outweighed by tales of unseemly communal strife and discord, chronic financial deficits, and declining standards of religious observance and education. The very first item in 'Events in Anglo-Jewry', in October 1947, set the tone by reporting that 'British Jewry, fighting the national crisis which threatens from outside, is also involved in a hardly less serious communal crisis', the long-running internal conflict between Zionists and non-Zionists over the succession to the late Chief Rabbi. Reports on the bitter and convoluted internal feuds that affected Anglo-Jewry were frequent.

Together with items that lamented the seriously inadequate supply of suitable teachers for London's Jewish schools and the general decline in Jewish education and culture, such reports hardly painted the reassuring picture of a united and harmonious community that would have attracted the refugees. They would have been further disquieted by 'Events in Anglo-Jewry' of August 1948, which reported the 'virtual excommunication' by the United Synagogue in Cardiff of a number of people described as 'new assimilationists' and 'camouflage Jews', designations that could well have been aimed at Central European refugees often noted for their relaxed approach to traditional observance.

Particularly numerous were items highlighting the chronic financial problems affecting the institutions of Anglo-Jewry. Thus, a long report in

'Anglo-Judaica' of September 1949, entitled 'A Tale of Deficits', began with the weary words: 'Since our communal finance appears to be condemned to everlasting deficits'; a report in December 1949 appeared under the title 'Living on the Overdraft'; and in July 1949 the United Synagogue presented what the journal resignedly termed 'the usual gloomy balance sheet [of] leading Anglo-Jewish institutions'. The frequency of such items contributed to a picture of Anglo-Jewry in difficulties. Though there were, it must be emphasized, many positive items in 'Anglo-Judaica', there were also enough depicting the problems affecting Anglo-Jewry to have deterred refugees who might have been drawn to it. Certainly, the image of Anglo-Jewry promoted in *AJR Information* in these years would have done little to impel them towards active participation in the existing Jewish community. Rather, their desire to preserve their own separate culture would have been reinforced by the mixed nature of the reports carried in 'Anglo-Judaica', and their sense of their own distinct community identity correspondingly accentuated.

The development of the communal identity of the Jewish refugees from Nazism in Britain was largely shaped by the crucial choices that they made in the immediate post-war years, choices that revealed a great deal about the nature of that identity both through what the refugees chose and through what they rejected. The option of returning to their homelands was decisively rejected by the overwhelming majority of the refugees, which meant that they discarded their German or Austrian national identity of pre-Hitler times, though they retained much of the German-speaking, 'Continental' culture in which they had been steeped. The great majority also opted not to emigrate to the USA or other third countries, thereby confirming that they had permanently transferred their allegiance to Britain as their homeland of choice, not just as a country of transit or involuntary exile. This was also reflected in their reluctance to emigrate to Israel, which showed that they mostly lacked the necessary level of commitment to the core values of the Jewish state, though they supported it warmly from a distance.

The decision to stay in Britain in turn profoundly influenced the development of the refugees' communal identity, as their situation was radically different from that of their fellow refugees who had settled in Israel or America. In Israel, the refugees from Central Europe were faced with a Jewish state dynamically intent on integrating all the varied groups of immigrant Jews into a society unified around a sense of common Jewish values and a common Jewish national consciousness. In America, the refugees from Central Europe were confronted by American Jewry, a far larger ethnic group than Anglo-Jewry, with a vibrant communal life into which they could easily be absorbed. America was above all else a society of immigrants (as was Israel), a society structured so as to facilitate the smooth and rapid integration of immigrant groups; whether or not the refugees retained an identity separate from that of American Jewry, they were soon able to don an American identity, as numerous groups of immigrants had done before them. This overarching American identity did not replace their original ethnic identity, for it was designed on the contrary to sit alongside it, as was the case with Irish, Italian or Hispanic Americans.

In Britain, by contrast, the refugees from Central Europe did not on the whole integrate into Anglo-Jewry, which was considerably smaller and less outward-looking than its American counterpart and from which they felt in large measure historically and culturally distinct. The refugees, who had begun to adapt to British society during the war, found it relatively easy to integrate instead into mainstream British society, as their eagerness to acquire British citizenship indicated. But one could not acquire a new identity along with the new passport: it was not possible to don a British – let alone an English, Welsh or Scottish – identity as quickly as an American or Israeli one, for Britain was not an immigrant society, and the notion of Britishness in those years accommodated only the home nations and, at a stretch, long-established British residents of Irish or White Commonwealth descent.

Consequently, the refugees were to develop their own brand of identity, which combined the Central European, 'Continental' social culture and values of the German-speaking lands with a wide-ranging acceptance and internalization of British social attitudes and practices. But they were the last generation to be able to draw on the German-language culture of the assimilated German and Austrian Jews, for there was no longer any interchange between them and their countries and communities of origin, as there is for the Afro-Caribbean, Pakistani or Cypriot communities in Britain. The children of the refugees, even those who learnt to speak German, were to grow up thinking of themselves as British. Indeed, the fact that the children of the refugees grew up and were educated overwhelmingly in the framework of British institutions was to contribute greatly to the integration of their parents into British society.[28]

NOTES

1. Freeden, who left for Israel in 1950, continued to report for *AJR Information* for many years in his 'Letter from Jerusalem', eventually returning to Britain, where he died in 2003.
2. See, for example, the interview with Helga Reutter at the Research Centre for German and Austrian Exile Studies for details of her father's return to Vienna when he got his factory back. When restitution

began in the 1950s, a number of former public sector employees returned to Germany because pension payments were initially easier to access there. See for example the correspondence between Professor Felix Jacoby, a refugee academic at Oxford since 1939, and the Dean of Christ Church, Oxford, February–November 1954, when Jacoby was deciding to return to West Germany for his pension (Christ Church Archives, file DPxx.c.1, Felix Jacoby).

3 *AJR Information* (December 1948), p.1.
4. In 1946 Ernst Lowenthal estimated the total number of Jewish refugees who had left Britain for the USA since 1933 at 13,000, with a further 500 leaving monthly. This amounted to nearly 60 per cent of total re-emigration, and also represented some 16 per cent of the Jewish refugees from Germany and Austria who had come to Britain before the war (*AJR Information* [June 1946], p.45; in 1946 the journal was paginated continuously throughout the year, thereafter from page 1 in each issue). If anything, the figures seem on the high side.
5. Interviews with Robert Norton and Gina Bauer-Gerson in the 'Refugee Voices' collection.
6. AJR circular (summer 1941), unpaginated (p.2).
7. As one example among very many, see the vehemence with which Gina Gerson rejects the very thought of assuming an Austrian identity or of being taken as an Austrian, the result of her traumatic childhood experience of Viennese anti-Semitism in 1938 (interview with Gina Gerson in the 'Refugee Voices' collection).
8. *AJR Information* (September 1953), p.3.
9. 422 *H.C. Deb.* 5s, col. 90.
10. *AJR Information* (April 1947), p.5.
11. *AJR Information* (March 1949), p.5.
12. *AJR Information* (January 1948), p.6.
13. *AJR Information* (March 1946), p.2.
14. Ibid., p.4.
15. *AJR Information* (October 1950), p.6.
16. *AJR Information* (November 1950), p.6.
17. Obituary of Edith Fairfield, *Jewish Chronicle* (19 March 2004), p.32.
18. For example, the front-page article 'The Hamburg Tragedy' in *AJR Information* (October 1947), one of several denunciations of the mistreatment of would-be immigrants to Palestine aboard the ship *Exodus 1947*; also the dramatic report on p.3 of the same issue about the poor conditions under which other would-be immigrants were held in refugee camps in Cyprus.
19. *AJR Information* (July 1947), p.4.
20. *AJR Information* (October 1950), p.6.
21. 'Anglo-Judaica' appeared on p.3 of the journal at this time, moving later to p.5.
22. *AJR Information* (April 1950), p.7.
23. *AJR Information* (April 1948), p.3.
24. *AJR Information* (August 1950), p.5. *Yekke* is an unflattering term used by Jews from Eastern Europe to describe the Jews from Germany and Austria, with their over-punctilious sense of order and inflated cultural pretensions.
25. Interview with Eva Sommerfreund at the Research Centre for German and Austrian Exile Studies.
26. The refugees' contribution to British society was already considerable by the late 1940s, and was perceived as such. To take but two examples: in 1945 Ernst Chain had become the first refugee scientist to win a Nobel Prize, while the Amadeus Quartet, Glyndebourne and the Edinburgh Festival, all in large measure refugee creations, transformed the British musical scene in the post-war years. See D. Snowman, *The Hitler Émigrés: The Cultural Impact on Britain of the Refugees from Nazism* (London: Chatto and Windus, 2002), especially pp.185–250.
27. *AJR Information* (July 1948), p.6.
28. As one example among very many, see the interview with Margarete Hinrichsen, née Levy, in the collection of the Research Centre for German and Austrian Exile Studies, where she makes the point very plainly: 'I made a lot of friends through the children, and I feel more British.'

5

The 'Continentals' and the British

Relations between the Jewish refugees from Central Europe and the British, the host community, are, for obvious reasons, fundamental to any analysis of the development of the refugee community in post-war Britain. But this is also an area of continuing controversy, as it is often linked in to the contentious issues of relations between the British and immigrant minorities and of British anti-Semitism. An academic history of the Jewish refugees from Hitler in Britain ought to remain neutral and objective, as far as possible in the highly charged areas of race and immigration. This study will therefore endeavour to stand aside from contemporary polemics relating to other groups of immigrants, though its overall stance is one of some scepticism towards the predominant line of sharp criticism of the British state and of British society taken by some scholars working on the refugees.

This is for the sound reason that this particular group of refugees was treated reasonably well in Britain, at least after the wartime hysteria that led to internment had subsided, and, perhaps even more importantly, that they *perceived* themselves to be reasonably well treated, certainly better than almost any other group of post-war immigrants. The refugees' perception of Britain as a predominantly benign place of settlement was an absolutely key factor: it helped them to overcome their own inhibitions and reservations about integrating, to varying degrees, into British society; it strengthened the resolve of a majority of them to adapt to a very substantial extent to life in the country they viewed as their new homeland; and it instigated a virtuous circle of appreciation of things British that fed into a growing sense of security and well-being and that in turn caused the refugees' pro-British attitudes, often already pronounced by 1945, to become more solidly rooted and their confidence in Britain as a permanent haven to flourish.

One cannot deny the existence of native British anti-Semitism and of barriers, both objective and subjective, that kept the refugees apart from the British and preserved their status as a small minority at a remove from mainstream society. The familiar refugee refrain that they feel 'British, but not English' is the most common evidence of this. Nevertheless, there are grounds for disputing the conventional academic wisdom that designates the refugees primarily as victims of British prejudice and xenophobia and locates their experience predominantly within a discussion of British anti-Semitic attitudes. It is, for a start, hard to believe that the picture of British anti-Semitism given collectively by such studies is accurate. We are told that anti-Semitism increased during the 1930s, when the entry of thousands of Jewish refugees fleeing Nazism fuelled anti-Jewish prejudices; we are told that anti-Semitism increased in wartime, during the morale-sapping months of the 'phoney war', during the panic months of internment and during the long years of privation and hardship that followed, when Jews could be scapegoated as black-marketeers and war-profiteers; we are told that anti-Semitism increased in the post-war years, when the strains of war were replaced by those of austerity, exhaustion and economic crisis and when anti-Jewish passions were inflamed by terrorist atrocities against British mandatory rule in Palestine.[1]

There is evidence for all these propositions, but taken together they can be misleading. For if anti-Semitism had been growing remorselessly since 1933, fuelled by a variety of changing factors, Britain would by 1950 have been a seething cauldron of anti-Jewish feeling. In fact, it is plain that in the late 1940s anti-Semitism was at the very most at levels similar to those of ten or fifteen years previously, probably lower, and declining. The problem is that it is very hard to measure anti-Semitism, especially when it is decreasing; and it is evident that there must have been periods between 1933 and 1950 when anti-Semitism declined or remained stable. Otherwise, its level in 1950 could not have been as relatively low as it clearly was. The familiar areas of anti-Jewish jokes, of public school quotas for Jewish pupils and of exclusion from golf clubs remained, along with what scholars have termed an 'amorphous' but pervasive dislike of Jews[2] in certain sections of society – genteel though no less injurious for that. But there was no quantum leap to widespread discrimination, and systematic, racist anti-Semitic discourse never spread beyond a radical fringe. It seems reasonable to conclude that in these years the graph of anti-Semitism in Britain did not rise in a straight line, but rather that it rose and fell in waves – with the falls being hard to spot.[3] 'No synagogues desecrated this month' was hardly the stuff of the newspaper headlines on which later historians would draw.

A further reason for treating the conclusions of academic studies of British anti-Semitism with caution as far as the Jewish refugees from Central Europe are concerned is that these studies tend to amalgamate the refugees too sweepingly with Anglo-Jewry, as common victims of native prejudice. As has already been shown, the refugees proved in the main unwilling to be absorbed into Anglo-Jewry; the abiding distance between the two communities is a recurrent theme in this study. To take one obvious point: whereas the East End of London was central to Anglo-Jewry in the 1930s and 1940s, and remains important in academic studies of British Jews, that area of London played only a very small part in the history of the Jews from Central Europe. A community that chose districts like Belsize Park and Swiss Cottage as its first areas of settlement plainly underwent a very different process of integration from one that settled in Stepney and Whitechapel – for one thing, there were no Cable Street-style confrontations with Blackshirt marchers in north-west London.[4]

Also to be treated with caution are scholarly attempts to understand the experience of the Jewish refugees from Central Europe solely by reference to an enduring and largely unvarying tradition of British xenophobia and hostility to immigrant minorities generally. That such attitudes were deep-rooted in Britain is beyond doubt, as is the fact that the refugees endured their share of British antipathy to foreigners, especially during the war when, as one refugee recalled, 'it was bad enough to be a German; even more to be Jewish; but most of all to be German-Jewish'.[5]

Nevertheless, to pitch the Jewish refugees from Central Europe into a single pot with immigrant groups that range from Eastern European Jews in the late nineteenth century to Afro-Caribbeans in the mid-twentieth and Somalis in the early twenty-first centuries is to risk such sweeping generalizations about the immigrant experience as to obscure the historical particularities of each group and the conditions under which it arrived. By and large, the refugees from Germany and Austria do not provide ready material for the writing of a history that highlights the illiberal, hostile and prejudiced nature of the reception accorded to immigrants in Britain. Nor is the end of historical accuracy always well served by viewing the experience of refugees who came and settled in Britain in the 1930s and 1940s from the perspective of very different groups who came many decades later, through the wrong end, as it were, of history's telescope.

After the Nazi years, the refugees from Germany and Austria were understandably sensitive to any manifestation of anti-Semitism, and *AJR Information* was always alert to the dangers of its resurgence in Britain. In May 1946, it published a lengthy warning about the growth in British anti-Semitism by Sidney Salomon, executive and press officer of the Jewish Defence Committee. That post-war conditions of austerity might be conducive to right-wing extremism was the ominous keynote of a *News Chronicle* article quoted in the journal's column 'What the Press Says' in October 1947:

Great Britain is moving with increasing momentum into deeply trou-
bled times. Anxiety and the strain of shortage will be our constant
companions for many weary months ... It is in times like these that
men of moderation and good will are apt to plead in vain, and that
extremists come into their own ... Incredible as it may seem, in the
last few weeks we have heard voices crying for Hitler in London
streets. Every week-end, in the old provocative way, Fascist meetings
are held in the East End of the city. The old gospel of hate is being
poured forth in the same strident accents as we used to hear before
the war.[6]

Though fears of economic crisis and political polarization never became
reality, there was a steady trickle of anti-Semitic incidents: Jewish reactions
to the activities of Mosley's Union Movement formed a staple item in the
journal's column 'Anglo-Judaica'. The attacks on Jewish property and buildings that occurred in several British cities in the summer of 1947 in reaction
to the murder of kidnapped British servicemen by Jewish extremists in
Palestine – the only instance of widespread anti-Jewish violence in Britain
since the war – were also reported, though quite briefly, as 'anti-Jewish
demonstrations in English towns'.[7] Racially motivated violence against the
refugees was almost unknown in those years, with the possible exception of
a report in September 1949, taken from the *Jewish Chronicle*, which spoke of
'alleged assaults' on elderly Jews in West Hampstead. Given the concentration
of refugees in that area, the victims could well have been former German or
Austrian Jews; but if the attackers picked on Jews who attended services at
the Hampstead Synagogue (in Dennington Park Road, West Hampstead),
then more likely not – for refugee participation in this traditionally minded
congregation was small.

AJR Information reacted with indignation to verbal expressions of anti-
Semitic prejudice, such as the allegation by a former aide-de-camp to the
king that the black market was chiefly run by Jews, or the storm stirred up
when a British general spoke of a 'Jewish conspiracy'.[8] More alarming, as
it originated with a senior Conservative politician, was the report of
remarks by Oliver Lyttleton MP, at a meeting convened by the Board
of Deputies' Trades Advisory Council, that 'at the bottom of most of
the scandals connected with clothing rationing were Jewish firms'. But this
was counterbalanced by a report, in the same column, of a statement by
Anthony Eden on behalf of the Conservative Party, which, he declared,
'entirely repudiates and rejects any policy of discrimination between one
citizen and another on the grounds of religion, race, class or creed'. He
added: 'It would indeed be a strange thing if the Party which honours the

name of Disraeli as one of its greatest leaders was not the first to condemn practices which are directly opposed to those on which the British Commonwealth and Empire are based and maintained.'⁹ Neither Eden nor the Conservative Party were known for their pro-Jewish sympathies (nor for that matter was the entire edifice of Empire), but this condemnation of the propagation of racial and religious hatred did show that the main right-wing party in Britain had in principle set its face against anti-Semitism.

Occasionally, *AJR Information* confronted its readers with extreme anti-Semitic views, such as those in a letter to the editor of *Truth*, a weekly organ of the far right:

> We all know – it is a matter of history – that a train of locked-in inter-nationals left Berlin non-stop to Moscow prior to the Russian revolu-tion! We all know – it is a matter of history – that thousands of German nationals entered England during the recent war, as peaceful (?) refugees. We all know – it is a matter of history – that Edward I, King of England, was obliged to invite these same people to leave England! We all know – it is a matter of history – that in A.D. 1300 these same people were, in Spain, massacred wholesale by the popu-lace for their misdoings! Would it not be wise of us to invite these same people to kindly leave England, and return to their country which our brave and gallant men have liberated? One would think that out of common gratitude they would offer to go, and leave place for our returning heroes to live in. Are they, perhaps, waiting until the English resort to the Spanish methods of A.D. 1300?

The editors of *AJR Information* had the confidence to let this snarl of hatred, decked out in a third-rate travesty of historical scholarship, stand without comment, allowing it to condemn itself out of its own mouth. They con-tented themselves with an icy editorial note: 'Truth, a weekly, is edited by Mr. Collin Brooks, at one time private secretary to the late Lord Rothermere. The deputy editor is Mr. A.K. Chesterton, who before the war was for some time editor of *ACTION*, the organ of Sir Oswald Mosley's British Union of Fascists.'¹⁰ Their confidence was justified: *Truth* (which later abjured its anti-Semitism) remained the voice of a political fringe.

By 1950, the refugees' increasing sense of security in Britain allowed their journal to treat the creation of a Jewish anglers' club by those exclud-ed from its gentile counterparts – a parallel to the oft-cited phenomenon of golf-club anti-Semitism – with humour. The column 'Anglo-Judaica', permitting itself a truly dreadful pun, entitled its item 'Anglers' Judaica':

> The variety of our social life was appreciably increased the other day

> when a bunch of Jewish anglers decided the time had come for them
> to form a club – a Jewish Anglers' Club, operating under the expressive
> name of 'Hadagim' ('The Fishes'). No doubt due regard will be had
> to the opinion conscientiously voiced by champions of orthodoxy
> that angling is a Jewish occupation only when attended by a Shochet
> [ritual slaughterer]. But with this proviso firmly fixed in mind, few
> will question the desirability of the happy venture, and none, at all
> sensible of the traditional glamour of gefilte fish, will underrate the
> angler's importance in Jewish affairs.[11]

This is not to say that the journal glossed over the anti-Semitism of golf
clubs and public schools. It evidently believed that these manifestations
indicated a level of anti-Semitism that could be dealt with, especially as it
was declining in both types of institutions mentioned, effectively dying
out by the 1970s.

By 1949, it was evident that naturalization did not always imply social
acceptance:

> Experience showed, however, that acquisition of citizenship, impor-
> tant as it may be, is only a milestone on the road the newcomer has
> to go, whereas the ultimate integration is a very slow process. If an
> advertiser in a local paper offers a furnished room 'for British people
> only', hardly any naturalised immigrant with common sense would
> apply for it.[12]

This was an example of the repugnant practices that the refugees might
face in everyday life. Overt discrimination was outlawed by the Race
Relations Act a decade and a half later, though by that time the journal had
long ceased to complain of such discrimination. 'Fortunately', this article
continued, 'the number of incidents which affect the Community as a
whole is, at present, comparatively small', a state of affairs that the journal
attributed to the ready adaptability of the refugees to their new environment and to the current state of full employment.

By 1950, the journal had less to report about racial discrimination and
anti-Semitic or neo-Nazi activity. One notable exception was its unusually
robust commentary on the disruption by Fascist rowdies of a film set in pre-
1948 Palestine, *Sword in the Desert*, and the apparent capitulation of the London
County Council, which tamely banned the film, in face of this threat of violence: 'The admirable British quality to tolerate another man's opinion, even
if one does not agree with it – moreover to fight for the right of that man to
say what he has to say, has not been displayed at the London cinema.'[13] This
unusually forthright condemnation of the British authorities, occurring over

a relatively trivial incident, drew its force from memories of the past: the disruption of the film version of Erich Maria Remarque's *All Quiet on the Western Front* by the Nazis in Berlin in 1930 had marked an important stage in their takeover of the public arena by violence and intimidation. In Britain, the disruption proved to be but a coda to the dismal failure of the Mosleyite right to make gains in London County Council elections in the late 1940s.

In the post-war years, the refugees were likely to encounter a certain degree of mostly low-level anti-Semitism in everyday life, while a rabid Mosleyite fringe remained active, but neither seemed likely to increase dangerously, certainly while unemployment remained low. This assessment is strongly supported by interviews with refugees, many of whom, when asked if they have encountered anti-Semitism in Britain, replied with a clear 'No'; others mentioned isolated instances. Asked whether they feared anti-Semitism, however, many replied in the affirmative: a case in point is Gina Gerson, who experienced the Nazi takeover in Vienna as a girl and was permanently affected by the accompanying orgy of anti-Semitism, though in Britain she met with a good deal of kindness as a young refugee.[14] Discussion of British attitudes to the refugees in *AJR Information* was also predominantly positive, reflecting no doubt a measure of unwillingness to cause offence to the refugees' hosts or to publish material likely to upset the readers, but also pointing to a genuine attachment to the new homeland.

Probably the most important article on British anti-Semitism to appear in the journal in these years was written in 1947 by one of its editors, Herbert Friedenthal (Freeden). Its principal argument was that the real danger of anti-Semitism did not emanate from fascist groups, which it enumerated in some detail, but whose activities it considered to be relegated to 'the outer fringes of public life'. Anti-Semitism, however, went considerably beyond fringe groups:

> It would be a good thing, indeed, if anti-Semitism were confined to those small and sharply distinguishable groups. The truth is that anti-Semitism has transcended the boundaries of political parties and formations. Hitler's teachings and practices have been rejected by the British – but they have made them Jew-conscious. In Britain there is no discrimination against Jews; but there is a subtle distinction between Jews and gentiles. Some would fervently object to being labelled anti-Semites but they might agree that they are 'Jew-minded' and even admit that they do not like Jews 'particularly'.[15]

To define more precisely this subtle and indirect form of anti-Semitism, Freeden used a recent exhortation to British Jews by the *Sunday Times* to be 'grateful': Jews in Britain, it claimed, had long possessed the full rights and privileges of citizenship, the offices and honours of the state were freely open to them, they were excluded from no profession or branch of industry, and if wronged, they could appeal confidently to the courts. But this absence of formal discrimination masked a subtler differentiation:

> Here, indeed, lies the crux of anti-Semitism among the British people: they have bestowed equality upon the Jews, they have equipped them with privileges but they do not expect them to take this for granted like other subjects of the King do. Not in a few Jew-baiter associations and Fascist journals lies the danger of anti-Semitism in Britain but in that unmistakable differentiation between Jewish citizens and British citizens.

In the case of the Jewish refugees from Central Europe, that sense of an intangible difference that separated them from native-born British citizens was to linger over the decades, often not vanishing until the generation of their children, and in some cases not even then.

Less impressive than Friedenthal's analysis was an article entitled 'Can It Happen Here?', published the following January, which suggested that something like a British version of Nazism might succeed in capitalizing on native anti-Semitism.[16] Its predictions were too vague and unsubstantiated for the writer Gabriele Tergit, who pointed out the very real differences between British and (pre-Hitler) German attitudes to the Jews, as experienced by the refugees, who were familiar with both. After detailing the anti-Jewish discrimination that permeated German society even before 1933, especially in the field of employment, she drew a powerful contrast with the treatment of Jewish refugee employees in Britain:

> On the other hand, let me give you an example of the situation in England. An elderly social worker from Germany was invited by a County Council to run a hostel for land girls. Not only the girls were delighted, the County Council did thank and praise her. Of course she is an exceptionally kind person. But anyhow, please imagine for one moment a Jewess from Warsaw [i.e. an immigrant] invited by a Landrat in Pommern [Pomerania] to run a hostel for agricultural workers. The whole thing is unthinkable. It would have been the same in the case of a Jewess from Berlin. Her life would have been hell, if ever there was a possibility of getting such a job. After 2,000 years of life in Germany the German Jews were not promoted lieutenants in the German army. There is more than one captain among the Jews who came to England 10 years ago.[17]

Most contributors to *AJR Information* were convinced that British attitudes and conditions imposed strict limits on the growth of anti-Semitism and xenophobia – though such elements undeniably existed within British society – and, like Gabriele Tergit, they were not slow to draw on their own experiences to prove the point. Martha Steinitz was a Jew from Germany who had been resident in Leeds since 1925 and a British citizen since 1933; teaching English to refugees enabled her to act as an intermediary between the two communities: 'From the time of [the refugees'] arrival it has been my object to get them into personal touch with my numerous English friends, with the result that all those Jewish refugees who wished to move out of their somewhat confined circle were able to form valuable friendships, widening their horizon and, incidentally, that of their Gentile neighbours and friends.'[18]

The impetus towards integration here was unmistakable, as was the explicit assumption that such social integration made for a valuable advance on the 'somewhat confined' life of an immigrant group. Evidently, refugees could expect a friendly welcome from Martha Steinitz's numerous acquaintances. She also pointed to the strength and vitality of resistance to anti-Semitism in British society, a factor sometimes underrated: 'I do not wish to deny the fact of the growth of anti-semitism in this country since the advent of Hitler, but I also beg to point out to you the strongly growing, organised and well-informed opposition to anti-semitism which is keenly sponsored by just the most influential section of British Public Opinion.'

The refugees' sense of being in some measure secure against racial prejudice and violence in Britain and their trust in British tolerance and traditions of freedom were often expressed in terms so unambiguous as to surprise today's readers. Louis W. Bondy, writing in 1946 on 'England and the Foreigner', produced a ringing defence of the British, or at least their thinkers and opinion-formers, against the charge of incurable xenophobia:

> Much is being written and said about the attitude of the English towards the foreigner. The old prejudices born of insular isolation and therefore of ignorance are fast disappearing in a world of improved communications and international cooperation. The war against Hitler's Germany has brought many thousands of foreigners to these shores, refugees from and allies against a common foe. They have worked and fought with the British. A few quotations from the writings of great Englishmen of the past have here been assembled showing that even in the old days when the uneducated were still strongly biased against anything foreign, eminent men spoke and fought for tolerance and understanding.[19]

Bondy quoted the clause in Magna Carta guaranteeing just treatment for those who would later be designated 'enemy aliens', Oliver Goldsmith's defence of cosmopolitanism, Macaulay's speech in parliament demanding the lifting of 'disabilities' imposed on the Jews, and Dickens's inspired tilt at xenophobic sentiments among the ill-educated in *Little Dorrit* – 'they had a notion that it was a sort of divine visitation upon a foreigner that he was not an Englishman' – sentiments that the refugees could still recognize. Beyond doubt, the balance of opinion in the journal was that the forces of tolerance, liberalism and civilized, humane attitudes were broadly in the ascendant in post-war Britain, at least where this group of refugees was concerned, a view supported by the overall experience of the refugees themselves, though with significant exceptions. Whether this opinion was accurate may be a matter for debate; but what is certain is that it greatly assisted the refugees integrating into a society that they perceived to be broadly welcoming and willing to let them live their lives in peace.

An interesting perspective on British hostility to minorities was opened up by an item in the column 'Anglo-Judaica' entitled 'Jews and Roman Catholics', which pointed to the fading of the virulent anti-Catholic prejudice once central to Britain's self-definition as a nation:[20]

> 'What do they know of England / Who only England know', says Kipling, and similarly one may venture the more prosaic query: What do they know of English Jewry who merely stroll about Woburn House, peruse the social columns of the [Jewish] *Chronicle*, or even occasionally call at the AJR? Jews are part of a larger body, and, everywhere the few among the many, they are inevitably concerned with all minorities. In the story of others they must recognise some features of their own. In England the 400,000 Jews will study with profit the condition of the three million Roman Catholics who have just been celebrating a memorable centenary – the restoration of the Hierarchy for the first time since the days when Henry VIII fell foul of the Pope and England became the head and front of Protestant Christianity. Much of the ancient zeal and passion is now spent. Reformation and counter-reformation has been superseded by revolution and counter-revolution, and Gladstone was probably the last to feel that anti-Popery was a basic article of English faith.[21]

The tone of this article was set by the quintessentially English opening quotation. Though it went on to detail the continuing disadvantages under which Catholics (and Jews) lived in Britain, its central thrust was the gradual lifting of disabilities and the dispelling of prejudice directed against racial and religious minorities, as demonstrated by the integration of

Catholics into the mainstream of British life. The sheer number of Catholics in Britain – and the proximity of the Irish, feared as a source of political unrest and derided as a butt for stereotyped jibes – gave anti-Catholic feeling a weight that anti-Semitism has never had. But for all that, the decline in anti-Catholic prejudice has been clear beyond question. The unexpressed hope of the article was plainly that anti-Semitism, and indeed all forms of prejudice against minorities, would in time abate, though as yet both Catholics and Jews were living 'in a society struggling valiantly to combine the freedom of conscience with the freedom from prejudice'.

The only concerted campaign organized against the refugees in Britain was the so-called 'anti-alien' petition of October 1945 in the borough of Hampstead, where a movement led by two women with far-right sympathies, Sylvia Gosse and Margaret Crabtree, sought to exploit the issue of shortage of accommodation to demand the repatriation of refugees resident in the area. Hampstead, and in particular the areas of Belsize Park, Swiss Cottage and West Hampstead on either side of Finchley Road, was home to the greatest concentration of refugees in Britain. The furore surrounding the petition and its subsequent inglorious failure have long lapsed into obscurity, but recently it formed the subject of two studies, on which this account draws.[22]

In October 1945, the petition, signed by over 2,000 residents of the borough, was handed to the Conservative MP for Hampstead, Charles Challen, at the House of Commons; it requested the 'prompt repatriation' of German and Austrian refugees so that their dwellings could be allocated to British-born people returning after the war. This showed how resentment directed against the refugees could be mobilized, especially when linked to issues such as accommodation, jobs or rationing, and how it held the potential for a direct and ugly threat to the core of the refugee community in Britain; for once, there arose something approaching a localized mass movement that crystallized around anti-refugee feeling. But it also showed the limits set to such agitation, for within a few weeks the petition had dwindled into disrepute and failure. It met with strong opposition, led by liberal notables prominent in Hampstead, who organized a 'Protest against Prejudice' meeting in the hall of Holy Trinity Church, opposite Finchley Road tube station, and circulated a counter-petition. When the borough council repudiated the petition after heated debate on 25 October 1945, it lost all momentum and sank rapidly from view.

The debate on the petition, and the thinly veiled anti-Semitism behind it, was largely fought out in the local press, in particular the *Hampstead & Highgate Express*. The paper published a number of letters and other items in its columns favourable to the anti-alien cause, though these did not necessarily represent accurately the level of support for it. When accused of publishing an undue number of letters opposing the petition, the paper's editor stated that he had printed fifteen letters from over fifty against the petition, and two in favour of it from only three received. The editor's attempt to give equal treatment to both sides, in itself distinctly questionable, thus gave an inflated impression of the support for the petition. It would appear that the petition gained a considerable but short-lived level of mass support, and that sections of the local Conservative establishment, including the mayor, Sydney Boyd, and at times Charles Challen MP, were receptive to anti-alien sentiment. But once the failure of the petition was plain, anti-alienism returned to its former status as the preserve of the extreme right. The episode demonstrated the potential for public hostility towards the refugees, but even more clearly the greater weight of the forces ranged against that potential. If an anti-refugee campaign was unsuccessful in an area where refugees were so heavily concentrated and at a time when resources like housing were under such stress, it was hardly likely to succeed elsewhere.

In the aftermath of the petition, the far right continued to try to capitalize on anti-alien feeling, but without success, their failure culminating in the miserable showing of the Mosleyite candidate in the local elections of 1949. In March 1946, *AJR Information* described under the caption 'Anti-Alien Meeting Ends in Fight' the fracas into which a meeting held at St Mary's Church hall in Primrose Hill had descended. Its organizer was Mrs Eleonora Tennant, leader of the Face the Facts Association, one of the xenophobic organizations prominent locally in anti-refugee activity. The meeting took a predictable course. Tennant launched into a diatribe as venomous as it was absurd. Claiming that German refugees were 'getting control' of Britain, she attacked the Home Office, the Foreign Office, the Civil Service in general and the press as 'being under German influence'. She excelled herself by calling Anthony Greenwood, a Labour councillor and candidate at a parliamentary by-election and later a Labour minister under Harold Wilson, 'the Hitler of Hampstead'. 'There were many cries of dissent and free fights started when a man jumped on the platform and shouted "This Fascist propaganda must cease". Police entered the hall, took a number of names and addresses and removed two men.'[23]

The extreme language and the violence at Tennant's meetings brought discredit on the anti-alien cause, as did its overt connection with known fascists. Crabtree and Gosse, the initiators of the petition, had sought to revive their campaign by involving Tennant and Jeffrey Hamm, leader of an active fascist group, the British League of Ex-Servicemen, and a rising star in Mosley's movement. Tennant invited Hamm to speak at a meeting that she had organized at St Peter's hall in Belsize Square on 30 November 1945. But, as with the meeting in Primrose Hill, her ranting and abuse led to the disruption of the meeting; nor were Hamm's anti-Semitic remarks well received. Hamm was refused permission for a meeting of his own by the vicar of St Peter's. Those familiar with the refugee community will not fail to note the symbolism of the venue, for only a decade and a half later the site of the hall was occupied by Belsize Square Synagogue, built for the largely refugee New Liberal Jewish Congregation; the architect was H.J. Reifenberg, husband of the writer Gabriele Tergit. The synagogue's hall now acts as the venue for Club 1943, the venerable refugee forum for cultural and political discussion named after the year of its foundation, and still flourishing under its current chairman, Hans Seelig, decades after Tennant and her fellow petitioners vanished into the footnotes of history.

Fascist attempts to whip up support in Hampstead, exploiting the issue of refugee settlement there, gained considerable public attention but little else. Mosley himself visited Hampstead in September 1946, and the area around the Whitestone Pond on Hampstead Heath became the scene for regular fascist meetings that provoked some public disorder. As the local elections in 1949 approached, the leading local Mosleyite Douglas Peroni stepped up activities. Hampstead borough council investigated the measures that could be taken to end the disturbances caused by fascist meetings, and the weekly meetings at the Whitestone Pond required a considerable police presence.[24] Scholars have noted the activities of Mosley's supporters in the late 1940s, emphasizing the distress and insecurity that such developments caused the refugees. They have been slower to note indicators that point in the opposite direction, like the nomination of a refugee and member of the board of the AJR, Eric Gould (Erich Goldberg), as Liberal candidate at the Hampstead borough elections, where the Liberal vote handsomely exceeded that for Mosley's Union Movement. Anxiety about the level of fascist support was relieved by the unequivocal rejection of Mosley's candidates all across London: Peroni secured eighty-one votes of nearly 25,000 cast in Hampstead, a derisory 0.3 per cent. This put an end to fascist activity in Hampstead, especially once Peroni bowed out not long after.

The Conservative candidate who was to replace Challen, Henry Brooke, later Home Secretary under Harold Macmillan, took care to lower the temperature in relations between the communities, while making his defence of the refugees against prejudice and discrimination plain. Asked at a meeting in 1949 why there were 'thousands of foreigners allowed to live in Hampstead when so many British ex-Servicemen cannot find a place to lay their heads', Brooke replied amidst applause: 'Personally, I am thankful a

refuge was provided for thousands of foreigners whose lives were in danger.'
He continued diplomatically:

> Hampstead has as large a proportion as is healthy for any borough,
> and I should be sorry to see it grow any higher and the proportion
> of British any lower. We are a cosmopolitan crowd and we have peo-
> ple from many parts of Europe and beyond. That being so, we must
> try to practise what we preach, for dangerous race feeling can most
> easily be inflamed.[25]

A year later Brooke, now the local MP, spoke at the Remembrance Day
meeting of the Hampstead Council of Christians and Jews, a body dedicated to improving understanding between the two faiths. Dealing with the
problems arising from the number of foreigners in the area, he said that
he received both pleas for help from naturalized constituents anxious to
bring relatives to Britain and complaints from British-born people about
the difficulty of finding accommodation. His view was that only a sound,
well-balanced compromise could resolve the problem; the idea of good-
neighbourliness was common to the Christian and the Jewish religions.[26]
Though falling short of what we would find acceptable today, Brooke's cautiously phrased remarks were, at a time when immigrant minorities were
still a comparative rarity among the dominant majority in Britain, about as
clear a statement as one could expect from a Conservative politician in support of mutual toleration and of harmonious coexistence across the racial
and religious divide. In 1953, furthermore, the integration and acceptance
of Jews in Hampstead reached a significant milestone with the election of
a British Jew, Emanuel Snowman, as mayor of Hampstead.

It is important to judge the impact of the Hampstead anti-alien petition
and its aftermath aright. Recent studies by those who work on British
fascism have tended to concentrate on the prevalence of anti-Semitic and
xenophobic attitudes among the native population and on the threat they
posed to the as yet comparatively unintegrated refugees. This is the lesson
drawn by Shepherd, while Macklin speaks of the Jewish refugee often
being viewed as 'a parasitic interloper depriving Hampstead's indigenous
citizens of scarce resources', adding: 'Against this backdrop of fear and
insecurity the callous inhumanity of the petitioners' demands and their
unwillingness or inability to comprehend the depths of suffering experienced by the refugees helped further undermine an already fragile sense of
belonging.' He concludes with the standard warning that these experiences
merely prefigured the greater hostility to which later generations of immigrants were subjected.[27]

This was not the picture that emerged from *AJR Information*. The journal

covered the anti-refugee activity in Hampstead as an alarming and dis-
tasteful manifestation of extremism, but not as an imminent threat to its
readers' settled existence in Britain. By the early 1950s, certainly, the
refugees in Hampstead felt themselves to be integrated well beyond a 'fragile sense of belonging'. Their perceptions of Britain as a predominantly
welcoming environment, which will be examined in the following section
of this chapter, determined their collective memory of post-war events: the
anti-alien petition disappeared from view with its rejection by the majority of local public opinion, while the Mosleyite threat was defused by its
utter failure at the polls. That is why those events have aroused no echo in
refugee consciousness down the decades comparable with the continuing
resonance of the election of a BNP candidate in the Isle of Dogs in the early
1990s, let alone the Notting Hill race riots of 1958, Enoch Powell's notorious 'River of Blood' speech in 1968, or even Norman Tebbit's 'cricket-
match' test of loyalty to Britain.

Those incidents relate to tensions and frictions that have not abated,
drawing their continuing hold over people's consciousness from divisions
as yet unresolved. The experience of the more fortunate refugees from
Central Europe was quite different, and it shaped different memories. The
symbolism of localities bears this out, an obvious example being the erec-
tion of Belsize Square Synagogue on a site cleared by the demolition of the
hall where an anti-alien meeting had been held in 1945. The Whitestone
Pond also held no terrors associated with a fascist threat. By the 1950s, far
from being invested with memories of anti-Jewish agitation, the pond was
a favourite starting-point for refugees taking weekend walks on the Heath.
Like the many children of refugees who grew up not very far from the
pond, I passed it times without number in the 1950s and was never aware
of any aura of danger.

The claim that there was 'enormous hostility' towards the refugees in
north-west London[28] would have been greeted with bemusement by the
great majority of refugees resident there, who on the whole lived on reasonably amicable and peaceful, if still somewhat distant, terms with their
British environment. Above all, that is predominantly how they *perceived*
their relationship to British society and how that relationship has been held
in their collective memory. The very fact that the episode of the Hampstead
anti-alien petition has had to be unearthed as a long-lost historical curios-
ity is eloquent proof of that proposition.

That the image of Britain and British society conveyed by *AJR Information*
was overwhelmingly favourable may surprise today's readers. One of the
journal's respected contributors was C.C. Aronsfeld, later deputy director of
the Wiener Library and the journal's editor for a time in the 1980s. By

1950, the refugees' integration was well enough advanced for Aronsfeld to urge them not to lose sight of the intangible values associated with the citizenship they had acquired:

> The erstwhile refugees are now, for the most part, soundly settled, and except for an occasional slip of accent and an awkward reference to the dictionary, the distinction of a new citizenship sits well on them. Some indeed seem now and then inclined to take the privilege for granted, finding satisfaction, sometimes understandably, more in its material advantages than in its moral significance. It is perhaps, therefore, well to be reminded of what it means to be a British citizen.[29]

He emphasized that Jewish refugees from Central Europe who had taken British nationality must remain mindful of 'the duties of that civilised citizen who, alive to his religious and historic tradition, bears the immemorial freedom of England under the stringent law of Israel'.

At a less elevated level, the journal frequently published items drawing on everyday life that expressed the refugees' admiration and affection for their adopted homeland. As some examples will show, the view of relations between the British and the Jews from Central Europe tended strongly to confirm the refugees' general image of Britain as a haven of relative freedom, decency and tolerance underpinned by habits of courtesy and consideration in day-to-day life. Fritz Ruhemann's one-page story 'Vorfrühling in Swiss Cottage' ('Spring Comes to Swiss Cottage')[30] captured this aspect of refugee life in the post-war years. The interplay between Continental and British manners forms a principal theme of this story, which follows an elderly refugee lady, lonely and depressed, walking towards Swiss Cottage one spring morning, steadfastly ignoring the polite Englishmen who seek to brighten her mood with remarks like 'Nice morning, Madam'. Lost in thought, she stops next to a building site and blocks the way:

> Die Passanten quetschten sich geduldig an den Bauzaun und nahmen sogar die Schuld auf sich, die guten Engländer, indem sie 'sorry' sagten; manche sagten 'thank you'. Plötzlich riss sie ein Heimatklang aus ihrer verlegenen Verwirrung: 'You, my lady, you hold ze whole traffic up.' Ja, das verstand sie! Ja, sie war fast angenehm berührt von diesem vertraut irdischen Ton und stammelte 'Oh, sorry!' (The passers-by squeezed patiently up against the hoarding and even took the blame on themselves, kind Englishmen that they were, by saying 'sorry'; some said 'thank you'. Suddenly a voice from her native land roused her from her embarrassed confusion: 'You, my lady, you hold ze whole traffic up.' Yes, that she understood! Yes, she was almost

pleasantly surprised by this familiar, down-to-earth tone and stam-
mered 'Oh, sorry!')

In her confusion, she steps straight out into the road, nearly causing an
accident, only for the driver to wave her politely across – 'After you,
Madam' – while someone else takes her by the arm to lead her over the
road, disappearing before she even has time to thank him. A workman
from the construction site provides her with a seat, where she reads a letter telling her that her children overseas are coming to London. The story
ends with an exchange between the lady, now much more cheerful, and
the workmen; though this is conducted on her side in heavily German-
accented English and on theirs in Cockney, the two parties communicate
with friendly good humour across the cultural divide.

The harsh realities of exile are not ignored here: the lady is living in
much reduced circumstances, she is in poor health and lonely, her husband
is dead and her children overseas, while she struggles to adjust to unfamiliar British modes of social interaction. But the depiction of her British
environment is, fog and damp apart, thoroughly positive. All the British
characters, from well-spoken gentlemen to Cockney workmen, treat the
lady with friendly politeness, and their courtesy comes so naturally that the
lady hardly notices it; only the curt tones of a fellow refugee remind her
of this difference between British and Continentals.

In reality, such displays of polite consideration would not have been the
rule, even in the London of 1953. But the repeated depiction of British
society as characterized by fair play and kindly manners arguably fulfilled
a need among the refugee readership: partly as a welcome contrast to the
brutality and inhumanity of the society from which they had fled, partly
as an idealized vision, a *Wunschbild*, of the new society into which they
could, by virtue of their qualities and abilities, hope to integrate, thus com-
pleting the process of integration that had been cut short in their homelands.

Another example of the readiness with which the refugees embraced
everyday life in Britain was provided by Werner Rosenstock, editor of *AJR
Information*, writing in his column as 'Narrator'. Like millions of others,
'Narrator' spent part of every Thursday evening glued to his radio, listen-
ing to the BBC comedy show *ITMA* ('It's That Man Again'); so great was the
hold of its quintessentially British humour over him that even Rosenstock's
devotion to duty was strained when he had to attend meetings that clashed
with it. In February 1949, the column lamented the death of Tommy
Handley, the star of *ITMA*. The item highlighted the way in which the
refugees had been brought closer to the host community by sharing in the

special brand of humour that the programme had made famous nation-wide:

> Refugee ITMA fans were made to feel that they were members of a
> large family of millions in this country, for whom ITMA's catch
> phrases had become a kind of code. It induced them to get better
> acquainted with the life and customs of the average Englishman and
> to sharpen their ears, lest they might miss the meaning of any of the
> precious cracks. They say with tears farewell to 'that man' who, in his
> unique way, taught them 'English without tears'.[31]

In this case, humour was a means towards social inclusivity.

Even the refugees' accents, a sensitive point with many, often furnished
the material for refugee jokes: after the closely contested general election
of 1950, *AJR Information* gleefully reported one of its readers as predicting
that Britain was heading for a 'collision government'.[32] That the refugees
felt relaxed enough to make fun of their own deficiencies in speaking
their adopted tongue pointed again to a growing sense of their security in
Britain. The election of 1950 was the first at which most refugees were
able to exercise their right to vote, and *AJR Information* urged its readers to
be sure to do so. A front-page article in February 1950 was lavish in its
praise of British political life: 'Political maturity is one of the outstanding
features of British public life. Party controversies are not as fierce as they
are on the Continent, and sound compromise is often preferred to doc-
trinarianism.' The journal emphasized that Jews, like other citizens, could
vote for any major party in Britain, whereas in Germany and Austria the
anti-Semitism of the right-wing parties had ruled them out of contention;
it went on to point out with evident satisfaction: 'This healthy state of
affairs is also mirrored in the fact that Jews are to be found amongst the
candidates of all parties.'

From the perspective of 1950, the contrast between the failure of parliamentary democracy in Germany and the ability of British institutions and
values to surmount the crises of mid-century would have weighed heavily
in the balance of the journal's judgement on Britain. Its editors appear to
have believed that an ingrained sense of justice, fair play and liberalism
made British society less fertile ground for extreme racist and nationalistic
prejudice than the lands of Central Europe, which had not enjoyed political
stability and settled institutions over many decades. Long experience of parliamentary democracy and a pragmatic tradition that distrusted ideological
extremes had, they considered, bred a spirit of tolerance and humanity that
provided a bulwark against totalitarian demagogues.

Qualities that the refugees especially admired were British individualism and non-conformism, to which Gabriele Tergit paid tribute by contrasting them with German obedience to authority, and British pragmatism, which Kenneth Ambrose saw as the moving spirit behind the success of the popular press: 'Like so many things in this country, it is hardly an ideal institution, certainly not a tidy one – but by and large it works better than in many other countries.'[33] Ambrose also charted the process whereby the refugees gradually came to appreciate the merits of the British system, having at first been dismissive of its apparent anomalies:[34]

> Why do people write letters to the editor? Haven't they anything else to do? What good do they think it does? This was one of the questions about which some of us were puzzled when we first arrived in this country. There were many other features which also appeared 'funny' to us in those days. Fancy having hospitals dependent on private charity, for instance; and a vital institution like the B.B.C. not controlled by the government! And then there was that 'farce' (as we thought) of Question Time in Parliament.

But experience taught the refugees that, far from being archaic quirks, such features in reality provided valuable safeguards for individual freedoms within the modern state:

> Your question in Parliament becomes an attempt to prevent a necessarily huge machine from crushing accidentally one of the individuals for whose benefit it was constructed. That is why, alongside trivial questions about the price of bananas and the shortage of nappies in Nottingham, we have others about the pension of an ex-serviceman, or the water supply of a village, or the internment or admission of aliens.

That the internment of 'aliens' had been debated in the House of Commons in August 1940, and government policy reversed, while invasion threatened and bombs were falling on London, lived on in refugee memory as striking proof of the fairness of British parliamentary government. 'Strange habits', Ambrose concluded affectionately, 'and not very effectual? Perhaps, but they will probably be recorded on the credit side of the ledger of history.'

Already in these early years, a considerable measure of refugee integration into British society was publicly recorded. As in the case of Johann Schneider, who had arrived in Britain in 1938 as a schoolboy, wartime experience often provided the impetus for post-war integration. With some pride, *AJR Information* reprinted an item from the *Leicester Mercury* entitled 'The Story of a Gallant Leicester';[35] this told how Sergeant John Taylor had joined the 1st Leicesters in 1944, after being interned and deported to Australia, had swiftly gained promotion, won the DCM, and was in 1946, aged 23, leading the intelligence section. Now the former internee was 'studying hard for a new life with our troops in Germany'; though the one certainty about that life was that it would not be lived in Germany, 'which holds such bitter memories'. The straightforward anglicization of his name – 'Schneider' means 'tailor' – was the prelude to a new phase in his life where the German past would be overlaid by the promise of an English future: 'Soon Sergeant Taylor hopes to receive British naturalization papers and start his life afresh.'

But the transition from the forces to civilian life was not always easy, especially for refugees, as a recently demobilized 'alien' officer made clear. He could look back with satisfaction on the achievements of refugees in the British forces, but lamented that 'the easy days in khaki, when nobody asked and cared for our nationality, are over'.[36] 'Civvy Street' was a rude awakening for those who thought that their military service entitled them to the same treatment as their British-born colleagues:

> Those of us who have served abroad cannot quite free ourselves from a feeling of disillusion. Yesterday, we were still members of that conquering British Army, true 'masters' in Germany; now, at the Dispersal Centre, it was driven home to us with a bang: Special questionnaires for Aliens! A few days later, we had to queue for our little grey identity book. We felt that we would be missing that close contact with British Army comrades. Our people at home were living in a world of their own, even talking their own language, 'Emigranto' [refugee admixture of English and German].

Refugee service personnel, he continued, faced particular barriers in adjusting to civilian conditions: few of them had been in settled employment in Britain before the war, and they were likely to encounter 'insular' prejudice from employers who gave preference to British applicants. This element of job discrimination should not be underestimated: refugees tended to seek employment in refugee-owned enterprises or, in British firms, to be kept at a distance by their British colleagues. But he predicted that such 'difficulties of adjustment' would eventually be overcome by refugees prepared to make the effort to adapt to British conditions, by committing themselves to a strategy of social integration and loyalty to Britain, hallmarks of the refugee drive towards close relations with British society: 'It will to a large extent be up to ourselves to make the best of it, to show the will to adjust oneself to one's British civilian surroundings, and again to prove a sense of loyalty.'

The classified advertisements section of *AJR Information* provided further evidence of settlement and integration. In June 1946, for example, there were a number of people either seeking or offering their services as cooks, housekeepers and home-helps, and of households needing nannies to help with small children – a sign of family formation in Britain. The commercial advertisements on the back page offered the services of a tailor, an optician, an insurance broker and a publisher of toy books for children, while in the following month a mortgage broker offered advice on home ownership, the clearest indicator of the intention to settle.

The issue of June 1946 also contained an article entitled 'To Which Schools Shall We Send Our Children?',[37] which proceeded from the assumption that refugees would put their children through the British educational system, that powerful mechanism for integrating the next generation into British society. The article, significantly, did not so much as mention the possibility of a Jewish education. Its detailed account of the British school system drew parents' attention to the differences between day and boarding schools and state and fee-paying schools; its emphasis on educational achievement reflected parents' ambitions for their offspring: 'Children with intellectual ability are sent to a Grammar School ("Realgymnasium"). There they have the opportunity of learning one to three modern languages and usually Latin as well, and there they sit for examinations necessary for University studies.' Surprisingly, there was a substantial section on the independent sector, implying that even at this stage there were not a few refugee parents with the aspiration and means to educate their children privately, thus giving them an entry to the higher echelons of British society.

The article warned parents that public schools charged substantial fees, and also that they had 'few vacancies for outsiders', a coded reference to the quotas for Jewish pupils maintained by some schools and to the general coolness in public schools towards pupils from other than established social backgrounds. This was one area where hurtful prejudice made itself felt; some children of refugees experienced coldness or hostility at school that stayed with them long afterwards. Nicholas Kent, director of the Tricycle Theatre in London and son of a refugee father who anglicized his name, would not be untypical in recalling 'antisemitic prejudice based on snobbery' at Stowe School.[38] It was possible for a child of refugee parents to go through the entire private system, from preparatory school to public school, without encountering any anti-Semitism (as was my own experience), but still to have felt an outsider in that most English of closed worlds. Not that anti-Semitism was uncommon in the post-war years in state and private schools: Gordon Shelton (Gunter Schnurmann) experienced it in crude form from a teacher at Haberdashers' Aske's Boys' School, and a teacher called the writer Anne Karpf's sister Eve a 'dirty Jew' at her state school.[39]

Awareness of outright anti-Semitism and, more widespread, a prevailing coolness towards immigrants from a different culture and background did not prevent *AJR Information* from emphasizing the successes of integration. The journal hailed the 'tremendous success' of the refugee actor Martin Miller in *Mountain Air*, an archetypal British farce, adding 'and nothing is so difficult as to break into this kind of national entertainment'.[40] Miller was to surpass even this feat of theatrical integration with his later success in that most British of productions, the long-running Agatha Christie thriller *The Mousetrap*. A high-point in the process of integration was the acceptance of works by the refugee sculptor Benno Elkan at Westminster Abbey, historic centre of the nation's religious and royal traditions. Though he was well over 50 when he fled Germany in 1933, Elkan made a fresh start in London, his busts of a long list of famous people, including Winston Churchill, earning him an OBE. His candelabra inspired by the Old Testament was placed in Westminster Abbey, at the wellhead of British nationhood, as early as 1939, an unprecedented honour for an exiled Jewish artist – though seldom mentioned in studies of the refugees. Elkan's candelabra inspired by the New Testament also found a place in the Abbey.

The rapid pace of integration led to the early winding up of organizations created to overcome barriers between the refugees and the British and to promote better relations between them. In 1947 the London Regional Refugee Council terminated its activities, as the adaptation of the refugees to British life meant that its work could not usefully be extended, and the following year the parliamentary committee on refugees dissolved itself. The refugees themselves plainly shared this view of generally successful integration, one indication of this being the drawing of historical parallels with earlier groups of immigrants. As early as 1946, Ernst Lowenthal described the experience of the Huguenots who had fled to England after 1685, making a comparison with the Jews from Central Europe too obvious to overlook:

> They all – men, women, whole families, people of many trades and professions, expelled from their homeland on account of their religious beliefs – found a refuge in Britain. Here they hoped to live in freedom and make a useful contribution to the country's development and wealth. Many were poor, having lost all their belongings and property; the English public came to their help. Whilst some of the newcomers subsequently went to the United States a considerable number settled in this country for good.[41]

Having dwelt on the generous reception of the Huguenots in England and the economic benefits with which they repaid it, Lowenthal concluded by depicting their descendants as having successfully integrated into British society while preserving key elements of their cultural heritage:

> It is almost two and a half centuries ago that the first Huguenots came to England. Their descendants have, of course, fully integrated into British thought and life and in many instances have held prominent positions in the service of this country. Huguenots can still be recognised by their French names which they faithfully preserve, being proud of the origin and fate of their ancestors. Huguenot immigration at the time was considered as a 'friendly invasion'. It has, in fact, been a most successful experiment.

This rose-tinted vision of happy acculturation owed as much to refugee expectations as it did to historical reality. But the Huguenot experience did provide a blueprint for the refugees: the Huguenots were a minority who had been partially integrated in their native country when the onset of religious intolerance drove them out, only for those who fled to the Protestant states of Germany to continue the interrupted process of integration and become loyal and respected citizens. The refugees hoped with some confidence to do the same in post-war Britain.

By 1949, a clearer and more differentiated view of the reality of refugee integration was emerging, as exemplified by two articles on 'The Second Generation' by Kenneth Ambrose.[42] Ambrose (who had left Stettin in 1936 aged 17 to study at King's College, Taunton) focused on those who had come to Britain as children or young people, standing awkwardly between the generation of their parents, still wedded to their Continental ways, and the anglicized generation born in Britain. He began by analysing the change in attitude to their parents caused by emigration, in particular the loss of confidence by this 'second generation' in the values and lifestyle of their parents, which were too geared to Germany to provide reliable guidance to life in Britain:

> Their scale of values and their social behaviour are no longer almost automatically adopted by us, for much of it is, or at first sight seems to be, a source of weakness rather than strength in their new environment. Those of us who were lucky enough to come here with their parents find that the answers to many of our daily problems are no longer found at home, but in our English surroundings ... many of us have had to look elsewhere for a sense of safety which we can no longer get from our elders.

The alternative of trying to pass as English was not open to those caught midway between British and German social cultures, so Ambrose advised his generation of refugees to recognize that their sense of discomfort, of not being firmly rooted in either camp, was part of their identity. The older generation was rooted in Continental values, a strength but also a limitation in a foreign society:

> The majority of the older generation can of necessity only make a series of external adjustments to an established way of life acquired beyond the Channel. We admire them for the striking success with which most of them have adapted themselves under the trying circumstances with which we have all been familiar. At the same time we know that our way is different in nature and not only in degree. We are not as firmly grounded as they are in another culture and most of us could be absorbed almost entirely by our new surroundings. Yet as we grow up we become conscious of the fact that we are not entirely a part of either the old way or the new, but could only be more or less poor imitators of either.

The British-born generation, on the other hand, had largely lost contact with German social culture, and was rooted in that of Britain, taking little interest in the culture of the former homelands and preferring 'the types of entertainment which their English school-mates enjoy'.

Ambrose's articles presented an easily recognizable paradigm: the older generation remained tied to the values and lifestyle of its native society, the transitional generation sought uneasily to combine elements from both the old and the new societies, while the younger generation was largely immersed in the social culture that surrounded it in Britain. The possibility of holding out against the insistent pressure to integrate was not mentioned, only that of adapting to it according to the varying sociocultural patterns that had shaped the three generations. Use of the German language was the key indicator of the older generation's adherence to Continental social values, with which the second generation was no longer comfortable ('Really, Mummy, you ought to speak English round here!'), while the British-born generation was already immersed in English culture and language.

The second generation, whose members had lived within two cultural patterns and were familiar with both, faced the choice between them. Ambrose advised his contemporaries against jettisoning either completely. Those who were tempted to opt for a purely British style of life, because it seemed safest and was urged upon them by the host community, were at fault insofar as they saw the values of their parents only as inadequate to the demands of emigration. He had even less time for those who were tempted to reject British society, 'our young Anglophobes, mercifully few, who would never dream of sitting down on the "New Environment" stool'. Instead, he gave preference to an intermediate position:

> Those members of the second generation who believe that some-
> thing of value is contained in both the old and in the new culture pat-
> terns have congregated there. They are not ashamed of the older gen-
> eration and do not artificially dissociate themselves from their past,
> nor do they turn their back on their new home. They try to remem-
> ber that in our effort to make life more worth living many English
> are on our side.

This led Ambrose to conclude on the optimistic note that the second generation was well placed to act as a 'hyphen between two culture patterns',
between two generations and two societies. Indeed, in October 1948 the
initial meeting took place under AJR auspices of an organization called The
Hyphen, a social club that catered for refugees between the ages of 21 and
35; this attracted a sizeable membership, branched out into cultural events,
and is still remembered by several married couples who first met there. For
Peter Singer, who met his wife Hanna through The Hyphen, it was 'the
connecting link between our former … state of being refugees and becoming full British naturalised citizens'.[43]

The difficulties faced by refugees of the older and younger generations
in their attempts to come to terms with their new environment also
emerged clearly from a front-page piece by Werner Rosenstock, 'Looking
Ahead', in the October 1949 issue of the journal. The article looked to the
future of the refugees, who had now mostly passed the first hurdle of integration by becoming British citizens, but who remained conscious of the
differences that separated them from the native British:

> It sometimes seems that amongst not a few of us the 'refugee-con-
> sciousness' has not decreased but increased after naturalisation.
> Before naturalisation, they could make themselves and others believe
> that they were British save the passport. Now they have the passport
> and all the other privileges of a British subject, which they grateful-
> ly appreciate, but has it any influence on their social intercourse or
> on their accent? Some of us may have been asked during the summer
> vacations by their fellow guests: 'Where do you come from?'; they
> will also have experienced that the answer 'from London' was not
> quite what the enquirer wanted to know.

The problem here was not one of discrimination or racial prejudice.

Though Rosenstock mentioned some cases of discrimination by employers and professional bodies, he felt able to state categorically: 'Fortunately, in the political field actions of general discrimination have been negligible in the recent past.' What concerned him was that refugees from Continental backgrounds were able to adapt only slowly to British society; this he had come to see as an inescapable part of the process of integration:

> We do not wish to minimize the achievements, or to lay the blame on anybody. There is no reason for complaints, nor for inferiority feelings, especially in the case of continental Jews with their proud past. It is only natural that, having spent their youth and adolescence in a different country, immigrants cannot be entirely identical with the majority population. Nobody wants to perpetuate refugeedom, but absorption must be an organic and, therefore, by necessity a slow process.

As the decade neared its end, Rosenstock did not question the desirability of absorption, seeing an organic process of integration as the natural path forward for the refugees. But he acknowledged that it would need a considerable period of time for the refugees' Continental identity to blend comfortably into a British environment, with distinguishing marks like their accents often remaining permanently and ineradicably foreign.

NOTES

1. See such standard studies as T. Kushner, *The Persistence of Prejudice: Antisemitism in British Society during the Second World War* (Manchester and New York: Manchester University Press, 1989), T. Kushner and K. Knox, *Refugees in an Age of Genocide. Global, National and Local Perspectives during the Twentieth Century* (London: Frank Cass, 1999), C. Holmes, *John Bull's Island: Immigration and British Society, 1871–1971* (Basingstoke: Macmillan, 1988), G. Alderman, *Modern British Jewry* (Oxford: Clarendon Press, 1998), and the numerous articles in journals such as *Patterns of Prejudice* and *Immigrants and Minorities*.
2. Holmes, *John Bull's Island*, p.145.
3. See for example Kushner's claim that anti-Semitism declined in the period before late 1943 (*Persistence of Prejudice*, p.98), neatly contradicted by Holmes's view that the same year, 1943, 'witnessed a marked upturn in antisemitism' (*John Bull's Island*, p.186).
4. Some studies of British Jewry, like Alderman's *Modern British Jewry*, give only a few passing mentions to the Central European refugees, presumably considering them a group apart.
5. Holmes, *John Bull's Island*, p.185.
6. *AJR Information* (October 1947), p.3.
7. *AJR Information* (September 1947), p.1.
8. *AJR Information* (August 1947), p.1; (February 1946), p.1.
9. *AJR Information* (April 1948), p.3.
10. *AJR Information* (February 1946), p.3.
11. *AJR Information* (June 1950), p.3.
12. *AJR Information* (February 1949), p.1.
13. *AJR Information* (March 1950), p.6.
14. See interview with Gina Bauer-Gerson, for example her teacher who helped her pay her way

through drama school; also interview with Sir Kenneth Adam (Klaus Adam), who went through a British preparatory school, public school, architecture college and the RAF without experiencing any anti-Jewish hostility, both in the 'Refugee Voices' collection.

15. 'Anti-Semitism in Britain', *AJR Information* (May 1947), p.3.
16. G. Warburg, 'Can It Happen Here?', *AJR Information* (January 1948), p.3.
16. Letter to the editor from Mrs Gabriele Tergit, *AJR Information* (February 1948), p.5. The social worker mentioned is probably Margarethe Jacoby, later chairman of the social club set up by the AJR for elderly and lonely members.
18. Letter to the editor from Martha Steinitz, *AJR Information* (May 1946), p.6.
19. *AJR Information* (September 1946), p.4.
20. L. Colley, *Britons: Forging the Nation 1707–1837* (New Haven, CT/London: Yale University Press, 1992), Chapter 1, 'Protestants'.
21. *AJR Information* (October 1950), p.3.
22. The first was an MA dissertation by C. Shepherd (Birkbeck College, University of London, 2001), summarized in two parts in *AJR Journal* of April and May 2002. This was followed by G. Macklin, '"A Quite Natural and Moderate Defensive Feeling"? The 1945 Hampstead "Anti-alien" Petition', *Patterns of Prejudice*, 37, 3 (September 2003), pp.277–300.
23. *AJR Information* (March 1946), p.3.
24. *AJR Information* (May 1948), p.3; (July 1948), p.7.
25. *AJR Information* (December 1949), p.6.
26. *AJR Information* (December 1950), p.8.
27. Macklin, '"A Quite Natural and Moderate Defensive Feeling"?' pp.298ff. In my experience, very few refugees indeed felt themselves cast as 'parasitic interlopers'.
28. Kushner, *Persistence of Prejudice*, p.118.
29. C.C. Aronsfeld, '"Civis Romanus Sum … "', *AJR Information* (August 1950), p.5.
30. *AJR Information* (August 1953), p.5.
31. *AJR Information* (February 1949), p.6.
32. *AJR Information* (April 1950), p.6. See also December 1948, p.6, for an account of a refugee audience heartily enjoying jokes about their accents.
33. G. Tergit, 'The Rebel – An Institution', *AJR Information* (February 1950), p.4, and K. Ambrose, 'Your Newspaper', *AJR Information* (January 1950), p.3.
34. K. Ambrose, 'John Citizen and His Government', *AJR Information* (July 1950), p.3.
35. *AJR Information* (April 1946), p.3.
36. A.R.H., 'A Demobbed Officer Writes: Problems of Adjustment', *AJR Information* (July 1946), p.1. Arnold Raphael Horwell (Horwitz) had served as an officer with the British occupying forces in Germany. The problems of adapting to business life mentioned in the article did not prevent him from founding Arnold R. Horwell Ltd, which became a leading supplier of laboratory and hospital ware. He held important offices in the Leo Baeck B'nai B'rith Lodge, Belsize Square Synagogue and the AJR.
37. *AJR Information* (June 1946), p.5.
38. R. Grunberger, 'Profile' of Nicholas Kent, *AJR Information* (December 2004), p.11.
39. Family communication between Gordon Shelton and the author; A. Karpf, *The War After: Living with the Holocaust* (London: Heinemann, 1996), p.13.
40. *AJR Information* (June 1948), p.5.
41. *AJR Information* (April 1946), p.4.
42. *AJR Information* (February 1949), p.5, (July 1949), p.3.
43. M. Malet and A. Grenville (eds), *Changing Countries: The Experience and Achievement of German-speaking Exiles from Hitler in Britain from 1933 to Today* (London: Libris, 2002), p.243.

6

Building New Lives, 1945–1955

The process of settlement in Britain was often difficult, prolonged and painful for the refugees. Following the traumatic experience of their forced emigration, the refugees from Germany and Austria had encountered considerable difficulty in acclimatizing themselves to Britain in the 1930s, where the reception accorded them, aside from a friendly minority, ranged from incomprehension and indifference to suspicion and outright hostility. To this had been added the stresses of war and the agonizing uncertainty about the fate of loved ones left behind, which was only resolved when the full extent of the Holocaust became known. The revelation of the extermination of family, friends and entire Jewish communities was a fresh trauma, with which many refugees could only cope by treating it as a taboo subject never to be discussed, thereby creating within families a painful legacy of subterranean and unresolved loss that could transmit itself to their British-born children.

Responsibility for most of this suffering – the persecution visited on the Jews before emigration, their brutal expulsion and the genocide perpetrated against those who stayed behind – rested with the Nazis. When analysing the experience of the refugees who settled in Britain, one should distinguish between those difficulties they encountered that were particular to Britain and those that applied to the émigré Jews from Central Europe generally (and to many other groups), primarily the trauma of forced emigration as such. Britain in the 1930s seemed an alien environment to most refugees, and many continued to find it so; that was not entirely the fault of British society, which was, unavoidably, different from German or Austrian society. But the nature of the refugees' reception in Britain was a British responsibility: the blinkered insularity with which they were greeted by much of the public, the press and the machine of government, the mass internment of 1940, or the persistence of anti-Semitic and xenophobic attitudes after the war. The initial experience of the Jewish refugees was fraught with difficulties in all countries, including Palestine/Israel, where the shortcomings in the treatment of refugees and Holocaust survivors have been well documented.[1] But the differences between the conditions obtaining in the various countries of refuge emerged more clearly as the refugees became more settled and integrated into the everyday life of the host societies.

Among the refugees who suffered most were elderly people unable to adapt to the demands of life in Britain, unaccompanied children and young people traumatized by the separation from their parents that left them in the care of strangers, and those who developed disabling mental or physical conditions as a result of their experiences. The workload of the Social Services Department set up by the AJR consisted in large measure of problems associated with old age and mental and physical disability in a strange country, while the AJR's Employment Agency, which was granted its first annual licence by the London County Council in March 1948, struggled to help those not equipped to survive economically in Britain. The most moving recollections are those of the Kindertransport children, memorably captured by Karen Gershon,[2] though it is often hard to judge to what extent their personal anguish, crises of identity and problems in later life were caused by the trauma of forced emigration from their homes and to what extent they were the result of the conditions they encountered in Britain; individuals were affected differently, by circumstances that differed from case to case and that were experienced in differing ways according to personality and temperament.

The settlement of the refugees in Britain must be seen in the context of the psychological disruption and suffering consequent on forced emigration. In 1956, an article entitled 'Healing the Wounds' discussed the long-term emotional problems common to refugees the world over, 'which quite a few of us have still not quite overcome and never will: the feeling of being uprooted or unwanted, the feeling of insecurity and suspicion, of being badly treated, or not fully acknowledged'.[3] The writer, H.H. Fleischhacker, also recalled that the incidence of nervous diseases among the German and Austrian Jews in Britain had been comparatively low at times of stress like internment or 'when the bombs began to fall'. Nevertheless, though the refugees themselves tended by the 1950s to see their settlement in Britain as a broadly successful story of obstacles largely overcome, the starting point for such observations always had to be the traumatic experiences they had undergone.

When Werner Rosenstock wrote a major retrospective article on the refugees' experience in Britain in September 1959, on the twentieth anniversary of the outbreak of war, he argued that one of the reasons why the refugees tended to congregate in certain areas (north-west London, Stamford Hill) was their legacy of suffering: 'Is it not understandable that the unique, inexpressibly tragic common experience forged a particularly strong link between all those who lived through it?'[4] Two decades, Rosenstock wrote, were a substantial span in a human life, and such a long period of residence in Britain had inevitably left its mark on the refugees. His reflections on this subject were highly pertinent, starting as they did with a consideration of what distinguished the refugees from the British and what they had absorbed from their new country:

> Though our different approach to many things and our accent will always remind us – and our environment – of our origin, we have all undergone fundamental changes, which we become particularly aware of if we pay a visit to our country of origin. We now live in a country where, in the course of several generations, democracy has struck roots. We have learned that differences of political opinions need not lose their weight if they are debated in an urbane manner and without personal invectives. In everyday life, the respect of the queue symbolises the knowledge that discipline may also be achieved by voluntary subordination instead of by order from above.

That was on the positive side of the balance.

Rosenstock also noted that the degree of the refugees' integration differed according to occupation and area of settlement, and especially according to age. In his view, those who were between 45 and 60 (born between the turn of the century and the First World War) were 'the most contented age group': 'They were not too young to benefit from the positive values of a German education and to participate in German or German-Jewish life before 1933. Neither were they too old to adapt themselves to a new way of life after their emigration.' Older people had greater difficulty in establishing themselves in Britain, where they often had to make do with a status and standard of living well below those they had enjoyed in pre-Nazi times.

The younger group, especially those who had come on Kindertransports, faced daunting problems, starting with a childhood overshadowed by Nazi persecution:

> For them, the memories of their childhood in Germany are haunted by the deprivations and degradations they and their parents had to suffer between 1933 and 1939. They are now in their early thirties and the English language, which they speak without a trace of an accent, is their mother tongue. However, to the surprise of many observers and possibly even themselves, some of them feel that their integration has not been achieved unreservedly.

It was dawning on commentators that such traumatic experiences would be one of the factors that made the transition from refugee status to a settled existence in Britain unexpectedly long and difficult: 'The lesson to be drawn from their position is that complete integration is a much longer and more complicated process than most of us realized when we were granted British nationality.'

From the material point of view, the bulk of the refugees in Britain had done reasonably well, even if not as well as those in America or South Africa (whom Rosenstock was not inclined to envy, given the lack of cultural opportunities there):

> But within the limitations of a country like England which, as a welfare state, has a comparatively level society, without extreme poverty and extreme wealth, those amongst us who were still able to work when they arrived have not fared too badly. The bed-sitters with their gas rings, where trunks served as wardrobes, orange boxes as cupboards and mantelpieces as bookshelves, have been replaced by flats. The house with a garden – an exceptional type of accommodation in the cities from which we hail – has also proved its attraction ... Honesty also demands that we record that many who started their careers as domestic servants in this country now run their own households with help from post-war immigrants from Germany and other Continental countries [that is, employing au pairs].

The education and skills that the refugees had brought with them, along with the values and ambitions absorbed from upwardly mobile, middle-class Jewish families, were doubtless great assets here.

But especially in these early years, the Holocaust cast a long shadow. Fresh in the memories of the Jewish refugees were the persecution and humiliation inflicted on them in the countries of their birth: they had been stigmatized as pariahs, then forced to flee for their lives, abandoning their homes, possessions and familiar surroundings; the communities in which they had grown up had been destroyed; and their loved ones left behind had almost all been murdered in conditions of unimaginable inhumanity. The Nazi years had created a permanent gulf between the refugees and their countries of origin. The ties that had bound them to their homelands had mostly been severed, leaving only a sense of loss and bittersweet memories of happier times. Many refugees suffered permanently from the loss of the rooted security they had once enjoyed. Some sixty years after boarding a Kindertransport train in Mannheim, Hans Seelig still felt affected by the sudden and terrifying separation from family and home:

> Fear drove away any feeling of hope. It was no longer a parting from

loving, self-sacrificing parents; it was parting from love itself, from everything that had still seemed secure: the embrace of one's parental home. We had no inkling of what was to come. This leave-taking, this feeling of uncertainty, of insecurity, this fear of the unknown would never leave the emotional life of the majority of these children; they would reappear in all crisis situations in the future.[5]

Such wounds would be hard to heal, in some cases impossible.

Inevitably, the early issues of *AJR Information* echoed to the aftermath of the catastrophe that had befallen the Jews in Europe. Though the Jews of Germany and Austria had not suffered losses on the same scale as those of Poland or Hungary, their experience of the Holocaust was the more bitter for the fact that it was in 'their' countries that Nazism had originated. The journal carried regular reports on the condition of the surviving Jewish communities in Germany and Austria, often, like the letter from a survivor in Hanover in its first issue, very moving:

Dear colleagues from Breslau,

I send my love to all of you who have worked together with me at the Jewish Hospital at Breslau. Up to now, I am the only nurse from Breslau who has returned from the Camps. With great difficulty I have gained my liberty, thanks to the British Army. I would be happy to obtain news from you and I am gladly prepared, as far as I can, to tell you of the whereabouts of your families. Day by day, we fought for our lives, and unfortunately only very few have survived the unspeakable horrors. I am the only survivor of a family of 9 members.

In the second issue, an article entitled 'Those Who Survived...' reported on the deportation of Jews from ten German cities to the east, with brief details of the fate that they suffered and of the pitifully few survivors who returned. In the same issue, the 'Missing Relatives' column carried an announcement that spoke for itself: 'Dr Käthe Laserstein wants to inform her relatives and friends that she has survived. Her present address is Berlin-Steglitz, Immenweg 7.'[6]

By the 1950s, the passage of time and the more immediate pressures of everyday life had caused the Holocaust to recede somewhat into the background. Nevertheless, it remained a presence in the journal, not least in the 'Missing Persons' column. The issue of June 1959 alone contained search notices from A. Silberman of Wycombe Gardens, London NW11, for his sister, Mrs Lina Simsohn of Königsberg, probably deported, and from Dr Cohn of Observatory Gardens, London W8, for Mr Jonas of Berlin-Schöneberg, who had succeeded in reaching Britain shortly before the war with his elder daughter, leaving behind his wife and younger daughter, who were subsequently deported. In August 1957, a bare announcement revealed a refugee's loss of her family: 'Mr Siegismund, Miss Else and Miss Laura Kiewe, of Schweidnitz, Silesia, dealing in ironmongery, died in a concentration camp. Would anyone who knew them contact Miss Erica Kiewe, 54, Belsize Park, NW3'.[7] The apparently unemotional style of these items rendered them the more moving: in an article entitled 'Lest We Forget', E. Gogarten of Berlin described his final visit, ten years previously, to relatives of his wife, conveying in almost lapidary terms the courage and dignity with which the elderly couple had faced deportation from the flat in which they had dwelt for over thirty years: 'We shook hands, and the vehicle with the men, women and children doomed to death drove away.'[8]

An account of a day's work at the AJR's Social Services Department in 1949 showed vividly how the after-effects of forced emigration, combined with the problems of daily life in post-war Britain, affected vulnerable members of the refugee community. The weight of the caseload, the despairing urgency of the enquiries and their sheer variety evidently impressed the writer, Werner Rosenstock, who witnessed the long procession of those with accommodation, employment and health problems. Predictably, a significant proportion of the more serious cases were not refugees but camp survivors, whose psychological problems were of a different order. But Rosenstock also saw suffering common among those of the refugees who could not cope with life in Britain: the middle-aged man who had lost his job, was consequently unable to afford his flat and was trapped in a vicious circle of unemployment and nervous decline; the tenant desperate because his landlord had given him notice; the lonely people dependent on volunteer visitors in the absence of relatives to look after them. These problems were not decreasing: 'Social casework was originally carried out on a comparatively small scale, but its urgency grew year after year – and where could people turn with their sorrows and their grievances, if not to helpers of their own background on whose understanding they can rely?'[9]

Most refugees faced considerable difficulties in building a stable new existence, and these extended beyond the pre-war and wartime years into the immediate post-war period. When Richard Chotzen, an accountant for the AJR and a popular member of its staff, celebrated his eighty-fifth birthday, *AJR Information* recalled that he had held very senior positions with two leading German banks, but had been forced to resign by the Nazis and had endured a spell in a concentration camp before emigrating to Britain. Here, the journal said, he had had to begin a new life at an advanced age and to find a new livelihood for himself, sustained by his devoted wife; he had maintained his equanimity and sense of humour through all the vicissitudes of refugee life, adapting himself to circumstances very different from those of his life before 1933. These difficult early years formed a standard theme in the life-stories of elderly refugees. The seventieth-birthday tribute to Kurt Friedlander, legal adviser to the United Restitution Organization in London, stated that his father had been one of only two Jewish members of the Prussian Herrenhaus (Upper House of Parliament before 1918) and that he had reached the rank of Regierungsdirektor at an early age; he had emigrated in 1939 and first found work in a factory, where according to the journal he had got on well with his Cockney workmates despite linguistic difficulties.[10]

Some refugees never overcame the barriers that emigration imposed on them. In his obituary of Willy Salomon, a gifted music teacher and musicologist, Ernst Kahn recalled meeting him at lectures on art at German universities and then at Onchan internment camp on the Isle of Man, where his large and enthusiastic audiences included the camp commandant and all his officers. But Salomon could never put the hardships he had endured behind him: 'Buchenwald and emigration uprooted this impressionable man, and he never really settled down to the full employment of his capacity, in spite of his coaching many well-known British artistes.' A sad case was that of Georg Chaim, a dental surgeon from Berlin, who fell victim to the stubborn refusal of the British dentists' professional body to allow dentists with German qualifications to register and was about to resume his career after years of frustration when he died in 1957.[11]

The conditions under which the leading Expressionist painter Ludwig Meidner lived as a refugee were vividly described by Leo Kahn in 1953:

> After the pogroms of 1938 Meidner, assisted by Augustus John and other English artist friends, was given refuge in this country. Refuge – but no more. Meidner, then in his fifties, was like most of us faced with the task of starting his career afresh; he did not succeed ... Whatever the cause, Ludwig Meidner, together with his wife Else – herself an artist of great talent and originality – has been living a life of artistic isolation and financial hardship for the last twelve years. There were very occasional commissions for portraits, like that of Dr Leo Baeck, and one or two exhibitions which received very favourable notices but failed to attract a wider public. Night after night the light burned in the barely furnished, though always neat and tidy, room where Meidner lives and works; his portfolios filled with hundreds of drawings and aquarelles known only to the small circle of his friends.[12]

It was hardly surprising that soon afterwards Meidner returned to Germany, where his work was appreciated.

The economic situation of the refugees in the post-war period varied greatly. On the one hand were the disadvantaged groups described above, but on the other were the businessmen, the owners of small factories, shops and other establishments, the professional people who had embarked on solid careers, as well as a smaller number of industrialists and major entrepreneurs, publishers, actors and people in the media who were enjoying a degree of prosperity even in the late 1940s. The high proportion of middle-class people in the refugee community caused it to assume an occupational profile different to that of the population at large, and consequently to do considerably better in economic terms, once wartime restrictions on its activities were lifted. This became even more marked in the 1950s, as the education and skills that the refugees had brought with them lifted more and more of them into relatively well-paid positions, while those who had come as children and young people also tended to acquire qualifications that equipped them considerably better than the average British worker for the economic opportunities that beckoned in the 1950s.

The economic situation of the refugees also changed very markedly over the years between 1945 and 1960, as did that of the population as a whole.[13] There can hardly have been a decade in which the economic condition of Britain improved more dramatically than it did in the 1950s, which began with rationing and austerity and ended with the mass consumption of the goods and services on offer to modern post-war societies. In the difficult years of the late 1940s, the majority of the refugees lived in straitened circumstances, along with most of the rest of the population; even the more prosperous minority enjoyed a standard of living that now appears modest. But as the post-war recovery fuelled the growth of the British economy in the 1950s, a significant section of the refugees, especially those established in middle-class occupations in London and other cities, began to experience a measure of solid affluence. It was probably in the 1950s that the socio-economic status of the refugees began to diverge unmistakably from that of the population overall. The ads in *AJR Information*, for example, indicate an undeniable level of prosperity among at least a section of the refugees; clearly, though, many still enjoyed only a modest standard of living, even struggling to make ends meet, until the economic upswing of the 'Never Had It So Good' years lifted the middle classes into the consumption-led affluence of the 1960s.[14]

'Are They Doing Well?' asked a front-page article in the January 1952 issue of the journal, and proceeded to set out evidence to counter the prevailing impression that the refugees had achieved a comfortable level of prosperity and security. Despite such indicators of affluence as car ownership, the article argued that there was an underside of hardship and distress – 'the average refugee has to struggle hard for his livelihood' – citing such factors as the refugees' decline from their formerly solid middle-class status, the need to make the difficult adjustment to new conditions, the loss of possessions and the fear of old age and the accompanying loss of income. The AJR's Social Services Department had to deal with a steady stream of cases of illness, loneliness, even suicide. The housing shortage badly affected refugees who had lost their furniture and could not afford to replace it, claimed the article, which went on to paint a picture of living conditions in Hampstead scarcely recognizable today: 'Dilapidated Victorian houses in the Hampstead district now accommodate twelve to fourteen different parties, each of them restricted to a small furnished bed-sitting room with a gas cooker.' Such makeshift arrangements underscored the insecurity of these tenants' situation, even twelve years after their arrival in Britain, with the resultant friction and tensions. A point repeatedly made was that the furnished rooms inhabited by many refugees were expensive, obliging refugees to spend an unduly high proportion of their income on rent.

Many refugees were at a disadvantage in the employment market because of their age and the language barrier. 'People of our background have hardly any chance of finding work through the local labour exchanges', stated the article, as they were not skilled manual workers; hence the need for the AJR's own Employment Agency. The article listed unemployment, housing difficulties, loneliness, sickness and loss of self-confidence as problems that made refugees especially vulnerable. While the legal side of the refugee problem had been solved 'by the generous naturalization policy of this country', the social difficulties continued, and might worsen as the refugee community aged.

In the absence of any official statistics on the social and economic situation of the refugees as a group, such sources as the reports from the Social Services Department and the classified advertisements published in the journal provide a rich vein of information. In April 1956, for example, the Social Services Department reported an increase in the number of applicants for home work on its books, most of whom were elderly and lacked work experience, so needed offers of unskilled work or work that could be easily learnt. The accommodation situation was bad, especially for elderly people who had lost their rooms when they stopped working and now needed accommodation at a moderate rent. The Department also appealed for a radio for an elderly lady who was unable to walk. In June 1956, the journal reported that members were increasingly calling on the AJR for legal advice, especially in cases of disputes between landlords and tenants and employers and employees; the psychiatrist who attended the

AJR in an honorary capacity was seeing a growing number of people; and the AJR's social worker, Dr Adelheid Levy, had visited lonely and disabled people unable to attend at its offices, an otherwise neglected group grateful for her attention.[15]

By piecing together information from the classified ads columns, one can build up a picture of the problems of housing, employment and health that most affected the refugees.[16] There is no other source of information on these daily aspects of refugee life that is remotely comparable. Well into the 1950s, there appeared a steady stream of ads requesting accommodation for vulnerable people, the elderly or those with health problems: 'Elderly Cultured Lady, blind but not very dependent on others, wants comfortable home in good surroundings. Daughter sends regularly parcels from America' (September 1947); 'German Jewish Refugee, concentr. camp 1938, urgently needs home as p. g. [paying guest] in family near Oxford. Mentally arrested, healthy, good natured, helpful in house and garden' (December 1947). Many elderly people tried to rent a room on a half- or full-board basis in a family home, where they would find company and care. Others tried to find lodgers or companions to share their homes, as a source of income or to care for them; others again looked to move into boarding houses.[17]

By the late 1950s, however, as poverty and distress lessened, the tone of the ads changed, as in this little gem of Continental culture transplanted to north-west London: 'Schönes Wohn-Schlafzimmer in modern block of flats, near Henlys Corner. Alleinstehende ältere Dame sucht eine möglichst berufstätige bessere Dame als Untermieter, die den Komfort einer erstklassigen Wohnung teilen kann.' ['Lovely bed-sitting room in modern block of flats, near Henlys Corner. Single elderly lady seeks a lady of good class, preferably professional, as lodger, to share the comfort of a first-class apartment.'][18] The economic upswing of the 1950s, though it brought a measure of affluence to the refugees as it did to the population at large, also caused the poor and vulnerable to lag even further behind. As AJR Social Services reported in 1957, the rise in house prices was inducing landlords to sell their houses, and the tenants to whom they gave notice turned in desperation to the AJR; but the parallel rise in rents, accelerated by the removal of rent control from some forms of rented accommodation, meant that rooms at affordable rents below £2 per week were hard to find. The rise in the cost of living, itself a reflection of increased spending power, forced retired refugees to seek work again, often as dressmakers, mending or altering clothes, or in domestic jobs, as cooks, 'sitters-in' or looking after the sick, invalids and children.[19]

The refugees had been at a disadvantage on the employment market since the end of wartime controls in 1945, as employers tended to give preference to British applicants for jobs, especially those returning from war service, over 'foreigners' whose English was faulty or who had difficulty in adapting to British conditions. Many refugees were unable to continue in their chosen professions in Britain, and had been forced to start again in far more lowly, sometimes menial, jobs. A front-page article in *AJR Information* of February 1952 went so far as to argue that the 'middle-class structure of German Jewry proved detrimental to their integration in the new countries', especially in the case of people in business and the professions who were over a certain age; competition on the labour market, the article stated bluntly, was impossible for bank managers and insurance brokers in their 60s.

In late 1948, when the AJR's Employment Agency had been functioning for eight months, no fewer than 1,000 refugees had sought employment through it.[20] Though some 850 vacancies were offered by employers, these jobs were often for young people, while the applicants were from the older age groups; and the demand was for skilled workers and craftsmen, while the applicants, though skilled in other walks of life, had no experience in such trades. Many applicants sought jobs as clerical workers, bookkeepers and storekeepers; even in these humble areas there were few vacancies, especially in London, and refugees were reluctant to move to 'the provinces'. Consequently only a quarter of the vacancies notified were filled. It was particularly hard to place former professional men, like lawyers, who had been used to positions of responsibility.

The Employment Agency's first report, in May 1950, showed where the difficulties lay.[21] It had not been offered many vacancies for men, and had on its books unemployed translators, interpreters, clerks, bookkeepers, store- and stock-keepers, packers, commercial artists, unskilled workers and home-workers. For women, on the other hand, many vacancies had been notified, but often for younger women or for those qualified as machinists; these could not be filled by older women seeking work as typists, shorthand-typists, translators, clerks, dressmakers, finishers, linen-repairers, cooks, companions, sitters-in and unskilled workers. The demand from women for jobs was concentrated in the areas of office and secretarial work, domestic work, including caring for people in their own homes, and the tailoring and dressmaking trades.

The report highlighted the plight of the disabled people on its records, who had great difficulty in finding work; it also emphasized the demand for trainee jobs from those unable to find work in their former professions and willing to retrain. The report ended with a list of special hardship cases: these were mostly people suffering from severe health problems or older people who could not exercise their chosen professions and were reduced to seeking employment in the drudgery of routine clerical or light manual work. The same categories of people predominated in the Employment Agency's subsequent reports and in the lists of those advertising in the journal's 'Situations Wanted' column; many required part-time jobs, for reasons of age or health, and many could only work from home. In an ageing community that had been through the ordeal of forced emigration, problems of health were predictably frequent and were often the root cause of unemployment, accommodation difficulties or chronic loneliness. The plight of the sick, the elderly and of invalids loomed large in the reports of the Social Services Department and, as has been seen, was reflected in the journal's columns devoted to housing and employment. It was exacerbated by the fact that many refugees had lost the family members who would have looked after them in Central Europe. So pressing did the problem become that in January 1959 a group of lady volunteers began to make weekly visits to invalids and hospital patients under the *Nachbarhilfe* ('Help Your Neighbour') scheme. At least the need to help the sick enabled the Employment Agency to place jobless people in work attending them, to the benefit of both categories of needy AJR members.

Loneliness was one of the psychological problems that affected the refugees far more widely than the host population. The AJR, conscious of this, did a great deal to combat the problem: it arranged a Seder during Passover for people who would otherwise have spent the ceremonial evening alone; it held tea-parties for elderly ladies, as the proportion of widows and single elderly women in the refugee community increased; and it founded its own AJR Club, first in Eton Avenue, then with its own premises in Adamson Road, both in Swiss Cottage, where the devoted work of Margaret Jacoby, the chairman, and Gertrud Schachne provided a warm, friendly ambience, a second home where lonely refugees could meet and enjoy congenial company and activities. But ads in the journal spoke a continuing language of poignant loneliness: 'Which nice family would take an old lady (German refugee) as paying guest? Bayswater district preferred' (March 1947); 'Lady, 40, very lonely in North of England would like acquaintance with gentleman re marriage. Widower with child considered' (February 1949).

Some refugees felt a sense of isolation that reflected a deeper inability to integrate into British society, especially after a certain age, as a letter to the editor put it in January 1951:

> Being 42 years of age, I feel sure that I left Germany too late, in order to ever assimilate in this country. My repeated visits to Germany and

Austria have proved this to me beyond doubt, in spite of the fact that the Germany of pre-Hitler days, as we knew it and which we loved, does no longer exist. One may be very happy professionally in this country, one may respect it greatly, but in one's very private and intimate sphere one does not and one cannot feel 'at home'. Therefore one either would have to return to the native country to be 'at home', a decision which can only be taken by a very few owing partly to professional and age reasons or partly to individual sentimental reactions, or else one has to live on here – lonely.[22]

In some cases, the sense of isolation would have been accentuated by the lack of a stable and permanent home, a common problem in the early years of settlement when most refugees were subject to frequent changes of residence.

The experience of having been uprooted from a world of stable security and exiled to a foreign country accompanied most refugees for the rest of their lives. The sight of a Huguenot grave in a church garden off Marylebone High Street brought home to the writer of a letter to the journal in May 1955 that it was part of the refugee's condition to end his life abroad and be buried in foreign soil: 'I thought of the many who rest in Hoop Lane and Willesden [cemeteries in north-west London favoured by the refugees], and as I saluted the Huguenot couple, across 250 years, the lines of Byron came into my mind: "But we must wander witheringly/In other lands to die;/And where our fathers' ashes be/Our own may never lie."' Entries in the journal's 'Family Events' column underscored the sundering of ties that had displaced the refugees from the pre-war world of Central Europe to a very different life in Britain. Ludwig Rosenthal from Heilbronn, whose seventy-fifth birthday was announced in March 1955, could hardly have expected to celebrate it in Wimbledon Park; and one can only speculate how Dr Julius Weinschenk, whose death at the age of 73 was announced in April 1955, felt about living out his last years in Mapesbury Court, on the crest of Shoot Up Hill, London NW2, instead of in his native Nuremberg.

The communal life of the refugees outside London appears to have followed a pattern similar to that in the capital, though on a considerably smaller scale and with certain predictable regional variations. On the evidence available in *AJR Information*, which devoted space in its regular column 'The AJR at Work' to the AJR groups outside London, the smaller communities in the regions looked to London and were much influenced in their development by new arrivals from London or, more frequently, by the departure of prominent local personalities to London. The local communities were almost all too small to maintain a broadly based, independent communal life of their own. The smaller ones tended of necessity to become absorbed into the British society around them, while even the larger ones, in Manchester, Leeds or Glasgow, survived by associating themselves with the existing local Jewish communities, lacking as they did the critical mass to survive as autonomous communities with their own distinct German-speaking culture and identity and with a full range of cultural life and activities.

None of the communities outside London was large enough to support a network of refugee organizations, businesses, retail outlets and other commercial enterprises comparable to that which developed across north-west London. The evidence for this is clear from *AJR Information*, where the only commercial advertisers from outside London were manufacturers and wholesalers who sold nationwide from a base in the regions – typically firms that had been established before the war with government support in depressed areas like South Wales, Lancashire and the North-East. But the local advertisers – the shops and small businesses, the builders and decorators, the cafés and restaurants, the firms dealing in clothing and textiles and those offering a multitude of other services – were almost exclusively London-based. Only in London, presumably, was there sufficient consumer demand from local clients with a refugee background to warrant the placing of an advertisement in the journal for retail goods and services from a local trader. When small refugee entrepreneurs were successful outside London, they mainly had to rely on a non-refugee clientele, as, for example, with the successful catering business that Henry Wuga set up in Glasgow, which was primarily dependent on custom from the city's wider Jewish community.[23]

The refugees spread across Britain fairly rapidly after the war. As stated at the end of Chapter 1, they had initially been heavily concentrated in London, but even before the outbreak of war some were scattered around the country. Wartime regulations restricted the mobility of 'enemy aliens', ensuring that many stayed in London, but at the same time the war disrupted the process of settlement there, causing some to leave the capital to escape the bombing, while others joined the forces and were despatched with their units to the four corners of the country. The end of the war appears to have opened the way for refugees to move out of London and settle across the country, and also for those wishing to return to London to do so. The overall movements of refugees between the capital and the regions at this time were complex and difficult to assess accurately.

As early as 1946, *AJR Information* listed twenty-seven local AJR branches.[24] These ranged from cities like Birmingham, Bradford, Glasgow, Leeds, Leicester, Liverpool, Manchester, Newcastle, Nottingham, Sheffield and

Stoke to the university cities of Oxford and Cambridge, where refugee academics congregated and which had also been centres of wartime evacuation. They included a few agreeable resort towns like Bath, Cheltenham and Harrogate, several towns within easy reach of London like Bedford, Epsom, Farnham, Guildford, Letchworth and Reading, and a scattering of places where refugees had settled for personal reasons or to set up businesses, such as Bishop Auckland, Blackburn, Cirencester, Northampton and Shrewsbury. But the coverage was patchy: Bristol and the south-west, Cardiff and Wales, and Edinburgh were not represented.

The same page of the journal listed six meetings to be held by local AJR groups in January 1946: three where speakers were sent from London (Werner Rosenstock in Nottingham, Louis Bondy in Cambridge and Rabbi Ignaz Maybaum in a church hall in Oxford), but also three events in Glasgow, a Skat tournament (Skat is a popular German card game), a dance at the Jewish Institute and a report on a visit to Holland, which were organized locally, independent of the head office. This indicated that Glasgow, with its larger refugee population, was to a greater extent able to mount its own activities and enjoy its own communal life.

During the 1950s the refugee communities across Britain stabilized, as the refugees put down roots and settled, with the high degree of mobility observable in earlier years decreasing markedly. By the end of the decade, refugees had spread widely across the cities, towns and even villages of Britain. In 1959, to take just two examples, *AJR Information* published a letter from Stella Kurrein, the widow of a rabbi from Linz in Austria now resident in Biggleswade, Bedfordshire, and a birthday tribute to Dr Walter Gordon, a geriatric specialist practising at St Mary's Hospital, Bury St Edmunds.[25] Refugees were also to be found in remoter locations: the cultural commentator PEM reported that the actress Irene Triesch, aged 80, was living in total obscurity in Scotland,[26] while Toni Goldstein advertised 'Arvonia', the rest and convalescence home she ran in Abersoch, North Wales, as early as 1946. Even in larger regional centres, refugees were being absorbed into British life: in 1956, the journal reported that the surgeon Dr Hans Korn had been invested with the Order of St John for his work over sixteen years for the St John Ambulance Brigade in Leicester, where he also served as a magistrate.[27]

In 1954, an article entitled 'Life in the Provinces' gave a detailed and informative insight into the settlement of refugees outside London. The author, Marie Sackin, described her initial reluctance to exchange life in a Hampstead boarding house for an isolated existence far away from her fellow refugees. But her experiences in S. (Sheffield) rapidly dispelled these fears:

In truth, however, London holds a maximum possibility for loneliness, and the provinces open up for you an insight into the English 'way of life' into which you are drawn and of which, unwittingly, you become part as the years go by. You realise that the English love their neighbours more than themselves. Life in a provincial town has a warmth for you to feel if you want to feel it. You know that Mrs. Huggins of No. 24 is weeping with you and rejoicing with you, though your topic of conversation has never gone beyond the weather.[28]

Even allowing for an element of idealization, this picture of refugees contentedly integrated into the friendly and neighbourly life of a provincial city plainly conveyed the refugees' underlying sense that they had settled in a predominantly benign environment and that their attitudes, manners and behaviour were readily compatible with those of the English, for all the latter's emotional reserve.

Conditions in Sheffield were conducive to a high degree of assimilation: 'The refugees here in S. have become completely absorbed. Their children do not speak German, and parents preserve their Saxon or Bavarian accent for use only in English.' Language was a key indicator of identity, as was religion; Sackin described in some detail how those refugees who preserved their Jewish faith tended to live near the synagogue and send their children to the Hebrew School, though her main point was the absence of anti-Semitism and the way in which the local population 'supports and respects Jewish activities'. The tolerance shown to observant Jews was but part of a wider acceptance of the refugees into the city's society, especially its professional life (Sackin mentions university lecturers, doctors and dentists and those engaged in research at the steelworks).

The refugees, by Sackin's account, had integrated to the point where they no longer frequented refugee circles only, but had built up wider, less exclusive networks of friends: 'You are not likely to meet all your local fellow refugees because you move in your own circle of friends, which may or may not contain refugees.' On the question of the refugees' national allegiance and identity, her conclusion was emphatic:

> Those I know, in spite of a deterioration generally in their financial position, are no longer 'refugees', but regard England [as] the country of their choice which they would not like to change back for the old Fatherland, Hitler or no. The mere thought of a return to Germany would be like a nightmare to the refugees in S., I know.

Though distinguished from the English by their accents and sometimes by customs preserved from Central Europe, these former refugees had opted decisively to put their past life in their native countries behind them and to adopt instead the path of assimilation into Britain, a path that most appeared only too willing to take.

The refugee community in the town of H., by contrast, attempted to maintain the ways of the past, in terms of language, social life and social exclusivity. Sackin saw this as a regressive attempt to carry on a communal lifestyle derived from the German-speaking lands; it impoverished those who practised it, 'for in H. the refugees form one harmonious family with Skat, Kränzchen [coffee circles] and the attachment of common experience. What English they learned in the first stage of emigration has atrophied by lack of use and is now not far removed from zero.' The irony with which Sackin described a community that sought to create a 'harmonious family' by shutting out the wider world around it indicated her distrust of its anti-assimilationist stance. She predicted that the continuing allegiance of these refugees to the attitudes and values of the past would lead to increasing isolation for those who stayed in Britain, while those who did not would be condemned to the 'nightmare' of returning to Germany: 'The wall of exclusiveness is shutting round them ever more tightly and it is no accident that from H., and never from S., refugees go on holiday to Germany and that one or two have returned for good.'

The attempt to preserve the communal life of pre-emigration times in near-entirety was doomed to failure, for it could have little attraction for the children of the refugees, who would abandon it: 'No doubt, the bond which holds together refugees in H. has been created by the past and will lose its magnetic power for a future generation.' Sackin plainly favoured the strategy of measured assimilation over that of refusing to integrate into British society. Whereas the former, which allowed refugees to maintain certain features of their past life within the framework of a broad accommodation to British society, created the conditions for a stable and contented existence, the latter, which was bent on re-establishing a German way of life with a minimum of concessions to British society, had no long-term future.

Bradford was another large city where a number of refugees had settled; as noted in Chapter 1, it played host to the Jewish Refugee Hostel housing boys from Germany and Austria, and Jewish immigrants had long been drawn to its textile industries. Bradford boasted an active AJR group, but as early as 1946 it was disrupted by the departure of its chairman, P.L. Goldschmidt, and its hon. secretary, P.E. Schwarzschild, for London. A new committee was formed, with H.O. Heymann as chairman, F. Heilbrunn as vice-chairman and F. Oppenheimer as hon. secretary.[29] But in 1953 Fritz Oppenheimer died, a severe loss to the group. Herbert Eger, the former warden of the boys' hostel, died in the same year; Eger's widow moved away to Harrogate, where she ran a guest-house. The loss of leading figures appears to have caused the communal life of the refugees to wane, at least as far as organized activities were concerned.

A familiar pattern emerged: the refugees developed their own private social and professional networks, no longer centred on other refugees. What remained were organizational ties between observant refugees and Jewish life in Bradford in general, principally through synagogues. When Rabbi Erich Bienheim, a rabbi in Darmstadt, then, after emigration, at West London Synagogue, and from 1949–61 at a synagogue in Bradford, died in 1962, *AJR Information* recorded a tribute from Hans Librowicz, a former Berliner, but in his capacity as chairman of the Bradford synagogues, not as a fellow refugee.[30] The organizations created specifically for refugees in Bradford appear to have atrophied, but the refugees remained: in 2004, Librowicz's son, Rudolf Leavor, was interviewed in Bradford for the 'Refugee Voices' collection.

In Leeds, a city with a large Jewish community where a substantial number of refugees settled, the development was broadly similar to that in Bradford.[31] But in a city like Oxford, with far less Jewish settlement, the refugees were absorbed into local British society. Yet Oxford, like Cambridge, was a city that had had a large refugee population, in relation to its size. Refugee academics congregated in the two university towns before the war, as did refugees offered support and accommodation by the liberal-minded academic community; and during the war, Oxford and Cambridge were favoured places of evacuation from London. The local committees set up to help the refugees were very active, and a network of refugee social life and activities developed. Yet this proved short-lived. After the war, many refugees left for London; the others developed social and professional circles of their own, especially the academics, who were absorbed into university life. By the time that Peter Pulzer arrived in Oxford in 1957, to begin a career that would culminate in a Chair at All Souls College, the refugees hardly featured as a distinct group; Pulzer only recognized his fellow refugees by the frequency with which they attended concerts.[32] The AJR group in Cambridge, led by Georg Schatzky, remained active, but only into the 1950s – probably because it was no longer needed after that.

The AJR group in Glasgow occupied a special place among the local refugee organizations, by virtue of its size and level of activity. It was founded shortly before the AJR itself, in late 1940, and could therefore consider itself to that extent an autonomous group equal in status to the London-based association, to which it had affiliated. The Glasgow Society for Jewish Refugees, as it was known, arranged a wide variety of events, provided support and assistance for lonely or needy refugees and acted as a forum for bringing the refugee community together. When a function was held in 1950 to celebrate the tenth anniversary of the founding of the group, it attracted a remarkable level of support and was attended by 135 members.[33] In July 1955, Leo Loewensohn, one of the Society's leading figures, reported that it had a membership of sixty to seventy, was active in the cultural and social fields, held fortnightly meetings with lectures, arranged functions on the Jewish festivals and played an active part in the affairs of Glasgow's Jewish community.[34]

The standing of the AJR Glasgow group was reflected in the tributes paid to its officers on occasions like their birthdays. In June 1953, *AJR Information* published an announcement of the 75th birthday of Ernst Levy, who had been the founder and president of the group and was now its honorary president; in July 1956, it published a tribute by Loewensohn, as chairman, to Curt Rosenberg, the treasurer, on his 80th birthday; and in November 1956, it reported that members of the Society had honoured its secretary, Herbert Levy, for his work for it and for the Mutual Refugee Aid Society, on his 70th birthday.[35] But the passing of time began to thin out the ranks of the founding generation. In October 1956, the journal reported that Max Doctor, a leading member of the Society, had died in a road accident aged 77.

Herbert Levy left for Israel in 1959, where he died shortly afterwards. In the issue of October 1959 alone, obituaries appeared for Leo Loewensohn, who had been the Society's chairman for thirteen years, and for Herbert Levy, who as well as acting as secretary of the Society had been founder and honorary president of the associated Mutual Refugee Aid Society.[36] Else Rosenberg, wife of Curt Rosenberg, who had been a member of the council of the Society and president of the Mutual Refugee Aid Society, had died a few months earlier.[37] Ernst Levy died in 1961, aged 83. In 1962, the Society, which the journal increasingly termed 'the Glasgow constituent of the AJR', elected a new committee, with B.N. Bergmann as chairman. Its officers were, compared to the founding generation, relatively unknown, with the exception of the historian Werner Mosse, but he left Glasgow in 1964 to take up a Chair at the University of East Anglia. The group would never recover its former dimensions.

The AJR group in Manchester was another local group that flourished in the post-war years, as a report in January 1946 on an address given to its members by Fritz Goldschmidt of the United Restitution Organization showed.[38] A feature unique to Manchester was the setting up of the Morris Feinmann Homes, which provided accommodation for elderly and lonely refugees well before similar homes were established in London. An article on the Homes, aptly entitled 'A Focus of Manchester's AJR',[39] stated that they were the first venture of their kind in Britain, an achievement all the greater because it had been accomplished by the 'comparatively small' refugee community in the city – a revealing comment, since Manchester and Glasgow contained the largest concentrations of refugees outside London. The first house, in Amherst Road, had been bought in 1947 and opened in 1948, with a second following next door in 1949. The Homes were named after Morris Feinmann, chairman of the Manchester Jewish Refugees Committee, who had died in North Africa in 1944, on a mission to provide relief for liberated Jews. The second house was given to the trust that administered the Homes through the generosity of Berthold Bochenek, then chairman of Manchester AJR.

But, as was the case in Glasgow, the AJR group in Manchester had by the early 1960s passed its high-point. When Werner Rosenstock travelled to Manchester to address a gathering of AJR members at Morris Feinmann House, *AJR Information* reported that an 'unexpectedly large number' of them had come to hear him speak, a comment that reflected less on Rosenstock's popularity than on the diminishing size of the audiences that were to be expected at the AJR group's meetings.[40] The transition from the founding generation was also evident in Manchester. On 7 December 1961, a farewell dinner was held in honour of Gertrude Blumenbach, the matron of Morris Feinmann House, who was retiring after thirteen years of service.[41] She had overseen the moving of twenty-six residents from the original 'austerity' home to new premises in Spath Road in December 1959, and she had successfully merged those residents with some twenty new arrivals 'into one large family'. Gertrude Blumenbach herself became a resident at Morris Feinmann House. The home is now part of general Jewish life in Manchester, retaining little of its refugee origins.

The period around the early 1960s appears to have marked a transition in the life of the refugee communities outside London, as the founding generation passed from the scene. The organizations that it had established gradually diminished in size and vigour, as their members either integrated increasingly into British society or became more closely associated with the local Jewish community. Their activities continued for some time, but eventually ceased, so that for a period the AJR had very little by way of local groups; indeed, it is now difficult to recreate anything like a full picture of the local groups, so completely did they disappear. Only in the 1990s did the AJR begin to promote local groups again, and then in a completely different form.

The late 1940s were a time of hardship and struggle for most refugees, as they were for the population at large. Britain had emerged from the war virtually bankrupt; much of the country's industrial resources and infrastructure was in ruins, and as production was inadequate to meet both consumer demand and the needs of reconstruction and exports, rationing and belt-tightening characterized these years of austerity. The cold and privation of the harsh winter of 1946/47, in particular, passed into refugee lore; in later days of affluence, they came to symbolize a bygone age of hardship, a period when the endurance of freshly settled refugee families was put to the test. This was the only time during which economic conditions featured in *AJR Information*, as shortages, fuel crises and sterling crises impacted on the everyday lives of the refugees. After 1950, economic conditions in Britain were hardly ever mentioned in the journal (aside from occasional apologies when strikes by postal workers or printers delayed delivery of the journal), evidence of the relative economic comfort achieved by the bulk of its readership.

AJR Information also showed evidence of the economic advance of the refugees. The post-war government's policy of full employment meant that there was a steady demand for labour, which was soon reflected in the journal's columns. In January 1947, for example, there were nine advertisements for vacant jobs (then still listed under 'Miscellaneous'), considerably outnumbering those seeking employment. Among these were ads for a highly skilled dental mechanic for a dental laboratory, for agents for a manufacturer of belts and shopping-bags, for agents with good connections with the wholesale dress and mantle trade and for local representatives nationwide for high-class leather goods. In October 1947, now listed under 'Employment', were ads for a salesman to visit the London shipping houses for an import/export firm, for a representative for a manufacturer of ladies' belts, for a travelling salesman in toys, games, sports and fancy goods, and for several travelling salesmen for a wholesaler in fancy goods, shopping bags, dolls, toys and stationery. This demand for travelling salesmen, representatives and agents indicated the lively commercial activity that had developed among the refugees, who were rapidly establishing a network of small businesses, manufacturing, import/export, wholesale and retail, concentrated in such fields as fancy goods, leatherwear, stationery, toys, belts, bags, buttons and all manner of textiles, clothing, tailoring and dressmaking.[42]

Many female refugees had learnt specialized skills in factories manufacturing clothing and uniforms during the war, and this benefited them subsequently. In July 1949, *AJR Information* contained ads for a designer/cutter for a newly opened skirt factory, for all types of labour ('machinists, tailoresses, finishers etc.') for a newly opened factory making ladies' coats and costumes, for felling hands, finishers and buttoners at 'good wages' for a factory making coats and costumes in the East End, and for instructors for evening classes in cutting and designing. While such jobs provided refugees with steady, if modest, wages, others were achieving higher salaries in professional positions; an ad in February 1949 from a firm of City solicitors for a Continental lawyer to deal with aviation insurance claims was one example of posts advertised that reflected the skills base that the refugees had brought with them and the consequent demand for their services in areas not normally the purview of recently arrived immigrants. Further indications of refugee entrepreneurial spirit, and a measure of prosperity, were advertisements from businessmen looking to invest capital into manufacturing or wholesale concerns.

The factories and other industrial and commercial enterprises set up by refugees have remained under-researched, with the exception of the work of Herbert Loebl[43] and Bill Williams's current project on the Greater Manchester area. Before the war, the government had sought to attract refugee industrialists to what were known as 'special areas' with high rates of unemployment, such as South Wales, the North-east and Cumberland. Refugee enterprises like Western Brush Co. Ltd were still flourishing on the Treforest Trading Estate, Pontypridd, Glamorgan, in the post-war period, to judge by an ad in the AJR's publication *Dispersion and Resettlement: The Story of the Jews from Central Europe* (1955), as were their equivalents on the Team Valley industrial estate, Gateshead, such as Loblite Ltd, manufacturers of lighting fittings and electrical accessories. Cumberland played host to one of the great refugee industrial success stories, Marchon Products, the chemical company run by Frank Schon, later Lord Schon of Whitehaven, and Frederick Marzillier, while Merthyr Tydfil in south Wales was the unlikely location for O.P. Chocolate Specialities, makers of the 'Original Viennese Dessert', 'Mozart Bon-bons' and Pischinger Torten to the original recipe.

Some idea of the number of refugee businesses can be gained from the wealth of ads from firms that supported the AJR's two publications, *Dispersion and Resettlement*, which contained twenty-five pages of ads, up to ten per page, and *Britain's New Citizens: The Story of the Refugees from Germany and Austria* (1951), which had seventeen pages of ads (though not all those advertising were refugee foundations). Among them were prominent concerns like Metalastik Ltd of Leicester, pioneers in the bonding of rubber to metal for the motor industry, whose founder was Mac Goldsmith (Max Goldschmidt). There were many firms making and selling textiles, mostly based in the garment trade's heartland around Oxford Circus, such as Schwarzschild Ochs Ltd, Hertie Ltd, W. Herz Ltd, H. Wertheim Ltd,

Strauss & Co., Dick & Goldschmidt Ltd, and S. Bischheim & B.E. Beecham Ltd (though few in the East End, where Anglo-Jewish firms predominated); many firms in the metals trade, especially metal merchants, where a clutch of businesses originally based in Frankfurt had resettled in Britain; and some manufacturers based in Lancashire, like Lankro Chemicals Ltd of Eccles, Emsa Works (moulded rubber goods) and Herbert Foot Appliances Ltd, and Newman's Slippers Ltd, both of Blackburn.

Firms like Corsets Silhouette Ltd of Park Lane, later Baker Street, Etam (Etablissements Mayer, hosiery) or Colibri of Warren Street, manufacturers of luxury cigarette lighters, added a further touch of class. Lennard & Tracy Ltd, manufacturers of fabrics, whose head office was in Hanover Square, W1, was evidence of the adaptability and business acumen of Manfred Altmann, a rabbi's son and law graduate who had built up a business and was an energetic promoter of Jewish causes. This ability of refugees to adapt and to switch between professions stood them in good stead; in his column 'Old Acquaintances', the cultural commentator PEM (Paul Marcus) described the career of Jan van Loewen, who had come to Britain from Berlin as an opera singer, become a teacher and coach for prospective tenors, worked in the German section of the BBC, and had then established himself as one of London's leading agents for writers and playwrights, responsible for such successes as Jean Anouilh's *Ring Round the Moon*.[44]

Whereas the refugees' achievements in the sciences, medicine and the world of scholarship, in the creative arts and related fields like publishing have been widely recognized, much of their contribution to British commerce and industry has not. Dunbee-Combex, once one of Britain's largest toy manufacturers, was co-founded by Richard Beecham, son of Simon Bischheim, a member of the AJR's executive who had emigrated from Frankfurt and re-established his textile business in Britain. Hans Peter Juda founded the textile export magazine *The Ambassador*, which he edited and published from 1935 to 1964, and whose profound influence on British industry and the promotion of British exports won him an OBE and the Bicentenary Medal of the Council of the Royal Society of Arts in 1965. These are just two of the refugees whose achievements were recognized at the time, but who are almost unknown to later scholars.

As early as 1946, an article in the journal estimated the number of factories established in Britain by refugees at 800, employing 50,000 workers:

> These refugees introduced the manufacture of many products never before made in this country, and trained labour for their production. Consumer goods of all kinds, such as metal alloys, surgical adhesives,

fine chemicals, food preservatives, toilet and hairdressing equipment, metal furniture, zip fasteners, plastic goods, buttons, paints and varnishes, spangles etc., are being produced by these manufacturers.[45]

The article stressed the benefits to Britain's export trade, at a time when the need to export was paramount, since the first of the post-war balance of payments crises that were to bedevil the British economy was looming. It cited the shift in the centre of the world fur trade from Leipzig to London: British fur exports had almost doubled between 1933 and 1938, becoming one of the largest items in UK export figures. A radio talk on refugee industries, reported in May 1948, highlighted their effect on the former special areas, where factories producing artificial flowers, slippers, bicycles and zip-fasteners had been built; one slipper factory had started with five workers and now employed 400, producing 8,000 pairs daily, the largest exporters in this line in Britain.[46]

Another indication of the importance of the industries founded by refugees was that the Committee for Industrial Development from Overseas, the renamed Refugees Industries Committee, was addressed at its annual conference in May 1948, at Caxton Hall, London, by Hugh Dalton, a prominent figure in the governing Labour Party.[47] A report on the British Industries Fair in 1948 proudly extolled 'the number of refugee firms who contributed to this parade of British industrial production and trade', in such areas as advanced scientific, medical and photographic equipment and plastic materials and mouldings, but also in cotton-finishing, knitwear, leatherwork and tile manufacture.[48] Many refugees had opted for trades requiring little initial capital, such as the manufacture of fancy goods, leatherwear, toys and buttons, but they were exposed to the adverse economic conditions prevailing on the home market, which hit sales of luxury goods hard.

Detailed evidence of the way in which the refugees from Central Europe were settling in Britain and integrating themselves and their families into British life can be gleaned from the ads and reports in *AJR Information*. It must be stressed, however, that refugees predominantly mixed socially among themselves; most found it easier to form friendships and social circles with people from a similar background, with a similar culture and interests, and correspondingly harder to establish such relationships with British people. An unmistakable sign of settlement was the starting of families and the establishment of family homes. The evidence of family building strongly suggests that the refugees participated fully in the baby-boom that accompanied the end of the war. The first notice of a birth in the 'Family Events' column of *AJR Information*, that of a daughter to Mr and Mrs P.Y. Mayer of Goldhurst Terrace, London NW6, appeared in its third issue, in March 1946; other children of proud refugee parents followed: 'A son (Peter Robert Leonard) was born on Sunday, August 24th, 1947, at the Princess Beatrice Hospital (Maternity Ward), Earl's Court, London, SW5, to Edith (née Daniel, formerly Kronisch), wife of Rudolph J. Friedmann, of 30, Parliament Court, London, NW3' (September 1947).

Children's needs featured prominently in the journal's ads. There were many ads both for nannies to look after children and from nannies seeking positions. The very considerable number of domestic ads, for maids, cooks, housemaids and daily helps, was also a sign of busy refugee households, where often both parents went out to work. In the absence of older family members to help with childcare, they depended on nannies or other domestics. Older refugee couples advertised for housekeepers, and single people, often widows, for companions, evidence again of a degree of settled residence. Photographers specializing in portraits of children advertised in the journal: Juvin Ltd of Muswell Hill, managed by a refugee, advertised regularly, while the issue of December 1949 contained an ad from W.G. Kaufmann offering 'charming and natural photographs of your children made in your home', as well as one from Elizabeth Bleichroeder for portraits and sketches for the Christmas season.

A prime necessity for children was education. Two schools founded by refugees before the war have become widely known: Stoatley Rough School in Haslemere, Surrey, founded in 1934 by Hilde Lion, former principal of the Akademie für soziale Frauenarbeit, Berlin, and Bunce Court School, whose staff and students the headmistress, Anna Essinger, brought over in 1933 from Herrlingen in South Germany to Otterden, near Faversham in Kent.[49] To these should be added Camphill School for the handicapped in Aberdeen, founded by Karl König.[50] Less well known is Regent's Park School, run by Bruno and Alma Schindler, which had its first premises in Maresfield Gardens, Hampstead, and settled after various wartime peregrinations in Horley, Surrey. This refugee foundation advertised in the journal, for instance in July 1948, when it announced that it would be open during August for boys and girls between 6 and 16 to enjoy 'its happy and carefree holidays'. The activities on offer were riding, tennis, cricket, gym, bathing, excursions and indoor activities; these typically English activities, in particular the initiation into the mysteries of cricket, marked the divide between those who grew up in Central Europe and those brought up in the English educational system.

There were also nurseries and kindergartens for younger children, of which the best known was Anna Freud's in Maresfield Gardens, Hampstead. To meet the demand from refugee parents, establishments like the House on the Hill, in Netherhall Gardens, Hampstead, run by Barbara

Bowler, a British friend of the refugees, and the Sherriff Day Nursery in Sherriff Road, West Hampstead, whose principal, Lily Collinge, held a Berlin PhD, advertised regularly in the journal. A high priority for refugee parents who had decided to make their homes in Britain was to secure the best educational opportunities for their children. So frequently did parents unfamiliar with the British system approach the AJR for advice that the journal published very early on an article entitled 'To Which Schools Shall We Send Our Children?', as assimilationist a document as one could find.[51]

Essential to the purchase of a family home was a mortgage. The habit of home ownership had not been widespread among the Jews of Germany and Austria, who preferred rented accommodation, nor was it anything like as common among the British as it later became. Nevertheless, refugees with families opted in some numbers to buy residential properties, sometimes suburban semi-detached houses of the interwar period, the clearest imaginable statement of intent to put down roots. The number of mortgage brokers advertising in the journal is evidence of this demand for home ownership. The first ad in this area was the saving plan for home ownership offered in July 1946 by the House Property Advice & Mortgage Association Ltd, which evidently scented business among the refugees even at this early stage, later introducing the name of Mr L. Sauer to attract them.

Refugee brokers were conspicuous. In January 1948, Merton Insurance Brokers Ltd, of Tottenham Court Road, advertised its services in the field of insurance and mortgages, adding for the benefit of refugee customers that Ludwig Pototzky, formerly of Pototzky & Co., Berlin and Breslau, was a partner. Family rivalry then ensued, as the following month's issue also carried an ad from Walter B. Pototzky, insurance brokers since 1938 at a prestigious address in Lombard Street in the heart of the City (the two were uncle and nephew). Insurance of residential and business premises and of personal property, as well as life assurance, was another necessary adjunct of settlement. Valentine & Wolff Ltd, insurance brokers of New Oxford Street, 'managed by Jewish refugee', advertised from the first issue of the journal, but the doyen of the insurance brokers was Leroi Flesch & Co. Ltd, of Mortimer Street, W1, run by Carl F. Flesch. There were also regular ads from a West End estate agent, M. Levison & Co. of Baker Street, while agents local to the Finchley Road area used the names of refugee personnel to attract refugee business.

Refugee homeowners were keen to repair and refurbish their properties, especially after years of wartime neglect. Consequently, the journal regularly carried ads from numerous firms of builders and decorators, some British, but others, like H. Woortman, 'the Continental builder and decorator', run by refugees. Other household needs were met by a veritable posse of upholsterers, mostly of refugee origin: Edmund Deutsch of Randolph Crescent, W9, H. Glaser (later M. Glaser) of Child's Hill, NW2, Herbert Zwillenberg (Felina Ltd, 'the Continental way fine class work') of Broadhurst Gardens, NW6, Leslie Shirley of Melrose Avenue, NW2, 'Manager L. Scheibe, formerly Polstermöbel und Matratzenfabrik, Berlin', while Paul Muller Ltd of Finchley Road NW3, formerly of Webgasse, Vienna VI, catered for the higher end of the market, offering 'high class furniture – interior decoration' and 'English, Continental and Antique Repairs – French Polishing – Upholstering'; and by several electricians and suppliers of electrical goods, who were refugees, like R. & G. (Electrical Installations) Ltd (Reissner & Goldberg), or enjoyed a close relationship with their refugee clientele, like Falcon Radio & Electrical and Gorta Radiovision Service, both of which were located among the many refugee businesses that clustered around the shopping parades on Finchley Road between Swiss Cottage and Arkwright Road.

Refugee businesses that responded to demand by placing ads in the journal included pharmacists, opticians, tailors, watchmakers, chiropodists, photographers, shoe repairers and a considerable number of Continental food shops and delicatessen, which advertised sauerkraut and a variety of German sausages that would have seemed exotic in the culinary wasteland of austerity Britain. No account of the restaurants and cafés in Finchley Road would be complete without the most famous of the refugee meeting-places, the Cosmo Restaurant, which numbered the Nobel Prize-winning writer Elias Canetti and a crowd of British literati amongst its patrons and whose last refugee owners were the Mannheimer family, and, on the other side of Finchley Road, the Dorice, a favourite haunt of the Amadeus Quartet in their early days, run for many years by the motherly figure of Doris Balacs. Typical of the establishments advertising in some numbers by the early 1950s was Patisserie Weil, of West End Lane, NW6, which offered Mandelberg cheesecake, Viennese Apfelstrudel and Zwetschenkuchen amongst its Continental specialities.

Clothing was also a lively area, with a large number of milliners, dress- and corset-makers and other specialists in ladies' wear offering their services: an example at the higher end of the market was Bratherton Ltd of Elgin Avenue, W9, managed by Betty Pagel, formerly Wollstein, which announced in April 1948 that the latest Paris fashions in hats were now in stock. In north-west London, Mme H. Lieberg in Golders Green was the best known of the discreet specialists in ladies' foundation garments, though these ranged from ladies who worked from home in Golders Green (Mrs E. Sonnenfeld) or West Hampstead (Mrs F. Wiener) to major concerns like Silhouette, manufacturers some years later of the 'Little X' range. There were a surprising number of ads from furriers, one of the signs of an early degree of affluence amongst a section of the refugees; as early as October 1946, the journal carried ads from C.D. Goldberg of New Bond Street, as well as from D. Silberman of Canfield Gardens, NW6, and from April 1947 from Mirro Furs Ltd. of West End Lane, NW6, managed by A. Spiegel of Berlin (*Spiegel* is 'mirror' in English). Ads from travel agents, jewellers and hotels all testified to the spending power of at least some of the refugees, as consumer demand began to revive after the war.

The journal's 'Family Events' column filled with announcements of births, marriages, birthdays and wedding anniversaries. Four months after the first birth, in July 1946, came the first marriage notice, that of Artur Heichelheim and Ingeborg Markowitz, of Lyndhurst Road, NW3, along-side the eightieth birthday of Moritz Weindling, of Howitt Close, NW3. There were also death notices: it was not long before stonemasons, like Leo Horovitz of Fawley Road, NW6, began to advertise the memorial stones that would mark refugee graves in Hoop Lane and Pound Lane cemeteries. The 'Personal' column displayed numerous notices for potential marriage partners and lonely-hearts ads, as well as a sprinkling of ads from rather unappealing marriage bureaux. A sign of the change in the community's status, from refugees fleeing persecution to settled 'new citizens', was that in February 1949 these notices for marriage partners for the first time outnumbered the enquiries under 'Missing Persons' for those lost in the Holocaust. Among those seeking partners women predominated, with a proportion of widows that increased over the years and occasional divorcees. They very often expressed a preference for Continental partners from the same German-speaking background as themselves, and not infrequently requested responses from non-Orthodox men only. Those advertising regularly emphasized their culture, education and intellectual refinement, qualities they also demanded of respondents.

The training courses advertised, ranging from dressmaking to shorthand for foreigners, were clearly popular with refugees wishing either to provide themselves with a settled livelihood or to move up the occupational ladder. Particularly noteworthy were the classes in English, offered by the AJR's Employment Agency among others. The refugees' eagerness to master the English language showed once again that most of them were determined to integrate into English life, professionally, socially and often in their own homes. An ad in May 1950 publicized an AJR meeting at the Blue Danube Club in Finchley Road, where Dr Ernst Perl was to speak on 'How To Improve Your English'. This gave rise to some humorous reflections in Werner Rosenstock's 'Narrator' column, where he recalled how the refugees had arrived 'quite certain of their perfect command of the English language', and continued:

> Some, to be sure, have not made much progress since and still insist on 'speaking Miss X' (in the accusative) and on pronouncing the Home Office address as 'High Holl-born'. Others, however, and they are fortunately in the majority, have by now considerably broadened their knowledge; they are now much too far advanced as not to realise their shortcomings. Compared with other newcomers, Jews from Germany and Austria have not done so badly in their linguistic adaptation.

It was taken for granted here that linguistic integration was desirable, indeed inevitable, and the refugees' progress a matter for congratulation.

Dr Perl, who quoted Somerset Maugham's dictum that 'only card sharpers and diplomats can speak several languages with the same proficiency', predictably found that there was room for improvement in the English of the German-speaking Jews.[52] For conscientious refugees were able to master English grammar and spelling, but the characteristic refugee accent proved an insuperable problem, as its Germanic tones were almost impossible to eradicate. To this day, refugees who have lived here for over sixty years, who pride themselves on their integration into British life and who have long considered themselves British are irked by the readiness with which their accent betrays their foreign origins to British ears.

One of the principal indications of the intention to settle permanently in Britain was the change of name that thousands of refugees hastened to make in the years after the war. Many had already anglicized their names during the war, to disguise their 'German' origins or simply in despair at the inability of the linguistically challenged British to cope with foreign names. Refugees in fighting units of the armed forces formed a special category, as they were ordered to assume English names in case they were taken prisoner by the Germans. This saved the life of George Lane (Lanyi), a member of an elite German-speaking commando unit, who was captured on a mission in France on the eve of D-Day and questioned by Rommel himself. The Field Marshal promised Lane that he would not be executed, the usual fate of captured commandos, but became suspicious of his accent. Lane, who had undergone training in North Wales, explained his Hungarian-tinged accent away as Welsh. Charles Danson (Danielsohn) was also captured by the Germans and had to undergo an operation to remove a damaged eye; the doctor who operated on him warned him that he had spoken German under the anaesthetic, giving him to understand that he must make sure to speak it with an English accent, to match his assumed identity in captivity.[53]

The formal process of registering a change of name, usually by deed-poll, took place after the war, and was often associated with the taking of British citizenship. *AJR Information* published an article guiding readers eager to rename themselves through the bureaucratic procedures involved.[54] There were long lists of such changes in the columns of the local and national press, as well as in Home Office files and records. Very often they were relatively straightforward renderings of German-Jewish names into English: Abrahamsohn turned into Ambrose, Kantorowicz into Kay, Lachmann into Lawrence, Deutsch into Dunston, Pretzfelder into Preston, Spielmann into Spearman, Oppenheimer into Overman, Heine into Howard, Wiesengrund into Willis, Männlein into Manley, Tarnowski into Tarnesby. This occasionally made it hard to differentiate refugees from the British: F. Ransome's name appeared in the journal, in connection with translation work, but only when he mentioned his brother, Dr Ernst Ransohoff, did his original identity became plain.[55] Sometimes names were translated, Schwarz into Black being a frequent example; to turn Rosenberg into Montrose showed linguistic sophistication, as well as adding a touch of distinction. Many chose to discard their German-Jewish names as the cause of complications in daily life, others in order to mark a clean break between themselves and the countries that had disowned them.

Carl Flesch lists one witty fellow who called himself Anders ('different' in German), two brothers who divided the surname Schwarzschild between them by calling themselves Black and Shield respectively, and a soldier called Giebel who was refused permission by his wartime commanding officer to change his name to the alluring Clark Gable (Giebel).[56] Sometimes the change of name was drastic: Joachimsthal into Steele or Leipziger into Bright. Fred Egon Berliner from Vienna transformed himself improbably into Egon O'Hara,[57] a name that he may have adopted in the army, perhaps from a friend or from a family that had befriended him, as happened commonly. Claus Ascher, who fought in the same commando unit as George Lane, was deciding what to call himself when an Avro Anson flew past, and he became Colin Anson.

In the November 1956 issue of the journal alone, the 'Family Events' and 'Missing Persons' columns recorded the crisply British names of L. Kemp (Ludwig Kluger), Jim Grant (Gratz) and Ernest Long (Ernst Loewenstein). So common was this kind of anglicization by abbreviation that a letter to the editor extolling the virtues of monosyllabic names appeared in 1954; it was signed 'Sam Ham (formerly Siegfried Hamburger)'.[58] A number of businesses evidently found it more advantageous to trade under English names. L. Scheibe of Berlin, 'Continental upholstery and repairs', became Leslie Shirley Ltd, and A. Spiegel of Mirro Furs Ltd used the name Spencer when he added a dyeing and cleaning business; other firms took English-sounding abbreviations as names, like the Rilo Shirt Co., managed by Richard Loebl, formerly of Vienna's First District, or Wolco Ltd, a firm of builders and decorators run by K. Wolff and H. Cohn. To keep their refugee clientele, such firms were often keen to publicize their German or Austrian origins as well.

Among the refugees themselves, the subject of changing names gave rise to numerous jokes and was mostly treated humorously. Those who abandoned their Central European names seldom seem to have suffered much heart-searching over it; their life in Germany and Austria was over, and they were fully prepared to make the external adjustment to their identity necessary for life in Britain. The adoption of a new name symbolized their ready acceptance of settlement in Britain, as the end of the war had enabled them to lay the foundations for a fresh life and to create a new identity for themselves and their families. It signalled their adaptation to British society, while allowing them to maintain the Continental elements that continued to form the core of their social being. If, as Tony Kushner claims, changing a Jewish name to an English one was to many British right-wingers 'an outrageous state of affairs',[59] then the refugees themselves seem to have been blithely unaware of it; probably because they saw their new names as just another step along the road to integration and because there were few, if any, reports of objections from the British to these post-war changes of name.

The light-heartedness with which most refugees approached the subject was exemplified by a review of Norman Bentwich's book on refugees in the British armed forces, I Understand the Risks, which cited the case of a refugee named Tischler who wanted to become known as Thistlethwaite, but was persuaded to make do with Thompson.[60] Writing as 'Georg Sch. (future name G.B. Shaw)', one correspondent even had the temerity to address Werner Rosenstock as 'dear Dr Rosecane', at the end of a not entirely serious letter lamenting the old names:

> When, in 1939, I visited a Jewish cemetery in England for the first time, I met on the tombstones the familiar names, such as Holländer, Kempner, Rosenblüth, Karfunkel and Silberstein. Addressing myself I said: 'I like that. Not much difference to Berlin-Weissensee or Breslau-Cosel. Old names, full of flavour, taken from geography, botany and jewellery. I'll feel at home here after my earthly days.' But no. Only a few years will pass and there will be no Miss Edelstein any more, and no Mrs Morgenstern. They will be Miss Eden and Mrs Morgan.[61]

With most of his friends unrecognizable by name, the writer concluded that they would not even stick to their original initials were it not for the monograms on their linen.

The novelist Gabriele Tergit remained a lone voice when she pleaded for retention of the old names in an article entitled 'Please Keep Your Identity'.[62] A response from W. Katzenstein, writing from Canfield Gardens in the refugee heartland of NW6, dismissed Tergit's case as unconvincing.[63] He pointed out that Pereira and Rothschild, which Tergit had cited as names that no Jew could imagine changing, had themselves been adopted in Portugal and Germany respectively, products of Jewish integration into those societies. Her argument that name changes made it more difficult to trace relatives separated during the Nazi years was 'somewhat beside the point': 'Surely, to be traced easily is not the paramount concern of people who, without any intention of undignified assimilation, merely wish to integrate into the life of a new homeland?' This was the crux of the matter: whereas Tergit detected an inferiority complex behind the desire to change names, Katzenstein maintained that Jews who rid themselves of names that caused them difficulty in their social and professional life were 'thereby following only a time-honoured Jewish tradition'. For him, as for the great majority of the refugees, 'assimilation' was the norm, and nothing to be ashamed of; a Jew from Central Europe could assume an English name and still remain proud of what he was.

'What's in a name', mused Werner Rosenstock in 1959, reviewing a book on name changes among Jewish refugees in the USA.[64] He noted that these were more common among refugees in Britain than in America, an ethnically mixed society where exotic names abounded; in Britain, a more homogeneous society, there was pressure on the refugees to integrate to a greater extent, by adapting themselves to the practices and characteristics of the majority community. But he did not overlook the many refugees who retained their former names: those who felt that their name formed part of their personality, those who feared that changing names would be seen as an attempt to conceal their origins, or those who felt under an obligation to preserve the family name.

Some refugees felt that a British name sat badly alongside a foreign accent, but even that was no longer an issue for the following generation, whose first language was English. In terms of ease of integration, the refugees from Central Europe were at an advantage compared to subsequent waves of immigrants from the Third World, whose colour would continue to betray their origins down the generations. British-born children of refugee families have been able to present a convincingly British face to the world thanks to a new surname, in many cases becoming effectively indistinguishable from the native British.

NOTES

1. See especially T. Segev, *The Seventh Million: The Israelis and the Holocaust* (New York: Hill & Wang, 1994).
2. K. Gershon, *We Came as Children* (London: Gollancz, 1966); the raw pain comes across less strongly in the more recent collections of memories, B. Leverton and S. Lowensohn, *I Came Alone: Stories of the Kindertransport* (Sussex: The Book Guild, 1990), and M. Harris and D. Oppenheimer, *Into the Arms of Strangers: Stories of the Kindertransport* (London: Bloomsbury, 2000).
3. *AJR Information* (June 1956), p.6.
4. 'Twenty Years After: German Jews in England', *AJR Information* (September 1959), p.1.
5. Quoted in *AJR Information* (August 2005), p.11.
6. *AJR Information* (January 1946), p.5, (February 1946), pp.5 and 8.
7. *AJR Information* (June 1959), p.12, (August 1957), p.14.
8. *AJR Information* (January 1954), p.5. The article was taken, in translation, from the Berlin *Tagesspiegel* of 11 November 1953.
9. *AJR Information* (June 1949), p.3.
10. *AJR Information* (January 1955), p.8; (October 1958), p.8.
11. *AJR Information* (October 1958), p.11; (March 1957), p.10.
12. *AJR Information* (February 1953), p.7.
13. On the early post-war years, see P. Hennessy, *Never Again: Britain, 1945–51* (New York: Pantheon Books, 1994), and D. Kynaston, *Austerity Britain, 1945–51* (London: Bloomsbury, 2007). On the British economy in those years, see C. Barnett, *The Audit of War: The Illusion and Reality of Britain as a Great Nation* (London: Macmillan, 2001), and *The Lost Victory: British Dreams, British Realities 1945–1950* (London: Macmillan, 2005), also B. Alford, *British Economic Performance, 1945–1975* (Cambridge: Cambridge University Press, 1995).
14. On the 1950s and dawning consumer affluence, see P. Hennessy, *Having It So Good: Britain in the Fifties* (Harmondsworth: Penguin, 2006), J. Benson, *The Rise of Consumer Society in Britain, 1880–1980* (Harlow: Longman, 1994), and T. Judt, *Postwar: A History of Europe since 1945* (London: Heinemann, 2005), Chapter X, 'The Age of Affluence'.
15. *AJR Information* (April 1956), p.11; (June 1956), p.11.
16. Commercial ads appeared on the back page of the journal, with some, mostly for hotels, guesthouses and boarding houses on the preceding page. The classified ads (employment, accommodation, miscellaneous and personal) were on the preceding page, as were the 'Family Events' and 'Missing Persons' columns. Where ads on other pages are cited, references are given in footnotes.
17. See for example *AJR Information* (August 1952), pp.6f.
18. *AJR Information* (September 1959), p.10. Henlys Corner was the junction of Finchley Road and the North Circular Road.
19. *AJR Information* (January 1957), p.11.
20. *AJR Information* (December 1948), p.5.
21. *AJR Information* (May 1950), p.7.
22. In the same year the AJR set up a club for the over-40s, to meet the considerable demand from refugees who felt isolated and desired closer contact with those from a similar background.
23. See the interview with Henry Wuga in the 'Refugee Voices' collection.
24. *AJR Information* (January 1946), p.8.
25. *AJR Information* (July/August 1959), p.19; (September 1959), p.9.
26. *AJR Information* (May 1957), p.7.
27. *AJR Information* (April 1956), p.11.
28. *AJR Information* (November 1954), p.6.
29. *AJR Information* (July 1946), p.7.
30. *AJR Information* (March 1962), p.12.
31. See for example the report on an AJR meeting in Leeds, *AJR Information* (June 1953), p.7, which gives a snapshot of communal life at that time.
32. See the interview with Peter Pulzer in the 'Refugee Voices' collection.
33. *AJR Information* (January 1951), p.7.
34. *AJR Information* (July 1955), p.9.
35. *AJR Information* (June 1953), p.6; (July 1956), p.12; (November 1956), p.11.

36. *AJR Information* (October 1959), p.7.

37. See the obituary, *AJR Information* (July/August 1959), p.10.

38. *AJR Information* (January 1946), p.7.

39. *AJR Information* (August 1955), p.5. The author was L.K. Sonneborn, a leading member of the Manchester group.

40. *AJR Information* (May 1962), p.15.

41. *AJR Information* (January 1962), p.11.

42. I observed this at first hand. My father established an import/export business in London, Arthur Grunfeld & Co., drawing on experience acquired through the family business in Vienna, to trade across the country and abroad in smokers' requisites, fancy goods and stationery.

43. H. Loebl, 'Refugees from the Third Reich and Industry in the Depressed Areas of Britain', in W. Mosse (ed.), *Second Chance: Two Centuries of German-speaking Jews in the United Kingdom* (Tübingen: Mohr, 1991), pp.379–403. This volume also contains articles on refugee engineers and on German Jews in British industry.

44. *AJR Information* (December 1950), p.5. On PEM, see T. Willimowski, '*Emigrant sein ist ja kein Beruf*': *Das Leben des Journalisten Pem* (Berlin: Wissenschaftlicher Verlag Berlin, 2007).

45. *AJR Information* (May 1946), p.5.

46. *AJR Information* (May 1948), p.6.

47. *AJR Information* (May 1948), p.7.

48. *AJR Information* (June 1948), p.3.

49. See H. Feidel-Mertz and A. Hammel, 'Integration and Formation of Identity: Exile Schools in Great Britain', *Shofar: An Interdisciplinary Journal of Jewish Studies*, 23, 1 (2004), pp.71–84.

50. On Camphill, see J. Ritchie, 'Dr Karl König and the Camphill Community', *Yearbook of the Research Centre for German and Austrian Exile Studies*, 10 (2008), pp.169–82.

51. See Chapter 5 above.

52. *AJR Information* (May 1950), pp.2 and 6; (June 1950), p.7.

53. Interview with Charles Danson in the 'Refugee Voices' collection.

54. *AJR Information* (July 1948), p.4.

55. Letter to the editor from F. Ransome, *AJR Information* (January 1956), p.11. Fred Ransome, who died in London in 1957 aged 65, had trained for the Bar there before the First World War, returning at the outbreak of conflict to Germany, where he became a translator and court interpreter in Berlin. After 1933 he re-emigrated to South Africa, then to London after the war, working for several years for the Allied Control Commission in Germany; there, as later in London, he applied his gift for translation to legal texts, including the Federal Indemnification Law, the most important piece of German restitution legislation (*AJR Information* [October 1957], p.10).

56. C. Flesch, *"Where Do You Come from?" Hitler Refugees in Great Britain Then and Now: The Happy Compromise!* (London: Pen Press, 2001), pp.77f.

57. *AJR Information* (March 1946), p.7.

58. *AJR Information* (October 1954), p.8.

59. T. Kushner, *The Persistence of Prejudice: Antisemitism in British Society during the Second World War* (Manchester and New York: Manchester University Press, 1989), p.91.

60. *AJR Information* (February 1951), p.5.

61. *AJR Information* (April 1950), p.7.

62. *AJR Information* (April 1948), p.5. Tergit (Elise Reifenberg, née Hirschmann) had herself changed her name in Germany for professional reasons.

63. *AJR Information* (May 1948), pp.5f.

64. *AJR Information* (May 1959), p.8.

13. Women refugees contributed to the war effort. Lorraine Allard (Lore Sulzbacher) served in the ATS. Courtesy of the Jewish Museum.

14. Robert Parker saw service with Seventh Armoured Corps in the advance into Germany, 1944–45. Courtesy of the Jewish Museum.

15. Josephine Bruegel, who had studied medicine in Prague, trained as a nurse during the war. Courtesy of the Jewish Museum.

16. Home from home? Refugees skiing on Primrose Hill, London, 1940. Courtesy of the Jewish Museum.

17. Two refugee families in West Hampstead, London, 1943. Courtesy of the Jewish Museum.

18. Certificate of naturalization granting British citizenship to Robert Simpson. Courtesy of the Jewish Museum.

19. Gerda Kaufmann with friends, Fulham, London, c. 1950. Courtesy of the Jewish Museum.

20. Trude Grenville and Klary Friedl walking on Regent Street, 1950s. In the possession of the author.

21. The house in Maresfield Gardens, Hampstead, where Sigmund Freud, his wife Martha (pictured) and his daughter Anna settled after emigrating from Vienna to London in 1938 is now the Freud Museum. Courtesy of the Freud Museum.

22. Former refugees, left to right, Trude Rothschild, Martha Goodman and Edith Rothschild, outside Swiss Cottage underground station, 1964. Courtesy of the Jewish Museum.

23. The coffee bar of the Cosmo restaurant, Swiss Cottage, London, 1965. Courtesy of Madeleine Mannheimer.

24. Doris Balacs (centre) at the Dorice restaurant, Swiss Cottage, London. Courtesy of Doris Balacs.

25. Ruth Sellers, née Hirsch, celebrates the Queen's Golden Jubilee, Stock, Essex, 2002. On the back of the photo is the inscription 'Continental Briton'. In the possession of the author.

7

Refugee Culture

The richness of German-Jewish culture has been the subject of so many studies that it needs little further introduction here: that it produced Heinrich Heine, Karl Marx, Sigmund Freud, Gustav Mahler and Albert Einstein during a cultural efflorescence that lasted only from the late eighteenth century until 1933 speaks for itself. The cultural achievements of the German-speaking refugees who came to Britain have also been very amply documented.[1] The purpose of this chapter is consequently not to roll out the familiar parade of celebrated refugees who made their names in the arts and sciences, academia and the world of culture generally. Rather, it focuses on the broader social stratum of the assimilated and educated Jewish refugees from Germany and Austria, who had brought a strikingly high level of German-language culture with them and from whom the prominent achievers in Britain emerged like peaks from a high plateau. This chapter covers a wide socio-cultural spectrum, but one that is more difficult to analyse than are famous individuals, since in the post-war years it drew on many thousands of mostly unknown refugees, with little public profile but with a distinctive and distinguished collective culture.

AJR Information, the journal that served this group, was one of the principal conduits by which they remained linked to the German-speaking culture of Central Europe that was disseminated abundantly in its pages. The journal contained any amount of evidence of the pride that the Jewish refugees in Britain took in the cultural achievements of their native communities. Rabbi Leo Baeck, the spiritual leader of the Jews from Germany, stated programmatically that *Geist*, the world of the mind, had always flourished in their communities; a love of art and learning and a strong sense of creativity had fuelled an intellectual dynamism that had given the name 'German Jew' its particular lustre in the world.[2] When Georg Landauer, a leading German Zionist, died in Israel in 1954, Hans Reichmann, chairman of the AJR, wrote a tribute almost exclusively devoted to Landauer's tenacious defence of the high standing of German-Jewish culture:

> Georg Landauer saw it as one of his responsibilities to secure for the great past and the achievements of the German Jews – a community

from which have sprung so many people who have enriched Jewish life in the world and in Israel across many spheres – the respect due to them by virtue of their past and their achievements. If anyone belittled the cultural heritage of the German Jews and sought to disregard the high standards that they were entitled to demand, it offended Georg Landauer's sense of justice, his feeling for tradition and honourableness ... His very last letter to us was devoted to his concern for the preservation of our cultural heritage.[3]

The preservation of their cultural heritage was a central preoccupation of the refugees. Characteristically, the agenda of the AJR's General Meeting for 1954 boasted an address by the scholar Rabbi Ignaz Maybaum on the subject 'Heritage and Obligation: Our Responsibility for the Spiritual Values of German Jewry'.[4]

The principal institutions founded by the refugees in Britain that remain to this day dedicated to the preservation of the culture and history of the Jews from the German-speaking lands are the London branch of the Leo Baeck Institute, which is responsible for the Institute's Yearbook; and the Wiener Library, which was brought over to London by its founder Alfred Wiener in 1939, and is the oldest established resource in the world for research on the Holocaust and National Socialism. The Wiener Library, associated with such names as Walter Laqueur, Eva G. Reichmann, C.C. Aronsfeld and Ilse Wolff, as well as Dr Wiener himself, remains a living repository of material relating to German-Jewish history.[5] The Leo Baeck Institute was expressly created by the Council of Jews from Germany, the organization that represented the refugees from Germany worldwide, as an institution which 'by research work and publications, is to save for posterity the cultural heritage of German Jewry'.[6] For many years, the editor of the yearbook of the LBI was Robert Weltsch, and the director of the London branch for nearly forty years was Arnold Paucker; the eminent refugee historians Peter Pulzer and John Grenville are closely associated with its work.

In July 1955, a front-page article in *AJR Information* proudly announced the setting up of the Leo Baeck Institute, which would record the history of German Jewry and uphold and preserve its heritage, going back to the emancipation without which modern Jewry would not have been possible: 'German Jewry had created unique institutions which were destroyed by the catastrophe brought about by National Socialism; their achievements and their traditions, however, must not perish and must not be forgotten.' The Council of Jews from Germany also considered the preservation of the cultural achievements of German Jewry to be among its prime obligations, as the Council's president, Leo Baeck, made clear in his presidential address

to the Council when it met in London in August 1956. He stressed that 'the
Jews from Germany had built up the Council not only in order to help one
another but also, and in the first place, because they felt an urge to preserve
and develop their precious heritage'.[7]

Looking back at the end of the 1950s, Werner Rosenstock drew a balance between the material and the cultural achievements of the Jewish
refugees from Germany. Of the four paramount tasks that had faced the
refugees in Britain after the war, three were material in nature: the consolidation of their political status in their new homeland through their naturalization; the campaign to secure restitution from Germany; and the creation of social welfare schemes to meet the needs of elderly, infirm and
impoverished victims of Nazi persecution. 'But man does not live by bread
alone', Rosenstock continued. 'Our spiritual heritage, shaped by Jewish life
in Central Europe in the course of five generations, must also find its
expression'; hence the decision by the Council of Jews from Germany in
1954 to set up the LBI. He concluded by stressing that that cultural heritage played a key part in the successful integration of the refugee community into British society: 'The integration of the immigrants into their
new environment would be unrealistic and impracticable if they tried to
shake off their past. Only by remaining aware of the forces which formed
them can they retain their spiritual balance and be accepted in their country of resettlement.'[8] A striking vision of Continental immigrants retaining
their own social culture and by that very token achieving acceptance in
British society, thus creating an identity which balanced Central European
and British components harmoniously.

'Books Have Their Fate' was the title of a moving confession by the
writer Friedrich Walter of his abiding passion for the literary culture in
which he had grown up.[9] In it he recalled the first German book that he
had bought in England in 1940, on leave in London in British army uniform. It was a paperback copy of Wagner's *Ring des Nibelungen* which, he
remembered nearly twenty years later, had been published by Schott in
Mainz and bought at a bookshop in Dessau. What drew Walter to the book
was not his love of Wagner, long since abandoned, but the silent testimony the volume bore to the deep emotional hold on German Jewry of its
dual allegiance to Judaism and to Germany and German high culture. The
book contained the inscription 'Der Herr segne und behüte Dich' ('May
the Lord bless and keep you'), addressed in German and Hebrew by a
Jewish mother to her son when he left for the front in August 1914, and
it had accompanied him until the end of the war; in it he had carefully
noted the Wagner operas that he had heard every year on leave in Germany.

It was this apparently inextricable interlinking of the German cultural

tradition with Judaism, so characteristic of German Jewry, that had attracted Walter with such force that he spent a whole shilling from his meagre
pay on the book. Since then, whenever he visited antiquarian bookshops
specializing in German books, he always looked first for the names of their
former owners, discovering a proud but melancholy list of unknown
German Jews who had inscribed their names on the entire canon of
German classics, from Goethe and the Romantics to Paul Heyse and
Theodor Fontane. The works on the bookshops' shelves mirrored an entire
era of German-Jewish intellectual, cultural and social history; and the
Jewish surnames of their owners 'spoke so eloquently, insistently and movingly' of the fate of their community, of its love of Germany and of a devotion to German-language culture that even forced emigration could not
eradicate. Walter reflected sadly that much of German literature, banned by
the Nazis, had survived only in exile: the works of the once renowned
writers of the *fin de siècle*, of the Expressionists and the Jewish novelists like
Jakob Wassermann or Georg Hermann lived on tenuously in Britain, where
the culture they represented had found a provisional haven.

The libraries from which these books came, almost all sold off by
refugees re-emigrating to America or simply too poor to keep them,
included the standard editions of Goethe, Schiller, Heine and modern
classics like Ibsen and Gerhart Hauptmann; these are familiar to anyone
who knows refugee living-rooms with their imposingly laden bookcases.
The very atmosphere and furnishings of those living-rooms seemed to
breathe the culture of the German-Jewish symbiosis, destroyed in its
homeland by twelve years of Nazi barbarism but still lovingly conserved in
exile, as the educationalist Nelly Wolffheim noted in her obituary of Clara
Sander, an important figure in the German women's movement who had
died in Britain in 1958: 'The very special atmosphere that surrounded her
never failed to impress me, when I entered her large living room, that
space in which the culture of a vanished era was preserved.'[10]

Indisputably, Nazi persecution and the Holocaust had had an indelible
impact on the refugees' attitude to the social culture that they had imbibed
in Germany and Austria before emigration. When Bruno Woyda represented the refugees from Germany in 1959 at the consecration of a Jewish
community centre on the site in Berlin where the Fasanenstraße Synagogue
had stood until the 'Kristallnacht' pogrom, his mind inevitably went back
to the destruction of Berlin's synagogues in November 1938: 'Unforgotten,
unforgettable memories will be alive till the last breath within the Jewish
refugees who grew up in Germany in the firm conviction that the barbarism of previous centuries could never recur in the civilized democracy
of the twentieth century, yet had later to face the unsurpassed horror of the

Nazi abyss.'[11] Many assimilated Jews had trusted almost as an article of faith in the liberal, progressive and highly civilized culture that they had partaken of in Germany, but, as Woyda conceded, that trust had suffered a shattering blow and could never be resurrected as it had been before 1933.

This did not mean that the German-speaking Jews rejected the entire German-Jewish culture of their homelands, seeing that cultural symbiosis as a historical aberration; in a sense, that would have proved Hitler right. When the Council of Jews from Germany began to be active in the cultural field, it very soon took the view that German Jews were defined by their culture, an inheritance that kept them in some measure separate from the Jewries of their countries of emigration, including Anglo-Jewry. The dry language of a report on Council business could not conceal the pride that the German-speaking refugees still took in their heritage and the degree to which it constituted the core of their identity: 'Without wishing to advocate any segregation of German Jews from the Jewish communities in whose midst they were now living, the Council took the view that German Jews can serve the wider community best if they are conscious of their history and if they realize the special position arising from their past.'[12] This was very far from jettisoning their past as irrevocably tainted with the evil of German National Socialism. But neither could that past ever be seen separately from the cruel caesura of 1933 and the years of suffering and loss inflicted on German Jews by their fellow countrymen.

Writing on the centenary of the birth of his father, Professor Moritz Schäfer (1857–1930), Ernst Schäfer recalled him as 'a man typical of those qualities which ... are characteristic features of German Jewry, both in the Jewish and the German sense'.[13] The details of Professor Schäfer's career recorded a life of academic achievement, of dedication to his profession and of proud and selfless public service, all qualities highly valued among German Jewry: before he became the first Jewish teacher to be appointed Oberlehrer at his Berlin Gymnasium (grammar school), he had to serve nine years in the subordinate post of Hilfslehrer.

He also shared the widespread and almost unquestioning faith in integration as the right path for German Jewry, and followed the line of the Centralverein deutscher Staatsbürger jüdischen Glaubens (Central Union of German Citizens of the Jewish Faith), the organization to which most assimilated German Jews belonged, which claimed for Jews the right to be considered fully equal German citizens, though of a different religious denomination: 'In his capacity as a master in a German school he never felt any conflict between his pronounced Jewishness and his quality as a "German citizen of the Jewish faith". The ideology of the "Centralverein" was the hallmark of his outlook.' But three years after his death his widow was to thank providence for having spared him the shattering shock of Hitler's assumption of power. Between those two poles lay both the greatness of German Jewry's achievement and its ultimate failure.

AJR Information refrained from taking a line on the highly controversial question of Jewish 'assimilation' into German society. In the wake of the Holocaust, some of its correspondents saw the attempt at social integration in Germany as a hideous mistake, the result of a self-deception that blinded many German Jews to the forces of anti-Semitism that were gathering to destroy them; for those who took this view, the culture produced by the German-Jewish symbiosis was little better than a decorative fraud. But most of the material in the journal proceeded from the standpoint that there had been much of value in pre-Hitler German-Jewish culture and that its heritage should be treasured and preserved in exile. There was an unmistakable note of pride in the many articles devoted to the intellectual and cultural achievements of the German-speaking Jews.

A survey of two areas, literature and music, will give an indication of the depth of culture among the refugee community. Literature, it must be said, was not a field where refugees were especially successful, since most established writers found it almost impossible to change languages after their emigration and to tailor their writing to a British readership. The towering exception was Arthur Koestler, the Budapest-born ex-Communist whose route to Britain via a death cell in one of General Franco's prisons set him apart from the general run of the refugees.[14] But even the much-translated Stefan Zweig, who was in Britain from 1934 to 1941, struggled to establish himself, while a number of distinguished writers like Hilde Spiel and Robert Neumann returned to the Continent, gaining greater recognition in the German-speaking world.[15] Elias Canetti, winner of the Nobel Prize for literature, continued to write in German and remained relatively unknown in Britain, eventually leaving for Switzerland.

Robert Neumann, who had made his name as a literary parodist, was as well equipped as any for the change of language, and he did indeed achieve some success with novels in English, especially *Children of Vienna* (1946). But Neumann too chose to move to Switzerland, and is now almost forgotten in Britain. Many other writers fared much worse. The great theatre critic Alfred Kerr cut a sad figure in exile, and the inimitable Austrian poet Theodor Kramer survived obscurely as a librarian in Guildford. The gifted Viennese writer Mela Hartwig, sensing the impossibility of a literary career in Britain, launched herself afresh as an artist under her married name Mela Spira, achieving success in a field not limited by language. Only in the special area of self-mocking humour did refugees gain early recognition among the British, most famously with the Hungarian George Mikes' *How*

To Be an Alien (1946), which inspired a series of exercises in affectionate Continental bafflement at British ways.[16]

Despite this, the level of literary culture in *AJR Information* was of an admirably high standard. Book reviews formed a substantial part of each issue, and a series of stylish and knowledgeable reviewers graced the journal's pages. One of these was Lutz Weltmann, born in west Prussia in 1901 and brought up in Berlin, where he became a noted theatre critic and literary journalist. After emigrating in 1939 and serving in the British army, he taught at grammar schools in the London area and lectured at North Western Polytechnic, not always happily according to his obituary.[17] Weltmann faced the usual difficulties of adapting to British conditions, but ended up as a valuable cultural intermediary between Germany and his adopted country, translating works by English authors and contributing to German literary periodicals. It was as a reviewer, however, that he came into his own, for he had the ability to focus his extensive knowledge succinctly, intelligently and readably into the short pieces required for *AJR Information*.

In the 1950s Weltmann reviewed a very large number of writers, such as the novelist Lion Feuchtwanger (April 1953), the poet Rudolf Borchardt (June 1957), and the playwright Paul Kornfeld, in a well-informed piece on three Prague writers. In the last of these Weltmann displayed his customary ability to empathize with his subjects, especially Kornfeld, who had once advised him 'Beware of everything that you find too easy', but could not be persuaded to emigrate in time.[18] Weltmann's work in the theatre equipped him to write expert and often moving appreciations of figures like the great director Max Reinhardt (October 1953) or the famous actor Albert Bassermann, whose performances Weltmann recalled, from Leopold Jessner's production of Schiller's drama *Wilhelm Tell* to the Michael Powell/Emeric Pressburger film *The Red Shoes*.[19]

Weltmann's familiarity with English culture was on show in an amusing review of an English translation of the nonsense poet Christian Morgenstern's *Der Mondschaf*, in which he also recalled several recitals of Morgenstern's verse, including one that interspersed the famous *Galgenlieder* with short extracts from Kafka. His conclusion was characteristically perceptive: whereas English nonsense humour was 'a humour of things', Morgenstern's was 'a humour of ideas, where every word has an idea at its core. It seems that the English like their nonsensical humour pure, not charged with deeper meaning'.[20]

Another piece that combined the two cultures was Weltmann's impressively knowledgeable appreciation of Siegfried Trebitsch, the translator of Bernard Shaw, who died in Zurich in 1956. His account of Trebitsch's career began with the encouragement he had received from the poet Rilke as a young man and went on to a fascinating and authoritative survey of Trebitsch's involvement with Shaw's plays, which eventually conquered the German stage through Victor Barnowsky's Berlin production of *Pygmalion* with Tilla Durieux. Weltmann described graphically his own involvement with a Shaw/Trebitsch production: 'Condensing for Barnowsky's production of Shaw's "Biological Pentateuch" for two evenings, with the knowledge that Shaw was against it and that Trebitsch did not risk committing himself, was the most difficult job in my theatrical career.'[21]

Weltmann was well able to review modern English writers, as a piece from October 1951 on Christopher Fry demonstrated. He recalled having reviewed Fry's *The Firstborn* four years earlier, when he was unknown; now Fry was a leading dramatist, and Weltmann praised *A Sleep of Prisoners*, comparing it aptly to Eliot's *Murder in the Cathedral*. Weltmann was an acknowledged expert on Shakespeare and, as the English representative of the German Shakespeare Society, was invited to address the Society's annual meeting in April 1957 on the 'Development of Shakespeare's Portrait in England'. His exceptional range was demonstrated by a scholarly piece on the figure of the Golem, complete with references to the German poets Achim von Arnim and Annette von Droste-Hülshoff, to Gogol, and to the related figures of Pygmalion's statue and the robot;[22] and a piece on Freud, which showed him to be familiar both with the latest psychoanalytical studies and with the interrelationship between literature, mythology and psychoanalysis, in German literature (Stefan Zweig, Thomas Mann) and in English (the Auden/Isherwood *Ascent of F6*).[23]

What would have struck a special chord with his readers was Weltmann's ability to evoke the books and writers of the immediate pre-Nazi past, an era that had been obliterated in Germany by the banning or burning of the books and the expulsion or extermination of the writers, but which lived on in the cultural memory of the refugees. He brought to life figures like the poet Oskar Loerke, whom he remembered from the offices of the great Jewish publishing house S. Fischer in 1938, ill and suffering.[24] In a memorable piece entitled 'The Dead Speak to the Living', Weltmann surveyed recent posthumous publications of writers who had not survived the war, like Alfred Wolfenstein, who committed suicide in Paris, and whom Weltmann had known well in Berlin; and the poet Gertrud Kolmar, who was deported from Berlin in 1943 and of whom Weltmann said that she should have inherited the mantle of Else Lasker-Schüler.[25] The works of these German-Jewish writers lived on through the exposure given them in the columns of *AJR Information*, even though the writers themselves and the culture they represented had vanished from central Europe.[26]

Other literary reviewers of high quality writing for the journal included Friedrich Walter, Ernst Kahn and the widely talented Egon Larsen. It
could also count on the services of historians like Erich Eyck, Hans
Liebeschütz and Bernhard Reichenbach, the economist Leon Zeitlin, the art
critic Alfons Rosenberg, the music critic H.W. Freyhan and the orientalist
Erwin I.J. Rosenthal, as well as early experts on the Holocaust like H.G.
Adler and Eva G. Reichmann, whose book on National Socialism was
reviewed by the celebrated sociologist Norbert Elias. In the issue of
February 1960 readers could enjoy reviews by Egon Larsen, by Ernst G.
Lowenthal on events in Germany, by Ida Herz, a long-time correspondent
of Thomas Mann's, and by Peter Zadek, a young refugee theatre director
about to embark on a triumphant career back in Germany; the following
issue contained pieces by C.V. Wedgwood on Schiller, by Alan Bullock and
Leonard G. Montefiore on Dr Alfred Wiener, and by C.C. Aronsfeld and the
noted Jewish genealogist Jacob Jacobson. By any standards a feast.

Books played a central part in refugee life: in January 1953 the AJR's
Social Services Department opened its own library of German books, to be
lent free of charge and intended particularly for elderly members less
familiar with English. Specialist booksellers were prominent among the
journal's regular advertisers: Hans Preiss in Bury Place, WC1, R. & E. Steiner
in Gloucester Terrace, W2, Lola Mayer in Lanhill Road, W9, and, most
famous of the German-language second-hand bookshops, Libris in
Boundary Road, NW8, a Mecca for academics and bibliophiles run from
1945 to 1971 by Joseph Suschitzky. No one who bought books at Dillon's
University Bookshop in Malet Street (now Waterstone's) would easily forget the formidable figure of Eva Dworetzki, who moved to its German section in 1959 from the well-known bookshop Bumpus.

Like Friedrich Walter, the novelist Gabriele Tergit was a lover of antiquarian book-dealers; in 1958 she wrote an article celebrating the sixtieth
anniversary of the founding in Berlin of the famous firm Breslauer &
Meyer, which Martin Breslauer restarted in Bloomsbury when he fled to
London in 1937 and which his son continued after Breslauer's death in the
Blitz in 1940.[27] The respect for books that was, according to Tergit, so
deeply ingrained in the Jews from Germany made refugees prominent
among London's book-dealers. An example was the music publisher and
antique book-dealer Otto Haas, who had run the antique book-dealership
of Leo Liepmannssohn in Berlin, which he re-established under his own
name after emigrating to London in 1936; the firm was acquired in 1955
by another refugee, Albi Rosenthal, who had originally set up the company that bore his name in Oxford in 1941. As is well known, British publishing was transformed by refugees like George Weidenfeld, Paul Hamlyn,

André Deutsch, Béla Horovitz (Phaidon Press), Walter Neurath (Thames and Hudson) and Tom Maschler.

Books also helped to cement the relationship between the refugees and their British hosts. As early as 1946, *AJR Information* reported that some 6,000 German books had been presented by Mrs Regina Kantorowicz and her two sons to King's College London. The library had belonged to her late husband, and his widow had brought them to Britain in 1939. The gift had been made 'in memory of the late Dr Ludwig Kantorowicz and in gratitude for the asylum the donors have found in this country'.[28] Later that year the journal announced that the music library of the musicologist Paul Hirsch, 'the completest and most important working collection of musical scores and literature in private hands', brought over to Cambridge by its owner when he emigrated in 1936, had been acquired by the British Museum, whose own music library thus became 'the most comprehensive in the world'. Agreeing to a grant of £60,000 towards the price of £120,000, the chancellor of the exchequer stated in parliament that the price was substantially less than Hirsch could have obtained elsewhere, 'and his offer, therefore, represents an act of generous gratitude to his adopted country which I am sure the House would wish to acknowledge'.[29] That the gift more than made good the damage inflicted on the British Museum's music collection by German bombing added to its symbolic significance in refugee eyes.

The importance of music in refugee life is well known, given the richness of the German and Austrian musical traditions from which they came. Many refugees were from a milieu suffused with musical culture, where music was part of daily life, and they were used to attending recitals, concerts and operas on a scale unfamiliar to the British. It was a living culture that they had brought with them, its influence still clear in such evocations of its roots as H.W. Freyhan's tribute to the conductor Bruno Walter on his seventieth birthday: 'Vivid memories reappear of unforgettable opera nights and concerts in Europe before the war. Indeed, to us Bruno Walter represents so much that was good and beautiful in those days; this loveable artist is one of the symbols of that past musical glory that was once in Berlin, Munich, Leipzig, Vienna, Salzburg.'[30]

There was hardly a sphere of British life that the refugees enriched more than music. Both Glyndebourne and the Edinburgh Festival were indebted to the contributions of refugees: Fritz Busch and Carl Ebert were instrumental in creating Glyndebourne, and Rudolf Bing was a key figure in both. Refugee musicians included the violinist Max Rostal, the pianist Franz Osborn, the pianist/composer Franz Reizenstein and the three refugee members of the Amadeus Quartet; conductors like Karl Rankl, the

first Musical Director of the Royal Opera House, Covent Garden, and Walter
Goehr; composers like Berthold Goldschmidt, Mátyás Seiber and Hans Gál;
and musicologists like Egon Wellesz and Otto Erich Deutsch. Through his
work at the BBC's Music Division, Hans Keller played a pivotal role in
British musical life, while refugee commentators like Peter Stadlen and
Mosco Carner influenced public attitudes and tastes. The music publishers
Boosey & Hawkes employed a gifted trio of refugee experts, Alfred Kalmus,
Erwin Stein and Ernst Roth, the last of whom rose to become chairman.
Probably the best-known refugee in the musical field was the tenor
Richard Tauber. When he died in 1948, *AJR Information* published an appre-
ciation by Magnus Davidsohn, Cantor at the New Liberal Jewish
Congregation (later Belsize Square Synagogue), who had first met the 9-
year-old Tauber in 1901, at his mother's funeral at the Fasanenstraße
Synagogue in Berlin.[31]

The extent to which musical culture permeated the lives of the mass of
ordinary refugees can be gauged by the wealth of items in the journal
relating to music. Advertisements for concerts and recitals appeared frequently. The very first issue carried a report on 'the by now almost traditional A.J.R. concert', which had filled the Phoenix Theatre to capacity in
November 1945. The conductor was the refugee Fritz Berend (who had
participated in the most notable contribution of British musicians to the
war effort, Dame Myra Hess's Lunch-Hour Concerts at the National
Gallery), with his International Chamber Orchestra, leader Norbert
Brainin, later of the Amadeus Quartet. With Franz Osborn at the piano, it
was hardly surprising that this was a sell-out.[32] The next AJR concert, in
December 1946 at the same venue, followed a similar pattern, with Berend
conducting and Reizenstein at the piano.

Local musical events were also advertised, for example the chamber
music and song recital held by the AJR's Golders Green Group at the
Hodford Hall in Golders Green in February 1946, with Berend at the
piano, Martin Lovatt, the non-refugee member of the Amadeus Quartet, on
the cello, and the soprano Inge Markowitz.[33] Outside London, AJR's
Manchester group organized a celebrity concert in March 1950, featuring
Max Rostal and the soprano Irene Eisinger. The journal was swift to inform
readers of refugee achievements; they were doubtless gratified to learn that
Norbert Brainin had been awarded the prestigious Carl Flesch Medal in
1946.[34] The journal first mentioned the Amadeus Quartet in an advertisement for a charity concert at the Wigmore Hall in May 1949 for Self Aid
of Refugees, a smaller refugee organization that was later absorbed into the
AJR.[35] Self Aid's annual concerts at the Wigmore Hall became an important
item in the refugee calendar. According to the journal, the concert held in

December 1954 'kept up a tradition by which these annual functions have become an artistic and social event for the Community'; the concert featured Franz Osborn and the Amadeus Quartet and reached its high-point with a 'delightful' performance of Schubert's 'Trout' Quintet.[36] The concert for 1955 featured the Melos Ensemble, and that for 1957, conducted by Peter Gellhorn, another distinguished refugee, raised the not inconsiderable sum of £5,000 for Self Aid.[37]

By 1967 the concerts had outgrown the Wigmore Hall and moved to the larger venue of the Queen Elizabeth Hall, which enthusiastic refugees promptly filled to capacity; Max Rostal made his first appearance in Britain after a long interval, Elisabeth Söderström sang Schubert and Beethoven, and £7,000 was raised.[38] As their economic position improved, refugees formed a significant contingent among audiences at musical events in London, especially the Wigmore Hall, which came to hold a special place in their affections. They also came to love British artists like Kathleen Ferrier, sadly missed after her early death, but fondly remembered by AJR members for the 'unforgettable' recordings of Mahler that she made with Bruno Walter.[39] The cellist Jacqueline du Pré was later to enjoy similar popularity among discerning refugees.

Classical music formed a regular accompaniment to life in a refugee milieu. In 1958 the homes for elderly refugees which the AJR co-managed with the Central British Fund celebrated the festival of Hanukah with concerts of high quality: at Leo Baeck House in The Bishop's Avenue, N2, Franz Reizenstein played; at Otto Schiff House in Netherhall Gardens, NW3, Johanna Metzger-Lichtenstern sang, accompanied by her husband Paul Lichtenstern, both of whom were regulars at refugee musical events; and at Otto Hirsch House in Priory Road, Kew, there was a concert by the Chandos Ensemble.[40] When civic dignitaries visited the homes, they were treated to high culture: in March 1960, the mayor and mayoress of Finchley heard trios by Mozart and Mendelssohn at Leo Baeck House, 'beautifully rendered' by Natalia Karpf and her London Alpha Trio, and the previous month the mayor and mayoress of Richmond heard piano works by Schubert, Beethoven and Chopin at Otto Hirsch House.[41]

A number of advertisements in the journal showed that music was woven into the fabric of refugee life. There was a brisk trade between those requiring instruments and those offering them for sale: in July 1947 a pianist wanted a 'good upright piano. German make', and on the same page a Bechstein grand in perfect condition was offered for sale, while in October 1952 two violins were on sale, with a lute in its case thrown in for good measure. In December 1951 a Blüthner grand piano was offered to let, while few British landlords would have thought of advertising a room to let with a piano as a main attraction, as a refugee advertiser with a Primrose Hill telephone number did in August 1958.

Music teachers offered their services in abundance in the 1950s: they included Helga Lewin, a piano teacher with German qualifications who had trained at the Stern'sches Conservatorium and was now living in St Gabriel's Road, NW2 (October 1959), and Alice Schäffer, the holder of a German State Diploma as a singing teacher, now of Belsize Park, NW3 (December 1956). Some of these were musicians of considerable standing in their own right: Hans Block of Hampstead, who advertised in September 1956 as a qualified piano teacher with his own German and foreign [sic] methods, gave a recital at the Wigmore Hall two months later, with a programme of Beethoven, Mozart, Schubert and Chopin; and Paul Blumenfeld of Mowbray Road, NW6, who offered 'cello lessons and chamber music' in June 1954, was a member of Dr Oscar Adler's Adler String Quartet alongside Hans Keller. Alice Schäffer also gave a recital to the AJR Club (set up by the AJR for elderly and lonely members), where her rendering of lieder by Schubert and Brahms 'left an indelible impression on the large and grateful audience'.[42]

One can document the refugees' deep involvement with music into the new millennium. In January 2005, Heinz Liebrecht, a refugee and music-lover from Mannheim who had lived in Holly Mount in Hampstead for sixty-two years, died aged 96. He had contributed as a factory worker to the war effort, while at the same time he and the musician family with whom he then shared his house 'regularly packed their home to the rafters with audiences who came to hear their chamber music concerts'. After the war, he set up an agricultural engineering business, which he moved to Norfolk in the 1970s. There he sought to build a wider audience for chamber music by founding, aged 80, the Society for the Promotion of the Arts in North Norfolk. At 90 he was awarded the MBE for services to the arts in Norfolk, his investiture taking place sixty years to the minute after his arrest on 11 November 1938, when he was sent to Dachau.[43]

But it is possible to go further than simply pointing to the high level of culture displayed by the journal and the refugee community generally. A deeper analysis reveals that refugee culture in Britain continued to draw specifically on core elements of the pre-emigration culture of the assimilated German-speaking Jews, on the structures of their thinking and on the socio-cultural identity of the secularized Jews of Germany and Austria as such. That cultural identity developed out of the age of the Enlightenment, the rationalist movement that in Germany reached its philosophical and intellectual peak in the later eighteenth century and its greatest cultural efflorescence in German classical literature, with figures such as Goethe and Schiller. Opposed to all superstition and prejudice, the Enlightenment sought to carry the banner of reason into all areas of human society, as a means of liberation in the name of human dignity. It proclaimed equality in place of hierarchy, freedom in place of subservience to established authority, humanism and cosmopolitanism in place of traditional social, ethnic, national and religious divisions. It especially advocated political and religious tolerance, freedom of religion, and equal rights for all; this directly affected the Jews, hitherto predominantly a marginalized, backward and impoverished minority, subject to discrimination and restricted in the interaction they were permitted with gentile society.

The Enlightenment marked the historic moment when the Jews were able to emerge from isolation into the mainstream of German social, economic, cultural and intellectual life; abandoning a style of life strictly defined by religious ritual, custom and practice, the newly emancipated Jews embarked on integration into German society. The Jewish Enlightenment, the Haskalah, marked the beginning of that extraordinarily fruitful conjuncture of Jewish thought and creativity with the ideas of the German *Aufklärung* that is often called the German-Jewish symbiosis. No group in Germany had more to gain than the Jews from the spread of the values of the Enlightenment, which promised them equal rights and freedom from discrimination. The emancipation of the Jews began with the Enlightenment, and emancipation provided the conditions for assimilation, for Jews to enter German society on an equal footing with the full civil and political rights of German citizens. Though we now know that this assimilation would ultimately fail catastrophically, it seemed only natural in the later eighteenth and nineteenth centuries that the German-speaking Jews should embrace the values of the Enlightenment, which promised them so much, with particular enthusiasm; and that they should make every effort to integrate into German and Austrian society on the basis of a progressive, humanist consensus.

As is well known, German-Jewish culture was characterized by a very rapid process of acculturation, in which traditional religiously determined values and practices were abandoned for the political values of liberalism and the cultural values of German literature, music and the arts. Reviewing his family history from his post-war exile in Britain, Rabbi Max Eschelbacher remarked in 1960 on the astonishing speed of the transformation from the generation of his grandfather, a devout, uneducated outsider, to that of his parents, eager participants in German culture; for the latter 'German culture was a formative force from the outset and later on it became, for many years, the only cultural expression by which they were shaped, whereas association with the values of Jewish culture receded more and more into the background.'[44]

The culture created by the German-Jewish symbiosis was predominantly that of a largely assimilated, highly educated, secularized, middle-class Jewish community for part of which traditional Jewish customs and religious rituals had lost much of their significance; the self-image of the assimilated German Jews, their sense of identity, had correspondingly changed radically during the period of emancipation, and that change was in good measure to last even beyond the Nazi period. That many refugees still remained true after 1945 to the cultural heritage that they had brought with them from Germany and Austria is clear from an abundance of evidence in *AJR Information*. Many continued to value the German-Jewish high culture that was the product of assimilation more or less unquestioningly. *AJR Information* contains a wealth of material showing how strongly the Jewish refugees from the German-speaking lands continued to be influenced in Britain by their cultural tradition, by the humanist values of the Enlightenment, its advocacy of tolerance, equality and individual freedom, and especially by its love of culture, education, of *Bildung*, to use the term developed in the classical period to denote education, with an added dimension of cultural development towards moral maturity. Secularized German-speaking Jewry showed an exceptional devotion to the classic art and culture of the German Enlightenment, a devotion that bridged the gulf of emigration.

The culture of the refugees in Britain continued to be permeated by veneration for the great works of the classical period: the trumpet call of freedom in Beethoven's *Fidelio* and the appeal for a universal brotherhood of humankind in his Choral Symphony; Schiller's dramas of liberation, from the early plays like *The Robbers* and *Don Karlos* – Marquis Posa's ringing appeal to King Philip of Spain to grant freedom of thought was often quoted – to his dramatization of historical figures like Wilhelm Tell, Joan of Arc and Mary Queen of Scots; Goethe's *Faust*, with its themes of striving, guilt and ultimate redemption; the philosopher Immanuel Kant's essay *Was ist Aufklärung?* (*What Is Enlightenment?*), in which he argued in the name of reason for the abolition of outdated barriers to progress and individual self-fulfilment; and works that demonstrated the individual's ascent towards personal, moral and cultural maturity, from Goethe's *Wilhelm Meister* to Mozart's *Magic Flute*. Many refugees were still proud to quote verbatim from Enlightenment poetry learnt by heart at school, especially Schiller's moralising epic poems with their message of virtue rewarded (*Die Bürgschaft, Der Kampf mit dem Drachen*) or crime punished (*Die Kraniche des Ibykus*).

Among the rich legacy that the Enlightenment and the German classical tradition bequeathed to the Jews from Germany, one play occupied a special place of honour: *Nathan der Weise* (*Nathan the Wise*) (1779) by

Gotthold Ephraim Lessing (1729–81), a militant philo-Semite and friend of Moses Mendelssohn, the father of the Jewish Enlightenment. Set in Jerusalem at the time of the Crusades, the play is both a highly effective plea for religious tolerance and a blistering indictment of prejudice and bigotry. Lessing took the bold step of making his hero a Jew, the wise, tolerant and humane Nathan, who stands by his faith in the universal values of humanism and tolerance despite having lost his family in a pogrom. Nathan has little difficulty in winning Sultan Saladin, a Muslim, to his cause, but the representative of Christianity, the Templar, constantly lapses barbarously into anti-Semitic prejudice, fired on by the bigotry of his co-religionist, the Patriarch, who believes that Jews should be burnt.

The high-point of the play is Nathan's parable of the three rings. At stake here is which of three rings, each of them allegedly given by a wise father to one of his three sons, is the true ring, and which son in consequence the entitled heir. As it proves impossible to tell which of the rings is the true one, each is ultimately endowed with equal value and each son equally entitled to regard himself as his father's heir. The parable enunciates the play's central theme: all three of the great monotheistic religions are equal; each must therefore tolerate and respect the others; and the ultimate criterion of the validity of a set of religious beliefs is not doctrine or dogma, but the goodness and good actions of its adherents. One would have to search far in world literature for a more effective plea for respect for the beliefs and customs of others, especially the perennially despised Jews.[45]

Given its advocacy of religious and racial tolerance, its abhorrence of prejudice and discrimination, particularly anti-Semitism, and its vision of different cultures united in a common humanism, it is not surprising that *Nathan der Weise* is mentioned more often and more prominently in *AJR Information* than any other German classic, including Goethe's *Faust*. Its iconic status is evident from the way in which it was attached to dates that marked milestones in the history of the German Jews. When the noted German-Jewish actor and producer Fritz Wisten died in 1963, *AJR Information* recalled that in 1933 he had commenced his work for the Jüdischer Kulturbund, the organization that courageously promoted Jewish culture inside Nazi Germany, with a production of *Nathan*; and that in 1945 he had resumed his work in the theatre by staging the same play at the reopened Deutsches Theater in Berlin.[46] Here Lessing's masterpiece stood at either end of the Nazi years, in 1933 as a counter to the onset of Nazi barbarism and in 1945 as a symbol of the survival, among the ruins, of humane, civilized values. It is also significant that when the Leo Baeck Institute planned a history of the Jews in Germany, it chose 1779, the year of *Nathan der Weise*, as the starting date for that history.[47]

But the significance of *Nathan* for the refugee Jews from Germany and Austria went deeper even than that. The play and its message of humane tolerance were embedded in their consciousness, influencing the very structures of their thinking, as some examples will demonstrate. In May 1963, on the ninetieth anniversary of the birth of Rabbi Leo Baeck,[48] *AJR Information* carried a long appreciation of the spiritual leader of the Jews from Germany by the distinguished Jewish philosopher Hermann Levin Goldschmidt, entitled 'Der junge Leo Baeck'.[49] Goldschmidt described graphically the young Baeck's debut at the Generalversammlung des Rabbinerverbandes in Deutschland, held in Berlin in June 1898. The 25-year-old spoke out on the contentious issue of the awarding of rabbinical diplomas, at that time limited in Germany to three Jewish educational institutions, one Orthodox, one Conservative and one Liberal. Baeck's argument was radical: he supported the restriction of the diploma-awarding institutions to three, but argued that students should be able to move freely between them. His audience, incapable of following this bold plea for the freedom of students to sample the best of each of the three rival trends in German Judaism on an equal basis, greeted his impassioned words 'Weshalb soll der Mensch nur eine Richtung haben?' ('Why should a person have only one orientation?') with hilarity.

But Goldschmidt, writing sixty-five years later, saw the wisdom and deeper humanity of Baeck's view:

> Why, according to the young Leo Baeck, should a person not have one orientation only? For methodological reasons! For the common world of all humankind consists of a number of orientations: both the world of humanity, where Judaism embodies only one of a number of orientations, and the world of Judaism, within whose framework there is likewise more than one basic orientation.

It is not difficult to relate this principled rejection of a narrow-minded insistence on the doctrinal correctness of one set of beliefs over all others to the tolerant, reasoned understanding of the value inherent in all morally based systems of belief, as advocated by Nathan in Lessing's play. Seen like this, the three contending trends in German Judaism became not mutually exclusive hostile camps, but three variants of a single morally and doctrinally valid core set of values, each of which contained, like Nathan's three rings, the presumed imprint of the greater truth that stood behind it. Goldschmidt emphatically denied that this open-minded approach to the beliefs of others implied disloyalty towards one's own beliefs, mere unprincipled relativism. On the contrary, it was precisely the stance of free, open-minded tolerance that gave Leo Baeck's position its underpinning of

principle: 'In order to have, as the young Leo Baeck demands, not one orientation only, but several, for methodical reasons, it is necessary to com-
mit oneself most clearly to a single orientation as one's own. Only someone who holds an unambiguous position, who is himself firmly rooted,
can be open-minded, tolerant, free.'

This could almost be a character sketch of Nathan, the convinced Jew
whose unshakeable faith gives him the moral and intellectual strength to
appreciate the beliefs of others. Goldschmidt celebrated Liberal Judaism,
the creed of the greater part of German Jewry, as the religious movement
that had the freedom necessary to approach its rivals in a spirit of tolerant
and sympathetic understanding, as Nathan approaches the representatives
of other religions in a spirit of brotherly love: 'Thus liberal Judaism always
remains true to its own orientation alone, the path of freedom, an unambiguous commitment, even though because of that path it also acknowl-
edges the other orientations in Judaism in their historical place and in their
contemporary significance, seeks to understand them sympathetically and
welcomes them joyfully as enrichments of Judaism as a whole.'

This rejection of any rigid insistence on one set of beliefs, of all dog-
matic bigotry, was also evident in a review by Rabbi Max Eschelbacher of
the German translation of the classic study of the Pharisees by R. Travers
Herford: 'In a splendid analysis of both religions he shows that they are,
each of them, different forms of the one truth – Christianity with its stress
on belief, Judaism on obedience to the Law. For him the Halakhah, the Law,
is the analogon to the Creed.'[50] Tolerance, the supreme virtue, could only
be achieved through an open-minded willingness to appreciate the merits
inherent in the systems of belief of others, by understanding the essential
truth underlying their beliefs. Eschelbacher quoted Travers Herford: 'For
the Jews their religion was as true, as real and alive, as it could be. Judaism,
rabbinic Judaism, is as deeply rooted in the hearts and souls of its believ-
ers, as is Christianity in those of the Christians, and this is the only true
standard that can be set.' When religions were seen as equal, religious discrimination could be ruled out, as it is in the parable of the three rings.
Thereby, to adapt Goldschmidt's words, the whole of mankind was
enriched.

One major article in *AJR Information* even attempted to apply the precepts
of the Enlightenment and its successor, nineteenth-century political liberalism, to the intractable problems of Israel and the Palestinians. Writing
in 1960 on the centenary of the birth of Theodor Herzl, the founder of
political Zionism, Robert Weltsch reinterpreted Herzl's ideas as those of 'a
Viennese Jew and a Liberal in the old nineteenth-century tradition of
Central Europe' who was 'rooted in an old cosmopolitan civilization'.[51]

Weltsch went so far as to claim that only those imbued with the values of German Jewry, 'people who originated from the same intellectual and cultural background', could fully grasp Herzl's message. A leading Zionist journalist in Germany, Weltsch had emigrated to Palestine in 1938 and came on to Britain in 1946; he was a prominent advocate of reconciliation with the Arab population of Palestine. For him, the Zionist project was ethically based, or it was nothing. When he wrote of Herzl's 'glowing vision of a Jewish life that should be perfect in every respect', the idealist and humanist nature of his thinking was clear: 'Zionism was to Herzl an "eternal ideal". It would not cease after the establishment of the Jewish State. "For in Zionism", he wrote, " . . . there is not only the striving for a legally secured soil for our poor people; there is the striving for moral and spiritual perfection".'

This vision of the Jewish state, which Weltsch saw as deriving directly from the values of German Jewry, was universalist rather than nationalist, ethical rather than political in inspiration:

> [Herzl's] Jewish State idea cannot be equated to the nationalist aspi-
> rations of other . . . nationalities, which were directed solely towards
> independence. To him, independence had to provide an opportunity
> of creating a form of community life in which the highest human –
> not nationalistic – ideals should be implemented ... For Herzl, the
> form of political independence was not as essential as its content, the
> establishment of what he called a *new society*.

In Weltsch's account, Zionism was inextricably linked, both ethically and aesthetically, with German classical literature and its advocacy of individual freedom and humanity:

> Herzl was rooted in the humanitarian idealism which was the secu-
> larised religion of the educated classes of his nineteenth-century gen-
> eration. He was convinced that an ethical appeal for a cause whose
> beauty and greatness should be obvious to all, was the most power-
> ful approach. As all people in German-speaking countries, he was
> educated under the influence of the dramas of Friedrich Schiller.
> When we read Herzl's own account of his interviews with the poten-
> tates of the world ... we cannot help thinking of the classical exam-
> ple of such an oration, namely, of course, Marquis Posa standing
> before King Philipp. The proud, free, idealistic hero arguing his case
> before this most powerful man, who had never before listened to
> such bold language. It was the entrancing Song of Songs of freedom
> and human dignity, which could not fail to make an impression on
> the most hardened soul.

In the stirring conclusion to his article, Weltsch drew on *Nathan der Weise* for moral guidelines by which to determine the relations between Jews and Arabs. Arguing that it was fundamental to Herzl's thinking that the implementation of Zionism would have to be carried out in accordance with the principles of humanity, Weltsch vehemently denied that Herzl ever conceived of the Palestine problem 'as a clash of nationalisms', contending that the expulsion of native peasants from their ancestral soil would have been utterly alien to his thinking:

> In so far as Herzl envisaged a mixed population in Palestine, he adhered strictly to the ideas of equality and tolerance. In this respect his Utopian novel *Altneuland* reads like a paraphrase of Lessing's *Nathan the Wise*. This eighteenth-century German anthem of religious equality was the stronghold of Jewish assimilationists in Germany in their fight for full emancipation; in Herzl's visionary Jewish State it got its first application in an opposite direction, namely justice and toleration not demanded by Jews for themselves but applied by Jews to their fellow-citizens of other denominations and races.

The purpose of this striking passage was effectively to claim the authority of the founder of political Zionism for a policy of reconciliation between Jews and the Arab population of what had been Palestine, on the basis of equal rights and mutual toleration. Though history had taken a very different course, Weltsch could still envisage the principles enunciated in *Nathan der Weise* as the blueprint for resolving the conflict between the two peoples.

It goes without saying that the refugees' attitude to classical German culture could not remain unaffected by the Holocaust and the chasm that it opened up between Germans and Jews. This too was reflected in refugee attitudes to *Nathan*, as an example taken from *AJR Information*'s reporting of one of the most significant events in post-war Jewish history showed. At the height of the trial of Adolf Eichmann in August 1961, the front page of the journal carried another article by Weltsch entitled 'Chosen People?'. As editor of the *Jüdische Rundschau* in the 1930s, Weltsch had been responsible for the famous leader that responded to the Nazi boycott of Jewish businesses of 1 April 1933 with the exhortation 'Tragt ihn mit Stolz, den gelben Fleck!' ('Wear it with pride, the yellow patch!'). Three decades later, as the headlines of the world's press again dwelt on the horrors of Nazi genocide, he turned to the legacy of Lessing's *Nathan der Weise* in the post-Holocaust world:

> Why do you call yourself the Chosen People? – The call sounds still

in our ears from schooldays, when we read the words of the Tempelherr in Lessing's *Nathan*. We heard it again these days, as this great drama has recently been recorded with Ernst Deutsch[52] in the leading part, and we may well discover that it is not as obsolete as many of us had thought. Seen in the light of our own experiences, it appears paradoxical that such a work was written in Germany, of all places, yet in some respect it is topical even today.

Weltsch compared Deutsch's performance with that of the celebrated Jewish actor Adolf von Sonnenthal, who died in 1909, finding Deutsch's reading of the part 'quite different, less sublime, more naturalistic and even slightly ironical', and his rendering of Nathan's response to a pogrom with a deed of love and mercy 'somewhat harder, and less convincing, as it ought to be in our age'. The optimistic confidence of the earlier age in the triumph of humane and tolerant values was no longer possible after the genocide perpetrated against the Jews; the play had to be reinterpreted accordingly. What Weltsch was addressing in his analysis of the two inter-pretations of its leading role was the survival, at least in part, of the values of the Age of Enlightenment and the German-Jewish cultural symbiosis into the post-Holocaust era, among that part of German and Austrian Jewry that lived on in countries like Britain. The gap between the 'human warmth ... and prophetic pathos' of Sonnenthal and the ironic distance that Deutsch put between himself and his role reflected the gulf between two historical worlds separated by the Nazi tyranny. But the refugees' continuing pre-occupation with *Nathan der Weise* showed how the culture that they had imbibed in their native countries, and the values underlying that culture, though shaken to their foundations by the Holocaust, survived in refugee society in Britain, as the legacy of classical humanism and *Bildung*.

If the German classics provided the foundations of refugee culture, ele-ments from British culture were soon integrated into it. The interpenetration of English and German elements in the new culture that the refugees devel-oped in Britain became very evident precisely in the sphere of classical culture. For the figure of Lessing's Nathan naturally led the refugees on to its most celebrated counterpart, the creation of an English playwright already familiar to many of them before emigration: Shakespeare. Emigration to England had further familiarized the refugees with *The Merchant of Venice*, and from an early date they showed a high degree of inter-est in the play and in the figure of Shylock. Their engagement with Shakespeare was a high-point in their integration of elements of English art and literature into their cultural canon, mirroring the integration of elements of British social culture into their attitudes and way of life generally. Among the refugees were Shakespeare experts like the writer, journalist and theatre critic Hermann Sinsheimer, formerly editor-in-chief of *Simplicissimus* and head of the 'Feuilleton' of the *Berliner Tageblatt*, who died in London in 1950.[53] His study of Shylock was first published in a shortened version by Gollancz in 1947; the full-length German version appeared only in 1960.[54]

The most remarkable contribution on Shylock by a refugee came, however, from a rabbi, the Viennese-born Ignaz Maybaum, who had been one of Berlin's three communal rabbis and who in emigration eventually secured a post at the Edgware and District Reform Synagogue. Maybaum's arresting analysis of Shylock appeared in a long essay, 'Shylock, the Tragic Champion of the Law', incorporated into his *Trialogue Between Jew, Christian and Muslim*, which was published in London in 1973 and whose title plainly echoes *Nathan der Weise*.[55] In March 1953, on the occasion of the great Jewish scholar Martin Buber's seventy-fifth birthday, *AJR Information* published an article by Maybaum entitled 'Dialogue with Buber'. Here Maybaum did not hesitate to criticize a recent work of Buber's for overemphasizing spiritual and doctrinal aspects in his analysis of good and evil and of just or righteous people (*Tsaddikim*) at the expense of legal and practical dimensions.[56] Shylock made an unexpected appearance in this theological forum.

In a stunning display of intellectual virtuosity, Maybaum first situated Buber's analysis firmly in the German tradition of Kantian moral absolutes and of Luther's denial of the possibilities of good works, which he traced back to Saint Paul. In Maybaum's view, Buber wrote as 'one whose surrounding Christian civilization is of German Pauline fabric', whereas he, Maybaum, now lived in an Anglo-Saxon world and could see what Buber had never been exposed to:

> Buber, though originally a native of Eastern Europe, is still a German Jew. Nowhere but in Israel could German Jews, intellectually and spiritually, remain to such a degree what they were before. There, no indigenous civilisation forced them to change. It is different with the German Jew who went to England. Here the Christian civilisation is not of Pauline but of Petrine fabric. Even if we think of the boy scout who sets out for the 'good deed of the day', we realise the difference in atmosphere from that of Luther's country.

The key difference, according to Maybaum, was that between Kant, the German philosopher who claimed that there was nothing in the world that could be called unconditionally good except the good will, thereby implying that once translated into action it of necessity became imperfect, and the English boy scout whose practical ethic was that of goodness in action. Not content with this startling pairing, Maybaum continued his vision of

Anglo-Saxon pragmatism contained within the supporting framework of the law by portraying Shylock as an exemplar of English values, citing his unconditional belief in the law: 'We understand Shylock, with the commentary of English daily life around us, as an English character. What Shylock says amounts to the often heard sentiment: The Law is the Law.' He then quoted from *The Observer*:

> '"We have to take the Law as it is", Lord Goddard, Chief Justice of England, once said, "always remembering that in Other and Higher hands mercy may be extended". When Lord Goddard refers to the Almighty, there seems to be the suggestion of another court, not unlike his own, but far away, and possibly slightly eccentric.' (*The Observer*). Shakespeare never met a Jew. Shylock is not a Jew but, being truly human, he has Jewish features; he is a hero who fights a moral battle for the validity of legal undertakings; he is an English character and he would not understand a German who called a contract 'a scrap of paper', as the disciple of Kantian philosophy, Bethmann-Hollweg, did. [This refers to the German Chancellor's notorious speech justifying Germany's invasion of Belgium in August 1914 by dismissing the treaty guaranteeing Belgian neutrality as 'a scrap of paper'.]

This comparison of German and Anglo-Saxon approaches to morality, ethics and law, spectacularly encompassing Kant, Shylock, the 'hanging judge' Lord Goddard and Chancellor Bethmann Hollweg, climaxed in Maybaum's interpretation of Portia's lines 'How far that little candle throws his beams,/So shines a good deed in a naughty world' as a triumphant vindication of morality translated into practical action:

> She does not speak of 'the word' (logos) which shines in the darkness, but she changes the words from the gospel and speaks of the good deed which shines in the darkness. In this light man can walk here on earth; he who does so is the Tsaddik. He exists. Middle-class 'respectability' is spoken of in England without the reproach of bourgeois hypocrisy. Integrity means not merely good motives, it means the success of a man, of a group, of a country of putting into practice what is honest and fair.

The social fabric of English society was here seen as underpinned by mutual trust between individuals and groups, based on respect for binding agreements. Maybaum invoked English legalism, albeit prone to harshness and rigidity, as the counterweight to 'German spiritualisation of morality', which he called 'dangerously unprotected against barbarism'. The pragmatic Anglo-Saxon ethic, buttressed by its firm faith in the ultimate validity of the law, would, one infers, have been better equipped to withstand the evil of National Socialism. Through his faith in the law, Shylock, its tragic champion, came to represent for Maybaum a quintessentially English vision of the sanctity of legal contracts, an invaluable supplement to German codes of pure ethics.

For the refugees, classical German literature formed a crucial area of cultural common ground with like-minded British people. Eva G. Reichmann, one of the first post-war historians of Nazism, recalled in a front-page article in *AJR Information* in May 1960 the dark days of the Second World War when Nazism threatened the civilized world, and when she had invoked classical German literature and its values as an antidote. This cultural counter to the Nazi menace had taken shape in a forum where British and German intellectuals met and united around a common admiration for the values associated with the greatest of the German classical writers, Goethe:

> It was in 1942. The outcome of the war hung in the balance. Then a number of academic researchers met together in London, at the instigation of my revered teacher Morris Ginsberg, Professor of Sociology and a Jew, to clarify their understanding of the nature of Germany. The lectures given at this study group were subsequently collected together in the volume *The German Mind and Outlook*. One of the participants, Professor Willoughby, concludes his contribution on 'Goethe in the Modern World' with these words: 'We must not allow the thought of what Germany has become today (as a result of National Socialism) to blind us, through the passions stirred up in us, to what Germany was and will be again.'[57]

What the Jewish refugees preserved was an outpost of a high culture much of which had been driven underground or obliterated by the Nazis, and which survived in exile almost as a memorial to its own past. The combination of their willingness to integrate into British society with their desire to preserve the bygone riches of German high culture emerged very clearly from an interview with Richard Grunberger, editor of *AJR Information* from 1988 to 2005, published in a special issue of the journal after his death:

> I see my role as the editor as somebody who is trying to bridge the gulf [between] where the refugees came from and where they have found themselves for the last 60 years. I want them not to lose contact with what they have left behind because there was a very rich German cultural Jewish life of which they are the last representatives. On the other hand, I want them to be more acculturated to English life and English culture. I am trying to act as a mediator between the two and as a propagandist for the amalgam of the two cultures.[58]

NOTES

1. See detailed studies such as D. Snowman, *The Hitler Emigrés: The Cultural Impact on Britain of the Refugees from Nazism* (London: Chatto & Windus, 2002), and W. Mosse (ed.), *Second Chance: Two Centuries of German-speaking Jews in the United Kingdom* (Tübingen: Mohr, 1991).

2. *AJR Information* (November 1957), p.1, quoting after his death from an address given by Baeck four years earlier, on the occasion of the fifteenth anniversary of the 'Kristallnacht' pogroms.

3. H. Reichmann, 'Dienst an unserer Gemeinschaft' ('Service to Our Community'), *AJR Information* (March 1954), p.3 (my translation).

4. 'Erbe und Verpflichtung: Unsere Verantwortung für die geistigen Werte des deutschen Judentums', formal notice of the General Meeting in *AJR Information* (June 1954), p.1.

5. B. Barkow, *Alfred Wiener and the Making of the Holocaust Library* (London: Vallentine Mitchell, 1997).

6. *AJR Information* (March 1955), p.1.

7. *AJR Information* (September 1956), p.1.

8. W. Rosenstock, 'A Link Between Two Ages: The Leo Baeck Institute', *AJR Information* (March 1959), pp.1 and 3.

9. F. Walter, 'Bücher haben ihre Schicksale ...', *AJR Information* (July–August 1959), p.14 (my translation). The title, from the Latin 'Habent sua fata libelli', was one of those literary mottos beloved of German-Jewish intellectuals and designed to evoke the cultural aura of their milieu.

10. *AJR Information* (January 1959), p.7 (my translation).

11. *AJR Information* (November 1959), p.6. Woyda had spoken several times at the Fasanenstraße Synagogue, as a member of the executive of Berlin's Jewish community. In Britain he became honorary secretary of the Council of Jews from Germany.

12. *AJR Information* (January 1951), p.2.

13. *AJR Information* (May 1957), p.6.

14. D. Cesarani, *Arthur Koestler: The Homeless Mind* (London: Heinemann, 1998).

15. R. Dove, *Journey of No Return: Five German-speaking Literary Exiles in Britain, 1933–1945* (London: Libris, 2000).

16. For example V. Ross, *Basic British* (London: Max Parrish, 1956).

17. *AJR Information* (December 1967), p.14. See also the appreciation of Weltmann that appeared on the occasion of his fiftieth birthday, *AJR Information* (March 1951), p.7.

18. *AJR Information* (March 1958), p.4.

19. 'In Memoriam Albert Bassermann', *AJR Information* (June 1952), p.4.

20. *AJR Information* (June 1954), p.4.

21. *AJR Information* (July 1956), p.7.

22. *AJR Information* (September 1957), p.12.

23. *AJR Information* (May 1956), p.6.

24. 'Words and Deeds behind a Veil', *AJR Information* (August 1958), p.4.

25. *AJR Information* (June 1956), p.4.

26. The rediscovery of the German Expressionist writers in the 1960s owed much to the efforts of the non-Jewish refugee Karl Otten, who spent over twenty years in Britain, and his seminal anthologies *Ahnung und Aufbruch* (1957) and *Schrei und Bekenntnis* (1961).

27. 'Das Volk des Buches und das Jubiläum von Martin Breslauer' ('The People of the Book and the Diamond Jubilee of Martin Breslauer'), *AJR Information* (October 1958), p.12.

28. *AJR Information* (June 1946), p.4.

29. 'An "Act of Generous Gratitude"', *AJR Information* (September 1946), p.4. Martin Breslauer had originally catalogued the Paul Hirsch music library, and Otto Haas had evaluated it prior to its purchase by the British Museum.

30. *AJR Information* (September 1946), p.4.

31. *AJR Information* (February 1948), p.4.

32. *AJR Information* (January 1946), p.7.

33. *AJR Information* (February 1946), p.7. The 'Refugee Voices' collection contains an interview with Inge Markowitz under her married name, Inge Heichelheim.

34. *AJR Information* (December 1946), p.4. The violinist Carl Flesch emigrated to Britain in 1934, but left for Holland, neutral at the outbreak of war, eventually reaching Switzerland. His son, Carl Franz Flesch, born in 1910, lived for many years in West Hampstead.

35. *AJR Information* (May 1949), p.7. This was sixteen months after the Quartet's debut recital at the Wigmore Hall on 10 January 1948.

36. *AJR Information* (January 1955), p.7.

37. *AJR Information* (January 1958), p.14.

38. *AJR Information* (December 1967), p.16.

39. *AJR Information* (September 1956), p.7, on the occasion of Walter's eightieth birthday.

40. *AJR Information* (January 1959), p.11. Johanna Lichtenstern had been the great friend of Dora Diamant, Franz Kafka's companion in his last months, with whom she had formed a close friendship while interned on the Isle of Man. See K. Diamant, *Kafka's Last Love: The Mystery of Dora Diamant* (London: Secker & Warburg, 2003).

41. *AJR Information* (April 1960), p.14. The 'Refugee Voices' collection contains an interview with Natalia Karpf.

42. *AJR Information* (December 1956), p.11.

43. 'Concentration Camp Survivor and Music Lover Dies Aged 96', *Hampstead & Highgate Express*, 14 January 2005, p.24, and 'Heinz Liebrecht', *Jewish Chronicle*, 18 March 2005, p.36.

44. *AJR Information* (March 1960), p.10.

45. On the parable of the rings see H. Nisbet, '*De Tribus Impostoribus*: On the Genesis of Lessing's *Nathan der Weise*', *Euphorion*, LXXIII (1979), pp.365–87, and R. Robertson, *The 'Jewish Question' in German Literature, 1749–1939: Emancipation and its Discontents* (Oxford: Oxford University Press, 1999), p.45. A standard study of Lessing's plays is F. Lamport, *Lessing and the Drama* (Oxford: Clarendon Press, 1981).

46. *AJR Information* (February 1963), p.9.

47. A. Paucker, 'Preserving Our Heritage: The Work of the Leo Baeck Institute', *AJR Information* (October 1962), p.13. Paucker stressed that the organizations of the Jews from Germany had the duty 'to preserve the best of German Jewry's cultural tradition'.

48. Born in 1873, Leo Baeck was elected president of the Reichsvertretung der Juden in Deutschland in May 1933. He opted to stay at his post and was deported to Theresienstadt. Liberated in 1945, he came to London, where he became president of the Council of Jews from Germany, the organization set up by the Association of Jewish Refugees and its sister organizations in the USA and Palestine to represent the rights and interests of the Jews from Germany. He died in London in 1956.

49. *AJR Information* (May 1963), pp.2f. (my translation).

50. M. Eschelbacher, 'Pharisaism Reassessed', *AJR Information* (August 1963), p.12. This is a review of R. Travers Herford, *Die Pharisäer*, translated by W. Fischel.

51. R. Weltsch, 'The Dream and the Reality: Some Reflections on the Herzl Centenary', *AJR Information* (June 1960), pp.1f.

52. Born in Prague, Ernst Deutsch was probably the most famous of the German-speaking Jewish refugee actors active on the post-war stage. He had returned from America to Germany, where he specialized in the great classical roles, also taking such parts as Anne Frank's father in the dramatized version of her diaries.

53. See G. Weber and R. Paulus (eds), *Hermann Sinsheimer: Schriftsteller und Theaterkritiker zwischen Heimat und Exil. Eine Auswahl aus dem Gesamtwerk* (Landau/Pfalz: Pfälzische Verlagsanstalt, 1986).

54. H. Sinsheimer, *Shylock. The History of a Character or The Myth of the Jew* (London: Gollancz, 1947), and *Shylock: Die Geschichte einer Figur* (Munich: Ner-Tamid Verlag, 1960).

55. See N. de Lange (ed.), *Ignaz Maybaum: A Reader* (New York/Oxford: Berghahn, 2001), where the essay on Shylock is reprinted, pp.137–50.

56. Dr I. Maybaum, 'Dialogue with Buber', *AJR Information* (March 1953), p.4.

57. Eva Reichmann published *Hostages of Civilisation: The Social Sources of National-Socialist Antisemitism* in 1950 (German translation, *Flucht in den Haß: Die Ursachen der deutschen Judenkatastrophe*, 1954). Her husband was Hans Reichmann, chairman of the AJR, 1954–63. L.A. Willoughby was a distinguished professor of German at the University of London, best known for his collaboration with Elisabeth Wilkinson. (The translation into English is mine, and I have followed Reichmann's rephrasing of Willoughby's concluding words.)

58. 'Richard Grunberger on Richard Grunberger: Extracts from an Interview with Bea Lewkowicz', *AJR Journal* (April 2005), p.1.

8

The Development of a Communal Identity: 'Continental' Britons

The large amount of research devoted to ethnic groups and ethnicity in recent decades has shown conclusively that ethnic identities are not solidly invariable and given once and for all, but are fluid, relative and negotiable according to conditions and situations. What one leading social anthropologist has said holds true for research across the range of academic disciplines: 'Instead of viewing 'societies' or even 'cultures' as more or less isolated, static and homogeneous units ... many anthropologists now try to depict flux and process, ambiguity and complexity in their analyses of social worlds. In this context, ethnicity has proven a highly useful concept, since it suggests a dynamic situation of variable contact and mutual accommodation between groups.'[1] This is the context in which the upsurge of interest over recent decades in ethnic minorities like the Jewish refugees from Nazism may be seen.

Ethnic groups, like individuals, do not have a single static and stable identity. Rather, their overall identities shift and develop over time, under the pressure of events and as the component layers and elements within them collide, interact and find a new balance. Of no group is this more obviously true than a group composed of refugees, whose former identity from their homelands has had to reach an accommodation with a new identity in their land of settlement, especially when that earlier identity has undergone the fracture of forced emigration. Social groups, like individuals, can have a number of identities and allegiances; as an individual can identify with a family, an ethnic group and a nation, so having a British identity was not incompatible for members of the refugee community with retaining a sense of themselves as Jews from Germany or Austria. Clearly, the balance between those identities and allegiances could shift. Events like the common struggle against Hitler had helped to blend the Jewish refugees into British society and to underpin their growing sense of a British dimension to their identity, whereas the German or Austrian element, already undermined by the Nazi years, receded over time.

This chapter will analyse the interplay between the German, Jewish and British aspects of the refugees' identity, but within the context of their settlement in Britain and with special attention to their relationship with

British society around them. It has often been assumed that the relations between the British and groups like the Jewish refugees were characterized by hostility or at least disparagement. But that is no more than an assumption; one can equally well take the view that there was a measure of mutual acceptance and toleration between the refugees and the British with whom they came into contact.

Theoretically, indeed, the very concept of an ethnic group presupposes some relation to another group: 'Notably, the use of the term "ethnic group" suggests contact and interrelationship ... By definition, ethnic groups remain more or less discrete, but they are aware of – and in contact with – members of other ethnic groups. Moreover, these groups or categories are in a sense *created* through that very contact.' And that contact will not always necessarily be hostile: 'Very often it is taken for granted that the groups in a polyethnic social system remain apart and different in most regards, and a great number of studies focus on the ways in which the groups manage to remain discrete ... However, since ethnicity is an aspect of relationship, one may equally well stress the mutual contact and the integrative aspect.'[2]

This is not to deny that the refugees encountered hostility and prejudice in Britain, especially in their early years in the country. But over the years the majority of them adapted reasonably smoothly to British society, as they settled permanently and established a rooted new life; by the late 1950s, most of them, with the exception of some of the older ones amongst them, would have found their new circumstances in large measure acceptable. As this chapter will show, that process went hand in hand with their adoption of a new identity in which British elements played a large part, while the German or Austrian and, in many cases, the Jewish elements receded. One can argue that since so many of the refugees were from an assimilated background, they were already predisposed to a degree of social integration with the majority community and to the assumption of an identity that reflected that integration.

The historian Eva G. Reichmann wrestled with the complexities of her identity in a speech given in Germany in 1960 and reprinted in *AJR Information*: 'I am no longer a German; and I will never be an Englishwoman, for all that England gave me the right to live when my native land denied it me.'[3] She now defined herself as a Jew, formerly German, subsequently of British nationality, and thus with three layers of identity struggling to resolve themselves into a new whole. But the German and the Jewish parts of her could never be reunited; what had once been a 'unified duality' (*geeinte Zwienatur*) had been dismembered and destroyed. She now looked to Britain to provide the framework within which the two sundered parts of her former identity could coexist, helped by her confidence in British society as a favourable setting for a new integrated identity to develop:

> But perhaps it is thanks to my anchorage on the British Isles, to the new horizon that opened up among the friendly, undemonstrative people over there, that what were formerly parts of a whole still feel related to one another, even after their undesired separation: that the Jewish part is most strongly conscious of itself in its sense of belonging to German-Jewish history, the formerly German part in its coming to terms with its guilt-laden relationship to its Jewish fellow human beings, and that both have gained a new dimension through their contact with the English world.

By 1960, when the refugees had been in Britain for some twenty years, a sense of tripartite communal identity, German, Jewish and British, had to a considerable degree established itself.

In that year, Kenneth Ambrose, formerly Kurt Abrahamsohn from Stettin, looked back on his life in Britain, with satisfaction, affection and some surprise, but certainly not in anger:

> Twenty-four years ago to the day I arrived at my English public school in Somerset, with a good knowledge of English, but otherwise a fairly typical German middle-class teenager of sixteen, who happened to have the wrong religion for his country of origin ... Twenty-four years after my arrival I am by all appearances one of the British middle-class. I live with my family in a small house with a garden, I work for a large Anglo-Jewish firm, my boys go to or are entered for a good public school ... I march off to work in the morning with briefcase and rolled umbrella to catch my train just like my neighbours, and on Sundays I wash my car, if necessary, do the minimum of gardening, and enjoy my family and home. My children only understand the few words of German which they have learnt from 'Oma' and 'Opa' ('granny' and 'grandpa').[4]

The touch of self-mockery in this suburban idyll did not detract significantly from Ambrose's conclusion, expressed in his title, 'The Best of Both Worlds', that he belonged to the generation of refugees that was both well enough integrated to enjoy British life and still familiar enough with the German past to draw benefit from its legacy. In terms of his external lifestyle, he had adapted smoothly to Britain, having come to appreciate the advantages of orderly queuing, a sense of social responsibility and neighbourliness without prying: 'I appreciate and have adopted many of the good characteristics of the British ... All generalizations are dangerous, and all countries have good and bad points, yet on the whole I feel that I would rather live here than in any other country I know.' However, his abiding sense of the past, his desire not to forget or allow the world at large to forget how the Jews of Germany had lived, distinguished him from his British neighbours.

Ambrose's article is remarkable for its relaxed tone, its feeling of well-balanced normality:

> If I try to stand back and take a look at myself at the gateway to middle-age and after nearly a quarter-century in this country, it seems to me that I have turned out surprisingly normal. I have become used to being judged not for where I come from, but for what I am ... I am just a relaxed, ordinary citizen now, but one, I hope, who has a good understanding of both the older generation of refugees who were unable to outgrow the habits and thoughts of their earlier days, and of the younger generation to which these habits are strange. I am, it seems to me, getting the best of both worlds.

But this integration into British life and the gradual grafting of a British dimension onto the refugees' collective identity had its limits. If refugees bent on a headlong rush into Britishness overstepped them, they risked criticism from those who, conscious of their refugee identity, were easily irritated by excessive self-identification with the British.

The sense of secure balance expressed by Ambrose should not blind one to the problems and conflicts that continued to beset the refugees' sense of identity, even within what they perceived as the largely benign setting of British post-war life. For a start, all but the youngest of them retained some sense of their German or Austrian identity in spite of Hitler and the Holocaust, if only because they found it impossible to discard the upbringing and education that had shaped them. Most refugees from Germany had experienced relatively little anti-Semitism before 1933 and had memories of a happy youth spent amidst familiar and well-loved surroundings; that many also came from relatively privileged, secure backgrounds was doubtless also a factor here. The image of life in pre-Hitler Germany conveyed in many refugee memoirs and interviews is predominantly one of tight-knit families proud of their German-Jewish social culture and well integrated, as they thought, into their sector of society and nation, as demonstrated by the number of Jewish fathers, brothers and husbands who had served the Kaiser in the First World War.

Refugees like Werner Rosenstock felt emotionally bound to their native cities, as his affectionate review of a book about Berlin, his home town, showed. The book vividly evoked the atmosphere 'between Spree and Panke', arousing fond memories in him of Berlin's inhabitants with their inimitable brand of humour.[5] Even the refugees from Austria, whose early life had often been soured by a higher incidence of anti-Semitism, remained in thrall to the beauty of their native land and especially to Vienna, home to the great majority of Austrian Jewry. Though some refugees refused ever to return to the country of their birth or to have anything to do with their former fellow citizens, many others did revisit the sites of their former homes, experiencing painful sensations of loss alongside happier memories of life before Hitler.[6] As shown in Chapter 7, the culture of Central Europe, expressed through the medium of the German language and drawing on a common stock of German literature, music and art, remained a treasured legacy for the refugees, one that continued to inform and permeate their identity and self-image in Britain.

But that sense of a secure identity, rooted almost as much in culture as in material prosperity or civic and political rights, had even before 1933 never been complete enough to unburden the assimilated Jews of the problems of being Jews in Germany or Austria. After 1945, the refugees were permanently separated from their native societies by the Holocaust, which made it impossible for most refugees to see themselves any longer as having a German or Austrian identity that they shared with their former fellow citizens. After their experiences in 1938/39, refugees from Vienna would react indignantly to English people insensitive enough to assume that they were 'Austrian' – though they would mostly have been content to be called 'Viennese', considering themselves to be heirs to the cultural tradition that had made their native city a great artistic centre.

Central to this loss of a sense of German or Austrian identity was the loss of almost all living connection with the towns and cities where they had been born. Those who made return visits were often overwhelmed by the absence of the many familiar faces forced into exile or deported. That absence was made the more poignant by the fact that the physical environment had remained much the same, allowing for wartime damage; the effect was that of a ghost-town where vanished faces populated streets otherwise empty of familiar human contacts. As in Werner Rosenstock's experience of the deserted Jewish cemetery at Weissensee in Berlin,[7] the living had disappeared, leaving the city to the dead. It was as if the reservoir of a living community, on which the former sense of identity had drawn, had been emptied, thus denying that identity the means to replenish itself and putting a historical as well as a geographical distance between the émigrés and their former selves. The chasm that the Holocaust had opened up between the refugees and their former homelands could never be bridged or forgotten; it had dissolved the community of identity between the refugees and the citizens of their former homelands.

The attitude of the refugees to the German or Austrian part of their identity was thus fraught with painful contradictions. On the one hand, it was bound up with the past that had shaped them and that lived on, often still much loved, in their memory; on the other, it was associated with the discrimination, persecution and genocide inflicted on them and their families by Nazism. Werner Rosenstock expressed this dilemma eloquently in 1951:

> A journey to Germany is bound to create conflicting feelings. Which Germany do we visit? Is it the country in which our relatives and friends were murdered, or is it the land where we spent our formative years? We would offend the memory of our nearest ones and we would sacrifice our self-respect if our emotions were not invariably determined by the horrors of the past decade. Yet we would deceive ourselves – and perhaps also succumb to Hitler's 'ideology' – if we did not become aware again of the deep roots we once had in that country. However, to make this clear beyond doubt, the past can never become present again. The view of the ruins reflects our own conclusions: our previous world has sunk once and for all, we cannot start again where we broke off in 1933.[8]

When the refugees looked back on the historical evolution of their identity, they encountered similar conflicts. On the one hand, they had enjoyed a secure identity as assimilated Jews in communities to which they felt they belonged. A review of a book about the Jews of Cologne, for example, spoke of 'the high degree to which the majority of Cologne's 20,000 Jews were affected in speech, habits and outlook by the strong local atmosphere and tradition; how proud they were of being "kölsch" [from Köln, German for Cologne]; how firmly convinced – call it folly or tragic illusion – that they were fully assimilated'.[9] But the Nazi assumption of power in 1933 had dealt a shattering blow to the foundations of their identity as Germans and Jews; Robert Weltsch recalled this in an article written for the twenty-fifth anniversary of the boycott of Jewish businesses on 1 April 1933, the first government-sponsored act of discrimination against the Jews:

> In this earthquake the edifice of concepts cherished by the German Jews collapsed. The ground was dragged away from under their feet. Most of them could not understand what was happening. They had been *bona fide* Germans, certainly law-abiding, patriotic citizens; Germany was their nation and their country, they were brought up in the German language and culture, they were grateful and loyal to the fatherland and had taken part in fighting its battles. They did not

know anything else, as far as political loyalty was concerned. Now suddenly they were confronted with a hostile world which taught them that they were Jews. Being a Jew had not had much meaning to many of them until that day. Now it was the only refuge that was left to them.[10]

That Nazi persecution had the effect of making the Jews of Germany more conscious of their Jewish identity is beyond question: Weltsch's ringing injunction in the *Jüdische Rundschau* in April 1933 to wear the Yellow Star with pride had epitomized it. In Britain, even the more secularized of the refugees were to retain a clear sense of their Jewish identity. Many others were conscientious in their observance of the Jewish rituals and practices they had learnt in their native lands, as their contribution to synagogues and other institutions showed; this was especially the case with Belsize Square Synagogue, which was founded by refugees and had a strong refugee contingent among its membership.[11]

AJR Information regularly carried articles on the occasion of the main religious festivals, emphasizing the legacy of Jewish identity that had been handed down to the refugees. For Rosh Hashanah in 1951, a front-page piece entitled 'Our Common Way' looked back to their spiritual roots in German Jewry: 'The High Festivals are bound to make us think in wider spaces of time. We remember how we spent these holy days in our former home towns. We realize that our outlook has changed since, but we also know that the heritage of several generations has left its mark on us once and for all.'[12] In September 1958, again on the front page, the journal published Robert Weltsch's 'Some Thoughts for the Holy Days', in which he emphasized what held the refugees together as a Jewish community, despite secularization and a decline in religious observance.

The AJR, created as the organization to represent all strands of refugee Jewry in Britain, had numerous devoutly observant members. The members of its founding Executive included Orthodox or Conservative Jews like Adolf Schoyer and Abraham Horovitz, as well as the Zionist Salomon Adler-Rudel, whose convictions led him to emigrate to Israel. When Horovitz died, Leo Baeck wrote that 'Judaism meant to him wholeness and fullness of his identity. He was the example of the pious Jew.'[13] There were many similar obituaries in the journal's pages over the years. But perhaps most significant was the journal's insistent appeal to the more secularized of the AJR's members not to lose sight of the Jewish aspect of their identity. In an article on the twentieth anniversary of the death of the Jewish thinker and activist Ludwig Tietz (1897–1933), Werner Rosenstock wrote that Tietz started from the knowledge that a Western Jew can only be a balanced personality if he develops his Jewishness instead of trying to suppress it. This may sound a little vague and unspecified. Yet we must remember that an increasing number of German Jews, especially of the younger generation, having lost their forefathers' natural religious loyalty, did not any longer stand on safe ground and tended to drift away. The split personality of the Jewish intellectual, detached from the community of his origin and yet not unreservedly accepted by his environment, was the most conspicuous and most tragic representative of this type. His spiritual position is reflected in Kurt Tucholsky's farewell letter, where he writes: 'Ich bin einmal aus dem Judentum "ausgetreten". Heute sehe ich, daß man so etwas garnicht kann' ['I once "resigned" from the Jewish community. Today I can see that one can never do that'].[14]

Tucholsky, however, had committed suicide in Sweden in December 1935, at a time of despair when it seemed that all options were closed to the German Jews: it was impossible to be either an observant or a secularized Jew in Germany, and not yet possible to find a community of former German Jews solidly established abroad (certainly not in Sweden). Conditions in Britain in the 1950s were vastly different; in particular, the assimilated Jews who had formed the majority of the Jews in Germany and Austria had re-established a viable community in Britain, where they were, very broadly speaking, continuing the process of social integration interrupted in their native lands by Hitler. As the Anglo-Jewish writer Emanuel Litvinoff put it in an article in the *Jewish Observer*: 'The rise of Hitler in the '30s brought to Anglo-Jewry a mass infusion of energetic, gifted, educated German Jews who anglicized themselves more quickly and with more thoroughness and skill than any other Jewish immigrants.'[15]

The sense of an assimilated identity that tended to downplay traditional Jewish elements predominated in *AJR Information*. This was evident in articles which, to take two examples from many, recalled the complete lack of interest in Judaism among many of the German-speaking Jews of Prague before 1914, or which claimed that the connection of the majority of non-observant German Jews with their synagogues had been social rather than religious in nature.[16] As usual, the reassertion of this strongly assimilated identity went hand in hand with a heightened awareness of what had divided the more secularized German-speaking Jews from their Orthodox co-religionists, with their strongly traditional values and identity. Nelly Wolffheim, an educationalist, kindergarten teacher and member of the Berlin Group of the International Psychoanalytical Society, recalled starting

work before 1914 in a kindergarten in Berlin. There she had been discon-
certed by the gulf between herself, an educated, assimilated, middle-class
Jew, and poorer Jews more recently arrived from the East, who maintained
a style of life utterly unfamiliar to her: 'When I came to work in a kindergarten near the Alexanderplatz, I found it very hard to establish contact
with the children and their mothers, and my attitude towards them was
rather like that of so many English people towards us, the "foreigners".'[17]

Nelly Wolffheim, a Jew whose identity had been shaped by a background steeped in the values and culture of middle-class Germany, could
describe traditionally observant Jews from the East as 'foreign', so strange
had the rituals and customs that underpinned their life become to the
socially integrated Jews of Berlin. The two groups almost literally spoke different languages, for those who saw themselves as assimilated Jews had
opted for German as their everyday language, very deliberately rejecting
Yiddish, the language of the old Jewish world that they wished to put
behind them. Language is of course a principal determinant of identity and
socio-cultural self-image; the banishing of Yiddish – it was by no means
unknown for children in assimilated households to be forbidden to speak
it[18] – was therefore a powerful statement of how such integrated families
saw themselves and how they wished to be seen.

The Jewish refugees in Britain also mounted a resolute defence of the
assimilationist policies pursued by the principal organization representing
the Jews in Germany before 1933, the Centralverein deutscher Staatsbürger
jüdischen Glaubens, whose willingness to embrace a Germanized identity
and culture, to declare its loyalty to Germany and to go a long way down
the road of integration into German society came under heavy criticism
from Jewish historians after 1945.[19] Despite the events of 1933–45, articles in *AJR Information* continued to present the assimilated life and culture
of the bulk of German Jewry as a legacy of lasting value and its termina-
tion in Germany as the destruction of a precious and substantial tradition.
A review of a book of essays by the writer Margarete Susman expressed this
continuing positive identification with the German-Jewish heritage:

> as Margarete Susman is herself a Jewish refugee from Germany she
> realises and tries to analyse the deep tragedy that emigration has
> meant for the Jews. Germany was the only country where the Jews
> had become so imbued with all that was beautiful and elevating in
> the land of their adoption and where they had themselves created
> immortal works in a language they had come to love.[20]

The AJR's pride in the achievements of the Centralverein (CV) was evident
in its tribute to Max Apt, one of the founders of the organization in 1893,

on the occasion of his eighty-fifth birthday in 1954: 'The AJR, which considers it a great privilege that throughout the years he has identified himself with its cause, conveys to Professor Apt its sincerest congratulations.'[21] One could say with equal justice that the AJR continued in many ways to identify with the values espoused by the CV, even though the cause of integration into German society had been fought and lost forever.

On the sixtieth anniversary of the foundation of the CV in 1953, *AJR Information* published a substantial article by Hermann Ludwig Berlak, Leo Baeck's son-in-law, on the organization's history and achievements. It started by considering the largely negative view of the CV and its assimilationist stance predominant among contemporary commentators:

> But for Hitlerism, the 'Centralverein deutscher Staatsbürger jüdischen Glaubens' would have celebrated its 60th anniversary on March 22, 1953. Today, the achievements of German Jewry are largely forgotten, the remnants of German Jewry are dispersed, their institutions dissolved, their ideas, ideals and organisations often misunderstood or even despised. So we ask ourselves if there is a place in history for this organisation, which once prided itself on being the largest of the many organisations of German Jewry.[22]

Berlak proceeded to answer this question in the affirmative, setting the record straight with a stout defence of the role of the CV in consolidating the advances made by the Jews of Germany since emancipation, in securing fully equal rights for Jews as German citizens and later in resisting Nazism. He admitted that the CV, a child of its times, had been affected by the nationalism of the nineteenth century, and that the discussions among the German Jews in those days 'speak a language which is not any longer our own'. But he believed that the ideology of the CV, combining national patriotism with an insistence on equal rights for Jews, still formed a living part of Jewish political identity in the countries of the West:

> The CV's postulate of Jewish pride, combining faithfulness to the Jewish heritage and loyalty to the country, and the belief in the duty of fighting for one's right have become generally accepted by Jews all over the world. In all countries of Western civilisation Jews live their lives ... as loyal citizens ... The world in which the CV worked does not exist any more, but wherever Jews, both the former adherents and the former opponents of the CV, may stand today, they can agree on one point: It has written a great chapter in the history of German Jewry.

Berlak's own life exemplified the values that he espoused. Born in Posen in 1896, the son of a wholesale grain-merchant, he volunteered for the

German army in 1914 and was decorated. After studying in Freiburg and Berlin, he became an accountant. He married Ruth Baeck in 1923. During his student years he had joined the KC (Kartell-Convent der Verbindungen deutscher Studenten jüdischen Glaubens), known as the most assimilated of the Jewish student organizations and modelled too closely for some Jews on German student corporations (often right-wing and anti-Semitic). The KC led on naturally to the CV, on whose executive he sat; in a spirit of open-mindedness, he was one of the CV officials who cooperated with the Jewish Agency for Palestine, though himself not a Zionist. Forbidden to work in 1933, he nevertheless stayed in Germany, emigrating to Britain only in 1939. He retrained as an accountant, founding his own firm in 1940. In that year he was interned, but later served in the Home Guard, loyal to his adopted homeland. After the war, he worked for a range of organizations that followed in the assimilationist tradition of the German Jews: the AJR, the United Restitution Organisation, the Council of Jews from Germany and the B'nai B'rith Leo Baeck Lodge. He died in the same month that saw the publication of his article on the CV.[23]

The majority of the Jews from Germany and Austria, who thought of themselves as assimilated, had thus assumed an identity that militated against their absorption into Anglo-Jewry; instead, they tended to integrate directly into British society. They were also aware of the historical barriers that separated them, as heirs to the middle-class, emancipated, secularized Jewry of the German-speaking cultural world, from the descendants of the Jews from Eastern Europe who had settled in Britain, where they had retained more of the values and customs of a traditional Jewish background and had developed a quite different social identity. As previously indicated, there was a considerable history to this. In Germany and Austria, the Western Jews had often been less than welcoming towards newly arrived Jews from the East, whose distinctive appearance and habits threatened to rekindle anti-Semitism, and whose traditional beliefs, time-hallowed lifestyle and limited horizons, as well as the associated poverty and backwardness, uncomfortably reminded their proudly assimilated cousins of the pre-emancipation world that they had left behind. The Eastern Jews, for their part, considered those whom they saw as assimilated Jews as renegades who had abandoned the Jewish faith and the world of Jewry for the lure of German culture and education and for social and material advancement.

In Britain in the 1930s, the boot had been on the other foot, with the descendants of the German Jews arriving as destitute refugees in a country where the descendants of Jews from the East formed the bulk of established Jewry. Though the refugees were duly grateful for the material assistance extended to them by Anglo-Jewry at the institutional and official level, their collective memory of their reception at the private, personal level was more mixed, given for example the treatment sometimes experienced by refugee women on domestic service visas in Anglo-Jewish households and the general sense that British Jews did not fully accept the refugees as fellow Jews or welcome them with corresponding warmth. The patterns of settlement of the refugees tended not to bring them closer to Anglo-Jewry, reinforcing the latter's view of them as over-keen to integrate and to assume a pose of social and cultural superiority.

The collective memory of the refugees was decisively influenced by experiences such as those of C.C. Aronsfeld, who came to Leeds in 1934 to work for a year and stayed for three. In a barbed account of his relations with Leeds Jewry, Aronsfeld was at pains to record those who behaved generously towards him, like Professor Selig Brodetsky, while making clear that they were exceptions: 'Naturally, the ordinary Jew did not always readily share in the breadth of his vision. Sympathy for the refugees from Germany was never entirely free from sentiments bordering on Schadenfreude, for all but a very few Leeds Jews had come from Russia and passed through Germany.'[24] Anglo-Jewry seemed to be bent on persuading the refugees to leave Britain as soon as possible, reflecting the same anxiety with which, ironically, the German Jews had formerly hurried the Eastern Jews on their way to the ports of emigration:

> On several occasions I was told by the Refugees Committee that it was extremely difficult, if not hopeless, to get a permit for England, that it would, in fact, be best not to come hither at all. When just six of our twelve months in Leeds had passed, a high Jewish official appeared from London to impress on us, with all the authority at his command, that any extension of the original licence was most unlikely; we should be well advised to seek our future elsewhere.

Aronsfeld recalled attitudes that the refugees came to see as typical of sections of Anglo-Jewry: their surprising indifference to the plight of fellow Jews who were victims of Nazi persecution, as in the case of his employer in the sewing-machine trade, who was 'severely unconcerned with any but business matters'; and their willingness to take advantage of the refugees' situation, as in the case of the young female domestic servants who had been 'kept all too busy in Jewish households'. He recalled with particular distaste the local representative of the Jewish Refugees' Committee, an affluent tailor who took exception to the fact that Aronsfeld had had an article published in a German-Jewish periodical:

> Mr. Micawbersky promptly summoned me into his august presence

and on the evidence before him, which he was no more able to read than to refute, he told me that being a mere factory hand, I had no business to write such articles, or for that matter any articles, and in appropriately high excitement, tempered only by the careful attention with which he was winding up the precious bulging bales of newly arrived cloth, he added: 'I am going to get rid of you! I send you back to Germany!'[25]

By Aronsfeld's own admission, matters improved in the later years of immigration. In addition, a refugee resident in Leeds published a letter in the journal the following month, vigorously disputing Aronsfeld's view of Leeds and disassociating himself from Aronsfeld's 'most unkind and sneering remarks'.[26] Nevertheless, the image of Anglo-Jewry conveyed in articles like Aronsfeld's was widespread, and it contributed greatly to the formation among the refugees of a separate, 'Continental' identity that developed almost in contradistinction to their perception of British Jewish identity. That the two groups in fact shared so much of a common heritage merely served to highlight certain key differences in their collective outlooks and identities.

This sense of distance from Anglo-Jewry undoubtedly influenced the development of the refugees' own communal identity, which, determined in large measure by their German-speaking, assimilated origins, set them apart from other groups of Jews. A parallel factor was the largely good relationship most of them came to enjoy with British society around them; this caused the refugees to adapt the way they led their everyday lives, and within certain limits their attitudes and values, more to British norms, bypassing Anglo-Jewry in the process of their integration into British society. Plainly, this did not mean that the refugees became British, other than in the formal sense of taking British citizenship, since they retained many elements of a Continental lifestyle: their accent and use of the German language, which immediately distinguished them from the British, their preferences in diet, dress, holidays or leisure pursuits,[27] and above all their Central European culture. Over the years of settlement, however, they plainly came to acquire what one can call a British dimension to their communal identity.

In 1959, the Association of Democratic Lawyers from Germany, a refugee organization, invited Dr Georg Blessin, a senior German civil servant from the compensation and restitution department of the Federal Ministry of Finance, to speak at a public meeting at Hampstead Town Hall. Given the sensitivity of the subject and the high feelings inevitably engendered by the appearance of a German government official, it was perhaps not surprising that proceedings became heated. Nevertheless, the lawyer Ernst Schäfer was sufficiently shocked at the behaviour of some members of the audience to write to *AJR Information*, protesting that in rudely shouting down a speaker they had 'violated the standard of good manners prevailing at public meetings in this country'.[28] This was a token of the internalization of British notions of courtesy, tolerance and fair-mindedness by the refugees, who had come from countries where public meetings in the 1920s and 1930s had often been anything but decorous and calm.

The refugees' experiences led them to become attached to British values as they perceived them in public life: the aversion to violence and extremism, the measured pace of evolutionary reform, and the spirit of consensus and willingness to compromise that ensured that reforms, once achieved, were not reversed. Writing in 1952, a year after the Conservatives under Churchill had returned to power, Lutz Weltmann described an earlier Tory prime minister: 'The cure Disraeli proposed was the English way: timely reforms and compromise with reality. He was not in favour of Utopian blueprints, but propagated good government, which meant for him government not for one class only, but trusteeship of an élite for the welfare and happiness of the governed.'[29] Behind this surely lay the refugees' admiration for a political system under which the creation of the Welfare State by Attlee's Labour government, a radical innovation that recast post-war British society, was accepted by an incoming Conservative government in the interests of the people as a whole. Less than a decade after the end of the Third Reich, this must have seemed a reassuring indication of security and continuity.

In a quite different area, Rabbi Ignaz Maybaum, attacking Martin Buber's 'nationalist theology' in relation to Israel, concluded that fifteen years of exposure to cool-headed British pragmatism had changed the refugees' very patterns of thought: 'German Jews living now in English-speaking countries and having become acclimatized to English empirical thinking will probably realize how estranged they have become to Buber's German argumentation.'[30] The classic declaration of a refugee's love for British society with its abhorrence of extremes, suspicion of ideologically charged manifestos and instinctive preference for the way of moderation, informed by a spirit of friendly, albeit strongly anti-intellectual decency, was to be found in the second volume of Arthur Koestler's autobiography, *The Invisible Writing*, published in London in 1954. Reviewing the book, the noted writer Hans Jaeger, a political exile, predictably chose to quote in full the well-known passage in which Koestler described his rejection of the 'arrow in the blue' (the title of the first autobiographical volume), symbol of utopian visions, ideological absolutes and perfect causes:

I adopted as my home a country where arrows are only used on dart-boards, suspicious of all causes, contemptuous of systems, bored by ideologies, sceptical about Utopias, rejecting all blue-prints, enamoured of its leisurely muddle, incurious about the future, devoted to its past. A country neither of Yogis nor of Commissars, but of potterers-in-the-garden and stickers-in-the-mud, where strikers played soccer with the police and Socialists wore peers' crowns.[31]

That Jaeger devoted almost half of his review to the few short pages of the book's epilogue, which contained Koestler's analysis of his relationship with Britain, was highly significant, for those nine or so pages (in a book of over five hundred) gave graphic expression to the way many refugees felt about their adopted homeland. Jaeger, like Koestler, began with Britain at war, citing the incident where a major at the Duke's Road recruiting centre agreed to postpone Koestler's call-up so that he could complete a book, suggesting 'that he calls at this Centre when he is at liberty to join His Majesty's Forces'. At first, this merely confirmed Koestler in his conviction that Britain would lose the war; later, he learnt to value the regard for the individual and the preservation of a measure of individual liberty even at a time of total war. Jaeger then retraced Koestler's gradual post-war realization that England had become home to him, at least in the sense that when living away from England, he became conscious of being 'abroad'; in England, he had felt a stranger, but abroad he now felt an Englishman, so he returned to London in 1952, vowing to live there ever after.

Many refugees shared Koestler's realization that, if they could never feel English in Britain, they certainly felt British when abroad. Though there were aspects of British life to which they could never accustom themselves, refugees routinely described the same feelings as Koestler on returning 'home' to Britain: 'The smug contentment that I feel each time I arrive at the Passport Control at Dover, joining the queue which says "For British Subjects" and casting a cold eye at the queue "For Foreigners" (the poor chaps can't help it), alternates with moods of impatience and fits of exasperation. But a relationship without ambivalence would be lacking in spice.'[32]

Jaeger quoted Koestler's memorable description of Britain as a country where refugees could recuperate after their experience of the totalitarian dictatorships that disfigured Central Europe: 'I have found the human climate of England particularly congenial and soothing – a kind of Davos for internally bruised veterans of the totalitarian age.' Evoking a Britain long vanished, Koestler continued with a warm tribute to its easygoing tolerance and dislike of violence: 'Its atmosphere contains fewer germs of aggression and brutality per cubic foot in a crowded bus, pub, queue or street than in any other country in which I have lived.'[33] Jaeger did, however, conclude with Koestler's recognition that the dislike of systems and ideologies that attracted him, the Continental intellectual, to the English could all too easily degenerate into an insular and philistine rejection of the realm of ideas and culture so prized by the refugees.

Koestler was in many ways an exception, as an ex-communist and a professional intellectual, and one must exercise caution in applying his self-presentation in *The Invisible Writing* to the refugees in general. But what Jaeger chose to highlight was the intriguing process by which this most *mitteleuropäisch* of figures had to a considerable degree integrated himself psychologically and in terms of his identity into the society of his adopted homeland, while preserving qualities and attitudes that would forever mark him as an outsider. Something not dissimilar could be discerned in the wartime reminiscences of the educationalist and child psychologist Nelly Wolffheim, though in her case the starting-point was her sense of alienation from British Jews, which caused her to rethink her relationship to non-Jews.[34] Seeing herself as an assimilated Jew from Germany, she was startled by the tendency of British Jews to isolate themselves from British society and to mix exclusively among themselves: 'In Germany I had not encountered their fear of assimilation and their rejection of any closer contact with non-Jews.'

Her description of her experiences with the English, by contrast, was predominantly positive, beginning with her emigration. Desperately seeking admission to Britain for her, some friends had hit on the bold expedient of putting an advertisement in the *Church Times*, and promptly found a guarantor, a devout High Anglican lady whose manifold kindnesses she listed; they included a bedroom with a private bath, breakfast in bed, afternoon tea in her own room and other favours not enjoyed by many refugees in British households. She went during the war to Oxford, where for twelve years she experienced friendliness and a tactful understanding of her situation as a refugee on all sides: from her first non-Jewish contact, the secretary of the local Refugee Committee, to various kindly households where she worked and the two sisters who offered Sunday hospitality to refugees, an oasis of civilization, kindness and cups of fine tea amidst the dreariness of life in furnished rooms.

She was particularly struck by the prevailing tolerance in these Christian houses, where her Jewish beliefs were never an issue: 'Here one did not feel an alien foreigner, one had the feeling of being able to behave exactly as one was used to ... Where differences in beliefs arose, they were bridged by the good manners and courtesy of the hostesses.' She never encountered any open anti-Semitism; those less-educated landladies who refused to let rooms to refugees were, she assumed, motivated by a wartime dislike of 'Germans'. Nelly Wolffheim's experiences, limited as they were to the progressive middle-class sections of Oxford society, were hardly typical, still less did her depiction of her reception in Oxford reflect the full reality of British wartime attitudes to the refugees. But by the eve of the 1960s an image, a *Wunschbild* almost, of British tolerance, courtesy and traditions of fair play had taken root among the refugees, attracted by such qualities as the (alleged) British ability to defuse potential conflicts by old-fashioned politeness and consideration.

'English' attitudes like this fed into the new sense of identity that the refugees were developing. Nevertheless, even Nelly Wolffheim concluded at a critical juncture that, for all her gratitude to her hosts and her willingness to adopt some of their ways, a gulf remained between her and the British. When news came through of the end of the war, she feigned illness to avoid attending the celebrations:

> I could not bring myself to celebrate the defeat of Germany, much as I had longed for it, with English people. I felt uncomfortable at taking part as one of them. A strange feeling for a Jew, who was certainly more pleased and excited by the announcement of victory than most of the surprisingly passive English people around me. An eternal contradiction lies hidden within the Jewish soul.

In 1958 Nelly Wolffheim was still writing in German, not English; and for all her fondness for English society, she moved into Otto Schiff House, one of the refugee Old Age Homes, preferring in later life to surround herself with the company of other German-speaking Jews.

The 1950s provided favourable conditions for the refugees to integrate into British society. It was a decade of growing prosperity, of stability and consensus, not of polarization and radicalism. Politically, the threat of anti-Semitism was receding: one of the most virulent foes of the Jewish refugees disappeared in 1954 when the weekly *Truth* repudiated its anti-Semitic stance, rejecting the racial discrimination that had previously disfigured its pages. *AJR Information* continued to carry reports of the usual kind of petty anti-Semitism: discrimination by golf clubs and medical schools, quotas at public schools, resistance to the adoption of Jewish candidates in the Conservative Party, or the antics of Hitler-loving members of the aristocracy like the Marquess of Bath. It must be said that fear of anti-Semitism declined in good measure because immigration from the Caribbean presented the racist right with a more immediately visible scapegoat, deflecting the reservoir of racial prejudice towards an alternative target.[35] It was nevertheless something of a milestone when in 1954 the Home Secretary, Sir David Maxwell-Fyfe, stated in reply to a parliamentary question that no instances of racial discrimination had been brought to his notice recently.[36]

If it is true that a man is to be known by his friends, then the British friends publicly acknowledged by the refugees in the 1950s say a great deal about the openness of the refugees' communal identity to assuming a 'British' element. In the immediate post-war years, the majority of the benefactors of the refugees mentioned in *AJR Information* were Anglo-Jewish, mainly those who had run the organizations responsible for the emigration and settlement of the Jews from Europe. Outstanding among these was Professor Norman Bentwich, alongside other Anglo-Jewish notables such as Leonard G. Montefiore, James de Rothschild and the Hon. Lily Montagu. The most prominent non-Jews were members of parliament like Eleanor Rathbone, Josiah Wedgwood and Oliver Locker-Lampson, political campaigners on behalf of the refugees who, however, had only limited personal contact with them.

In the 1950s this changed, with non-Jews outnumbering British Jews among those to whom the refugees recognized a debt of gratitude. The former continued to include public figures like the Oxford academic Gilbert Murray, the composer Ralph Vaughan Williams or the Bishop of Chichester, George Bell, but ordinary British names came to the fore, reflecting the increasingly easy interaction between the refugees and the everyday British world in which they moved and the development of friendly personal relations. In April 1956, for example, *AJR Information* paid warm tribute on her seventy-fifth birthday to Dorothy Buxton, a doughty crusader for often unpopular liberal causes, who had worked tirelessly after 1933 for the rescue of Jews and for the removal of prejudice against the new arrivals: 'It has been the good fortune of our Community that this country has always been conspicuous by the great number of liberal minded personalities who identify themselves with the cause of minorities.' Under the title 'The Mother of the Cambridge Refugees', the journal celebrated the eightieth birthday of Hilda Sturge, honorary secretary of the Cambridge Refugee Committee from 1933 to 1945, who was gratefully remembered by her 'former charges [who] still remember her unfailing devotion and care in the days of their need'.[37] These were 'ordinary' middle-class people, distinguished only by their generosity of spirit.

Another family that showed kindness to refugees was the Attenborough family of Leicester, one of whose sons grew up to be the actor and film director Richard (later Lord) Attenborough. He recalled in 1955 how his father, chairman of the local refugees' committee, had taken into his home two German-Jewish girls who had been stranded in Britain by the outbreak of war, en route to America.[38] Most of these benefactors were from the middle class, the sector of society with which most refugees established contacts, often progressive in outlook, and not infrequently Quakers (like Hilda Sturge). Hospitality from a grander background came from Mary Beeton, on whose eighty-fifth birthday Nelly Wolffheim wrote: 'For many in our midst the name of Mary Beeton is inseparably linked up with memories of pleasant days of recreation. An invitation to "Handsmooth", her beautiful country seat, was for a great number of former refugees a ray of light during the first difficult years of our stay in this country.' Miss Beeton always had two or three refugee guests at her house, the number having enjoyed her hospitality between 1938 and 1945 rising to some seventy-five, many of whom made return visits after forming real friendships with her.[39]

Those who put themselves at risk for the German Jews included a genuine aristocrat, Sir Michael Bruce, who was asked by leading figures in Anglo-Jewry to go to Germany at the time of the *Kristallnacht* pogroms to bring back a record of what was happening there. Bruce succeeded in smuggling the reports out, but at the cost of being imprisoned and badly beaten by the Gestapo. The highlight of Werner Rosenstock's review of Bruce's autobiography, *Tramp Royal*, was Bruce's account of his efforts to persuade Rabbi Leo Baeck and Wilfrid Israel, an Anglo-German Jew who later died on a wartime rescue mission, to take two free seats on a private plane out of Germany:

> He begged Wilfrid and Dr Baeck to be those two passengers. 'Wilfrid said quietly: "I will go when Dr Baeck goes." Dr Baeck looked at him and smiled, and said: "I will go when I am the last Jew alive in Germany." ... The world is a better place for having given birth to two such gallant men. I am proud and honoured to have worked for a brief space at their sides', he writes.[40]

Rosenstock's satisfaction at this recognition of German-Jewish qualities by a member of the British upper class reflected a broader integrationist expectation that the two groups could meet, as in this instance, on the common ground of mutual appreciation and acceptance.

At the other end of the social scale was Charles Coward, an ordinary soldier from Edmonton, North London, who was taken prisoner at Calais in 1940 and whose attempts to escape landed him in the Monowitz camp adjacent to Auschwitz, where he ingeniously contrived to rescue several hundred Jews from the death camp. Sergeant Coward's heroism first came to the refugees' attention in 1952 when he and another British prisoner-of-war, Robert Ferris, were commended by a Frankfurt court in its judgement on the case of *Wollheim v. I.G. Farben*, in which it recognized the claim of Norbert Wollheim, a former slave-labourer, against the firm that had exploited him at Auschwitz. In 1953 the AJR wrote to the two men, paying tribute to them for their humanity. Two years later, Werner Rosenstock reviewed *The Password Is Courage* by John Castle, which documented Coward's wartime experiences, and recalled the AJR's letter of thanks to the two British ex-soldiers 'for their courageous attitude which helped the Jewish prisoners to retain their belief in humanity'.[41]

On 24 October 1960, Coward was the subject of a programme in the popular BBC television series *This Is Your Life*. Among those appearing was Norbert Wollheim, by then well known as a leading figure among the Jews in Germany, and a hero in his own right in the eyes of the Jewish refugees for his selfless courage in accompanying Kindertransports to Britain and then returning to Germany. As *AJR Information* put it, the programme brought together the ordinary Londoner and the Holocaust survivor: 'It was certainly the climax of the broadcast, when, at the end, Norbert Wollheim, himself a former Auschwitz prisoner, appeared. In a most dignified and impressive way Wollheim paid tribute to this unassuming Cockney, who, out of a sense of unshakeable decency and at danger to his own life, single-handedly conducted his rescue work.'[42]

The journal was at pains to point up the bond that existed between an apparently typical working-class Englishman like Coward and the Jewish victims of Nazism. Tellingly, no historian has yet picked up the fact that a man with a record like Coward's was watched by millions of viewers being hosted by Eamonn Andrews on prime-time TV. The refugees, on the other hand, were clearly concerned to keep the memory of Coward's rescue of Jews alive, as the reports about him in their journal over a period of years showed. *AJR Information* had extended its thanks to the two British ex-soldiers in the context of its members' growing sense of values and experiences shared with the British.

The refugees' sense that they were becoming accepted in British society, with friends and benefactors across the range of the social classes, reinforced their feelings of gratitude to Britain for taking them in and their admiration – often tempered by amusement – for the British. This formed part of the process of identification with the adopted homeland and the development of a communal identity influenced by integration into British society. A consequence of this was that *AJR Information* published a striking number of eloquent tributes by former refugees to Britain that expressed real affection, even love, for their adopted homeland.

It is often argued that such expressions of gratitude and of high regard for the British were motivated by a residual fear among refugees of being cast as outsiders, and were thus little more than servile gestures aimed at propitiating potential British hostility aimed at them as 'aliens' and Jews. But in fact the tributes read very differently, with no hint of any uneasy currying of favour with a potentially malevolent host population. This was plainly the case with the farewell tribute paid by Rabbi Alexander Altmann, one of the outstanding refugee ministers, when he left Britain to take up a Chair at Brandeis University: 'I found refuge in this country, and it is entirely due to the humanity which this country represents that my family and I were able to be transplanted to England.'[43] Altmann, never the kind of man to kowtow to hostile pressure, had no need to make concessions to British prejudices when he was about to leave for America.

The same argument applied, if anything more strongly, in the case of the journal's report that Adolf Heikorn, of Adamson Road, Swiss Cottage, had stated in his will that he wished to place on record 'my heartfelt thanks for the hospitality which I have enjoyed in England as a refugee from Nazism and to express the wish that God's blessing may ever be on England'. One's will is, after all, a place where one can speak without fear of human retribution. Such warm testimonies of affection were a regular note in obituaries of refugees who had arrived in Britain well into middle age, overcome the difficulties of the early years of settlement and become deeply attached to their new homeland. In 1956 Leo Baeck wrote an obituary for Rabbi Bruno Italiener, who had served as minister in Darmstadt and Hamburg before coming to Britain, 'the homeland of the refugees, and he learnt to love it so affectionately'; as Rabbi at West End Synagogue, Italiener had developed a special love of Regent's Park. Neither Baeck, after surviving Theresienstadt, nor Italiener could have felt much need to parade a synthetic attachment to Britain and the British.[44] The unadorned simplicity of these tributes gave them both force and authenticity, not least as evidence of the perceived lack of barriers separating the refugees from the culture and society around them.

As the refugees grew into British society around them, the culture of that society was taking root in them. When Dr G.J. van Heuven Goedhart, United Nations high commissioner for refugees and winner of the Nobel Peace Prize, died in 1956, *AJR Information* started its tribute with an image steeped in English associations: '"Goedhart" might well be a figure taken straight from *Pilgrim's Progress*, a companion of Greatheart and Faithful and the rest who struggle against all kinds of troubles as they seek the Celestial City. Goedhart, therefore, was a fitting name for a man charged to take care of those war victims who had lost their homes.'[45]

While Werner Rosenstock was drawing on John Bunyan as if it were the most natural thing in the world, Kenneth Ambrose found himself, rather to his own surprise, preferring British books for children to *Struwwelpeter*, a classic of the German children's literature that had helped to mould the imagination of generations of German-speaking readers. 'It seems strange criticizing a book one had taken so completely for granted. Sacrilegious, almost', mused Ambrose, before explaining why 'such a horrid book' now seemed to him quite unsuitable for his own small British-born son.[46] To abandon figures like Struwwelpeter or Max and Moritz, integral parts of a German child's world, for Alice in Wonderland or Winnie the Pooh was to replace the earliest reference-points of German-language cultural consciousness in the formation of identity with their British equivalents – no small step, if one thinks what it would take for an English person to do the reverse.

There appeared to be a growing sense that the refugees were becoming embedded in the British world around them. A report on the centenary of the birth of Heinrich Hertz, whose discovery of electromagnetic waves had made radio transmission possible, seemed to take it as a matter of course that Hertz's two daughters were now living in Cambridge, a transplantation that was a source of pride to the refugee community and re-established a link to earlier achievements bridging the gulf of forced emigration.[47] A striking indication of how much at ease many refugees now felt in Britain appeared in a review by Alfons Rosenberg of a book about Walther Rathenau, the multi-talented Jewish industrialist and intellectual who became foreign minister in the Weimar Republic and was assassinated by right-wing extremists in 1922. Rosenberg entitled his review 'Sir Walther', as Rathenau's friend the writer Gerhart Hauptmann used to call him, concluding with the remarkable claim that in Britain Rathenau would indeed have received a knighthood for his achievements, instead of the hand-grenade that killed him in Germany – evidence of a strong sense of an underlying compatibility between German-Jewish and British attitudes and values.[48]

A particularly significant indicator of the refugees' sense of identity was the name of their own organization, which called (and still calls) itself an association of refugees. Since the post-war years, the possibility of changing the AJR's name has repeatedly been mooted, often in conjunction with the question of publishing *AJR Information* in German. Both these issues relate fundamentally to the refugees' self-image and sense of identity, as well as to the degree of their integration into British society. The two issues were discussed vigorously in the early 1950s, starting with suggestions at the AJR's general meeting in 1952 that the term 'refugees' be dropped from its designation and that the journal be published in German. This gave rise to a lively correspondence where, as always, the view of the membership was clearer on the second of these issues.

The first response in the journal was a letter from Ernst Schäfer, in which he declared himself strongly opposed to publishing *AJR Information* in German.[49] He believed that the refugees could be expected to have the necessary fluency at least to read English, considering that even the elderly were 'eager clients of the public libraries and subscribers to the English press', and that it would be a retrograde step to 'relapse into German' just when the appearance of the AJR's twenty-first anniversary publication, *Britain's New Citizens*, had signalled the success of the community's integration into British society. Schäfer was not, however, convinced by the argument that the term 'refugees' should be dropped, even though 'most members of our group have by now settled in this country, acquired British nationality and consider themselves at home in what was first a country of refuge'. For him, the designation 'refugees' had lost the negative connotation of a minority group of outsiders, potential targets of discrimination and prejudice, and become a matter of pride: 'We are still a special group within the larger community, represented as such by our Association. We should be proud of the quality of refugees, a term with honourable significance in history.'

This letter gave rise to a substantial correspondence, which the editor tried to summarize in the following issue of the journal.[50] The great majority of these replies were opposed to changing the Association's name. One of the few in favour commented: 'Should we earmark ourselves as refugees for the rest of our lives? ... If one wants to be a useful member of the Community one has to take root and should not be reminded all the time that one does not really belong to it.' But the bulk of the correspondents felt that, as they had indeed come to Britain as refugees, there was no good reason to change the name, since they evidently did not associate it with any kind of second-class status.

One lone voice spoke up in favour of publishing the journal in German. Many others saw no reason to switch away from English; some considered that it would run counter to the development of their community away from its German origins and towards integration into British society: 'We are not a German Community living in this country, but Jews expelled from Germany who have found refuge and try to integrate in the British Community.' A further batch of replies published in September 1952 took the same view on both issues.[51] This showed again how the refugees had switched their loyalties from their native lands to Britain, adopting in this country the same strategy of integration, but with greater chances of acceptance.

A fresh bout of correspondence ensued in 1954, sparked off by a witty polemic by Georg Schatzky, chairman of the AJR's Cambridge group, against the suggested inclusion in the Association's title of the inelegant phrase 'ex-refugees' or 'former refugees', as if the AJR's members had become 'Refugees a.D.' [*außer Dienst*, retired].[52] The apparent impossibility of finding a replacement that was both as concise and as accurate as the original name has indeed been one of the main reasons why it has remained in place to this day; alternatives like that suggested in August 1954 by Alfred Lindemann, 'Association of Jewish New Citizens in Great Britain', were simply too clumsy. Schatzky argued in defence of the original name that the refugees from Central Europe in Britain could only divest themselves of their identity as refugees with great difficulty, if at all: 'But tell me: by what means may I resign my humble status as a refugee poor and simple and become a "former refugee"? Is it the length of residence in this country that counts, or the naturalization, or my Oxford accent, or my high prosperity?' Alfred Lindemann, on the other hand, preferred to look to the future in Britain, not to dwell on the refugee past; his proposed new name was intended 'to imply our willingness to become integrated into our new community', adding that 'to help our members to find a rightful place in this country was and is the main *raison d'être* of our Association'.

In a letter published in September 1954, Peter Johnson also argued for a change of name, claiming that Schatzky spoke only for those who were still too emotionally attached to Central Europe to be able or willing 'to become acclimatized in their new country of domicile'. Though still proud of his 'Continental-Jewish heritage', Johnson belonged to a younger generation of refugees born after 1914, many of whom had served in the British forces during the war, and he found the term 'refugee' unsuitable:

> In my humble view, once we have been given naturalization in a country different from that of our birth, we cannot in all truthfulness be classified as 'refugees' any more. That, on the other hand, we may remain strangers within our newly found domicile and alien in outlook is an entirely different matter. The same, though possibly to a smaller degree, applies to a Welshman or an Irishman in England, or to a larger degree to a Jew – of whatever nationality -- when he comes up against xenophobia in this country.

But Johnson had no new name to suggest, thereby dooming his plea for change to failure.

There was in truth more common ground between Johnson and Schatzky than first meets the eye. Both saw that the refugees were and would remain a group marked by its Central European origins and somewhat separate from mainstream British society, just as Johnson's Welshman felt something of a stranger in England. This was predictable when the host population was as homogeneous as Britain's still was in the mid-twentieth century; in an immigrant society like the USA, by contrast, a group of first-generation newcomers could come to feel fully integrated on an equal basis with other groups, for these too were mostly relatively recent arrivals still conscious of their original ethnicity and culture. American Jews who express surprise that the word 'refugee' still figures in the AJR's name over-look this fundamental difference between the two countries; American society is composed of a multitude of minority groups, all (except Native Americans) immigrants, whereas British society in the post-war period, though divided on class lines, was dominated by a single ethnically stable, homogeneous majority. This did not excuse the host population from wel-coming immigrant minorities correctly – rather the contrary; but even assuming that they received a proper reception, minorities like the Jews from Central Europe would still remain conscious of the differences that distinguished them from the native majority.

Neither Johnson nor Schatzky wished these cultural differences to delay the refugees' integration into British society, while Lindemann was con-cerned that it should proceed as quickly as was practicable. The desire of the overwhelming majority of the refugees that the journal of their Association should be published in English was clear evidence of their acceptance of the strategy of integration, within the limits indicated above. The fact that the journal's American equivalent, *Aufbau*, was published in German pointed again to the different situation facing minority groups in the two countries: in America, the Jews from Central Europe could integrate as one ethnic group among many, all maintaining much of the culture, identity, practices and language that they had brought with them; whereas in Britain integration necessarily meant the adoption, among other things, of the majority language.

In Britain, the refugees integrated, but they integrated as a refugee minority culturally distinct from the majority; in America, the majority into which the refugees integrated had itself developed from an agglom-eration of culturally disparate minorities. The communal identity of the refugees in Britain accordingly developed along different lines from its American counterpart; its German-Jewish identity became permeated with British elements, to the extent that the generation of the refugees' children has a public identity almost indistinguishable from that of its British peers.

NOTES

1.   T. Eriksen, *Ethnicity and Nationalism: Anthropological Perspectives* (London and Boulder, CO: Pluto Press, 1993), p.9. I have also drawn on M. Banks, *Ethnicity: Anthropological Constructions* (London: Routledge,

1996), B. Anderson, *Imagined Communities: Reflections on the Origin and Spread of Nationalism* (London and New York: Verso, 1999), N. Glazer and D. Moynihan (eds), *Ethnicity* (Cambridge, MA: Harvard University Press, 1975), and, for identity and memory, A. Assmann, *Erinnerungsräume: Formen und Wandlungen des kulturellen Gedächtnisses* (Munich: Beck, 1999).

2. Eriksen, *Ethnicity and Nationalism*, pp.9f. and pp.26f.
3. *AJR Information* (May 1960), p.1 (my translation).
4. *AJR Information* (June 1960), p.11. Ambrose attended King's College, Taunton.
5. *AJR Information* (June 1954), p.4.
6. See on this complex subject C. Brinson, 'Facing the Facts: Relations with the "Heimat"', in M. Malet and A. Grenville (eds), *Changing Countries: The Experience and Achievement of German-speaking Exiles from Hitler in Britain 1933 to Today* (London: Libris, 2002), pp.184–216.
7. See Chapter 4.
8. 'Journey into the Past', *AJR Information* (October 1951), p.5.
9. *AJR Information* (March 1960), p.8.
10. *AJR Information* (April 1958), p.1.
11. A. Godfrey, *Three Rabbis in a Vicarage* (London: Larsen Grove Press, 2005), and B. Lewkowicz, 'Belsize Square Synagogue: Community, Belonging, and Religion among German-Jewish Refugees', *Yearbook of the Research Centre for German and Austrian Exile Studies*, 10 (2008), pp.113–36.
12. *AJR Information* (October 1951), p.1.
13. 'In Memory of Abraham Horovitz', *AJR Information* (January 1954), p.3.
14. *AJR Information* (November 1953), p.5.
15. Quoted in *AJR Information* (February 1956), p.7.
16. *AJR Information* (January 1954), p.4, (May 1960), p.10.
17. 'Jüdische Beziehungen zu Nichtjuden: Autobiographische Notizen' ('The Relations of Jews to Non-Jews: Autobiographical Notes'), *AJR Information* (January 1958), p.10 (my translation).
18. An example was Lucie Schachne (Lucie Kaye) from Berlin, whose father made donations to Jewish charities supporting poor Jews from the East, but would not allow her to speak Yiddish. See interview with Lucie Kaye, in the possession of the author.
19. For an expert analysis of the C.V. from a positive perspective, see A. Paucker, *Deutsche Juden im Kampf um Recht und Freiheit: Studien zu Abwehr, Selbstbehauptung und Widerstand der deutschen Juden seit dem Ende des 19. Jahrhunderts* (Teetz: Hentrich & Hentrich, 2003).
20. *AJR Information* (July 1954), p.4.
21. *AJR Information* (July 1954), p.4. Max Apt lived in Britain for fifteen years before returning to Germany in 1954, where he died in 1957.
22. 'A Chapter in Our History', *AJR Information* (March 1953), p.5.
23. See the tribute by W. Rosenstock in *AJR Information* (April 1953), p.3.
24. *AJR Information* (February 1952), p.3.
25. According to the Online Database of British Archival Resources relating to German-Jewish Refugees 1933–1950 (BARGE), www.sussex.ac.uk/Units/cgjs/barge, the real name of the Leeds committee representative was David Makofski (information kindly supplied by Samira Teuteberg of BARGE).
26. *AJR Information* (March 1952), p.6.
27. These aspects of refugee life have been thoroughly investigated by M. Berghahn, *Continental Britons: German-Jewish Refugees from Nazi Germany* (Oxford: Berg, 1988).
28. *AJR Information* (May 1959), p.14.
29. *AJR Information* (March 1952), p.4.
30. *AJR Information* (March 1951), p.4.
31. Quoted in *AJR Information* (October 1954), p.4, with some divergences from the published text, which I have amended.
32. A. Koestler, *The Invisible Writing: The Second Volume of an Autobiography: 1932–40* (London: Hutchinson, 1969), p.522.
33. Ibid., p.519.
34. *AJR Information* (March 1958), p.12 (my translation).
35. The first major statement on this subject in *AJR Information* was a front-page article by C.C. Aronsfeld, entitled 'Coloured Immigration: The Challenge of Racial Prejudice', published in March 1955 in connection with the first Immigration Regulation Bill.
36. *AJR Information* (March 1954), p.8.
37. *AJR Information* (April 1956), p.6; (July 1956), p.13.
38. *AJR Information* (December 1955), p.5.

39. *AJR Information* (February 1961), p.10.
40. *AJR Information* (November 1955), p.7.
41. *AJR Information* (August 1953), p.3; (April 1955), p.4.
42. *AJR Information* (December 1960), p.3. Roger Ryan, currently researching a dissertation on Coward at University College London, kindly provided me with details, including the date of the broadcast.
43. *AJR Information* (July 1959), p.5.
44. *AJR Information* (November 1956), p.6; (August 1956), p.3.
45. *AJR Information* (August 1956), p.1.
46. *AJR Information* (February 1954), p.8.
47. *AJR Information* (April 1957), p.5.
48. *AJR Information* (September 1959), p.4.
49. *AJR Information* (June 1952), p.6.
50. 'Our "Gallup Poll"', *AJR Information* (July 1952), p.6.
51. *AJR Information* (September 1952), p.7.
52. Letter from Georg Schatzky, *AJR Information* (July 1954), p.6, followed by letter from Alfred Lindemann; (August 1954), p.7, and from Peter W. Johnson (Wolfgang Josephs), (September 1954), p.6.

9

Patterns of Settlement, 1955–1970

By the mid-1950s, when the war had been over for ten years and the pre-war refugees resident in Britain for more than fifteen, the process of building new lives that had characterized the first post-war decade of refugee life in Britain was giving way to permanent settlement. The next decade and a half, encompassing the late 1950s and the 1960s, arguably saw the high point of the refugee community; then a change of generations set in as the British-born children of the now ageing refugees began to reach adulthood. The period between 1955 and 1970 was marked by a growing stability, as the bulk of the refugees adapted, on the whole successfully, to the society and way of life around them and created the material conditions for a settled life for themselves and their families.

Fundamental to the smooth long-term settlement of the refugees was economic security, manifest in the degree of at least modest prosperity which most of those not disadvantaged by specific handicaps achieved during the later 1950s and the 1960s. This showed itself across a wide spectrum of refugee activities and refugee life, including spending patterns, employment, housing and the founding of businesses. During those years it was, for example, very evident that the consumer spending power of the refugee community was rising strongly, as advertisements in *AJR Information* showed. One very visible sign of this was the growing demand for and availability of Continental foods, which had been rare during the period of post-war rationing and austerity but which were now becoming more widespread.

Already in *AJR Information* of March 1954, P. Morris & Son of Charlotte Street, W1, was targeting the refugee market by offering to deliver 'all types of Continental foods to you counter fresh', including Knackwurst, Leberwurst, Wiener Würstchen, salami and sauerkraut. In September 1955, Green's Ltd of Cricklewood, who had two stores in NW2 (Willesden Green), advertised their Continental delicatessen and specialities, including Continental bread fresh every day, while Cohen's (Smoked Salmon) Ltd of Finchley Road announced the opening of a Continental cooked meat department offering a range of Central European delicacies that were exotic by the

(British) standards of the day: Hungarian salami, Cervelat, liver sausage, ox tongue, Teewurst and Debrecziners. By the 1960s shops catering for Continental tastes had multiplied; typical was an ad in September 1962, inviting readers to 'Shop in Comfort at Rawel's Super Food Store' (in Fairfax Road, off Finchley Road) for their Continental delicatessen.

Further evidence that refugees now had money to spend on Continental comforts was the interest in acquiring Continental quilts, in place of English blankets; individuals placed ads seeking to buy or sell quilts, while one regular advertiser, Dawson-Lane Ltd of Wembley Park, declared Continental down quilts to be their speciality and promised refugee customers the personal attention of Mr W. Schachmann (later anglicized to Shackman). Growing prosperity also enabled the refugees to remedy the deficiencies of British domestic heating by installing central heating in their homes. Among the ads for these systems was one in November 1962 for Comfortair, heating consultants and installers of West Heath Drive, NW11, offering 'Tailor Made Central Heating by oil, gas, solid fuel or electricity'.

The journal's columns filled with ads for the classic consumer durables of the period: cars, television sets and washing machines. Cars, new and used, could be purchased from a number of firms located in areas of refugee settlement, such as Bray Motors of West End Lane or Cavendish Motors of Cavendish Road, both in NW6; other firms offered to meet the demand for repairs, parts and servicing. Refugees keen to take to the road for the first time could avail themselves of driving lessons from the Academy of Motoring in West End Lane, which offered complete courses from £4 16s. Car ownership became part of everyday life for many refugees, while some added a touch of luxury. Norwest Car Hire of Finchley Road, a firm run by refugees, advertised saloon cars for hire by those willing to pay for the convenience of being driven to stations, airports or country destinations. In July 1954, James R. Walsh Ltd of Tottenham took an eye-catching ad covering almost a column for their upmarket motorcycles, 'the cream of Continental motorcycles', priced from £106 16s to £188 8s for the 350cc model.

Firms offering to sell or repair television sets, like Electric Comfort Ltd of Haverstock Hill, NW3, advertised in some numbers in the early 1950s, but it was in 1952/53, with the coronation of Queen Elizabeth II, that the boom in sales took off. A large boxed ad from Mott & Reynolds Ltd of Church Road, Willesden, declared: 'Be Tele-Wise! Television at its best will be a source of pleasure during the long Winter Evenings', and offered part-exchange for old radio and television sets, free demonstrations in customers' own homes, as well as a large selection of fridges, radiograms and other electrical appliances.[1] Refugees were also taking advantage of new labour-saving devices. As early as November 1951 a Yorkshire firm advertised a brand of detergent for electric washing machines (though in the primitive form of two-gallon kegs at 25 shillings), which showed that the refugees would be in the forefront when taking up the new range of electrical appliances that appeared on the market from the mid-1950s.

By the 1960s firms that had been advertising simple electrical goods began to trade in the larger domestic appliances that became known as 'white goods'. In February 1963 the electrical retailer Gorta, restyled as Gorta Radiovision Service, announced that it stocked refrigerators and washing machines and that it had the agency for major manufacturers like Bush, Pye, Philips and Grundig, catering for the boom in record players and transistor radios; in December 1962 a competitor, R. & G. (Electrical Installations) Ltd, advertised its agency for such brands as Hoover, Frigidaire and Kenwood.

Probably the most significant indication of the relative affluence that sections of the refugee community now enjoyed was the demand for a range of luxury goods and services, which firms advertising in the journal hastened to meet. Dobrin Chocolates, with shops in the Hampstead Garden Suburb and on Edgware Road, W2, was a refugee business specializing in Continental chocolates; another was Ackerman's Chocolates, which started out in Kensington Church Street, W8, and in December 1956 announced the opening of its shop in Goldhurst Terrace, NW6, one of the best known and longest lived of refugee retail outlets. Ackerman's advertised a range of mouth-watering confectionery, such as their de luxe Easter eggs, evidence both of the refugees' taste for expensive delicacies and of their adaptation to non-Jewish practices. In 1968 Ackerman's received the Royal Warrant; thereafter, the ads for its chocolates proudly bore the royal crest and the designation 'By Appointment to H.M. Queen Elizabeth the Queen Mother Confectioners'.[2] The refugees could also indulge their appetite for Central European coffee and pastries at establishments like the Café Vienna in Cleveland Street, W1, or in the upmarket surroundings of the Schubert Coffee Lounge in Blenheim Street, W1, off New Bond Street.

Besides the Cosmo and the Dorice on Finchley Road, there were refugee establishments in more exclusive areas, like Balsam's Restaurant in Down Street, Mayfair. This was more expensive, as befitted its surroundings, and in the 1950s was offering three-course dinners by candlelight to the accompaniment of entertainers as well known as the singer Alma Cogan. It also served Continental specialities, as did a potential competitor, the Wayfarer's Restaurant in Granville Place, W1, which in July 1952 announced the opening of its Tokay Grill 'with gypsy music and exotic cuisine'.

Connoisseurs of fine wines could patronize the well-known refugee wine dealers, S.F. & O. Hallgarten of Crutched Friars, EC3, which played an important role in raising the public profile of German wines in Britain, as *AJR Information* recalled on the occasion of the founder's sixtieth birthday in 1962.[3] Bernard Sachs of Old Bond Street, W1, advertised itself as the successor to the German firm of Sachs & Hochheimer, with a range of fine wines from France and Germany at up to £1 a bottle, no small price then.[4] A number of catering firms sprang up to meet the demand from those who entertained at home: M. Oberlander & Son of Finchley Road, NW11, advertised as 'caterers with that fine Continental touch';[5] Mrs Mandl, 'well known for high-class catering', advertised her special dishes for parties in customers' homes; and for many years Mrs Illy Lieberman promised 'catering with a difference'.

Ads for genuine luxury articles demonstrated how refugee spending power had grown, though not many could have afforded Jean Patou 'Cocktail Dry' perfume, advertised at 157/6 (just under £8) for two ounces, with French phrases to appeal to a supposedly more sophisticated market segment. Often placed next to these illustrated boxed ads were those from Colibri Lighters, which in February 1959 advertised a diamond and ruby studded gold lighter at the staggering price of £1,200; in the mid-1950s even their standard models cost from 32/6 to £24.[6] The pattern of increased spending on expensive consumer goods and services was clear: from the mid-1950s watchmakers switched the emphasis of their ads from repairs of old watches to the sale of new ones, often from Switzerland; furriers brought in furs from France; the ads for ladieswear moved towards haute couture and those for menswear towards made-to-measure shirts and suits; and several beauticians offered cosmetic and beauty treatments, following the first 'creative hair stylist and tinting specialist', Marion Dessauer, 'late of Mayfair', who announced her availability for home visits in November 1951.

In the 1960s the number of people advertising expensive luxury items increased considerably. In March 1969 a ladies' wardrobe was advertised, consisting mostly of new two-piece suits, coats and dresses with top brand names like Aquascutum, and with a new Persian lamb jacket and black calf-skin fur coat, both with black mink collars; this was followed in November 1969 by a mink coat at £90, a dark mink stole at £75, and a light beige musquash jacket at £55. Another indicator of increased spending power was the demand for recreational and sporting goods, like the golfing accessories advertised in May 1967; it would have been hard to imagine many refugees taking to the golf course fifteen or twenty years earlier.

One of the most striking developments in the field of consumer spending was the transformation of foreign travel from a preserve of the few into an industry of mass tourism, so that by the 1960s the package tour was firmly established. The refugees were quick to take advantage of the opportunities for travel to Europe, partly because many of them visited Germany or Austria for personal, family or business reasons or for holidays. On the other hand, others refused to set foot there again or returned reluctantly, experiencing real emotional difficulties on crossing the border into a realm that still evoked nightmares of Nazism.[7] But the ads in the journal testified to a lively demand for travel abroad from refugees, often to upmarket, relatively expensive resorts. As early as May 1952, UNA Travel of Tottenham Court Road, W1, advertised their expertise in travel to Israel and offered all-Jewish tours to Switzerland, Spain, Belgium, France and the Riviera; the following month it offered fourteen-day holidays in a private villa in Juan-les-Pins, a mountaineering break in Zermatt or touring Barcelona and the Costa Brava, then still exotic and unfamiliar destinations.

Airlines like El Al and Sabena occasionally advertised flights to Israel, but the bulk of the ads were for Europe. Peltours of Duke Street (later Wigmore Street), W1, advertised regularly from June 1952, starting with crossings to the USA and Canada by luxury liner or by air, but then concentrating on the closer European destinations, including winter sports resorts.[8] In December 1954, Superways Continental Coach Cruises of Sherwood Street, W1, advertised coach tours to Paris and Brussels, the French and Italian Riviera and Switzerland, from twenty-nine to thirty-nine guineas, while in January 1955 the Wayfarers Travel Agency of Russell Square, WC1, sought to brighten the winter gloom by offering holidays in the sun on the Costa Brava (fifteen days at £29 15s) and on 'the lovely unspoilt island of Ibiza', in Lugano and on Lake Garda, as well as a grand tour of Yugoslavia at £54 7s 6d.

For the many music lovers among the refugees, Gardiner Travel Service of Regent Street, W1, offered in December 1952 to arrange travel, accommodation and tickets for the 1953 Wagner Festival at Bayreuth and for other European festivals, as well as luxury motor tours along the Rhine and the Danube and to Italy and Switzerland. (Wagner, Hitler's favourite composer, would have been anathema to most Jews, but for some refugees, with their deep attachment to German culture, the magic of the operas with which they had grown up outweighed the composer's notorious anti-Semitism.) By the 1960s there was no shortage of travel agencies like Seven Seas Services of Queen's Grove, NW8, run by Miss I. Kaiser, which advertised its services in July 1962 in making reservations for clients at personally inspected Continental hotels.

Foreign travel was becoming an accepted part of life for many refugees;

the journal's classified ads columns carried offers of holiday flats and villas to rent, like that in April 1960 for Mrs Hilde Lorenz's villa near Locarno on Lago Maggiore, Switzerland. Holiday destinations became more expensive: those desirous of spending autumn or winter on the Côte d'Azur were offered in October 1963 the chance to rent a furnished luxury flat in Nice, close to the vaunted Promenade des Anglais, while in July 1964 those who preferred the mountains could take a holiday chalet in the French Alpine resort of Mégève. By the mid-1960s this class of ads was appearing regularly, as one in January 1966 for a flat on the Riviera and another two months later for a cottage in the Roman Hills showed.

As the 1950s wore on, it became very apparent that the proportion of the refugees enjoying economic security was increasing further and that their standard of living was rising, albeit from the low level of the austerity years, helped by the full employment and economic growth of the decade. By the late 1950s the number of those seeking employment through the journal's classified columns had fallen significantly. Already by the mid-1950s the AJR Employment Agency was reporting that the number of situations vacant notified to it exceeded the number of those seeking employment.[9] The journal quoted from the annual report for 1956 of the Reading and District International Advice Bureau and Refugee Committee, which had decided after seventeen years to concentrate its efforts on post-war arrivals in Britain, as the refugees from Central Europe were successfully settled:

> It is pleasant to report that almost all the original refugees from Nazi oppression are now British citizens and that not only are they fully acclimatized but doing well, including among them distinguished scientists, professional workers, artists and musicians or being themselves large employers of labour. Once again it is proving true that people at first admitted from charitable motives have proved an asset to the country of their adoption. More slowly, the same thing is beginning to be the case with their successors of certain, but not all, original nationalities.[10]

The integration of the refugees from Central Europe was already perceived as having proceeded quickly and smoothly, by comparison with other groups of immigrants now beginning to settle in Britain.

In the 1960s the numbers of those seeking employment fell sharply, an unmistakable sign that refugees in economic difficulties were a declining minority. At the meeting of the AJR Board in 1967, it was reported that the Employment Agency had dealt with 400 employers in 1966, but with only 220 employees, about four a week, a figure that contrasted with the fifty members a day visiting the AJR Club, and showed that the Employment

Agency was itself becoming redundant. In July 1964 no jobseekers advertised for posts in the journal's employment column.

The situation across the entire age range of the refugee community had improved vastly by 1970. The great majority of men of working age were in employment, with a heavy proportion in professional and managerial positions or self-employed; single women and working wives were largely in secure jobs, some in part-time employment and others in full-time careers. Those who were retired mostly enjoyed second pensions (denominated in German Marks or Austrian Schillings) significantly more generous than the British old age pension. Among the refugees' British-born children now coming on to the job market, unemployment was at a minimal rate, thanks to their parents' insistence on equipping them with educational or vocational qualifications and to the aspirations instilled in them in the family home. The economic and occupational profile of the second generation was overwhelmingly middle class.

The quality of the jobs on offer improved correspondingly. By the late 1950s, as the lists of elderly men seeking employment as packers or bookkeepers and of women seeking jobs as typists or seamstresses shortened, some well-paid executive positions began to be advertised. In December 1958 a starting salary of £900 was offered to attract an intelligent young man who would eventually fill a responsible position; in April 1959 an international manufacturing company with its head office in Mayfair advertised for a general manager who could expect handsome remuneration; and in May 1958 a retail executive with a public school education, service in the RAF and a BSc (Econ.), at present earning £1,500, advertised his interest in changing to a more interesting or challenging post. Even the situations vacant columns came to reflect the prosperity of refugee employers. In June 1957 all four positions advertised were domestic: a cook was wanted for a private household in Belsize Park, a woman experienced in baking for a private household, a part-time help to assist a housewife in Golders Green with weekend tea parties, and a resident housekeeper for an elderly lady with a flat in the West End. The days when a significant proportion of women refugees had been domestic servants were long gone; now they were more likely to be able to afford domestic help in maintaining a comfortable middle-class lifestyle.

Patterns of employment had changed greatly since the post-war years. No longer were refugees seeking employment largely confined to run-of-the-mill clerical, secretarial and semi-skilled or unskilled positions. Instead, more attractive options were emerging. In April 1968 a chemical engineering company in the Manchester area required an experienced young man with drive, organizing ability and a sound grounding in engineering practices for a job with 'excellent prospects'. This firm was very likely Lankro Chemicals Ltd of Eccles, a highly successful refugee enterprise producing chemicals for the plastics, detergent and leather industries. Founded in 1937 by Falk Heinz Kroch from Berlin, it employed 700 people by 1967, when Dr Kroch was awarded the freedom of the town of Eccles.[11]

A similar trend was discernible even in the area of domestic employment. As the number of more menial domestic jobs on offer to refugees declined, there was an increase in more desirable positions with better pay and conditions. Particularly noticeable was the demand for companions, German-speaking ladies from a Continental background, to share accommodation with elderly widows. In June 1963, for example, an advertisement asked for a companion/help for an elderly lady in a flat in Hampstead; the position offered a high salary, good conditions and the promise of a daily help to take care of domestic chores.

By the late 1960s such advertisements were frequent. In May 1969 several good residential positions in comfortable surroundings were on offer: one job advertised was in a centrally heated house with a cleaning lady in the pleasant seaside resort of Paignton, one was as housekeeper for a childless couple in Hampstead, and one as housekeeper for an elderly couple in a four-room luxury flat in Sloane Street, Chelsea. 'Own room, daily help kept, no rough work, simple cooking, mainly supervision of general household and personal assistance', read the terms for the last of these. These advertisements reflected the growing number of elderly refugees in an ageing community, but also the ability of some of those refugees to pay for expensive domestic assistance and companionship.

The standard of the accommodation occupied by the refugees also improved dramatically. No longer did many of them live in rented rooms, bedsits and cheap flats; instead, a significant proportion now owned their own homes, where they settled and brought up their families. This pattern of home ownership had begun in the first decade after the war, as noted earlier, as part of the integration of a substantial section of the refugee community into the British middle class, and by 1970 it was well entrenched. The accommodation advertised in *AJR Information* also came to reflect the more affluent circumstances of much of the readership: in October 1963, an advertisement offered 'first-class accommodation' in a flat 'in [a] newly built villa close to Hampstead Heath'; in June 1967, a 'beautiful self-contained flat in [a] private house' in a 'first-class neighbourhood' was offered at eight guineas a week; and in September 1965, a mere bedsit was offered at five guineas a week, though it was in a well-appointed block of flats in Hampstead. Expensive locations like Hampstead and St John's Wood featured quite frequently, as did the leafy outer suburbs of north-west London.

At the meeting of the AJR Board in 1970, the Social Services Department reported that more vacant rooms were on offer than were required, a situation barely conceivable fifteen or twenty years previously and evidence that the perennial problem of accommodation had been substantially resolved.[12] One unexpected way in which refugees benefited from the financial security provided by home ownership was revealed in the advertisements from widows and single ladies that became a regular feature of the journal in the 1960s. They used their houses, sometimes inherited from their late husbands, to demonstrate their solid financial status, as in the case of two items in the journal's personal column in November 1969: 'Attractive widow, beautiful home in London suburb, German born, well-to-do, seeks companionship/marriage with educated, cultured gentleman about 65/71'; and 'Cultured Continental lady, early fifties, own home and income, would like to meet cultured gentleman not older than 64. Object companionship/marriage'.

The terms of exchange implicit in these advertisements said much about refugee values: the lady offered her home, hoping in return to meet a partner with a matching level of culture. While such items showed a prosperous and well-settled community, they also showed, on the sadder side, the losses that befell it as it aged. An item from November 1969 even made light of the burdens of advancing years: 'Three intelligent, lively sisters (two widows), 60 to 65, German-Jewish background, not Orthodox, own houses (Highgate and near), of independent means, interested in concerts, theatre, etc., dining out and dancing occasionally, would like to meet escort-companions in similar circumstances.' With their insistence on their German-Jewish background, with its emphasis on high culture rather than traditional Judaism, and their settlement in a fashionable part of north London, these high-spirited ladies brought echoes of Lehár's *Merry Widow* to Britain; certainly, they hardly resembled Chekhov's three sisters, stagnating in a backwater far from metropolitan culture.

AJR Information also contained evidence of the high level of business activity among the refugees, in particular the number who founded new businesses. The entrepreneurial drive characteristic of the refugees led many to consider setting up a business; they then sought advice on unfamiliar aspects of English commercial law and practice. This happened so often that in November 1952 the journal's legal expert published a piece on the subject in response entitled 'Shall I Form a Limited Company?' in his 'Law and Life' column. This column also discussed the alternative of buying an existing company. It had previously published an article on the registration of business names, giving details of the procedure to be undertaken and notable for the almost palpable air of excitement surrounding the setting up of new business ventures by newly naturalized refugees.[13]

A trade in businesses sprang up. In April 1955 the journal carried an enquiry from a prospective purchaser: 'Advertiser wishes to acquire sound, well-established business (over 3 years) in Greater London area from owners who want to retire, considered also active partnership. Investment £10–£15,000.' This was followed by an ad from a prospective vendor: 'Leather handbag manufacturing business for quick sale in London. Going concern with good accounts and agent. Substantial orders in hand. Seven employees and outdoor workers. All figures and details available.' The AJR was well aware of the number of its members who ran businesses, and sought to benefit from it. In advance of the appearance of its anniversary publication *Britain's New Citizens: The Story of the Refugees from Germany and Austria*, the AJR targeted the owners of firms through a 'special advertisement scheme' under which they could buy space in the publication to advertise their businesses and products: 'Attention of readers who have built up firms in this country is drawn to the advertising facilities of the forthcoming Jubilee Publication', which would be widely read beyond the refugee community.[14] The response, as noted earlier, was gratifyingly large.

Items aimed at those who had recently set up in business proliferated in the 1950s. 'Law and Life' offered professional advice from an accountant on 'bookkeeping for small traders', covering such areas as writing up ledgers and filing invoices and receipts, and explaining the different functions of accountants and auditors. Inevitably, the less welcome aspects of business life intruded, as in the same expert's advice on how to deal with income tax demands for the year 1952/53. By the mid-1950s, however, some relief was at hand, in the form of advice on tax exemptions: the insurance brokers Leroi, Flesch & Co., a refugee business, pointed out in an ad that the Finance Act, 1956, offered considerable advantages to directors of companies and the self-employed by allowing them to pay premiums for pensions free of tax, and offered their expertise to business people looking for financial security in retirement.[15] In the 1960s, once refugee businesses had become established, the emphasis switched to expansion: advertisements appeared like that from a small import/export firm of Continental origin announcing that it wished to expand its activities and would welcome enquiries from similar businesses with a view to amalgamation or absorption.[16]

It was hardly surprising that the journal contained details of any number of refugees who founded, owned, ran, managed or acted as directors of business enterprises. The following examples appeared in the columns celebrating the achievements of individual refugees, marking their birthdays or mourning their deaths. Nathan Schmidt, a well-known figure in pre-war German Jewry, celebrated his seventy-fifth birthday in Darlington, County Durham; in Germany, he and his brother had founded a leather factory under the name Alligator, which they refounded after emigrating as Alligator Leather Goods Co. Ltd of Bishop Auckland and built up successfully until its products were widely known in Britain and the Commonwealth.[17]

Walter Erlanger, a native of Nuremberg, died in 1957 aged 64; he had been particularly helpful to the AJR as a director of the London printing firm De Vere Press Ltd, which printed the AJR's two publications, *Britain's New Citizens* and *Dispersion and Resettlement*. Siegfried Cahn from Frankfurt was an industrialist whose services to his adopted country earned him a CBE in 1957; he came to Britain in 1936 and joined Goodlass Wall and Lead Industries Ltd, and his expertise was of such value during the war that he was, exceptionally, naturalized in 1941 at the request of the Ministry of Supply, one of the ministries that he advised on matters concerning non-ferrous metals. He acted as British delegate to the International Tin Study Group and the International Tin Council, and became managing director of Goodlass, chairman of associated companies, and a member of the board of several more companies.[18]

Even refugee lawyers, whose training in Germany was of no help when it came to practising British law, found a new field of activity when the process of restitution began to generate large numbers of claims that required legal expertise. The United Restitution Organisation, which was set up by the Council of Jews from Germany with its headquarters in London and which shared premises with the AJR for some time, employed a number of lawyers full- or part-time, while others set themselves up independently as advisers on restitution claims. One example among many was Dr Albert Schneider, who had followed in his father's footsteps in building up a practice in international law in Berlin, but had to learn a trade to keep himself alive after he emigrated to Britain; only when he joined the URO as a legal adviser was he able to return to his chosen calling.[19] Other lawyers who made fresh careers for themselves with the URO included Dr Kurt Friedlander, who after a difficult start in Britain worked there as a legal adviser for many years, and Dr Frederick (Fritz) Goldschmidt, the lawyer in charge of the London office for some twenty years until his death in 1968.

In the decade and a half from 1955, the overall impression that the refugee community was enjoying new and increasing levels of prosperity was unmistakable. Looking back on the early years from the vantage point of 1962, one commentator declared unambiguously:

The time when the majority of refugees had still to fight for their living is by now left far behind for most of them. The courage and self-sacrifice of those who, as former doctors, lawyers and members of other free professions, had to find work as domestic help, office clerks and in other positions outside their vocational training belongs to history.[20]

Speaking two years later, on the occasion of a banquet held at the Empire Rooms to celebrate the twenty-first anniversary of the founding of the Leo Baeck (London) B'nai B'rith Lodge, a leading member struck an almost identical note: 'It is a far cry from the small beginnings during the war, when most of our people were still unsettled in this country and had to struggle very hard, and the present days, when for the majority of them, these difficulties are a matter of the past.'[21] In July 1968 more than 600 people attended a banquet at the City of London's historic Guildhall to celebrate the Lodge's silver jubilee. This prompted Werner Rosenstock to contrast the Lodge's humble beginnings with the grandeur of the later banquet: the guest speakers were Home Secretary (and future Prime Minister) James Callaghan, Shadow Home Secretary (and future Lord Chancellor) Quintin Hogg and the Anglo-Jewish grandee and former Lord Mayor of London Sir Bernard Waley-Cohen; the messages of congratulation included one from the Queen.[22]

From the mid-1950s, a process of psychological acclimatization to Britain and of adaptation to British life took place, in parallel to the economic security and growing prosperity detailed above. Though the settlement of the Jewish refugees from Hitler was almost without exception regarded as a success story by contemporary commentators, it also defied easy categorization, as an article by two refugee authors argued:

> On the whole integration, at least in Britain, presents a most spectacular and unique social phenomenon, full of interesting examples and personal stories; in fact, most of these 'cases' are so different from one another that it is hard to generalise, except that by saying that success is their common denominator. 'Emigration' is by no means an immutable event with a certain predictable result. We, the 'results', have been shaped by the interaction of our individual personalities with the situation in which we found ourselves. Therefore, the results are as different as our personalities, circumstances, and background.[23]

They singled out age as the main differentiating factor, contrasting the experiences of children who had arrived in their new environment aged under 10 years, young people who came aged 18 or over, and mature people who were over 50 when they emigrated. Whereas young children could absorb the language and customs of the new homeland completely and 'melt into its community', many of the over-fifties, the unhappiest group, 'despaired right from the start, and never made a real effort to penetrate the language-and-customs barrier because they felt that it would be beyond their capacities'. Age at arrival was almost certainly the most influential factor determining the degree to which successful integration was possible.

Complete integration was not possible for the generation of the older refugees. Many appeared to harbour a certain regret that they could never fully achieve the status of Englishmen or women. When Egon Larsen wrote a review of the refugee artist Fred Uhlman's autobiography *The Making of an Englishman* in 1961, he gave it the slightly rueful title 'Not Quite an Englishman'. He began his review with the familiar phrase that refugees often used to express their awareness of the gulf that separated the naturalized citizen from the native Englishman: 'You can become a British citizen; but you have to be born an Englishman.'[24] Within these limits, however, most refugees had little hesitation about assimilating; their integration into British society proceeded apace.

In the later 1950s and 1960s refugee life became ever more permeated with British elements. This showed up particularly clearly in the small details of everyday life that appeared in large numbers in *AJR Information* during the 1960s. In October 1963 the AJR reminded its members that it was running a National Savings Group and that members wishing to join could obtain savings stamps from the AJR offices, thus doing their patriotic duty by strengthening the National Savings movement while at the same time avoiding the British chore of queuing at post offices.[25] Two months later, a Triang OO model railway set, that most British of toys, was offered for sale, in time to delight a child at Christmas.[26] Bringing up children in Britain provided refugee parents with a powerful impetus to familiarize themselves with British ways. Writing in 1964 about the generation of refugees born between 1918 and 1933, Miriam Brassloff described how their attachment to the customs and lifestyle of Central Europe was being eroded by the pervasive influence of the British environment to which they were exposed through their children: 'They are in fact trying to assimilate to their English surroundings. If the ladies still have the ambition to learn to bake *Zwetschgenkuchen* [plum cakes] this must be considered as a family tradition. The parental teachings of manners and behaviour patterns are slowly being superseded by those which conform to the expectations of their own children.'[27]

This interpenetration of British and refugee life sometimes took unexpected forms, as when *AJR Information* reported that for the second time the AJR had received a generous donation from a Carmelite Monastery in Quidenham, Norfolk, where the responsible officer, the sister procuratrix, had heard of the AJR and its charitable activities from a member.[28] Even more improbably, the renowned Schubert expert Otto Erich Deutsch – who gave his name to the 'D' (for Deutsch) numbers by which the composer's works are designated – conceived a passion for the comic operas of Gilbert and Sullivan; in his obituary of Deutsch, H.W. Freyhan related how the musicologist had returned from Britain in the 1950s to Vienna, 'where, besides his other activities, he sought to promote the cause of "G and S" with a new translation of *The Mikado* for the Vienna Volksoper'.[29]

In the 1960s refugee authors commonly engaged with familiar British practices, often with affectionate humour. Egon Larsen, a refugee from Munich who had changed his surname from Lehrburger, co-edited an anthology of English humour, *Laughter in a Damp Climate*, that appeared in 1964 to favourable reviews.[30] Larsen was a frequent contributor to *AJR Information*, as was another mediator between British, German and refugee social cultures, Egon Jameson, whose book *London, wie es nicht im Wörterbuch steht* (London as You Won't Find It in the Dictionary) was described by PEM on its appearance in 1961 as a very funny guide to the peculiarities and traditions of Londoners.[31]

Jameson, who was born Egon Jacobsohn, was resolute in his adoption of the identity of a refugee who had left Germany for Britain. He even wrote a history of 10, Downing Street. PEM entitled his obituary of Jameson 'Der Mann, der zweimal starb' (The Man Who Died Twice), referring to an incident in 1948 when a reporter in Berlin had asked him if he was Egon Jacobsohn, only to receive the answer that he was Egon Jameson, and that Jacobsohn had died on 30 January 1933, the day that Hitler was appointed chancellor.[32] Richard Friedenthal, who wrote a famous biography of Goethe, spent some twenty years in London as a refugee; he also wrote a book about London, which was published in Munich in 1960. In his review, 'A Remarkable Book on London', Lutz Weltmann compared it to *The Survey of London* by John Stow, a contemporary of Shakespeare, as both authors were conscious of writing at a turning point in history, in Friedenthal's case the transformation of the British Empire.[33] Arguably, refugee authors were well placed to write about British topics and institutions, which they could view sympathetically as well as knowledgeably, while at the same time preserving a measure of distanced objectivity about subjects like the end of Britain's imperial era, a development with which the British have struggled to come to terms ever since the war.

Another indication that the refugees had, so to speak, come in from the cold was the number of them who became popular public figures. Among them were the inimitable musician-humorist Gerard (Gerhard) Hoffnung and the great cartoonist Vicky (Victor Weisz), both of whom died early, and Fritz Spiegl, erstwhile principal flautist in the Liverpool Philharmonic Orchestra, who became a much loved authority on the correct use of English. Sir Clement Freud became part of the furniture of British public life to such an extent that it overshadowed the fact that he was the grand-son of Sigmund Freud (and brother of the artist Lucian Freud). Sir Clement was active in a startling variety of areas: in the theatre (he was involved with the Royal Court Theatre in its great days), as a sports writer and as a cookery expert for various newspapers and magazines (his lugubrious image was famously used to good advantage in advertisements), and as Liberal MP for the Isle of Ely from 1973 to 1987. He was also the last sur-viving member of the original team on the long-running BBC Radio Four programme Just a Minute, which included such notable humorists and word-smiths as Kenneth Williams, Derek Nimmo and Peter Jones.[34]

The refugees were absorbing and being absorbed into the social culture of Britain. When the painter Frederick Feigl died in London in 1966, aged 81, Adele Reifenberg-Rosenbaum lamented the loss of 'one of the most outstanding painters amongst the refugees from Central Europe'.[35] Born and educated in the intellectual hothouse of Prague, where his friends and schoolmates had included Franz Kafka, Max Brod and Franz Werfel, Feigl had also lived in Antwerp, Berlin and Paris, where he had been influenced by the Fauves. Even this cosmopolitan artist, whose works were set in loca-tions ranging from Paris to Jerusalem, had, according to Reifenberg-Rosenbaum, found his creative home in London: 'But I think he was at his best when he depicted the life around him, people in Hampstead cafés, or the change of the seasons, trees in bold brush strokes, the lush green of the summer, the yellow fires of autumn, the shimmering water of Regent's Park or the river.'

The substantial refugee contribution to the Festival of Britain in 1951 was a matter of enduring pride, a demonstration of participation in an event of symbolic national importance. When the Viennese-born sculptor Georg Ehrlich died, also in 1966, AJR Information was quick to recall that he had exhibited two bronzes at the Festival.[36] The numerous refugee contrib-utors had included the architects Peter Moro and Heinz Reifenberg, hus-band of Adele Rosenbaum, and the designer F.H.K. Henrion.[37] An item from PEM's column of November 1966 epitomized the extent to which refugees were becoming part of the British scene: Irene Prador, sister of the actress Lilli Palmer, was conducting her new radio series, It's Continental, on

the Home Service of the BBC; Martin Miller celebrated his sixty-seventh
birthday and the forty-fifth anniversary of his first role on stage by appearing in *Arsenic and Old Lace*; and at the higher end of the cultural spectrum, the
academic, poet and translator Michael Hamburger had translated Georg
Büchner's drama *Lenz* for the avant-garde publishers Calder and Boyars.[38]
Refugees were also making their mark across the country: Dr W.K.
Bernfeld, a Cardiff medical consultant born in Leipzig, learnt Welsh, studied the flute at Cardiff College of Music and Drama and won prizes as a
flautist at the Welsh National Eisteddfod.[39]

The narrative of successful adaptation to their new homeland by no means
encompassed all the refugees. Many, especially the elderly and the lonely,
remained at a disadvantage in British society, where they felt unhappy,
unwanted and unloved. Some younger refugees retained a lifelong sense of
grievance against Britain for having denied them the education they would
have received in their native lands or the chance to exploit their gifts successfully in later life. Some experienced hostility or prejudice in Britain,
and a number left the country, unable to adapt to life in Britain or to build
a secure existence for themselves. These groups formed the less visible
reverse side of the conventional refugee success story; they tended to lack
a voice to record their experiences, though Annette Saville's *Only a
Kindertransportee*, which appeared in 2002, is one of several autobiographical
texts to articulate such sentiments.

Nor did the overall increase in the prosperity and security of the
refugee community diminish the plight of those suffering from mental
problems, as the opening in 1968 of Charles Jordan House, a home in
Finchley Road offering aftercare for victims of Nazi persecution discharged
from mental hospitals, showed. Those suffering from mental conditions
remained an enduring problem. In the year ended February 1968, Self Aid
of Refugees distributed almost £25,000 to former refugees, according to its
annual report. It provided assistance not only to the old and lonely, but also
to people who had arrived in Britain on Kindertransports and were now
middle-aged: 'Mental instability is still the greatest of many problems', said
the report.[40] The shortage of suitable accommodation for the elderly
remained another intractable problem. Margot Williams of the AJR's Social
Services Department gave a detailed account, the more moving for its sober
tone, of the difficulties faced by families trying to cope with elderly people
and by single elderly people whose health was deteriorating.[41]

A survey of refugee mental health problems was more optimistic, reporting that the main categories of patients treated by the medical adviser to the
Social Services Department no longer suffered from psychological problems
specific to refugees, but rather from physical illnesses, the after-effects of

hospital treatment or such difficulties as being in unsuitable employment. The overall number of patients dealt with had not decreased, but the number of elderly people 'has nearly disappeared', thanks to such factors as restitution, residence in Old Age Homes, membership of the AJR Club, a greater sense of stable settlement or simply the removal of the need to work. Those whose nervous strain derived from the 'refugee situation' were also far fewer, the survey stated, as they had mostly found the means to overcome their problems.[42] When a German television film about the refugees, Sie kamen nach London (They Came to London), was shown to a refugee audience in 1966, some agreed with its view that the settlement of the Jews from Central Europe in Britain had been a success. Others were more critical: 'Some viewers felt that the reference to the initial difficulties had been inadequate and also pointed out that there were quite a few whose lives had been broken beyond repair and that the tragic happenings had left their indelible marks on everybody.'[43] Werner Rosenstock concluded that it was very hard to present a balanced picture, given that failure did not lend itself to portrayal as easily as success.

No history of refugee settlement would be complete without a consideration of one of its most characteristic establishments, the refugee boarding house. These were set up by refugees for other refugees, starting soon after 1933, and became social centres for those who lived there, oases of familiar Continental life and culture; an example was Dr Lily Wagner's boarding house in Hampstead, mentioned in Chapter 1. They provided a source of income for those who ran them, often ladies who had been widowed or were without other means of support,[44] and board and lodging at affordable prices for refugee lodgers on meagre incomes. Some of these boarding houses became focal points of refugee life in the pre-war and wartime years; they were numerous in the 1950s, when they tended to cater for poorer, more elderly refugees, often single people, who had not been able to move into their own accommodation.

Boarding houses had at first been a congenial environment for refugees struggling to cope with the accommodation problem in a strange country. They offered the company of people from a similar background, speaking the same language and facing the common hardships of forced emigration, and they served Continental food to those unaccustomed to British cooking. They reflected the special needs of a refugee community, many of whose members were at a disadvantage in finding settled, private accommodation and, when elderly, lacked relatives to look after them and homes to which to go.

The two best-known refugee boarding houses were those run by Mrs Adam and Mrs Sachs, established before the war on either side of Finchley

Road near Swiss Cottage. Mrs Adam's boarding house in Greencroft Gardens, NW6, was renowned for the refugee artists, intellectuals and professional people it accommodated and for the high cultural tone set at dinner every evening – an echo of the social world that her family had inhabited in Berlin, before emigration and the death of her husband. Her son Klaus, now Sir Kenneth Adam, became an Oscar-winning designer of film sets.[45] At the time of writing, her daughter, Mrs Loni Charlton, still lives in a flat in the building in Greencroft Gardens.

The boarding house that Lilli Sachs ran with Bertha Pick, on the corner of Eton Avenue and Adamson Road, NW3, lasted into the 1960s. By the end of that decade, rising costs were making permanent residence in boarding or guest houses prohibitively expensive. Margaret Jacoby's piece in AJR Information in memory of Lilli Sachs, on her death in 1965, conveyed something of the atmosphere of the house:

> With the death of Mrs Lilli Sachs, founder of the well-known Boarding House at Swiss Cottage, a chapter of our community's history has come to a close. For thirty years, hundreds of Jewish refugees from Central Europe found a home again in the cheerful and protective atmosphere of the House. In the early days and during the war, the House was exclusively staffed by Jewish refugees, thus providing for many a working permit and livelihood.

Starting with one building, the establishment expanded to fill no less than six houses. It became an institution in its own right: visitors from all over the world spent holidays in London there, Mrs Sachs arranged the celebrations for residents' wedding anniversaries, and also an annual bridge party for the benefit of the League of Jewish Women. 'The personality of Mrs Sachs, with her love of music and literature, gave the house the atmosphere of old cultural tradition', concluded the article.[46] The obituary of Bertha Pick, who died in 1963, also emphasized her devotion to her refugee guests and to the staff, for whom she bought Christmas presents.[47]

The refugee boarding houses that advertised in the journal formed a cluster in West Hampstead (NW6) and across Shoot Up Hill in Willesden Green (NW2). In July 1951 a 'first-class Continental boarding house' in Mapesbury Road, NW2, advertised vacancies, and another in (West) Hampstead also stressed its 'Continental' credentials in March 1955. It was probably a boarding house that advertised in the journal in May 1955: 'West Hampstead. In gepflegtem Haus Wohn- und Schlafzimmer, Voll- oder Halbpension, geeignet für ältere Damen oder Berufstätige. Auch Einzelzimmer mit Frühstück' ('Living room and bedroom in good-class house, full or half board, would suit elderly ladies or professional people.

Also single rooms with breakfast'). Other 'Continental' boarding houses were in West Heath Drive, Golders Green, and The Avenue, NW6, and there was a 'comfortable home for old ladies' in Shoot Up Hill, NW2.

In May 1952 there appeared the first of the regular advertisements for Rosemount, in Parsifal Road, NW6, which welcomed elderly people and promoted itself as ' the boarding house with culture', as only a refugee establishment could have done. The boarding house run by Mrs Wolff in Hemstal Road, West Hampstead was typical in its appeal to those with Central European tastes: 'Do you want comfort and every convenience, first-class accommodation, room with own bath, excellent Continental food, TV, lounge, gardens?'[48] Central heating, still uncommon in British homes, was essential.

Refugee guesthouses, similar to boarding houses, but with more short-term guests, also abounded. As they were more akin to hotels, they were often situated in coastal resorts and holiday locations, as well as in north-west London. One of the earliest of such establishments was Loxwood Hall in Loxwood, West Sussex, managed from 1939 to 1949 by Egon and Trude Goliat, and much favoured by refugees seeking a break from London. After the war the Goliats returned to Munich, where Egon became director of the Theater am Gärtnerplatz and Trude, under the name Kolman (the anglicised version of Kohlmann, her maiden name), managed the theatre Die Kleine Freiheit, where her authors included the poet and humorist Erich Kästner, best known outside Germany for *Emil and the Detectives*.

Ashdale Guesthouse in Bournemouth was run by Mr and Mrs Bruder from Linz in Austria until Hilde Bruder's death in 1951 after which her husband continued alone. Clifton House, in Clifton Place, Brighton – 'We still cater Continental' (ad of July 1952) – was run by Mr and Mrs Atkins (Abraham), moving upmarket to Hove in 1954. In 1951, the announcement of the sixtieth birthday of Dr Fritz Schwarz, formerly a lawyer in Berlin, where he had been chairman of a Jewish youth education institution, and still a loyal member of a German-Jewish student association, noted that he had for the last ten years run Furzedown, a guesthouse in Hindhead, Surrey, a meeting place for refugees.[49]

The Continental Hotel in Bournemouth betrayed its origins through its name, even though it offered such upper-class English pursuits as golf, riding and fishing. It was run by Mr and Mrs Schreiber, who had previously run Schreiber's Guest House in Blenheim Gardens, NW2, a Continental establishment where German was spoken; in January 1954, it advertised single rooms from £6 and double rooms from £10 10s. Other south-coast establishments were the Picardy Hotel in East Cliff, Bournemouth, which advertised in May 1959 as a 'first-class family hotel, Continental cuisine';

the proprietors were E. and R. Kerpner, 'late of Vienna and London'; and the Melrose Hotel, Regency Square, Brighton, 'the home from home with Continental cooking at its best', run by Mr and Mrs Andy A. Vogel, according to an ad in June 1960. Hotels were less numerous than the more modest guesthouses, like Simar House, the 'new Continental Guest House in Bournemouth', whose opening was announced in July 1956; by February 1958 it also boasted a sun lounge, though it took care to remind potential customers that it remained 'the house with the Continental atmosphere'. In August 1959 the journal carried the notice of the death of Simon Gustav Smith; his wife Margot carried on alone.

Guesthouses formed part of the refugee economy, and were bought and sold as going concerns on which refugee owners could live. A guesthouse in Swiss Cottage, offered for sale on a long lease in May 1954, gave an insight into the finances behind such establishments. It had twelve rooms, a garage, yielded 'a net income of £30 per week (without food)' and had scope for development; the asking price was £6,500, fully furnished and equipped. One refugee who decided to make a living in this way was Mrs M. Eger, who ran Oakbrae Guest House in Harrogate, Yorkshire, whose opening was announced in an ad in August 1954. She was the widow of Herbert Eger, formerly a lawyer in Berlin, who had been warden of the hostel for refugee Jewish boys in Parkfield Road in Manningham, Bradford. His death, the notice of which appeared in July 1953, left his widow to fend for herself and her children. The guesthouse, situated close to the Royal Baths in the centre of the genteel spa town, would have secured them a modest, if hard-working living.

In March 1954, Mrs Lotte Schwarz's guesthouse in St Gabriel's Road, NW2, advertised 'first-class rooms with radiator heating', best Continental cuisine, TV, a lounge where the Central European passion for bridge could be indulged, good transport connections, and above all a 'Continental atmosphere' (this in bold type). By May 1959, when it had acquired the name Arlet, Mrs Schwarz was bidding permanent guests and visitors to London welcome 'in my exquisitely furnished and cultured Private Guest House'. From the ads and other items in *AJR Information*, it is still possible to reconstruct something of these establishments, an important feature of refugee life in the period of settlement, but one that has almost entirely disappeared from view.

A factor that became significant in refugee life from approximately the mid-1950s was restitution, as West Germany and later Austria (but not East Germany) began to pay compensation to the Jewish victims of Nazi persecution. The process of restitution for the losses incurred and the suffering endured by Jews under Nazism had been started by the Allied Powers, who had put differing measures in place in their respective zones of occupation in Germany; these were followed by laws enacted by the West German *Länder*, including West Berlin, and by the federal government after 1949, together forming a complicated patchwork of piecemeal legislation.

The two main laws enacted by the Federal Republic of Germany in this field were the *Bundesentschädigungsgesetz* (Federal Law on Compensation, BEG) of 1953 and the *Bundesrückerstattungsgesetz* (Federal Restitution Law, BrüG) of 1957, on to which were tacked numerous pieces of secondary amending legislation. Restitution is a highly complex area demanding specialist legal knowledge and will not be dealt with in detail here, except insofar as it is necessary to estimate correctly the importance of restitution payments to the economic situation of the refugees. It is mistaken to see the relative prosperity of the refugees in the 1950s and 1960s as largely dependent on restitution payments. For a start, these took a long time to come through: the German authorities had to set up a complex new apparatus to deal with restitution claims, and the customary slowness of the government machine was aggravated by a degree of bureaucratic obstructionism and some residual anti-Jewish sentiment, not to mention the length of time required to process the huge number of claims (nearly three million were lodged under the BEG alone by 1960).

The large number of refugees from Austria had to wait even longer for adequate restitution, as that country steadfastly maintained that it had itself been invaded and occupied by Hitler's Germany. Citing the Moscow Declaration of 1943, in which the Allies declared Austria to have been the first victim of Nazi aggression, post-war Austrian governments sought to deny any guilt attaching to their citizens and proved stubbornly reluctant to acknowledge their obligations to their former Jewish citizens. *AJR Information*, which generally regarded the West German government as conscientious in the legislation it had enacted to compensate German Jews and in the implementation of that legislation, frequently had reason to complain of the delaying tactics employed by the Austrian authorities to evade their responsibilities. As late as December 1969, nearly a quarter-century after the end of the war, C.K. (Charles Kapralik) reported that a recent piece of legislation had brought benefits to former Nazis who had been Austrian state employees superior to those conceded to their Jewish counterparts who had been forced to emigrate; Nahum Goldmann, on behalf of the Conference on Jewish Material Claims against Austria, had had to demand that the Austrian government take steps so that the position of the refugees should not remain worse than that of the ex-Nazis.[50]

A crucial factor in the value of restitution payments was the rate of exchange at which payments made in Deutschmarks or Austrian Schillings were converted into pounds sterling. Until the mid-1960s, when the pound was valued at around DM11, the value of most regular monthly payments made under the BEG was relatively modest, but from 1967, as the pound was devalued repeatedly over the years, losing more than three-quarters of its value against the Deutschmark by 1992, payments from Germany increased greatly in value to recipients in Britain. The same applied to those from Austria. In the 1950s the Schilling had stood at seventy-two to the pound, but this fell to less than twenty by the 1990s, with the result that by the 1990s a monthly pension that would have been worth £250 at a constant exchange rate had increased in value to about £1,000.[51] While £1,000 per month was a significant income then, £250 was barely enough to keep a refugee at subsistence level. The impact of restitution payments on refugee old age pensioners, the largest recipient group, was dramatically greater in the 1990s than it had been in the 1950s and 1960s; and the proportion of the refugee community that benefited from pension payments in those earlier decades, though considerable, was far smaller than in the mid-1990s, by which time even those who had come as children in the late 1930s were reaching retirement age.

The great majority of the refugees benefited considerably more from monthly payments – apart from old age pensions, these included widow's and disability pensions, other social insurance benefits, payments to widows and orphans of those who had died in the Holocaust, compensation for loss of liberty in prisons or camps, for damage to health and for loss of professional advancement, among others – than from one-off payments for the restoration of property. Payments under the BEG, broadly representing the former kind of compensation, greatly exceeded those made under the BrüG, which dealt, broadly speaking, with the restoration of property. Whereas almost all refugees from Germany and Austria eventually became eligible for payments under the BEG, in particular old age pensions, the number of those who received substantial lump sum payments in compensation for the loss of businesses, factories or other assets was relatively small. The bulk of the restitution payments were therefore regular, but relatively modest in the earlier decades.

The degree to which the financial situation of refugees in the 1950s and 1960s improved as a result of restitution payments, once they began to receive them, was determined by their overall financial circumstances. The majority of refugees who earned a reasonable income from their employment would in those years have found restitution payments a welcome bonus, but little more. But for the less well-off minority, especially the elderly and those unable to find employment, restitution payments were essential to escape from real need; in its articles on restitution, AJR

Information frequently adduced the poverty of such refugees as an urgent reason for speeding up the process of legislation and its implementation. Only in recent decades, as the value of restitution payments rose and as the number of refugees dependent on old age pensions increased, did it become common for elderly refugees, often widowed ladies, to depend on their pensions from Germany or Austria to provide them with a level of comfort that the British state pension could not supply.

This chapter has sought to investigate in detail some key aspects of the settlement of the Jewish refugees in the late 1950s and 1960s, especially their material circumstances, an area on which hardly any research has yet been carried out. From what has been shown above, it will be clear that the refugees, far from being largely dependent for their wealth on restitution payments, had mostly created the conditions of their own prosperity themselves, by using their skills, energy and initiative to find gainful employment, by their ability to advance themselves in their professions or by setting up businesses. Those who could mostly engaged willingly and energetically with British society, pursuing their integration into it purposefully. This is not to deny that there were a considerable number of refugees who remained poor and achieved at best the shabby gentility of the uprooted exile who has come down in the world. It also remained the case that most refugees preserved important elements from the pre-emigration past in their identity and lifestyle, elements that marked them out as 'Continental' and that they would keep, mostly with a degree of pride, all their lives.

NOTES

1. *AJR Information* (December 1952), p.8.
2. See PEM's account of Werner Ackermann's transformation from Berlin theatre enthusiast to London confectioner, on the occasion of the latter's sixtieth birthday, *AJR Information* (September 1961), p.6.
3. *AJR Information* (June 1962), p.15.
4. *AJR Information* (June 1953), p.6.
5. *AJR Information* (November 1952), p.5.
6. *AJR Information* (November 1955), p.9; (February 1959), p.11.
7. See for example the description of a first post-war visit to Germany in the interview with Elisabeth Rosenthal, in the collection of the Research Centre for German and Austrian Exile Studies.
8. *AJR Information* (June 1952), pp.4f.
9. See for example *AJR Information* (October 1955), p.9.
10. *AJR Information* (May 1956), p.11.
11. *AJR Information* (February 1967), p.10.
12. *AJR Information* (March 1970), p.1.
13. *AJR Information* (November 1952), p.4; (July 1951), p.4.
14. *AJR Information* (April 1955), p.6; (November 1951), p.7.
15. *AJR Information* (December 1951), p.4; (December 1952), p.6; (September 1956), p.7.
16. *AJR Information* (September 1967), p.10.
17. *AJR Information* (August 1956), p.10.
18. *AJR Information* (September 1957), p.13; (February 1957), p.5.

19. See his obituary in *AJR Information* (June 1955), p.9.
20. W. Schindler, 'The New Citizens' Contribution to Economic Demands', *AJR Information* (October 1962), p.17. This was a special issue marking the twenty-first anniversary of the founding of the AJR in 1941.
21. *AJR Information* (November 1964), p.14.
22. *AJR Information* (August 1968), p.11.
23. K. Ambrose and E. Larsen, 'How They Settled: Some Aspects of Integration', *AJR Information* (October 1962), p.20.
24. *AJR Information* (May 1961), p.ll.
25. *AJR Information* (October 1963), p.8.
26. *AJR Information* (December 1963), p.14.
27. 'The AJR and the Younger Generation', *AJR Information* (December 1964), p.14.
28. *AJR Information* (December 1967), p.16.
29. *AJR Information* (January 1968), p.11.
30. See the interview with Larsen's sister Marion Smith in the 'Refugee Voices' collection.
31. *AJR Information* (June 1961), p.7.
32. *AJR Information* (February 1970), p.5.
33. *AJR Information* (April 1961), p.10.
34. On the remarkable success of the Freud dynasty in Britain, see D. Snowman, *The Hitler Emigrés: The Cultural Impact on Britain of the Refugees from Nazism* (London: Chatto and Windus, 2002), pp.356f.
35. *AJR Information* (February 1966), p.8.
36. *AJR Information* (August 1966), p.2.
37. On refugee contributors to the Festival of Britain, see Snowman, *The Hitler Emigrés*, pp.256ff.
38. *AJR Information* (November 1966), p.5.
39. *AJR Information* (November 1961), p.3; (September 1962), p.15; and (June 1963), p.9.
40. *AJR Information* (January 1969), p.3.
41. *AJR Information* (September 1961), p.14.
42. H.H.F[leischhacker], 'Recuperation of the Mind: Observations of a Psychiatrist', *AJR Information* (October 1962), p.12.
43. *AJR Information* (May 1966), pp.1f.
44. The wife of the distinguished historian Erich Eyck had run a boarding house, thus providing him with some means in the early years of emigration (*AJR Information* [December 1958], p.4).
45. Interview with Sir Kenneth Adam in the 'Refugee Voices' collection, also C. Frayling, *Ken Adam: The Art of Production Design* (London: Faber and Faber, 2005).
46. *AJR Information* (August 1965), p.15. See also the description of life in the boarding house in the interview with Ludwig Spiro in the 'Continental Britons' collection.
47. *AJR Information* (October 1963), p.9.
48. *AJR Information* (June 1958), p.15.
49. *AJR Information* (February 1951), p.7.
50. *AJR Information* (December 1969), p.2.
51. This was the amount of the monthly pension that my mother received after my father's death in 1992.

10

The Refugees in the 1960s

Writing in 1969, at the end of a turbulent decade that had seen social change in Britain on a scale that transformed attitudes and lifestyles, two of the old guard of refugee commentators attempted to draw stock. Herbert Freeden, who had been co-editor of *AJR Information* from 1946 until his departure for Israel in 1950, paid a visit to London, which he described in an article entitled 'An Israeli's View of London'.[1] Freeden was startled at the changes he observed, which began even before he entered Britain, with entry regulations that required him to obtain a new stamp in his passport. The reason behind this was mass immigration into Britain, especially from the Caribbean and the Indian subcontinent, one of the most immediately visible changes to affect British society from the 1950s, and the subsequent imposition of controls on immigration from the New Commonwealth countries. Given the high profile of the issue, Freeden was prepared for coloured faces in what he had known as a solidly white city; in fact, coloured immigrants were less prominent among the London crowds than he had expected, though he noted that many worked on the buses and the Underground, where they had been recruited by London Transport.

Freeden was struck by the new cosmopolitanism evident in some of the capital's formerly more insular aspects, such as the profusion of foreign restaurants offering a wide variety of cuisines. 'The days of the Yorkshire puddings, prunes and nondescript vegetables boiled in water have gone', he wrote, as had some of the familiar old teashops, like the ABC chain. Though welcome from a culinary point of view, these changes were also a matter of regret to Freeden; he was shocked to find that Lyons Corner House on Tottenham Court Road, whose Vienna Café had been a favourite meeting place for 'Continentals', was now a small tea shop surrounded by gambling establishments. When he emerged from Swiss Cottage tube station, he was confronted by a six-lane highway, product of 1960s urban engineering, 'which appeared to be good old Finchley Road'; he looked in vain for 'the grey, little, quiet houses in one of which the "Blue Danube Club" [a Viennese cabaret popular with refugees] had its domicile and which had given way to impersonal apartment buildings'.

Behind the article's carefully cultivated atmosphere of nostalgia for the London of bygone years lay a more profound sense of ambivalence, widespread especially among older refugees, towards the changes wrought by the 1960s.[2] British society was by 1970 more affluent, more tolerant and open, more liberal and less conformist, more diverse and cosmopolitan; but it was also less cohesive, less united by a sense of shared values, more selfishly assertive and materialistic, harsher and more impersonal in the anonymity and bustle of its urban life. As the 1960s marked the end of the post-war period, and a generation that had not known the war matured into adulthood, there was among some refugees a certain feeling of loss, an undertone of regret for the passing of a society in some ways cosier and more human, quintessentially if sometimes quirkily British, with which they had become familiar and in which they had, once settled, mostly grown to feel comfortable.

Freeden was evidently relieved to find some familiar landmarks amidst the vista of change evoked by his article, though these were to be found in the world of the refugees rather than in that of the British: 'But something did remain. I went into a familiar restaurant [the Cosmo in Swiss Cottage] – the cuisine was still Continental and nourishing, and on my left and right elderly gentlemen in heavily accented English or unaccented German were having a conversation from table to table.' The AJR's offices in nearby Fairfax Mansions had also remained much as they had been. Preserved as if in a Continental bubble, the now ageing refugees held to their ways, while the British-born younger generation took its own path, responding to the tide of change in British society as a whole.

Looking for elements in British society that had remained as the refugees remembered them, Freeden lighted on the familiar figure of the British bobby, pronouncing himself impressed by the lack of violence with which the police had handled the large anti-Vietnam demonstration held outside the American Embassy in Grosvenor Square. This image of the friendly British policeman was one of those most deeply embedded in the refugees' consciousness of their adopted homeland, and one that appears very frequently when refugees are asked to comment on the differences between Britain and the countries from which they had fled.[3] Testimony to the refugees' attachment to a vanishing era, it, too, owed more to memories of the past than to the reality of the Metropolitan Police Force in the late 1960s.

In December 1969, on the eve of a new decade, C.C. Aronsfeld, another prominent contributor to the journal, took a more wide-ranging view of what he called 'The Changing Face of Britain: Prospects of the Permissive Society'.[4] Compared to such momentous advances as the landing of a man on the moon earlier that year, Aronsfeld found the pace of change in Britain more measured, as befitted a country that proceeded by reasoned debate rather than revolution, but nonetheless unmistakable. One of the greatest changes in Britain's position in the world was the withdrawal from empire, which had reduced Britain from a world power to a regional European power. Anticipating Britain's accession in 1973 to what was then the European Economic Community, he claimed that 'many who once swore that they did not have it in their bones to enter Europe are looking at their bones again'.[5]

Aronsfeld saw that many of the problems besetting Britain were problems of adjustment to her changed post-war situation, in which old imperial attitudes were hampering attempts to improve Britain's economic competitiveness, productivity and efficiency. One of the principal reasons for a loss of confidence in Britain's future prospects was indeed her depressingly poor economic performance, compared to the faster-growing economies of her European competitors. Britain's post-war history was marked by a succession of economic crises, mostly caused by the weakness of the pound sterling, which imposed a 'stop-go' cycle of unsustainable expansion and abrupt contraction on the economy. Aronsfeld would not have needed to remind his readers of the crisis that had ended with the humiliating devaluation of the pound in November 1967. Britain had been a great imperial power when the refugees had arrived, and had been one of the 'Big Three' Allied Powers during the war; but wartime victory had been followed by peacetime failure, and the fact that the erstwhile 'workshop of the world' was now struggling to compete with Germany, France or Italy saddened and unsettled the refugees.

Aronsfeld adopted a studiously neutral attitude when he came on to discuss the 'permissive society', as British society in the 1960s was commonly called. The decade had seen social inhibitions loosened and social taboos lifted, a relaxation in attitudes to sexual behaviour, including the legalization of abortion and homosexuality, the liberation of individual lifestyles from the restrictive conformity of the 1950s, and the toleration of activities previously condemned as immoral or anti-social. Aronsfeld commented on a correspondence in *The Times* that had been triggered by a letter calling for a halt to 'destructive and demoralising trends' that were 'threatening the stability of the traditional British way of life'; the letter cited the usual litany of crime, drug addiction, gambling, abortion, venereal disease and hooliganism and, more generally, the tide of immorality, sensationalism and debasement of values that was allegedly undermining the social order.

Aronsfeld did no more than set out the arguments on both sides: on the one hand, the need to defend the established moral order, even if it needed some regeneration, and on the other the benefits brought about by the new tolerance and its rejection of prejudice and discrimination. No doubt conscious that his readership would have had divided views on the subject, he retreated to safe ground, citing 'the central tradition of Western civilisation, the dignity of the individual, based on liberty under the law', concepts that few readers would have been likely to dispute. This enabled him to conclude, inoffensively, that 'it may then be that the permissive society is no more than a phase on the road towards a maturer stage', a formula broad enough to satisfy most parties to the debate. Many refugees would have shared Aronsfeld's reluctance to side unambiguously with either the 'progressive' or the 'reactionary' faction; though they would have welcomed much of the reforming and liberalizing trend of the decade, they also retained a certain attachment to older British traditions, values and manners.

The new individualism of the 1960s, with its emphasis on free self-expression and the fulfilment of individual desires and aspirations at the expense of traditional conventions and rules of behaviour, ran counter to the orderliness, self-discipline and understated self-restraint that had characterized British society. The Second World War had reinforced the collectivist tendency to subordinate personal feelings and interests to the greater good of society as a whole, but this was incompatible with the new spirit of individualistic self-assertion, which demanded radically new forms of freedom and created a cult of 'alternative' non-conformism – the 'counter-culture' – in defiance of the conventional codes and values that had bound society together. As already noted, many refugees had been strongly influenced by their experience of Britain at war; they were accordingly likely to be hesitant to embrace the very different attitudes and values that emerged in the 1960s to challenge those of the 1940s, not least the later decade's scorn for patriotism and pride in British achievements.

AJR Information is a plentiful source of information about everyday refugee attitudes and concerns in the 1960s, which are otherwise well-nigh impossible to ascertain in detail forty years later. Already in the early 1960s, a number of the issues that were to dominate the decade made themselves apparent. In October 1961, PEM's column referred to the film *Victim*, in which a young barrister is blackmailed over a homosexual liaison; the reason for the report was that the film had a refugee cameraman, Otto Heller, but PEM made a point of calling the film 'the courageous Rank picture [Rank was the film's distributor] starring Dirk Bogarde'.[6] *Victim* is often seen as the first British film to treat the subject of homosexuality seriously and sympathetically, a sign of the more liberal attitudes that would lead to its legalization in 1967. The new frankness about sex in the permissive society also enabled Frank Wedekind's sexually explicit play *Spring Awakening* (*Frühlings Erwachen*) to be performed for the first time in London, at the Royal Court Theatre, as PEM noted in June 1965.[7] A new note of openness also crept into some of the advertisements in the personal columns of the journal: an expression of feelings as intimate as 'MARTITA PFLMCHN. Everything has changed, I have changed, everything will be as you want it. Let us discuss things. Please telephone' (March 1968) would have been inconceivable in a personal ad ten years earlier.

One of the most striking features of the decade's rejection of established authority was the satire boom of the early 1960s. Following on from the revue *Beyond the Fringe*, in which Jonathan Miller, Peter Cook, Dudley Moore and Alan Bennett made their names, a wave of savage political satire found expression in the magazine *Private Eye*, the television show *That Was the Week That Was*, presented by David Frost, and the Soho club 'The Establishment', where the political and social establishment was mercilessly lampooned. Reviewing the refugee performer Agnes Bernelle's one-woman show at 'The Establishment', in which she sang songs by Brecht and other writers of the 1920s, Egon Larsen saw London as rapidly catching up, in theatre and satire, with Berlin of the 'Roaring Twenties'.[8] The comparison between the cultural ferment of that decade in Germany and the 'Swinging Sixties' in Britain, both remarkable for their exuberance, innovation and impatience with established authority, was to become routine: interviewed on the BBC before the first night of the musical *Cabaret*, which probably did more than anything else to perpetuate the image of Berlin in the late Weimar years, PEM inevitably found himself asked to compare Berlin's 'golden years' in the pre-Hitler period with London of the 'Swinging Sixties'.[9]

The 1960s were memorable for radical innovations in fashion and style that transformed the grey, nondescript London of the 1950s into a trend-setting centre of eye-catching experimentation in dress and in styles in hair and make-up. Even *AJR Information*, which took little interest in fashion, commented on the shortness of skirts, an indicator of a new freedom that did not escape its (male) correspondents' eye. The bold new styles were evident in the advertisements, some of which were accompanied by graphics influenced by changing fashions in design and image. In July 1962 a new-look ad for Corsets Silhouette – 'Look specially slim front and back in the new special X by Silhouette' – carried an image of two slim, youthful models, in the streamlined, uncluttered outline then considered the height of modernity. These smart new ads were continued in October 1963 with an ad for Silhouette's Little X line, featuring a model upside down – 'You'll

go head-over-heels for the new Silhouette Little X' – and adding, 'yet it
never restricts your freedom'. The emphasis on freedom, ease of movement
and ease of use – the product 'machine-washes in a wink' – hinted at the
new freedom that women were to enjoy.

In August 1965, with the decade in full swing, a striking new Silhouette
ad showed a free-moving young woman, very much in tune with the new
mood of the times; its youthful vitality plainly reflected the cult of youth,
one of the dominant features of the period, when the gulf between the
older and younger generations was unusually wide and the younger generation's demand for its voice to be heard unusually strident. By September
1966 this new look spread to Colibri, the manufacturer of cigarette lighters,
whose ad showed two lighters leaning against each other and lighting a
common flame, with a human couple embracing in the background; such
an unmistakable, if discreet, evocation of physical passion was very much
of the new era, as was the 'adspeak' language of the accompanying motto,
'Colibriness'. By the end of the decade, in March 1969, Etam was using
the slogan 'The Shops with the Flair for Fashion!' to advertise its range of
clothes, the words printed in the full and ornate print and the flowery
script familiar from the record covers and posters associated with the
Hippies and 'flower power' and with the 'psychedelic' image favoured by
underground rock bands and publications. Etam and Silhouette used
quintessentially 1960s images of 'with-it' young women for their ads in
1970, the former a girl with a late-1960s hairdo in classic 'flower power'
style.

References were also to be found in the journal to television pro-
grammes that drew strongly on 1960s trends: the Frost Show, which grew
out of its presenter's success in That Was the Week That Was; and the cult
series The Prisoner (1967), starring Patrick McGoohan as 'Number Six', the
lone rebel held captive in the mysterious surroundings of a resort – in reality Clough Williams-Ellis's Portmeirion – by the impersonal agency of a
remote, but menacing technocratic authority. One area notably absent from
AJR Information, however, was popular music. It was perhaps here that the
generation gap of the 1960s made itself felt: pop music was then the preserve of teenagers and those in their early 20s, whereas even those refugees
who had come as children in the 1930s were now at least ten years older,
and those who had come as adults were over 50. Instead of the Beatles and
Rolling Stones, neither of whom rated a single mention, the only two pop
stars referred to were minor figures from the early 1960s: Mike Sarne
(Michael Scheuer), who had a hit single, 'Come Outside', in 1962 and was
the son of a refugee, and Frank Ifield, a yodelling Australian who also
reached the top of the pop charts in 1962, but whom the journal only

mentioned because he appeared in a West End show in 1965 with the refugee actor Martin Miller.[10]

Although Jewish refugees from Central Europe were immensely influential in the British cultural scene of the 1960s as a whole, they were far less prominent in the specific areas of radical counter-culture and 1960s youth culture. Unlike the USA, where such luminaries of the Frankfurt School as Theodor W. Adorno, Max Horkheimer and Herbert Marcuse exercised considerable influence on the radical intellectual currents of the 1960s – even though Adorno and Horkheimer were by then back in Germany – the refugee community that settled in Britain produced no trend-setting figures in radical politics or in the underground arts world associated with the ferment of the late 1960s. Even the children of the refugees produced nobody to compare with Daniel Cohn-Bendit, son of German Jews who had fled to France and a leader of the Paris students in May 1968.

In truth, the refugees, like most of the older generation in British society, looked on at the explosion of youth culture from a distance, with a mixture of incomprehension and somewhat derisive humour. The obsession of 1960s culture with fashion, its ability to create ever-newer and more outrageous trends, seemed to them ephemeral, insubstantial and infatuated with its own trendiness. When Alfons Rosenberg wrote a piece to mark the eightieth birthday of the Czech-born refugee Bruno Adler, who under the pseudonym Urban Roedl had published studies of such literary figures as Matthias Claudius and Adalbert Stifter, he stressed that these were writers who tended to live in their own private worlds, free from the fads and fashions of their time: 'They were in a way timeless, putting everything that was fleeting, easy, "with it", superficial in its place i.e. nowhere.'[11] The use of the currently fashionable term 'with it' left no doubt that the target here was 1960s culture. Reviewing an exhibition of paintings by Inge Sachs, Rosenberg again signalled his reservations about the novel formulations of the day even as he used them himself: 'There is something – to use the fashionable jargon – psychedelic about her work', he wrote, with an almost audible gritting of his teeth.[12]

More serious was the refugees' lack of sympathy with the political radicalism that characterized the late 1960s, coming to a head in May 1968 with the student revolts that broke out in Paris and other Western cities.[13] In March 1968, PEM reported that Egon Jameson had given a lecture to Club 43 with the title 'Auf die Barrikaden, ihr Greise!' ('To the Barricades, Old Men!'), a clear jibe at the slogans of the student revolution, with its self-regarding vision of itself as the exclusive bearer of new political truths that justified revolutionary action against the established order. Jameson's lecture, claimed PEM, brought out the element of conflict between the generations: 'His attack on today's overrated youth received an enthusiastic reception from his audience.'[14] What was emphasized here was not the idealism, spontaneity and desire for change of the student activists, but their empty rhetoric and the radical posturing that passed for a political strategy.

The propensity of student radicals for extremism and violence, their doctrinaire fanaticism and impatience with Western parliamentary democracy reminded some refugees uncomfortably of the intolerant radicalism that had swept Germany in the 1930s. In April 1968, *AJR Information* reported that Oskar Seidlin, a German Jew who had emigrated in 1933 and now held a chair at Ohio State University, had refused the offer of a professorship at Munich University because of the latest 'excesses' in West Germany; the student demonstrations were too reminiscent of 1932/33.[15] Refugees were particularly shocked when student radicals disrupted events connected to the Holocaust. In May 1968 the journal reported that a joint meeting of Christians and Jews in West Berlin, part of the 'Brotherhood Week' that was held annually in West Germany to promote reconciliation and tolerance, had been the object of a left-wing demonstration protesting against neo-Nazism and the rise of the NPD, a far-right party, and against the 'hypocrisy' of Brotherhood Week itself.[16] As the AJR supported Brotherhood Week, and as refugees like the historian Eva Reichmann regularly spoke at meetings held under its auspices, readers of the journal would have been shocked to find it associated with neo-Nazism, as well as aggrieved by the suggestion that they had been taken in by an exercise in German hypocrisy.

Worse was to follow. Werner Rosenstock wrote an article on the ceremony held on 15 September 1968 to mark the unveiling of the memorial at Dachau concentration camp. He had represented the AJR and the Council of Jews from Germany at the ceremony, alongside delegates from fifteen countries. A small number of protesters, mainly students, carrying banners with anti-Vietnam War or anti-NATO slogans, had disrupted the proceedings and tried to shout down Klaus Schütz, mayor of West Berlin and president of the Bundesrat, the upper house of the West German parliament, when he delivered a message on behalf of the federal government. This looked like a gratuitous insult to the memory of the many thousands who had died at Dachau. Rosenstock's dislike for what he saw as modish anti-Establishment gestures came across clearly when he compared the protestors' juvenile antics with the experiences of those delegates who had engaged in real resistance to the Nazis and had often suffered grievously for their courage. The instigators of the demonstration, Rosenstock wrote, 'not only showed disrespect to the memory of tens of thousands of heroes but were also oblivious of the fact that, but for the courage of those anti-Nazis, freedom of thought and speech would have vanished from the European continent'.[17]

Expressions of support for student radicalism received short shrift from a refugee readership, as C.C. Aronsfeld discovered when he wrote an ill-judged article in June 1968 on what he saw as the parlous state of West German politics. Beginning with the stark pronouncement 'Something is rotten in the State of Bonn', he described the opposition offered by democratic forces to the neo-Nazi NPD as feeble even by comparison with resistance to Hitler under the Weimar Republic. Greatly exaggerating the crisis facing West German democracy and the threat posed by the NPD, he argued that, should a revolutionary situation arise, or should the ruling coalition of Christian Democrats and Social Democrats break down, the extra-parliamentary opposition of the young should 'supplant, or at the very least supplement' parliamentary democracy.[18] In effect, Aronsfeld was arguing that West Germany in 1968 faced a situation like that facing the Weimar Republic in the early 1930s, where, with the democratic system weakened beyond repair, the only choice was between the Communists on the extreme left and the Nazis on the extreme right.

The response to this dubious historical comparison, especially its negative attitude to West Germany's democracy, was predictably hostile. A letter to the editor from R. Graupner took issue with Aronsfeld, defending the Grand Coalition as a stabilizing factor in West German politics that had been absent in Weimar and pointing out that the government had not deviated from policies acceptable to Jewish interests and to Israel.[19] But Graupner's main target was Aronsfeld's tolerant view of the radical left. He dismissed the latter's argument that the students' movement was extra-parliamentary, but not anti-parliamentary, citing their frequently stated hostility to parliamentary democracy and their eagerness for a revolution to overthrow it. Heavily critical of Aronsfeld's indulgence towards revolutionary youth, with its openly anti-democratic aims and its Maoist or anarchist tendencies, Graupner concluded by questioning whether such contentions belonged in the journal at all. This was doubtless the view of the majority of its readers, and no more was heard of sympathy for the neo-Marxist left. Within a few years, the student protest movement had run its course, and political radicalism itself became yesterday's fashion.

The consolidation of democracy in West Germany contributed greatly to the emergence during the 1960s of a more settled attitude among the refugees towards Germany (and to a lesser extent Austria). While one cannot speak of a 'normalization' of relations between the Jewish refugees and the countries indelibly associated with Nazism and its crimes that had driven them out, it is nevertheless the case that with the passage of time a more conciliatory attitude towards Germany established itself among many refugees, though by no means all. By the mid-1960s, twenty years had passed since the end of the Nazi period; long enough for a generation of young Germans to have grown to adulthood with no direct experience of Nazism, and for the stability of democratic institutions in West Germany and that state's official rejection of anti-Semitism to have stood the initial test of time. With the experiences of the Nazi years receding gradually into the past, it became possible for the refugees to arrive at a more distanced perspective on their former homelands, less immediately influenced by the painful memories evoked by the events of 1933–45.

The two principal contending views of Germany were clearly defined by Werner Rosenstock in December 1967. In a front-page article in *AJR Information*, he stated that the AJR had to respect two schools of thought about Germany among its members: those who were 'irrevocably antagonistic' because they had been expelled by the country they had considered their homeland, and those who continued to 'lay stress on the formative impact of their past lives in Germany'. According to this view, one should note, even those who maintained a relationship to Germany did so for reasons connected to their pre-emigration past; few refugees saw Germany as a country congenial and sympathetic enough for 'normal' close or friendly relations to develop in the post-war present.

Refugee attitudes to Germany varied from individual to individual, according to the almost infinite permutations of personal experience and temperament. It is, however, possible to identify age at emigration and the degree of integration as key factors influencing later attitudes. Younger refugees, those born after 1920, had little awareness of pre-Hitler Germany, knowing it only as a society hostile and threatening to Jews. Older refugees, on the other hand, had frequently experienced years of relatively untroubled and contented life in Germany, enjoying friendly relations with Germans who were not yet solidly anti-Semitic. It was predominantly these more integrated German Jews, those who had had most in common with German society, who retained an awareness of its better side.

Conversely, as the interviews in the 'Refugee Voices' collection show very clearly, refugees from more traditional, Orthodox Jewish families tended to take a far less forgiving line towards Germany, retaining a deep-seated dislike of Germans that was often expressed with considerable bit-terness.[20] Arguably, the enduring refusal of such refugees to have anything to do with a country they abhorred stemmed from their more pronounced sense of their own Jewishness, the very quality that the Nazis had sought to exterminate; the more that group identified with its Jewishness, and the less it was open to values like those of the assimilated German Jews, the more comprehensively its attitude to Germany and the Germans would be determined by the Holocaust and the Nazi attempt to destroy every last vestige of Jewish being.

Most refugees were permanently affected by their losses in the Holocaust; this applied also to thoroughly assimilated German Jews like Lotte Berk, who declared half a century after the war: 'I have got such a hate for the Germans. I think all Jews have.'[21] Some of these refused to set foot on German soil, reducing relations with anything German to a minimum; others returned reluctantly to Germany as visitors, finding the experience deeply disturbing.[22] Such people could never, or only with great difficulty, be reconciled to Germany; almost all refugees shared, at some level, a sense of the unbridgeable rupture that had been brought about by their expulsion and by the fate of the Jews who had stayed in Germany. On the other hand, a degree of nostalgia for Germany was not infrequently detectable among older refugees. A case in point was Bernhard Weiss, a deeply patriotic assimilated Jew who had been deputy police president of Berlin until 1932 and had been a particular foe of Joseph Goebbels. He fled in 1933 and spent seventeen years in Britain, a sad shadow of his former self, until his death in 1951. He longed to return to Germany, and might well have done so had his health permitted it.[23]

But by the 1960s one can detect a broad consensus attitude towards Germany that was beginning to crystallize at least among those refugees, mostly the formerly more assimilated, who were willing to accept that a new situation required a new response. *AJR Information*, though always concerned to keep the Nazi past fresh in its readers' minds, broadly took a conciliatory line towards West Germany, influenced by the development of the Federal Republic since its foundation in 1949 and by the growing body of evidence that 'Bonn was not Weimar'. The stability of West Germany's democratic institutions, the marginalization of the parties of the far right in its electoral politics, its support for the state of Israel and its adoption of policies acceptable to Jews were increasingly difficult to dispute by the 1960s.[24] Underpinning this new departure in German history was economic success, the 'economic miracle' (*Wirtschaftswunder*) that had transformed a nation in ruins into Europe's most powerful economy. For many refugees, that at least guaranteed a peaceful Germany; better fat, complacent Germans than the lean and hungry ones of earlier decades.

Some aspects of West German public life continued, however, to disturb the refugees. Foremost among them was the steadfast refusal of most Germans, especially during Konrad Adenauer's chancellorship (1949–63), to face up to the reality of Germany's crimes and the responsibility that they themselves bore for their varying degrees of participation in the Nazis' activities. The entire question of *Vergangenheitsbewältigung*, of coming to terms with the Nazi past, was to remain a running sore in relations between refugees and the Germans, whose tendency towards convenient collective amnesia and dubious self-exculpation, where the years of Hitler's Reich were concerned, caused bewilderment, fury and pain among their former fellow countrymen. The latter saw that the post-war process of de-Nazification had never been carried through. The reappearance of extreme right-wing, anti-Semitic and anti-democratic groups, whose spokesmen did not hesitate to make wounding and inflammatory pronouncements under cover of the constitutional guarantee of freedom of speech, added to the impression that the sensitivities of Holocaust survivors counted for little in Germany.

In West Germany of the 1950s, it seemed as if a veil of silence had been cast over the persecution and deportation of Jews. The marked reluctance of the authorities to prosecute Germans for crimes committed against Jews, at least until the late 1950s, and the lenient sentences sometimes passed on those convicted were further serious causes for grievance. The impression that West Germany tolerated ex-Nazis was reinforced by the reintegration of such people into the machinery of state at almost every level: Adenauer chose as his chief aide Hans Globke, author of the official commentary on the Nuremberg race laws of 1935; Theodor Oberländer, minister responsible for the Germans who had been expelled from Eastern Europe, had served with a Ukrainian unit suspected of massacring Jews. Ex-Nazis were to be found among civil servants, in the police and security establishment, in the universities, among judges and public prosecutors, doctors and teachers, and at all levels of management, business and commerce. Particular bitterness was aroused by cases where it emerged that former concentration camp personnel and doctors involved in medical experiments in the camps had lived for years as respected members of society, sometimes under assumed names, without being held to account.

In the late 1950s a change set in. In August 1958 the *Ulmer Einsatzkommando-Prozess* ended with ten former members of the *Einsatzkommando Tilsit* being sentenced at Ulm to long prison terms for their part in mass shootings, especially of Jews. This was the first of a series of trials which, receiving added impetus from the trial of Adolf Eichmann in Jerusalem in 1961, led on to the Auschwitz trials at Frankfurt, 1963–65, and other major trials of those involved in the Holocaust. Four months after the end of the Ulm trial, the Zentralstelle der Landesjustizverwaltungen zur Aufklärung nationalsozialistischer Verbrechen (Central Office of the Judicial Authorities of the Federal States for Investigation of National Socialist Crimes) was established in Ludwigsburg; as the agency coordinating at national level the efforts of the judicial authorities of the Länder, it brought a more vigorous and systematic approach to the investigation and prosecution of Nazi criminals.

Starting with the daubing of a synagogue in Cologne at Christmas 1959, a wave of anti-Semitic graffiti and desecration spread across German cities, arousing deep concern in the Jewish community, and beyond, throughout the world.[25] However, it rapidly became clear that those responsible were young delinquents with no coordinating organization behind them. More importantly, the outrages prompted a countervailing reaction in mainstream German society of far greater proportions, finding its expression in large public demonstrations of protest and of opposition to all forms of anti-Semitism. During the 1960s the West German authorities ensured that the Nazi period took its place in the school curriculum; the general education of the public about the Holocaust, which spread throughout the population, served further to inoculate public opinion against anti-Semites and Nazi apologists.

The impression sometimes created in the foreign press that West Germany was a powder-keg of Nazism, militarism and anti-Semitism just waiting to reignite could be subjected to a reality check, at least under a democratic system. This was demonstrated by the electoral fortunes of the neo-Nazi NPD, the party that in the 1960s posed the most serious challenge from the far right in the history of the Federal Republic. From 1966, *AJR Information* reported regularly on the electoral advances of the NPD, which won enough votes (over 5 per cent of those cast) to secure representation in the *Landtage* (regional parliaments) of several Länder, starting with Hesse, where it won 8 per cent of the vote and eight seats, and Bavaria, where it won fifteen seats. The unspoken fear behind these reports was plainly that the NPD would emulate the example of the Nazi party, which had been propelled from obscurity to government in less than five years by an apparently unstoppable stampede to the far right.

This gave rise to a serious overestimation of the reality of the threat posed by the NPD. In February 1967 a front-page article in *AJR Information* reported that the NPD leadership expected to win 'only' fifty to sixty seats in the next Bundestag. On the following page, the prominent West German politician Ernst Lemmer was quoted as warning that the number could be as high as seventy to eighty. The following month, an article entitled 'Extremists in Germany' took up the whole of the fourth page of the journal; it predicted that two million Germans would vote for the NPD at the next election, 6 per cent of the total vote, compared to the 2.5 per cent it had received in 1965. Under the West German system of proportional representation, such outcomes would have had a very serious effect. The NPD would have displaced the Liberal FDP as the principal third party whose votes were needed to provide a coalition government with a parliamentary majority; it would to some extent have been able to dictate its terms to its coalition partners. C.C. Aronsfeld even envisaged the effective collapse of West Germany's democratic institutions, with the NPD gaining 8 to 9 per cent of the vote.[26]

The Bundestag elections of 1969 did indeed turn out to be a historic turning point, but not as the prophets of doom had foretold. The NPD failed to gain 5 per cent of the vote and won no seats. Instead, the Social Democrats, under Willy Brandt, became the principal party of government for the first time, in coalition with the FDP, with a new, progressive agenda of liberalization. The changes that West Germany underwent under Chancellor Brandt and his successor, Helmut Schmidt, consolidated it as a democracy where the far right remained a marginal phenomenon. Surveying the election results, the historian and commentator Heinrich Fraenkel dismissed the NDP as 'this rather ridiculous little party', which had only won what votes it had because of left-wing demonstrations against it and the worldwide publicity it had attracted. Fraenkel predicted that 1969 marked a major turn for the better in Germany.[27]

It was only to be expected that any resurgence of neo-Nazism in Germany would arouse anxieties among the Jewish refugees. But by the 1960s the predominant line taken by *AJR Information* was that West German democracy deserved to be given its chance. Observers who travelled to West Germany could hardly fail to be struck by the change in attitudes, especially among the young. Werner Rosenstock, reporting on the mass rally held in Cologne in March 1964 as the climax of 'Brotherhood Week', was very impressed:

> If we try to turn our minds to the pre-1933 days in Germany we can hardly imagine that at that time more than 10,000 Christian citizens of one town would have been prepared to forego the leisure of a Sunday morning to attend a meeting, initiated solely by Christians, in order to express their feelings of brotherhood with the Jews.[28]

He added, however, that before 1933 it had been equally inconceivable that a German government would set about the planned extermination of millions of Jews. That was the context in which, unavoidably, the pro-Jewish manifestations had to be seen.

Eugen Mayer also experienced a warm welcome when he visited Frankfurt in 1961, but his suspicions about the past behaviour of some older Germans left him with a painful sense of alienation from his native city:

When I met others, perhaps an official, a headmaster, or a waiter, I wondered how they had behaved during those years. This may be the reason why I walked through the familiar streets of this town, where my mother-tongue is spoken, as if I were a foreigner ... In spite of all the hospitality – and it was almost overwhelming – and in spite of the genuine and often deeply moving warmth of the sentiments, I could scarcely ever rid myself of the feeling that I was in a spiritual No-Man's-Land, my only connection with which was the cemetery of a past history.[29]

Rosenstock's visit to Cologne in 1964 prompted a carefully balanced response, rejecting as oversimplifications both the view that unreservedly condemned all Germans for all time and that which considered the Nazi period an isolated chapter in German history that was now closed. No such clear-cut decisions were possible, he felt:

Certainly German gestures of atonement cannot eradicate the past, nor can they make us overlook symptoms of its political legacy in present-day Germany. We know that the catastrophe has been indelibly inscribed into German and Jewish history. Yet the position would be considerably worse if post-war Germany did not even try to make amends both in the material and in the spiritual sphere.

It was in that spirit that he was prepared to set such store by the efforts at atonement of the young Germans in Cologne, in whom he discerned a genuine desire for reconciliation.

By the 1960s some refugees were accepting that Germany had changed and that it was not immutably wedded to the aggressive militarism, expansionism and racialism that had long marked its history. In February 1969 *AJR Information* published an article that squarely took issue with the concept of an unchanging national character, arguing that in the case of relations between Germans and Jews the old cliché that 'the German leopard does not change its spots' did not hold water. The article recalled that during the First World War Germany had been regarded as the protector of the Jews of Eastern Europe against Tsarist oppression; for that reason, many uncommitted Jews had supported Germany. Now, Germany was again entirely different from what it had been twenty-five years ago; it would be a serious mistake to burden the new generation of Germans with the guilt for crimes that they could not have committed.[30]

As the years passed, it became clear that the refugees from Germany were on the whole more prepared to take a balanced view of their native land than were British Jews, most of whom expressed only blanket condemnation of

Germany. In a sketch by Francis Treuherz depicting two generations of a refugee family in 1964, the son realizes that the children of refugees can go to Germany and discuss it 'without exploding', while their Anglo-Jewish contemporaries cannot: 'Maybe this is because, although there is the unmentionable side to Germany which we all abhor, I have been educated with a certain gloss of German culture which my Anglo-Jewish counterpart hasn't got, and he therefore sees only the anti-German viewpoint.'[31] The socio-cultural links to Germany continued to influence refugee attitudes across the generations.

Because they knew German culture and society, the refugees were well placed to defend them. When a letter from a synagogue in Hendon appeared in the *Jewish Chronicle* asserting that 'hardly any expression of regret had been forthcoming from Germany', it met with a robust rebuttal from the eminent refugee jurist Professor Ernst J. Cohn. 'Every attentive reader of your columns will immediately recognise that this statement is utterly false', declared Cohn roundly. He proceeded to give a large number of examples of actions and statements of goodwill by Germans and concluded: 'A complete list of such expressions, some in extreme terms, by post-1945 statesmen, scholars, journalists, and other leaders of public opinion would, no doubt, fill many pages of *The Jewish Chronicle*.' *AJR Information* promptly published detailed extracts from Cohn's counterblast, leaving little doubt that it concurred with his views.[32]

The refugees were also ready to protest at unjustified criticism of Germany from British sources. When the BBC TV series *European Journal* broadcast a feature on Jewish life in Germany that was almost exclusively negative – it intercut shots of young Germans dancing at Carnival with shots of an urn containing ashes from a concentration camp – the review in *AJR Information* was strongly critical; it claimed that the programme ignored the degree to which Jews were integrated into German life and declared that it fell below the standards expected of a responsible broadcasting company.[33]

Some refugees made exceptional personal contributions to the task of reconciliation. Ilse Josephs, a refugee from Berlin, undertook the first of a series of concert tours of West Germany in 1967, giving a number of violin recitals, often in homes for elderly Germans. Though her own children had died at Auschwitz, *AJR Information* reported that 'she feels that hatred should not be perpetuated and that efforts of mutual understanding would be the best safeguard against the recurrence of catastrophes as experienced by the present generation of Jews'. When she explained to her audience that this was the motive behind her tour, it was greatly appreciated. During her tours, she always introduced her recitals by expressing the hope that

her efforts might help to overcome the past and to promote mutual understanding between peoples. According to German press reports, her appear-
ances made a considerable impact.[34] Such forgiveness in the face of such a
loss represented an extraordinary assertion of faith in the possibility of
German-Jewish reconciliation; admirable as it was, it almost certainly went
beyond what much of the rest of Jewry would have found acceptable.

At the official level, relations between the West German government
and the organizations of the Jews from Germany in Britain were cordial.
Successive ambassadors in London established friendly relations with the
AJR, and *AJR Information* regularly carried warm appreciations of their work
when they moved on to new posts. That West German diplomats should
seek to win over the former Jews from Germany was predictable, but less
so were the efforts by the Jews from Germany to reach out to Germans living in Britain. In 1961, a group of prominent refugees under the chair-
manship of Alfred Wiener, the founder of the Wiener Library, set up the
'Arbeitskreis 1961' ('Discussion Group 1961'), which organized talks for
young Germans in London. The first programme of talks, entitled
'Deutschland gestern und morgen' ('Germany yesterday and tomorrow'),
began with one on democracy. Speakers included the writer Hans Jaeger,
the historian Eva G. Reichmann and Rabbi Dr Georg Salzberger; subjects
included the Eichmann trial.[35]

Alfred Wiener and Eva Reichmann were among the prominent refugees
who were at the forefront of efforts to build bridges between Germans and
the Jews from Germany. When Wiener died in 1964, Reichmann, who had
worked with him at the Wiener Library, wrote an eloquent obituary in
which she highlighted his attempts to improve relations between the two
groups.[36] In his determination to strengthen the liberal, humanitarian and
freedom-loving forces in German society, Wiener was one of the first
refugees to embark on a series of visits to Germany, where he spoke to
those who shared his values, above all to young people, an undertaking
that met with considerable disapproval in the early days. But Reichmann's
tribute left no doubt of her admiration for Wiener's efforts to promote
understanding with Germans of goodwill. There were certainly many
refugees who had serious reservations about this; but among the leaders
and opinion-formers in the refugee community, the majority were clearly
willing to espouse a strategy of cautious reconciliation and a measured
renewal of contact and dialogue.

Probably the most significant initiative undertaken by the refugee com-
munity in the 1960s was the setting up of the 'Thank-You Britain' Fund.
This evolved out of a proposal in 1963 that the Jewish refugees from
Central Europe should make a public gesture of thanks to their adopted

homeland, to be paid for by their donations. The idea originated with Victor Ross, a former refugee who was a senior executive with *Reader's Digest*. The AJR, which had been thinking along similar lines, joined forces with him. The AJR took on the administration of the fund-raising, and Ross became co-chairman of the fund's organizing committee, alongside Werner M. Behr, AJR vice-chairman. The first mention of what was to become the Fund, in a report on the meeting of the AJR Board held on 27 January 1963, implied that the fund grew out of an initiative that the Association adopted: 'Inter *alia*, it was suggested that an appropriate scheme should be launched by which the former refugees should express their gratitude to the British nation for having admitted them to this country twenty-five years ago.'[37]

This was amplified by a statement that autumn, issued on the eve of the Jewish New Year and recalling the *Kristallnacht* pogroms of November 1938, which had destroyed any hope that Jewry could somehow survive in Germany:

> In November, twenty-five years will have elapsed since the mass exodus of the Jews from Central Europe started. During the few months between the pogroms and the outbreak of war, this small island, then in an economic crisis, rescued more Jewish persecutees than any other single country. The Executive is considering ways of visibly expressing the gratitude of the former refugees to the British people, and it is hoped that details of an appropriate scheme will be announced shortly.[38]

Three months later, a boxed announcement appeared in the journal, headed: 'Former Refugees' Thanks to Britain: Collective Gesture of Gratitude Planned'. It began: 'As already mentioned in this journal, the AJR Executive plans to mark the twenty-five years' stay of the former refugees in this country by a visible expression of their gratitude to the British people.' Readers were informed that Victor Ross had published a letter in several national papers proposing such a gesture of collective gratitude and that the response to this letter had been most encouraging. The AJR and Ross were therefore considering several proposed schemes, and, once one was chosen, intended to launch an appeal 'on the widest possible basis'.[39]

The scheme adopted became known as the 'Thank-You Britain' Fund, the proceeds of which were to be used for the awarding of research fellowships and the holding of lectures, both under the auspices of the British Academy, a highly respected institution that supports and promotes research and scholarship in the humanities. Ross approached the Academy, as the minutes of the meeting of its Council on 27 May 1964 recorded:

A proposal had been received from Mr Victor Ross, on behalf of refugees from Nazi oppression who had settled happily in Great Britain, that a Fund should be established to commemorate their welcome into Britain. The suggestion was that the Fund should be named 'The Thank-offering to Britain' Fund, and that this Fund should be used for the establishment of a Lecture and Research Fellowship under the auspices of the Academy.[40]

The Academy, adding gravitas, used the title 'Thank-Offering to Britain' Fund.

The minutes incorporated the conditions proposed by the Fund's sponsors. These stated that a fund had been established to enable a gesture of collective gratitude to be made by refugees from Nazi oppression towards Britain as the country of their adoption; that the fund was intended for use by the Academy to provide a periodical lecture and to establish a research fellowship; and that the subject of both of these was to 'relate to "Human Studies", widely interpreted in their bearing upon the welfare of the inhabitants of the United Kingdom'. The 'Thank-Offering to Britain' Fund Lecture was to be given every two years, for a fee of not less than £100; in the event, the lectures were given annually from 1966 till 1974, and thereafter mostly biennially until 2004. The 'Thank-Offering to Britain' Fund Research Award was to enable a Fellow selected by the Council to work for a period not exceeding three years at a university approved by the Council.

With the cooperation of the British Academy secured, the AJR proceeded to publicize the scheme to its members and to raise funds. In a front-page article in *AJR Information* of September 1964, entitled 'A Quarter of a Century: Days of Remembrances', Werner Rosenstock introduced the 'Thank-You Britain' Fund to his readers, again setting it in the context of the arrival of the refugees in Britain and their subsequent settlement:

> Thus it can be stated that, with unavoidable exceptions, the immigration of the Nazi persecutees has been a success. However, things would have taken an entirely different course had not this island admitted us to its shores during the darkest period of our history. It cannot be stressed often enough that between the pogroms of November, 1938, and the outbreak of war, Britain admitted more Nazi victims from Central Europe than any other single country. We should not forget either that this rescue work was carried out at a time when the country was going through an economic crisis. Now, as we have struck roots in our country of adoption, the time has come to express our thanks in a tangible way.

Rosenstock explained that the proceeds of the Fund were to be used for the awarding of research fellowships and the holding of lectures under the auspices of the British Academy, 'as a perpetual memorial of our gratitude'. The research sponsored was to contribute to the welfare of the country.

The Fund's patrons could scarcely have been more eminent. They were the distinguished economist Lord Lionel Robbins, President of the British Academy and author of the Robbins Report of 1963 that revolutionized higher education; Sir Isaiah Berlin, a member of the Academy's Council and one of the great intellectual figures of his day; Professor (later Sir) Ernest B. Chain and Sir Hans Krebs, the two refugees from Nazism who had won Nobel Prizes by 1964; and a third refugee, Professor (later Sir) Ludwig Guttmann, Director of the Stoke Mandeville Spinal Injuries Centre. The nineteen members of the Fund's committee included leading figures in the AJR and other refugee organizations. Among them were AJR chairman Alfred S. Dresel, Werner M. Behr, Victor Ross, Arnold Horwell, Egon Larsen, Hans Blumenau, Hans Jaeger and the indispensable Werner Rosenstock.

The organising committee of the Fund sent out to all AJR members a letter, signed by its two co-chairmen, inviting them to contribute to the Fund.[41] The Fund was to be administered from the AJR offices at 8, Fairfax Mansions, NW3. According to the letter, the original aim was to raise between £40,000 and £60,000, an amount equivalent to not far short of £500,000 in today's money, to be invested 'to create a perpetual income for the benefit of British scholarship and research'. The pressing terms in which members were exhorted to contribute to it indicated the organisers' sense of its exceptional importance. As Rosenstock put it in his article of September 1964: 'The present opportunity to make a gesture of collective gratitude is without precedent in the history of our community and also unlikely to arise again. It is, therefore, unique in the fullest sense of the word.'

The reaction to the appeal was gratifying. Already in October 1964, *AJR Information* reported that the response had been very encouraging. The following month, it reported that the Fund was making good progress: many members had made donations, sometimes accompanied by expressions of enthusiasm for the scheme, and the addresses of thousands of potential contributors had been received.[42] The appeal evidently struck a chord in the refugee community, as a letter sent by a contributor who was now deputy head of a college in Jamaica showed:

> I read in the *Manchester Guardian* about the 'Thank-You Britain' Fund. I was one of those who after the Kristallnacht was sent to Oranienburg [concentration camp] but managed to come to Britain in time before

the outbreak of war. I will never be able to repay all the kindness and understanding that was shown to me from simple Lancashire cotton workers to Quaker refugee workers and Jewish manufacturers. I am now a British subject and could not wish for anything better. I am trying to repay part of my debt by teaching as a British subject in Jamaica. What I can send is totally inadequate, but I try to say 'Thank you' every day by my work.[43]

In January 1965 a report stated that the appeal had met with a wide response from all sections of community, including prominent scholars, artists and scientists, and also former refugees who were not members of the AJR or any other sponsoring organization; even those who had little contact with fellow immigrants were responding.[44] Payments were flowing in steadily, and the lower target limit had already been reached, but the report emphasized that the Fund would only be commensurate with the size and standing of the community if the final amount raised was much higher. The report urged all those who had not contributed to do so, thus making the Fund truly representative of the community as a whole. To reinforce its impact, the report quoted from a letter attached to a contribution received from New Jersey, USA:

> I was only eight years old when we came to Britain from Germany. The ways in which we were accepted in those difficult times can never be repaid financially, but the heartfelt gratitude that so many of us felt for many years needed a form of expression. I am delighted to be able to contribute to your fitting memorial.

The British Academy also became aware of the unusual enthusiasm with which refugees reacted to the 'Thank-You Britain' Fund. On 21 July 1964, Miss D.W. Pearson, assistant secretary at the Academy, wrote to Victor Ross, enclosing a specimen form for a deed of covenant, a tax-effective way for contributors to increase the amount of their donations at no extra cost to themselves. Evidently, the printers (Oxford University Press) moved too slowly to keep pace with the eagerness of potential donors: before they had returned the proof of the form to the Academy, a handwritten note to Doris Pearson from another member of staff informed her that Ross had phoned to ask for the forms as quickly as possible, to send to contributors impatient to use them.[45]

The British Academy was involved in a considerable amount of correspondence about donations to the Fund. In May 1965 Rosenstock wrote to Pearson about Eva Kaul, a refugee who had used her restitution money from Germany to make out a covenant for £102.18.0 the previous December, in memory of her late husband. She had since received a further payment from Germany and wished to pay another £100 into the Fund. It would have been more beneficial to the Fund if this, too, were made under covenant, but it was not possible to increase a covenant already made. However, there was no regulation against making out two covenants for the same cause at different times, but before advising Mrs Kaul to that effect, Rosenstock requested Pearson to check with the Academy's accountants that this was in order.[46]

In July 1966 Werner M. Behr wrote to Pearson, enclosing a cheque for $50 from Fred Lang of Illinois, USA, as a contribution to the Fund. Lang had also requested more leaflets about the Fund, for distribution to potential donors in America. A note of admiration for the response aroused by the Fund crept into Doris Pearson's customary businesslike style: 'The way in which new donors are still coming forward from time to time to add their contribution to the Fund is really rather impressive', she wrote in her reply to Behr. She would probably also have been impressed by a letter she received from the eminent Classical scholar Günther Zuntz, Professor of Hellenistic Greek at the University of Manchester, saying somewhat sharply that he had learnt about the Fund only from Lord Robbins's presidential address and asking to be put in touch with the Fund's treasurer: 'For I want to do my modest bit.'[47] Sir Isaiah Berlin had sent his donation to Rosenstock, as treasurer of the Fund, in October 1964, through N.M. Rothschild & Sons, but this attracted the attention of the Inspector of Taxes, who demanded a copy of the rules of the Fund, as evidence of the purposes for which it would be used. Rosenstock forwarded this request on to the Academy, and the Academy replied to Rothschild's, setting out the academic aims for which the Fund had been established and confirming its status for tax purposes.[48]

Donations were also received in the form of bequests. Rosenstock passed on to Pearson a letter from a firm of solicitors in Pall Mall, stating that a client wished to make a bequest to the Fund in his will, and she suggested an appropriate form of words.[49] It was a source of pride to the AJR that shortly before his death in London in 1965, the internationally known economist, political scientist and government adviser Moritz J. Bonn had stipulated in a codicil to his will that a substantial legacy should go to the Fund. An editorial note attached to Bonn's obituary in AJR Information declared that it was a lasting honour for the Fund to be linked with the name of a man who on several occasions before 1933 had acted in negotiations between the German and British governments and after 1933 was one of the first German scholars to be appointed to a university position in Britain.[50]

By April 1965 the Fund had made remarkable progress, as a front-page article in the journal, 'Joint Efforts Bear Fruit: Response to "Thank-you Britain" Fund', testified. Rosenstock was able to report that some £67,000 had been raised, £46,000 from payments under deeds of covenant and the rest from outright donations. The amounts contributed ranged from £1 to £2,000, according to a later article.[51] In his article of April 1965, Rosenstock responded at some length to critics of the Fund who argued that the refugees had already amply repaid any debt that they might owe Britain and that the Fund was excessive as an expression of gratitude, criticisms that he felt able to refute confidently. The arguments presented on both sides here gave every appearance of emanating from entrenched positions, with neither side likely to retreat from its strongly held views.

Two underlying positions can be discerned: on the one hand, those who felt a strong sense of gratitude to Britain, who had settled by and large happily and integrated by and large smoothly into British society and who felt at ease with their part-British identity, and on the other hand those who felt that Britain had admitted them grudgingly, that British society had hardly gone out of its way to make them feel welcome and who preserved a sense of alienation and marginality in their daily life in Britain. These two contending positions are to be found throughout the refugee community, and the works of literature and scholarship devoted to it. From the evidence of the 'Thank-You Britain' Fund at least, one can say with some confidence that the majority of the refugees espoused the standpoint more favourable to Britain.

The clearest evidence for this proposition is the sheer number of refugees who contributed to the Fund, and the amount they gave, which in the end came to over £96,000, or nearly £1 million in today's money; that was a remarkable sum for a community of some 50,000 people who had had barely twenty years of peacetime conditions to build up a degree of prosperity. The April 1965 issue of the journal carried as an appendix a list of donors to the Fund, as of 15 March 1965. This ran to five solid pages of names, with six columns per page, totalling some 3,000 contributors. It did not include those who wished to remain anonymous and those whose contributions came in later, who together would have increased the final total substantially; in early 1966 that reached 4,500.[52] Famous names included Anna and Ernst Freud; scholars like Francis Carsten, Eduard Fraenkel, Ernst Gombrich, Otto Kahn-Freund and Claus Moser; scientists like Hans Kornberg, Nicholas Kurti, Heinz London and Max Perutz; Mosco Carner, Peter Gellhorn, Franz Reizenstein and Peter Stadlen from the musical world; writers like Hans Jaeger, Egon Jameson and Egon Larsen; and the cartoonist Vicky (Victor Weisz), the industrialist Mac Goldsmith, the actor Martin Miller and the rabbis Ignaz Maybaum and Jakob Kokotek.

But most significant were the serried ranks of ordinary refugees who formed the vast majority of the contributors; as many of them represented entire families, the number of donors came to form a substantial proportion of the refugee community, unmistakable evidence of the popularity of the Fund and the eagerness of the refugees to contribute to its gesture of gratitude to their adopted homeland. The most common surnames in the list were the German-Jewish names Stern (24) and Rosenthal (16). There were twelve Goldschmidts, but this increases to twenty-two if one adds the ten who had anglicised their name to Goldsmith. Indeed, the number of anglicised or English names, the Newmans, Newtons and Newhouses, the proliferation of Allens, Godfreys, Gilberts, Haywards, Kennedys, Kingsleys or Nortons showed again the extent to which many refugees had come to identify with Britain and to assume a part-British identity. It was their support that fuelled the success of the Fund.

The money raised by the Fund was formally handed over to the British Academy in autumn 1965. In September Rosenstock wrote to Pearson to tell her that the handing-over ceremony would take place on 8 November 1965, in the appropriately grand setting of Saddlers' Hall, just off Cheapside in the heart of the City.[53] In response to his request, she sent him the names of members of the Academy to be invited to the ceremony. The number of highly distinguished members was so large that she sent two lists, one of which, the priority list, consisted of the officers and council of the Academy and other eminent personalities, including members of the committee appointed by the Academy to administer the Fund.

The dignitaries on this list included Lord Robbins, Professor Roy Allen of the London School of Economics (treasurer of the Academy), the archaeologist Sir Mortimer Wheeler (its secretary), Sir Isaiah Berlin, the art historian (and spy) Sir Anthony Blunt, Sir Maurice Bowra, master of Wadham College, Oxford, the historian Sir Denis Brogan, the economist Alec Cairncross, Professor Henry Chadwick, Dean of Christ Church, Oxford, the senior judge Lord Devlin, the historian Sir Goronwy Edwards, Professor Helen Gardner of St Hilda's College, Oxford, H.L.A. Hart, professor of Jurisprudence at Oxford, the economist Sir John Hicks of All Souls College, Oxford, Dr Kathleen Kenyon of St Hugh's College, Oxford, the ancient historian Professor Arnaldo Momigliano, himself a former refugee from fascist Italy, John Pope-Hennessy of the Victoria and Albert Museum, Sir Ian Richmond of All Souls College, Oxford, and Dr Lucy Sutherland of Lady Margaret Hall, Oxford.

Relegated to the reserve list were such famous names as Sir Roy Harrod, the biographer of Keynes, Nicholas Kaldor, Prime Minister Harold Wilson's economic adviser, Sir Karl Popper and Professor Friedrich Hayek, the leading

proponent of monetarism and the inspiration behind the free-market doc-
trines later associated with Thatcherism. The committee appointed to
administer the Fund initially consisted of Lord Robbins, Sir Mortimer
Wheeler, Sir Isaiah Berlin, Sir Denis Brogan, Professor Raymond Firth of
the London School of Economics, Professor H.L.A. Hart, Sir John Hicks and
Professor Momigliano.

The response of the British Academy to the Fund would have been a
matter of profound pride and satisfaction to its organizing committee and its
supporters generally. The ceremony at Saddlers' Hall was attended by the
cream of the British academic establishment, and the committee appointed
by the Academy to administer the Fund consisted of scholars of international
distinction, two of them (Wheeler and Berlin) household names. *AJR
Information* reported the reception at which the Fund was handed over to the
British Academy prominently, quoting from the opening address given by
Werner M. Behr and reproducing in full the addresses of Sir Hans Krebs, who
handed over the cheque in the name of the refugees, and of Lord Robbins,
who accepted it on behalf of the British Academy.[54] Victor Ross and Werner
M. Behr, co-chairmen of the 'Thank-You Britain' Fund Committee, formally
signed a document giving the proceeds of the Fund to the Academy:

> THE 'THANK-YOU BRITAIN' FUND has been raised by men and
> women who, having come to Britain as refugees from Central
> Europe, were able to build up their lives anew. As a token of their
> gratitude to the people of this country, the Fund is now handed over
> to the BRITISH ACADEMY to be used for the award of research fel-
> lowships in the field of the humanities and the holding of an annual
> lecture.[55]

Twenty-three 'Thank-Offering to Britain' lectures have been held, start-
ing in 1966, when Lord Robbins spoke on the subject 'Of Academic
Freedom'. Among the lecturers were such outstanding public figures as
Roy Jenkins, Ralf Dahrendorf, Conor Cruise O'Brien, Arnold Goodman,
William Armstrong, Robert Blake, Stuart Hampshire, Lord Woolf and Lord
Irvine of Lairg, as well as three refugees, Arthur Koestler, Otto Kahn-Freund
and, in 2004, Claus Moser.[56] The first Research Fellowship was awarded in
1967 to John Patmore of Liverpool University, for his work on leisure and
land use, and the second in 1968 to Dr (now Lord) Robert Skidelsky of
Nuffield College, Oxford, for his research on Sir Oswald Mosley and British
fascism. In 2008/09 the recipient was Dr Patricia Clavin of Jesus College,
Oxford, for research on the League of Nations, and in 2009/10 Dr
Alexander Lingas of City University, for his research into Byzantine chant,
work that builds on that of the great refugee musicologist Egon Wellesz.

The impression that the refugee community had integrated into British society relatively smoothly, that it had gained a large measure of acceptance and that its achievements were valued was reinforced by such gestures of official recognition as the opening by the Queen of the sports stadium attached to Stoke Mandeville Hospital, the centre for spinal injuries where Sir Ludwig Guttmann, one of the patrons of the 'Thank-You Britain' Fund, carried out his pioneering work. *AJR Information* made this point explicitly in its report:

> If we had been told thirty years ago that one day someone in our midst would walk side by side with the Queen and act as her host at a public function, most of us would have dismissed the story as the product of wild and unrealistic imagination. And yet, it came true a few weeks ago, when Sir Ludwig Guttmann welcomed Her Majesty who had graciously consented to open the Stoke Mandeville Sports Stadium for the Paralysed and other Disabled on August 2.[57]

By the end of the 1960s, the refugees from the German-speaking lands had mostly been resident in Britain for over thirty years and had during the quarter-century of peace that had elapsed since 1945 gradually but steadily accommodated their lifestyle to that of their adopted homeland. For most of the refugees, that process of integration into British society had been broadly successful, though they retained enough of their former refugee status to remain distinct from the British around them, and to perceive themselves as distinct in terms of their identity. Most, though by no means all, refugees were broadly content with their life in Britain as British citizens, though that could never erase the memories of their treatment under Nazi rule, their expulsion from their homelands, the losses they had suffered in the Holocaust and the hardships and indignities of their early years in Britain.

By the late 1960s there were signs that the refugees were, in many cases, reaching a new and more settled relationship with Germany, the country primarily responsible for Nazism and the suffering that it had brought them. But they remained aware of their Jewishness, which set limits to the extent to which reconciliation with Germany was possible. Since the German-Jewish and Austrian-Jewish identities of most of the refugees had already been strongly assimilated before emigration, they were more easily able to continue the process of integration in Britain and to adapt themselves to British life. That process of integration was even more marked in the generation of their children. By 1970 many of the second generation were young adults, British by birth and incapable of recreating the Central European social culture of their parents, which in subsequent decades was gradually but inevitably to dwindle and disappear from the areas of British life that the refugees had inhabited and enriched.

NOTES

1. *AJR Information* (January 1969), p.5.
2. On the 1960s, see especially B. Levin, *The Pendulum Years: Britain and the Sixties* (London: Cape, 1970), A. Marwick, *The Sixties: Cultural Revolution in Britain, France, Italy, and the United States, c. 1958–c. 1974* (Oxford: Oxford University Press, 1998), and T. Judt, *Postwar: A History of Europe since 1945* (London: Heinemann, 2005), Chapter 12, 'The Spectre of Revolution'.
3. See for example the title of B. Turner's study of the Kindertransports, *...And the Policeman Smiled: 10,000 Children Escape from Nazi Europe* (London: Bloomsbury, 1990), and M. Malet and A. Grenville (eds), *Changing Countries: The Experience and Achievement of German-speaking Exiles from Hitler in Britain from 1933 to Today* (London: Libris, 2002), p.122.
4. *AJR Information* (December 1969), pp.1f.
5. He was referring to the statement by Anthony Eden, then foreign secretary, in a speech in New York in January 1952 on Britain's decision to stand aside from the European Coal and Steel Community and hence from the founding stages of the European project: 'This is something which we know, in our bones, we cannot do.'
6. *AJR Information* (October 1961), p.5.
7. *AJR Information* (June 1965), p.7. PEM mentioned the production because the cast included the refugee actor Peter Illing.
8. *AJR Information* (March 1963), p.9. Agnes Bernelle was the actress daughter of Rudolf Bernauer, a famous Berlin theatrical manager, producer and playwright who emigrated to London in 1935 and died there in 1953.
9. *AJR Information* (April 1968), p.5.
10. The show was called 'Up Jumped the Swagman', a quotation from the unofficial Australian national anthem, 'Waltzing Matilda'.
11. *AJR Information* (November 1968), p.9.
12. *AJR Information* (December 1968), p.7.
13. On the student revolution of 1968, see D. Caute, *The Year of the Barricades: A Journey through 1968* (New York: Harper and Row, 1988).
14. *AJR Information* (March 1968), p.7.
15. *AJR Information* (April 1968), p.10.
16. *AJR Information* (May 1968), p.11.
17. 'Dachau Pilgrimage', *AJR Information* (October 1968), p.11.
18. *AJR Information* (June 1968), pp.1f. Extra-parliamentary opposition (APO) was the term used by left-wing radicals for their opposition to the Grand Coalition that ruled Germany from 1965 to 1969.
19. *AJR Information* (September 1968), p.12.
20. Interviews with Eli and Chava Fachler, among others, in the 'Refugee Voices' archive.
21. Malet and Grenville (eds), *Changing Countries*, p.216.
22. See the examples in the section 'Postwar Encounters with the "Heimat"', ibid., pp.201ff.
23. J. Rott, *Bernhard Weiß: Polizeivizepräsident in Berlin – Preußischer Jude – Kämpferischer Demokrat* (Teetz and Berlin: Hentrich und Hentrich, 2008), pp.54ff.
24. For the history of post-war Germany, see M. Fulbrook, *History of Germany 1918–2000: The Divided Nation* (Oxford: Blackwell, 2002), P. Pulzer, *German Politics, 1945–1995* (Oxford: Oxford University Press, 1997), and A. Nicholls, *The Bonn Republic: West German Democracy, 1945–1990* (Harlow: Addison-Wesley, 1998).
25. See for example E.G. Lowenthal, 'When the Swastikas Returned to Germany', *AJR Information* (February 1960), pp.1f., and W. Rosenstock, 'The Watchword is Vigilance!', *AJR Information* (March 1960), p.1. The epidemic of daubing (*Schmier-Epidemie*) rapidly died out, and various perpetrators were charged and convicted; one was sentenced to read Eugen Kogon's classic study *Der SS-Staat* and submit a ten-page essay on it to the court (*AJR Information* [April 1960], p.10).
26. *AJR Information* (June 1968), pp.1f.
27. *AJR Information* (November 1969), pp.1f.

28. *AJR Information* (May 1964), p.1.
29. *AJR Information* (December 1961), p.8.
30. *AJR Information* (February 1969), pp.1f.
31. 'The Younger Generation and the A.J.R.: Another Contribution to the Debate', *AJR Information* (October 1964), p.11.
32. *AJR Information* (October 1961), p.3.
33. '"Jews in Germany Today": A One-Sided TV Broadcast', *AJR Information* (June 1965), p.9.
34. *AJR Information* (September 1967), p.9; (September 1969), p.15.
35. *AJR Information* (December 1961), p.15.
36. *AJR Information* (March 1964), pp.6f.
37. *AJR Information* (March 1963), p.1.
38. 'A New Year', *AJR Information* (September 1963), p.1.
39. *AJR Information* (December 1963), p.2.
40. The British Academy, 'Extract from Council minutes, 27 May 1964', headed 'Thank-Offering to Britain Fund. Memorandum on the proposed Lectureship and Research Fellowship relating to human studies', in folder 'ARCHIVES TOB', British Academy, London.
41. Copy (undated) in the folder 'ARCHIVES TOB' at the British Academy. The letter was accompanied by a donation form, which asked donors to enter the names and addresses of refugees who were not members of the AJR, so that they could also be approached.
42. *AJR Information* (October 1964), p.1; (November 1964), p.13.
43. *AJR Information* (December 1964), p.2.
44. *AJR Information* (January 1965), p.7.
45. Letter from DWP (Pearson) to Victor Ross, 21 July 1964, and handwritten note from EJR, presumably to Pearson, 21 September 1964, in folder 'ARCHIVES TOB'.
46. Letter from Rosenstock to Pearson, 14 May 1965, in folder 'ARCHIVES TOB'.
47. Letter from Behr to Pearson, 26 July 1966, and her reply, 27 July 1966, and letter from Professor Günther Zuntz, F.B.A., to Pearson, 2 August 1965, in folder 'ARCHIVES TOB'.
48. See letter from N.M. Rothschild & Sons to treasurer, 'Thank-You Britain' Fund, 8 April 1965, letter from Rosenstock to Pearson, 12 April 1965, and letter from the Academy to Rothschild Executor & Trustee Co., 11 May 1965, in folder 'ARCHIVES TOB'.
49. Letter from L.M. Doffman & Co., 123, Pall Mall, SW1, to secretary, 'Thank-You Britain' Fund, 16 June 1966, letter from Rosenstock to Pearson, 17 June 1966, and her reply to Doffman's, 5 July 1966, in folder 'ARCHIVES TOB'.
50. See the obituary by H. Jaeger, *AJR Information* (March 1965), p.12. On Bonn in exile, see P. Clavin, '"A Wandering Scholar" in Britain and the USA, 1933–45: The Life and Work of Moritz Bonn', *Yearbook of the Research Centre for German and Austrian Exile Studies*, 4 (2002), pp.27–42.
51. *AJR Information* (March 1966), p.1.
52. Ibid.
53. Letter from Rosenstock to Pearson, 24 September 1965, in folder 'ARCHIVES TOB'. The function was held in the Livery Hall of the Saddlers' Company, in Gutter Lane, EC2.
54. 'A Memorable Occasion: "Thank-You Britain" Fund Handed Over to British Academy', *AJR Information* (December 1965), pp.1f.
55. Copy in folder 'ARCHIVES TOB'.
56. List of lecturers kindly supplied by Dr Ken Emond of the British Academy.
57. *AJR Information* (September 1969), p.16.

Bibliography

PRIMARY SOURCES

Association of Jewish Refugees Information, 1946–2000 (from 2000, *Association of Jewish Refugees Journal*).

Unpublished Memoirs
Geernaert, M., 'Marianne: The First 30 Years...' (typescript, 2004).
Rosenstock, W., unpublished autobiography, 1941–1986 (typescript, 1986).
Wagner, L., 'Emigrants' Daily Life' (typescript, c. 1940).

Recorded Collections
Refugee Voices: The AJR Audio-Visual Testimony Collection, a digitalized archive that is accessible at a number of institutions in the UK and abroad; the original tapes are held securely at the AJR offices at Stanmore. To access recordings, refer in the first instance to the Wiener Library, London.
The Oral History Collection of the Research Centre for German and Austrian Exile Studies is held at the University of London Library, Senate House, London.
The 'Continental Britons' collection is held by Dr Bea Lewkowicz, London.

SECONDARY SOURCES

Alderman, G., *Modern British Jewry* (Oxford: Clarendon Press, 1998).
Argy, E., *The Childhood and Teens of a Jewish Girl in Inter-war Austria and Subsequent Adventures* (Charleston, SC: BookSurge, 2005).
Barkow, B., *Alfred Wiener and the Making of the Holocaust Library* (London: Vallentine Mitchell, 1997).
Bearman, M., C. Brinson, R. Dove, A. Grenville and J. Taylor, *Out of Austria: The Austrian Centre in London in World War II* (London and New York: I.B. Tauris, 2008).
Bentwich, N., *I Understand the Risks: The Story of the Refugees from Nazi Oppression Who Fought in the British Forces in the World War* (London: Gollancz, 1950).

Berghahn, M., *Continental Britons: German-Jewish Refugees from Nazi Germany* (Oxford: Berg, 1988).

Blend, M., *A Child Alone* (London: Vallentine Mitchell, 1995).

Bolchover, R., *British Jewry and the Holocaust* (Cambridge: Cambridge University Press, 1993).

Borchard, R., *We Are Strangers Here: An 'Enemy Alien' in Prison in 1940* (London and Portland, OR: Vallentine Mitchell, 2008).

Brinson, C., '"In the Exile of Internment" or "Von Versuchen, aus einer Not eine Tugend zu machen": German-Speaking Women Interned by the British during the Second World War', in W. Niven and J. Jordan (eds), *Politics and Culture in Twentieth-Century Germany* (Rochester, NY and Woodbridge, Suffolk: Camden House, 2003), pp.63–87.

Brinson, C. and R. Dove (eds), *'Stimme der Wahrheit': German-language Broadcasting by the BBC: Yearbook of the Research Centre for German and Austrian Exile Studies*, 5 (2003).

Brinson, C., A. Müller-Härlin and J. Winckler, *'HM Loyal Internee': Fred Uhlman in Captivity* (London and Portland, OR: Vallentine Mitchell, 2008).

Britain's New Citizens: The Story of the Refugees from Germany and Austria. Tenth Anniversary Publication of the Association of Jewish Refugees in Great Britain (London: Association of Jewish Refugees, 1951).

Cesarani, D., *Arthur Koestler: The Homeless Mind* (London: Heinemann, 1998).

Cesarani, D. and T. Kushner (eds), *The Internment of Aliens in Twentieth-century Britain* (London: Frank Cass, 1993).

Clare, G., *Last Waltz in Vienna: The Destruction of a Family 1842–1942* (London: Macmillan, 1981).

Clavin, P., '"A Wandering Scholar" in Britain and the USA, 1933–45: The Life and Work of Moritz Bonn', *Yearbook of the Research Centre for German and Austrian Exile Studies*, 4 (2002), pp.27–42.

Cooper, R., *Refugee Scholars* (Leeds: Moorland Books, 1992).

Cousins in Exile: An Anthology. Poems by Adolf Placzek and Ernst Philipp, with an introduction by M. Ives (Lancaster: Lancaster University, Department of European Languages and Cultures, Occasional Papers in German Studies, 2005).

De Lange, N. (ed.), *Ignaz Maybaum: A Reader* (New York and Oxford: Berghahn, 2001).

Diamant, K., *Kafka's Last Love: The Mystery of Dora Diamant* (London: Secker and Warburg, 2003).

Dove, R., *Journey of No Return: Five German-speaking Literary Exiles in Britain, 1933–1945* (London: Libris, 2000).

Dove, R. (ed.), *'Totally Un-English'? Britain's Internment of 'Enemy Aliens' in Two World Wars: Yearbook of the Research Centre for German and Austrian Exile Studies*, 7 (2005).

Dubrovsky, G., Six from Leipzig (London: Vallentine Mitchell, 2004).

Eberstadt, W., Whence We Came, Where We Went: From the Rhine to the Main to the Elbe, from the Thames to the Hudson (New York: W.A.E. Books, 2002).

Elsley, M., A Chance in Six Million (privately published, 1989).

Eriksen, T., Ethnicity and Nationalism: Anthropological Perspectives (London and Boulder, CO: Pluto Press, 1993).

Fachler, Y., The Vow: Rebuilding the Fachler Tribe after the Holocaust (Victoria, BC: Trafford Publishing, 2003).

Feidel-Mertz, H. and A. Hammel, 'Integration and Formation of Identity: Exile Schools in Great Britain', Shofar: An Interdisciplinary Journal of Jewish Studies, 23, 1 (2004), pp.71–84.

Flesch, C., 'Where Do You Come from?' Hitler Refugees in Great Britain Then and Now: The Happy Compromise! (London: Pen Press Publishers, 2001).

Friedländer, S., Nazi Germany and the Jews. Volume I: The Years of Persecution, 1933–1939 (New York: HarperCollins, 1998).

Fry, H., Jews in North Devon during the Second World War: The Escape from Nazi Germany and the Establishment of the Pioneer Corps (Wellington: Halsgrove, 2005).

Fry, H., The King's Most Loyal Enemy Aliens: Germans Who Fought for Britain in the Second World War (Stroud: History Press, 2007).

Gál, H., Musik hinter Stacheldraht: Tagebücher aus dem Sommer 1940 (Berne: Lang, 2003).

Gedye, G., Fallen Bastions: The Central European Tragedy (London: Gollancz, 1939).

Gershon, K., We Came as Children (London: Gollancz, 1966).

Gillman, P. and L., 'Collar the Lot!': How Britain Interned and Expelled its Wartime Refugees (London: Quartet Books, 1980).

Godfrey, A., Three Rabbis in a Vicarage (London: Larsen Grove Press, 2005).

Göpfert, R., Der jüdische Kindertransport von Deutschland nach England 1938/39: Geschichte und Erinnerung (Frankfurt-on-Main and New York: Campus, 1999).

Grenville, A., 'The Association of Jewish Refugees', Yearbook of the Research Centre for German and Austrian Exile Studies, 10 (2008), pp.89–111.

Harris, M. and D. Oppenheimer, Into the Arms of Strangers: Stories of the Kindertransport (London: Bloomsbury, 2000).

Holmes, C., John Bull's Island: Immigration and British Society, 1871–1971 (Basingstoke: Macmillan, 1988).

Karpf, A., The War After: Living with the Holocaust (London: Heinemann, 1996).

Kerr, J., Out of the Hitler Time: One Family's Story (London: Collins, 1995).

Koestler, A., The Invisible Writing: The Second Volume of an Autobiography: 1932–40 (London: Hutchinson, 1969).

Kramer, L., 'At Dover Harbour', in The Shoemaker's Wife and Other Poems (Sutton, Surrey: Hippopotamus Press, 1987).

Kushner, T., The Persistence of Prejudice: Antisemitism in British Society during the Second World War (Manchester and New York: Manchester University Press, 1989).

Lafitte, F., The Internment of Aliens (London: Penguin, 1940).

Leighton-Langer, P., The King's Own Loyal Enemy Aliens: German and Austrian Refugees in Britain's Armed Forces, 1939–45 (London and Portland, OR: Vallentine Mitchell, 2006).

Leverton, B. and S. Lowensohn, I Came Alone: Stories of the Kindertransport (Brighton, Sussex: Book Guild, 1990).

Lewkowicz, B., 'Belsize Square Synagogue: Community, Belonging, and Religion among German-Jewish Refugees', Yearbook of the Research Centre for German and Austrian Exile Studies, 10 (2008), pp.113–36.

London, L., Whitehall and the Jews, 1933–1948: British Immigration Policy, Jewish Refugees and the Holocaust (Cambridge: Cambridge University Press, 2000).

Macklin, G., '"A Quite Natural and Moderate Defensive Feeling"? The 1945 Hampstead "Anti-Alien" Petition', Patterns of Prejudice, 37, 3 (September 2003), pp.277–300.

Malet, M. and A. Grenville (eds), Changing Countries: The Experience and Achievement of German-speaking Exiles from Hitler in Britain from 1933 to Today (London: Libris, 2002).

Mikes, G., How To Be An Alien (London: Allan Wingate, 1946).

Mosse, W. (ed.), Second Chance: Two Centuries of German-speaking Jews in the United Kingdom (Tübingen: Mohr, 1991).

Muchitsch, M., Österreicher im Exil – Großbritannien 1938–1945: Eine Dokumentation (Vienna: Österreichischer Bundesverlag, 1992).

Paucker, A., Deutsche Juden im Kampf um Recht und Freiheit: Studien zu Abwehr, Selbstbehauptung und Widerstand der deutschen Juden seit dem Ende des 19. Jahrhunderts (Teetz: Hentrich und Hentrich, 2003).

Pelican, F., From Dachau to Dunkirk (London: Vallentine Mitchell, 1993).

Pross, S., 'In London treffen wir uns wieder': Vier Spaziergänge durch ein vergessenes Kapitel deutscher Kulturgeschichte (Frankfurt-on-Main: Eichborn, 2000).

Ritchie, J., 'Dr Karl König and the Camphill Community', Yearbook of the Research Centre for German and Austrian Exile Studies, 10 (2008), pp.169–82.

Robertson, R., The 'Jewish Question' in German Literature, 1749–1939: Emancipation and its Discontents (Oxford: Oxford University Press, 1999).

Roseman, M., The Past in Hiding (London: Penguin, 2001).

Ross, V., Basic British (London: Max Parrish, 1956).

Rott, J., Bernhard Weiß: Polizeivizepräsident in Berlin – Preußischer Jude – Kämpferischer Demokrat (Teetz and Berlin: Hentrich und Hentrich, 2008).

Schleunes, K., The Twisted Road to Auschwitz: Nazi Policy toward German Jews 1933–1939 (Urbana and Chicago, IL: University of Illinois Press, 1990 [1970]).

Seeber, U. (ed.), *Ein Niemandsland, aber welch ein Rundblick!: Exilautoren über Nachkriegswien* (Vienna: Picus, 1998).

Segev, T., *The Seventh Million: The Israelis and the Holocaust* (New York: Hill and Wang, 1994).

Sharples, C., 'Kindertransport: Terror, Trauma and Triumph', *History Today* (March 2004), pp.23–9.

Shatzkes, P., *Holocaust and Rescue: Impotent or Indifferent? Anglo-Jewry 1938–1945* (Basingstoke: Palgrave Macmillan, 2002).

Sherman, A., *Island Refuge: Britain and Refugees from the Third Reich 1933–1939* (London: Frank Cass, 1994 [1973]).

Shirer, W., *The Rise and Fall of the Third Reich: A History of Nazi Germany* (New York: Fawcett Publications, 1962 [1959]).

Sinsheimer, H., *Shylock. The History of a Character or The Myth of the Jew* (London: Gollancz, 1947), German version *Shylock: Die Geschichte einer Figur* (Munich: Ner-Tamid Verlag, 1960).

Smith, M., *Foley: The Spy Who Saved 10,000 Jews* (London: Hodder and Stoughton, 1999).

Snowman, D., *The Hitler Émigrés: The Cultural Impact on Britain of the Refugees from Nazism* (London: Chatto and Windus, 2002).

Spiel, H., *Die hellen und die finsteren Zeiten: Erinnerungen 1911–1946* (Munich: List, 1989).

Stent, R., *A Bespattered Page: The Internment of 'His Majesty's Most Loyal Enemy Aliens'* (London: Deutsch, 1980).

Tausig, O., *Kasperl, Kummerl, Jud: Eine Lebensgeschichte* (Vienna: Mandelbaum Verlag, 2005).

Tucker, E., *Becoming English* (London: Starhaven, 2009).

Turner, B., *… And the Policeman Smiled: 10,000 Children Escape from Nazi Europe* (London: Bloomsbury, 1990).

Walsh, B., 'From Outer Darkness: Oxford and Her Refugees', *Oxford Magazine* (eighth week, Michaelmas Term, 1992), pp.5–11.

Wasserstein, B., *Britain and the Jews of Europe, 1939–1945* (Oxford: Oxford University Press, 1988).

Weber, G. and R. Paulus (eds), *Hermann Sinsheimer: Schriftsteller und Theaterkritiker zwischen Heimat und Exil. Eine Auswahl aus dem Gesamtwerk* (Landau/Pfalz: Pfälzische Verlagsanstalt, 1986).

Weindling, P., 'Medical Refugees as Practitioners and Patients: Public, Private and Practice Records', *Yearbook of the Research Centre for German and Austrian Exile Studies*, 9 (2007), pp.141–56.

White, I., *I Came as a Stranger* (London: Hazelwood, 1991).

Willimowski, T., *'Emigrant sein ist ja kein Beruf': Das Leben des Journalisten Pem* (Berlin: Wissenschaftlicher Verlag, 2007).

Index

Names of publications beginning with the letters 'A' or 'The' will be filed under the first significant word. Page references to endnotes will be followed by the letter 'n'.